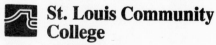

OVER THE RAINBOW

Hats off to Hollywood

Yes, it's the Wicked Witch of the West's hat from *The Wizard of Oz*. And, that is not all that is featured in Sotheby's Collectors' Carrousel auction on December 16. We also have a piano used in the filming of *Casablanca* and Clark Cable's script from *Gone with the Wind*.

For catalogues and more information, please call Dana Hawkes at (212) 606-7424. Sotheby's, 1334 York Avenue, New York, New York 10021.

SOTHEBY'S
FOUNDED 1744

Frontispiece

OVER THE RAINBOW

The Wizard of Oz
As a Secular Myth of America

Paul Nathanson

State University of New York Press

McGill Studies in the History of Religions,
A Series Devoted to International Scholarship

Katherine K. Young, editor

Published by
State University of New York Press, Albany

For information, address State University of New York Press,
State University Plaza, Albany, N.Y., 12246

Production by: Marilyn Semerad
Marketing by: Dana E. Yanulavich

Library of Congress Cataloging-in-Publication Data

Nathanson, Paul, 1947–
    Over the rainbow : the Wizard of Oz as a secular myth of America /
by Paul Nathanson.
        p.   cm. — (McGill studies in the history of religions)
    Includes index.
    ISBN 0-7914-0709-8 (cloth). — ISBN 0-7914-0710-1 (pbk.)
    1. Wizard of Oz (Motion Picture) 2. United States—Religion.
3. Myth. 4. United States—Popular culture.   5. Paradise.
6. Secularism. I. Title. II. Series.
PN1997.W593N38   1991   90-10163
791.43′72—dc20   CIP

        10 9 8 7 6 5 4 3 2 1

I dedicate what follows to the memory of Judy Garland, Ray Bolger, Jack Haley, Bert Lahr, Margaret Hamilton, Frank Morgan, Billie Burke, and the Munchkins, along with the composers, writers, artists, costume designers and everyone else associated with *The Wizard of Oz*. Their combined efforts have given the world something of enduring value. Not even the passage of over fifty years has dimmed the luster of its beauty.

CONTENTS

LIST OF ILLUSTRATIONS

FOREWORD

I stared at the small brass plaque on the bench atop Telgraph Hill that tourists climb for the panoramic view of San Francisco Bay. It said: "Toto, I have a feeling we're not in Kansas anymore." Was it a coincidence that this was 1989, the fiftieth anniversary of the movie from which these words were taken? And was it a coincidence that I had just finished reading Paul Nathanson's monumental work on it which begins with three simple words: "Only in America"? In any case, such synchronism was suddenly revelatory, as if it provided evidence for Nathanson's basic thesis: *The Wizard of Oz*, with its enormous and lasting popularity, can be understood only as a kind of myth.

In the past, cosmic myths were associated with hierophanies at sacred centers. These sacred centers were replicated elsewhere to extend the link between macrocosm and microcosm into the world of everyday life. This oriented the individual or community in space and time. And this, in turn, made the world preeminently meaningful. In a similar manner, Americans identify Kansas, through *The Wizard*, as the symbolic center of America. And this center is replicated, as it were, by a mere phrase on an ordinary bench. Just reading those words allows us to touch base, if only for a second, with something quintessentially American. In some elusive manner, Nathanson suggests, it also taps the symbolic worlds of both childhood fantasy and religious myth.

But how? To what kind of myth is Nathanson pointing? Besides, is it not presumptuous to use religious language for something secular, not to mention something that seems to be trivial or even bizarre? Myths are about Vishnu or Ishtar, after all, not Bugs Bunny or Dorothy Gale. Mircea Eliade (who did so much, through his study of patterns in comparative religion, to recapture the significance of myth, ritual, and sacred geography) mourned the loss of the sacred in modern times, especially in America. He would have spoken of

the plaque on that bench as a mere "survival" of religion, a cipher
for "situations and types which the consciousness does not want or
is not able to recognize."[1] Nathanson rejects this particular assumption of Eliade in no uncertain terms. How could the notion of a
banalized or camouflaged vestige account for the place of this film
in the psyche of Americans of all ages? How could a mere "fallen
myth" be so popular for so long? With such disarmingly simple
questions, Nathanson has thrown down the gauntlet for the next
generation of students in the fields of religious studies, film studies,
popular culture, and American cultural history.

Although *The Wizard* may be approached initially through the
genre of the folk tale, suggests Nathanson, it must be viewed in the
final analysis as a "secular myth." He explores this oxymoron by
examining the use of cinematic properties such as dialogue, color,
music, mise-en-scène, dramatis personae, space, and time. From this
formal analysis, it becomes clear that these cinematic properties are
used in a consistent pattern. This cinematic pattern is then related
through cultural analysis to symbolic patterns prevalent in the larger
culture. Nathanson does so, moreover, at three levels: individual (the
child or adolescent grows up and goes home), collective (the nation
"grows up" and "goes home"), and cosmic (the soul "grows up" and
"goes home").

Nathanson's thesis will have to be tested and his transdisciplinary
approach reviewed. Whatever the scholarly debate sparked by this
new and provocative view of the relation between religion and secularity, or tradition and modernity, this book has something for everyone. Some will be delighted by its storehouse of Oziana (both nostalgic and satirical). Others will be fascinated by its treasury of
Americana (both religious and secular). Readers will find discussions
in it about everything from Judy Garland's obituary to Dorothy
Gale's ruby slippers, from Christmas Day to Memorial Day, from
"Over the Rainbow" to "America the Beautiful," from Kansas to the
Kingdom, from Busby Berkeley musicals to Film Noir, from hymn
books to comic strips, from Thomas Cole and the Hudson River
School of landscape painting to Grant Wood and the Regionalists,
from grand opera to vaudeville, from the Western Wilderness to the
Eastern Metropolis. . . .

Our fascination with *The Wizard* and, indeed, with the whole
year of 1939 seems to be increasing. At no time has this been more
evident than in 1989. *Time*, for instance, entitled one feature story:
"1939: Twelve Months of Magic" and noted that Hollywood was

"beginning the greatest year of its Golden Age."[2] *Gone with the Wind,*
Wuthering Heights, Gunga Din, Beau Geste, Drums Along the
Mohawk, Intermezzo, Goodbye Mr. Chips, Young Mr. Lincoln, Mr.
Smith Goes to Washington, The Women, Juarez, and *The Wizard of*
Oz itself, were just some of the 388 films released that year. Then,
too, MGM boasted of having under contract "more stars than there
are in heaven," stars such as Clark Gable, Vivien Leigh, Maureen
O'Sullivan, Norma Shearer, Robert Young, Greer Garson, Lionel
Barrymore, Joan Crawford, Greta Garbo, Mickey Rooney, and Judy
Garland.

No wonder pundits in 1989 were still pondering the magic formula
of 1939. There had been important technological improvements in
film production, to be sure. And there had been superb talent both
in front of the camera and behind it. But one "secret" may have
been the simple acceptance of fantasy as a healthy part of human
existence. If so, then the same "secret" seems to be effective today.
"I think people are more romantic than they really want to say that
they are," opines one commentator on the continuing popularity of
old movies, "so they respond to these films. The films are more
idealistic, the basic human needs are better portrayed than they are
now...you see an idealism about people and the country. It was
innocence more than anything else. The films are not cynical. They're
larger than life....You don't get that now."[3] According to another
commentator:

> Though it liked to think of itself as the capital of sophistication, Holly-
> wood was in fact, just as unworldly as such places as Topeka, or Twin
> Falls, Idaho, where most of its inhabitants came from. The movies
> they made reflected and gained much of their strength from that
> innocence, and they resounded with a sincerity that no amount of
> artifice can duplicate. Would any scriptwriter today dare to type a
> corny line like this? "If I ever go looking for my heart's desire again, I
> won't look any further than my own backyard, because if it isn't
> there, I never really lost it to begin with." The writers of *The Wizard*
> dared and thereby helped make a great film. They were the mirror of
> the country, those men and women who made the movies of 1939.
> Like the country, they were confident, certain of themselves and their
> future. They knew, or thought they knew, the difference between good
> and bad, right and wrong, and that confidence, which they took for
> granted, was the rock upon which they built.[4]

But what kind of innocence was this? To answer, we must remember that the Depression was like an experience of death for many

Americans. According to a government investigator, providing relief for the destitute was "a kind of desperate job like getting the wounded off the battlefield so that they can die quietly at the base hospital."[5] Wherever one turned, there was emptiness. President Roosevelt knew just what Americans needed: self-confidence. "The only thing we have to fear," he said in his first inaugural address, "is fear itself." Just two years earlier, as the economy hit rock bottom, gangster films such as *Little Caesar* (1930), *Scarface* (1931), and *The Public Enemy* (1931) had abounded. These films had posed the problem of order and chaos in the starkest possible way. Then, too, people had identified with the gangsters who flourished while almost everyone else floundered. Gradually, the economy improved and hope revived. By the mid-thirties, Hollywood musicals were once again playing in theatres all over the country. Films of this genre and many others reaffirmed the nation's belief in itself and in its ability to endure.

> The yearning for the world as it had been—or as people liked to believe it had been—was the expression of hope for what it might become. Radical, revolutionary, and reform movements have often been based upon a myth of a "golden age" in the past. When, in *How Green Was My Valley*, Huw says: "it makes me think of so much that was good, and is gone," the viewer is likely to feel sadness, but the film also builds up anger that the goodlife of yesterday has been destroyed. The result can be an increased desire to change things. In such ways, the myths of the past become the agenda for the future. This is to say that it was precisely because the myths about American culture *were* myths that they served a progressive rather than a reactionary function. People looked back to see in front of them.
>
> The longing for an imagined golden age, for a feeling of security, for an identity, was evident in the thirties quest for a sense of place...[a] search for security in history or on the land.[6]

The Wizard was such a myth. It created a sense of security both in history and on the land. Nathanson shows how it fondly recalled an agrarian golden age in the recent past (although he also shows how it eagerly anticipated a technological golden age in the immediate future.) In short, it resonated with the experience of a people emerging from ten years of gloom.

But what is behind the mood of nostalgia gripping America *now*? Is it possible that the nation is finally turning its back on the future as old frontiers become distant memories and new ones become sinister threats? Whereas the country has long been in love with everything new—a New World, a New Deal, a New South, A New Frontier, a New Left, a New Right, even a New Easy Off—is it now in love with everything old? This takes the interpreter of contemporary culture straight to the heart of Deconstruction, a school of thought that is now de rigueur in philosophical and literary circles. According to C. Hugh Holman, "The concept of thing, substance, event, and absolute recedes, to be superseded by the concept of relation, ratio, construct, and relativity....Once one realizes that what seems to be an event is really a construct of a quasi-linguistic system, then one is in a position to undo the construct or to recognize that the construct, by its very nature, has already undone, dismantled, or deconstructed itself—with far-reaching implications for thought of every sort."[7]

Theoretically, this way of thinking should lead to relativism or even nihilism. But hardly anyone follows it to its logical conclusion. Deconstruction is generally done more selectively. Instead of denying privileged status to everything, those who adopt this method confer privileged status on what had previously been subordinated. This merely inverts the established order and creates a new hierarchy of values. Nevertheless, they see this as redemptive. With that in mind, they dismantle ideas or ideologies they do not like by pointing to their relativity but leave their own ideas or ideologies intact so that previously suppressed "voices" may now be heard. The underlying assumption is that they have some sort of ethical and intellectual immunity to deconstruction. Whereas those who lived through the Great Depression were able to survive by defying the *abuse* of cultural norms, we who are living through the Great Deconstruction may only be able to survive by defying the *lack* of cultural norms. For scholars interested in the history of religions or the history of consciousness (*mentalités collectives*), current nostalgia for *The Wizard* may well be examined as a popular response to this situation.

In any case, Nathanson sheds new light on our continuing affection for movies such as *The Wizard*. He leads us confidently into the enchanting, haunting, dreamlike universe of myth.

KATHERINE K. YOUNG

PREFACE

Virtually every book on American film history (to say nothing of American popular culture in general) mentions *The Wizard of Oz*. For technical, aesthetic, and other reasons, it was a cinematic landmark. Not surprisingly, therefore, it has also been the specific subject of several books. These are historical and descriptive. That is, they describe the actual production of this movie and some of the phenomena associated with its popularity over the past few decades. Some minor critical articles have also been written. Attempts have been made, for example, to interpret *The Wizard* from Marxist, Freudian, and theological points of view; these are discussed in the Introduction. My own attempt to interpret *The Wizard* is quite different. It is a semiotic study that includes both formal analysis (a systematic examination of the way its formal properties have created specific cinematic patterns) and cultural analysis (a systematic examination of the relation between these cinematic patterns and the symbolic patterns of both American culture and Western religion). Unlike earlier studies, in other words, this one examines *The Wizard* on a multidimensional basis. Consequently, the evidence presented is multidisciplinary.

Although many studies have revealed links between popular movies and myths, or between popular culture and popular religion, this one is (to my knowledge) the first systematic analysis of one popular movie with this in mind. I have found evidence suggesting not only that *The Wizard* is reminiscent of myth in general but also that it is directly derived from a specific tradition of myth. More important, I have found evidence suggesting that *The Wizard* functions as a myth in the context of an ostensibly secular culture. In doing so, I have raised new questions about the ambiguous relation between religion and secularity. As a result, the scope of religious studies may be considerably broadened. So far, this field has focused attention primarily on the teachings of theology or philosophy, the history of

xvii

churches or other institutions of organized religion, and the exegesis or evolution of classical texts. Systematic study of the way myth and ritual function in everyday life is generally left to the sociologists or anthropologists. Systematic study of popular religion is generally left to the sociologists or historians. And systematic study of the visual and musical expression of religion is generally left to the art historians and ethnomusicologists. This book, however, suggests that the religious life of a community cannot be understood adequately except in the context of all these manifestations of its "collective mentality"—including phenomena that are usually assumed to be secular.

*

Readers should bear several things in mind. (1) Passages from the Bible are quoted from the Revised Standard Version. (2) Even though it is the filmed version of L. Frank Baum's classic book for children that is under discussion here, I have used another "book," in addition to the movie itself, as a primary source: Noel Langley, Florence Ryerson and Edgar Woolf's *The Wizard of Oz: The Screenplay* (1939; New York: Delta, 1989). Reference to the page numbers appear immediately after quotations from the dialogue. (3) All other references are provided in the section devoted to notes. Because the notes also include extensive discussions of related subjects, though, readers are encouraged to consult them often as a kind of running commentary on the text. Good reading is not only like traveling on the interstate, as it were, moving quickly and efficiently from one point in the argument to another; it is also like exploring the countryside, pausing every now and then for detours along interesting byways—as Dorothy herself does on her way down the Yellow Brick Road.

ACKNOWLEDGMENTS

It could be argued that the years of effort required for a doctorate culminate in a coming of age; entry into the world of learning as a full-fledged scholar. To come of age, every fledgling must have a mentor, someone to show the way by acting as a model to be imitated. It was my privilege to have Katherine Young as my mentor. Katherine has been remarkably generous with her time. I have never understood how she manages to accomplish so much—teaching, writing, presenting papers, reading, keeping house—and still be so accessible to me. She has boundless energy. I am impressed most of all, however, by her delight in scholarship. For her, new ideas or ways of thinking are challenges to be enjoyed. Not every scholar in the field of religious studies would be willing and able to see connections between myth and film or even connections between elite and popular culture—to say nothing of connections between the Bible or the Ramayana and *The Wizard of Oz.*

What Katherine is to scholarship, Kendal Wallis is to librarianship. On several occasions, I came to him at the McLennan Library with the most incredibly obscure questions. And he was always able to help. Always. What impressed me most, however, was the sheer joy with which he approached his work. It was a pleasure to "do business" with him.

Due to the interdisciplinary nature of my research, inquiries took me less frequently to the Religious Studies Library. When they did, however, I was well served. More often than most students, I depended on the interlibrary loan service. At one point, five or six books were arriving for me every week. If Jennifer Wheeler ever felt burdened by so many requests, she never let on. The chief librarian, Norma Johnston, deserves a special note of gratitude. Over the years, I have spent many hours working for her in the library. Every once in a while, when I was running short of money, Norma would offer me a little more out of her own pocket. On one occasion, she said: "Go and have yourself a steak dinner tonight." Clearly, she was much more than just my boss.

I am also indebted to Robert MacAlear. How fortunate I was to meet someone with a special interest in the American tradition of musical comedy. My analysis of music in *The Wizard* could not possibly have been written or even conceived without his help. Similarly, I am very grateful to Jordan Peterson for checking my Jungian analysis of *The Wizard*. Without his help, it would surely have lacked integration.

For my subsistence while working on this project, I must thank the McConnell Foundation. Even after working for several years, I could not have returned to McGill without a substantial bursary. But I also owe a great deal to the Faculty of Religious Studies. Not only did Donna Runnalls, the dean, provide me with bursaries to supplement my income from other sources but, on more than one occasion, she came to my rescue in emergencies. When I came to her for help, the transaction was never conducted in purely business terms. Donna always made it clear that she believed in me and my project. That, along with her personal warmth and graciousness, meant as much to me as her generosity.

I was fortunate to have had the opportunity of learning Word-Perfect at the Faculty of Education's Computer Lab. I demanded more time from the staff than any three other students. Julie Lake and Chris Legault did not have to get me out of trouble over and over again. But they did. And I am grateful.

Finally, where would I be without my own family? I owe a great deal to my parents for encouraging me, sometimes nagging me, to complete what I had begun. But they offered me much more than words. Even though the subject of this study is far removed from their own fields of interest, they proofread every page of my work. Without their financial help, moreover, I could never have entered the computer age. And when I lost an entire chapter by pressing the wrong key, they watched over me with the kind of tenderness no one has a right to expect. Finally, I must thank my sister, Beverly, for having taken me to see *The Wizard* that first time. I was six years old. And the rest, as they say, is history.

1 INTRODUCTION

...the film which a quarter-century of ritual telecasts (not to mention its own natural charm) has made the most universal cult movie of them all... [is] clearly an integral part of the national collective unconscious.

—From a review of *The Wizard of Oz*[1]

Only in America.... When this phrase first became popular, it was used by Jewish immigrants discussing the marvels of life in the New World. Very quickly, however, it took on slightly humorous connotations. America was the land of freedom and opportunity, to be sure, but also of *mishegass* in this case, (disorienting but charming nonsense). It was with this in mind that Harry Golden entitled his collection of nostalgic anecdotes about growing up on the Lower East Side of New York, *Only in America*.[2] What can one say, after all, of a nation in which grown men and women gather every year to discuss a fantasyland called Oz? What can one say of a nation in which a disintegrating pair of "ruby slippers" is auctioned off for $165,000? What, indeed, can one say of a nation in which "We're off to See the Wizard" is by now as familiar as any traditional hymn or even the national anthem? Only in America....

In fact, a great deal can be said. Over fifty years after it was first released in 1939, *The Wizard of Oz* has become much more than a cult classic. By definition, cult classics are restricted to small groups of aficionados; this movie, on the contrary, has earned a place in the hearts and minds of ordinary men and women (not to mention boys and girls) across the length and breadth of America.[3] Its popularity, indeed, is so massive and so enduring that the phenomenon demands an explanation. What is really so extraordinary about this movie?

1

Can its popularity be explained solely in terms of technical virtuosity, fine performances, and the mystique of Judy Garland? Many movies are well produced yet remain of limited appeal (or of great appeal to a limited number of people). This is the case, for instance, with *Citizen Kane* (Orson Welles, 1941). Because of its many innovative techniques, it is generally considered by film critics and historians to be a cinematic masterpiece. A great deal has been written about it. Nevertheless, it is seldom shown on television and has not become part of the popular imagination in the same sense as *The Wizard.* Although many Americans have seen *Citizen Kane* and even more have heard of it, few would be able to quote lines from the script, tell the story or even identify the major characters. Aside from a single shot that is sometimes used to parody politicians (Kane standing on the stage with his campaign poster looming ominously in the background), visual references are seldom quoted or exploited for commercial purposes. In spite of its artistic value (or, some would say, because of it), *Citizen Kane* has been celebrated primarily in academic circles. *The Wizard,* on the other hand, has become the cultural property of almost every American. According to Aljean Harmetz, *"The Wizard of Oz* has become an American artifact, a piece of pop culture as tangible as a pottery shard. Over the last twenty-nine years, it has been seen in 436 million homes."[4] Not surprisingly, it continues to be massively popular whenever it is broadcast on television. According to Mike Eisenberg, director of audience measurement of CBS, "This movie will always work....It's one film that we put on regularly that we don't get concerned about how it's going to do."[5] Apparently, *The Wizard* "destroys the conventional wisdom that theatrical movies, particularly repeats, are not thriving on commercial television because of the competition of pay-cable and videocassettes."[6] Marvin Mord of ABC, includes it with *Gone with the Wind* (Victor Fleming, 1939) and one or two others as the most consistently successful productions. Market researchers, in fact, have understood that references to it on television commercials will be immediately understood by almost everyone. Moreover, it is associated with phenomena that look something like liturgy: audiences are filled with people who recite the dialogue and sing the songs as the movie is shown.

What makes this possible, of course, is the frequency with which *The Wizard* is shown on television. It is broadcast annually as a special event (which is to say, it preempts regular shows). This does not make it unique. Several other movies are also broadcast regularly as special events. These include *Gone with the Wind* (Victor Fleming, 1939), *The Ten Commandments* (Cecil B. De Mille, 1956), *It's a Wonderful Life* (Frank Capra, 1946), *Miracle on 34th Street* (George Seaton, 1947), and one version or another of *A Christmas Carol* (Edwin L. Marin, 1938; Brian Desmond Hurst, 1951; Ronald Neame, 1970; Clive Donner, 1984). This link between movies with no obvious reference to religion (such as *The Wizard* or *Gone with the Wind*) and those movies that are explicitly associated with religious festivals such as Passover, Easter, and Christmas suggests the possibility that they have come to function in similar ways.

Television has clearly made *The Wizard*'s popularity possible. Without repeated broadcasting, far fewer people would see it. But has television actually caused this popularity? Aljean Harmetz points out that some of the actors involved were themselves convinced that the success of this movie owed more to exposure on television than to any intrinsic cinematic merit. According to Jack Haley, for example, "It's like a toy. You get a new generation all the time because of television. The film didn't bowl anyone over when it first came out. It was never the big smashing hit that television made it."[7] But according to Harmetz, "the movie is repeated each year *because* it has become part of American culture."[8] In other words, being broadcast on television every year has been both a cause and a result of its popularity. In fact, it would be unreasonable to assume that popularity can be generated merely by showing a movie repeatedly. If network executives at CBS agreed to broadcast *The Wizard* annually at $225,000 for each of the first two years—an astronomical amount in 1956—and for several more years at $150,000, it was because they expected the deal to be profitable. And from the beginning, ratings for *The Wizard* have indicated exceptional popularity.[9] Because popularity is normally exhausted, not enhanced, by repeated broadcasts at close intervals, the continuing success of *The Wizard* is noteworthy. In short, television is only one factor, and not necessarily the most important one, involved in placing *The Wizard* somewhere near the heart of American culture.

*

The phenomenon under discussion is based on two cultural productions: a book, *The Wonderful Wizard of Oz* (written by L. Frank Baum, published in 1900) and a movie, *The Wizard of Oz* (directed by Victor Fleming in 1939). In addition, there have been several spinoffs;[10] these are interesting in their own right but the fact remains that this particular book (along with a few others in the series by Baum) and this particular movie version remain the passports to Oz for most people.

In 1900, Baum wrote the first in his long series of Oz books. (His success was such that the series was continued even after his death; indeed, it continues to this day.) According to estimates, it had been read by around 80 million people by 1939. "It is one of the fifteen best-selling books of this century," writes William F. Brown, "with more than ten million copies now in print in twenty-two languages—including Tamil and Serbo-Croatian."[11] And according to Martin Gardner's introduction to a recent reprint, *The Wizard of Oz* has become the country's greatest, best-loved fairy tale. It has never been out of print, and so many editions have been published, in the U.S. and abroad, that no one knows how many millions of copies have been sold."[12]

Baum had a great deal of respect for the works of the Grimm brothers, Hans Christian Andersen and other traditional stories for children. In his introduction to the first Oz book, he made his aims quite explicit. He wanted to write a fairy tale.

> Yet the old-time fairy tale, having served for generations, may now be classed as "historical" in the children's library; for the time has come for a series of newer "wonder-tales" in which the stereotyped genie, dwarf and fairy are eliminated, together with all the horrible and blood-curdling incidents devised by their authors to point a fearsome moral to each tale. Modern education includes morality; therefore the modern child seeks only entertainment in its wonder-tales and gladly dispenses with all disagreeable incidents. Having this thought in mind, the story of "The Wonderful Wizard of Oz" was written solely to please children of today. It aspires to being a modernized fairy tale, in which the wonderment and joy are retained and the heartaches and night-mares are left out.[13]

This however, has not prevented controversy over Baum's work. Recently, for example, parents in some communities have asked that their children not be exposed in the public schools to the "unchristian" messages of these stories.[14] For generations, in fact, librarians considered the Oz books to be hackwork and refused to make them available to children. One explanation for the hostility of educators and librarians is that the style is too simple to be considered literature. Nevertheless, psychoanalyst Justin Call suggests that "the thinking processes in the book are similar to the thinking of a child. There is a great deal of primary process thinking—thinking dominated by wishes, fears, and visual imagery; magical thinking with no respect for time, or causality, or logic."[15] This may be why children themselves have always been so fond of the Oz books no matter what the authorities on children's literature said. Baum himself had no intention of writing a series of Oz books. Because few of his other books were successful, he kept returning to Oz. Indeed, children kept writing him letters asking for more Ozian adventure stories and even offering suggestions.[16]

There are several important differences between the book and the movie. Carol Billman has described these in "I've Seen the Movie: Oz Revisited." She prefers the filmed adaptation to the original. This is surprising because most literary critics prefer original novels to filmed versions; the latter are usually attacked as superficial renderings of the former. In this case, however, Billman points out that the movie is a significant improvement over the book in several ways. As a professor of children's literature, she notes the following:

> Each semester I learn anew the omnipotence of the MGM film. Students inevitably come to the prose after the film version has been firmly impressed upon them, and they continue to read and analyze *The Wonderful Wizard of Oz* in terms of the later visualization. Secondly, the extraordinary number of plays and films based on the Oz fiction and especially the unequivocal success of the 1939 film raise interesting questions about the inclination to and the possibilities inherent in actually creating in visual form the world Baum imagined. The Victor Fleming film reworks both the strengths and the weaknesses in Baum's first Oz novel and in so doing earns the position it occupies in my students' minds as the authoritative work to which all other tellings of the story, even the original one, must answer.[17]

The film eliminates many of the charming but distracting episodes, for example, that do nothing to advance the story. Then, too, the movie provides a single narrative point of view: that of Dorothy. We see events unfold through her eyes. In the book, no perspective is clearly defined. Readers are not encouraged to identify themselves with any particular character. The book portrays Kansas as a place of unrelieved grayness and gloom. Why, then, is Dorothy so eager to return? Her attempts to do so are quite inadequately motivated. The movie, on the other hand, represents Kansas nostalgically as a cozy, turn-of-the-century farmhouse. Dorothy's family and friends are overworked but not unloving. Her desire to return is, therefore, adequately motivated. Apart from stylistic flaws in the book that are "corrected" in the film, however, there is another reason why the latter is more successful. Baum's work relies heavily on visual imagery and color. These, of course, are used with spectacular results in the movie.

> The urge to visualize children's fantasies in live action film has long been in evidence, from the adaptation of Frances Hodgson Burnett's *The Secret Garden* (which also blends color with black-and-white scenes) to more recent attempts like Disney's *Mary Poppins* and *Chitty Chitty Bang Bang*. But none of these efforts is as technically creative or as popular as *The Wizard of Oz*. Cinematic adaptation of children's fantasy is not as easy to do successfully as it is likely to do in the first place, as the furor over Disney's animated interpretations demonstrates. But *The Wizard of Oz* transcends its original in American popular culture, and by acts of both omission and commission the makers of the film produced a vision that deservedly overlays and conditions readers' responses to L. Frank Baum's *The Wonderful Wizard of Oz*. The film's inventive approach to make-believe is, after all, what wizardry is all about.[18]

Harmetz describes the care lavished upon MGM's production of *The Wizard*. Apparently, no expense was spared; in the end, it cost $2,777,000. It "was from the outset considered an important film," she writes. "It cost more and took longer to make than any other MGM film made that year."[19] And although it took over twenty years to make a profit, according to Harmetz, "the picture was probably never intended to make money. . . . *The Wizard of Oz* was intended as a prestige picture that would more or less break even."[20] As a result of the time and money lavished upon it, this movie is a piece of cinematic virtuosity. Not surprisingly, almost everyone associated with its production is now remembered primarily for working on it.[21]

Popular culture is saturated with references to Oz. Countless games, toys, books, articles of clothing, postcards, souvenirs and other artifacts are based on it. Consequently, it is only to be expected that references to Oz abound in other movies and even in advertisements and commercials. Possibly the most striking illustration of its place in American life was provided by an Independence Day concert in Boston. On July 4, 1987, the Boston Pops Espalanade Orchestra, directed by John Williams, played "The Star Spangled Banner" and then launched immediately into selections from *The Wizard*—"We're Off to See the Wizard," "If I Only Had a Brain" and "Over the Rainbow" (see Figure 1). (For a fuller discussion of *The Wizard* in popular culture, see Appendix 2.) The success of *The Wizard* has been so massive and so enduring that its place in American life (quite apart from that of the book) requires an additional explanation, one that goes beyond its ability to provide casual entertainment. What is it about this movie that transcends the boundaries separating races, classes, sexes, generations, and regions? This is the question to be answered here.

At issue, then, is not whether anyone involved in producing *The Wizard* consciously set out to create a secular myth. The conscious motivations of the MGM team may well have focused on more worldly aims. It is safe to assume that studio officials were interested primarily in making a profit at the box office (or, as Harmetz points out, earning prestige that would be translated into box office revenues from other studio productions). Their subconscious motivations are another matter. If this movie was not the result of their conscious decision to create a secular myth, it was not the result of pure chance either. Hollywood has always been famous for its ability to reflect the values and give expression to the collective daydreams of America. To a large extent, this can be explained by the fact that intuition is rewarded in the movie industry. Movies are financially successful, after all, only when millions of people find that their needs or desires are satisfied. And they become classics (or myths) only when millions of people over several generations find that their deepest needs or desires are satisfied. If *The Wizard* has become part of the collective mentality, it is at least partly because it was produced by people who were sensitive to symbolic associations deeply embedded in the fabric of American culture. Like those responsible for every other great work of the imagination, the creators of this movie were guided by impulses they themselves may not have fully understood. But whatever they were trying to do, consciously or unconsciously, is not the main issue here. This book is not about the few hundred people who produced *The Wizard* in 1939 except insofar as they were like the millions of people who have loved it ever since. It is not about why decisions were made but about why those decisions have succeeded so brilliantly.

*

To date, very little research has been done on *The Wizard*. Virtually every book on the history of American film mentions it, of course, because of its continuing popularity and its technical virtuosity. In other words, it is generally taken at face value as a movie that entertains children superbly but does little else. It is true that several works on Oziana have appeared recently.[22] In addition, several books and articles on the movie itself have been published. These include: *The Munchkins Remember*, by Stephen Cox; *Down the Yellow Brick Road*, by Doug McClelland; *The Making of* The Wizard of Oz, by Aljean Harmetz; and *The Official 50th Anniversary Pictorial History*, by John Fricke, Jay Scarfone, and William Stillman.[23] Unlike some beautifully illustrated but anecdotal works, the last two provide thorough accounts of the movie's production during the halcyon days of Hollywood's studio system—scripts, music, casting, directors, costumes, sets, special effects, and so forth—the reception given it by critics at the time, and the countless spinoffs that have been associated with it ever since. But they are historical rather than analytical in approach. Some attempts at analysis, though, have appeared in collections and journals.

The most common analytical approach seems to be psychoanalytical.[24] David Magder[25] suggests that *The Wizard* be considered a "parable of brief psychotherapy." In his words, "The Scarecrow, the Tinman and the Cowardly Lion represent syndromes with which most therapists are familiar: low self-esteem based on the sense that one is not intelligent or capable of dealing with the world as one would like to, or sense of inability to respond emotionally or affectively, and anxiety or fearfulness in dealing with the day to day problems of living."[26] Consequently, they seek therapeutic help from the Wizard. When he points out that all they lack is belief in themselves and that they have already demonstrated the very qualities they imagine are lacking, they are immediately cured.

Apparently, the three friends—Magder does not discuss Dorothy herself—are just like his own patients. Since the disorder in question is not traumatically induced, therapy based on cognitive readjustment is effective. He cites several case studies. A graduate student, for example, worried about not being intellectual enough; believing himself incapable of doing original work, he plagiarized the work of others. A university professor, on the other hand, worried about being too intellectual; believing himself incapable of sustaining emotional ties with his wife, he was ready to give up on his marriage. And a clerk in the cancer ward of a hospital worried excessively about her own mortality; believing herself incapable of functioning under stress, she relied on tranquilizers. In each case, the patient failed to observe behavior that contradicted the negative self-evaluation. The student devoted so much time to concealing his plagiarism that he was, in effect, producing original work; the professor's distress over marital problems revealed him as anything but unfeeling; and the clerk's performance in the hospital indicated that she was very much in control of the situation. As in the book or the movie, then, therapy depended on showing patients that "their worst fears about themselves were not only groundless but totally the reverse of the situation."[27]

Magder also notes several other parallels between the book or the movie and psychotherapy. Even after the Wizard is exposed as a charlatan, Dorothy and her friends are still impressed by his confident, persuasive, commonsensical approach to their problems. Magder says that "This reflects the idea...that expectancy and beliefs in a therapist play a major role in any therapeutic endeavor."[28] Moreover, he notes that there is a link between success in the task of killing the Witch and the cognitive-behavioral shifts that take place later on in connection with the Wizard. In successfully completing the task, each of the friends has had occasion to do something that disproves his former self-image. The Scarecrow demonstrates cunning; the Tin Man demonstrates devotion and loyalty to his companions (not to mention anger at possible harm to them); and the Lion demonstrates ability to overcome fear in the service of others. As a psychotherapist, the Wizard had only to remind his patients of what they had obviously done for themselves. These parallels with psychotherapy "could be considered just a whimsical footnote in the history of behavioral change," writes Magder, "except for the fact that the popularity and familiarity of the story make it a useful metaphor for illustrating and teaching therapeutic techniques which have major clinical application."[29]

Daniel Dervin and Harvey Greenberg are more ambitious. They use Freudian psychology to probe subconscious levels of meaning in *The Wizard*. In "Over the Rainbow and under the Twister,"[30] Dervin explains that Dorothy is troubled by conflicts over identity that arise from witnessing the "primal scene" (that is, sexual intercourse between her parents). Her adventure in Oz represents every young girl's passage through the phallic and oedipal phases of psychological development. In *"The Wizard of Oz:* Little Girl Lost—and Found,"[31] Greenberg takes a revisionist approach to Freudian analysis. This allows him to present a somewhat richer and more convincing interpretation. For him, Dorothy is not an infant of three or four but an adolescent moving quickly into adulthood (which corresponds to the age of Judy Garland when she played the role of Dorothy). Since I discuss both of these psychoanalytical interpretations in detail later, I will indicate here only that they are both flawed for similar reasons. The former depends on evidence not supplied in the movie itself while the latter ignores evidence that is supplied. Even though both are very suggestive, they are only partially satisfactory.

At least one Marxist interpretation has appeared. In "Over the Rainbow: Dialectic and Ideology in *The Wizard of Oz,"* Gregory

Renault argues that *The Wizard* is a response to advanced capitalism. It is a "critique of false values, a denunciation of the reification of the goal of an activity, and of the purely instrumental rationality used in pursuit of that goal."[32] In other words, all the major characters in Oz, except for Glinda and the Wizard, are seeking something they already have or are in the process of discovering in themselves. They mistake the quest for a means to some other end instead of realizing that the quest is an end in itself. Renault's interpretation is based on the assumption that Oz is unreal. Although Dorothy learns a great deal about means and ends, about interdependence and so forth, she is left to work out the implications of this alone when she wakes up in Kansas, which, for Renault, is the real world of everyday life. What troubles him is the fact that although *The Wizard* correctly identifies a major source of alienation in American life, it fails to solve the problem. By suggesting that alienation can be ended by simply looking into oneself and changing one's own attitude, the movie implies that external and systemic forms of evil and alienation are inconsequential. In fact, he says that this

> amounts to an affirmation of the essential benevolence of the existing order of things. The emphasis is on the self-sufficiency of the micro-cosmic, private, sphere of life. The message is clearly that we need not seek outside for what is already inside—that one should not envision as an end-object what is already present within the very process of seeking....Thus the ethical stance of the Judaeo-Christian tradition preserved in liberal theology is perpetuated within the film's contemporary analysis of alienation....The Procrustean reduction of social problems to matters of individual cause in *The Wizard of Oz* leaves the film's basic issue unresolved.[33]

Renault is too hasty in assuming that Oz is unreal. As a dream, of course, it could be considered unreal. This may have been the way it was intended to be understood. And this is certainly the way most people think about it. But I have found that, on a deeper level, Oz corresponds in many ways to conditions in the real world of everyday life. Implicitly, if not explicitly, the situation is more complicated than Renault allows. If I am correct, then his conclusion is superficial. It is precisely in Oz—a confusing, alienating, and dangerous world that, not unlike our own, offers glimpses of the sacred—that Dorothy cooperates with friends to defeat and even transform evil.

Linda Hansen, on the other hand, argues that *The Wizard* is a theological reflection, disguised in secular terms, of the classic religious quest. In "Experiencing the World as Home: Reflections on

Dorothy's Quest in *The Wizard of Oz*",[34] she argues that the goal is Home. By this, she refers not merely to Dorothy's particular home on a farm in Kansas but to the state of being at home in the world. Home is the state of mind in which we feel joy at simply being alive, being who we are and being with others. On the quest, we learn that being truly at home in the world means empowering others and being, in turn, empowered by them. For Hansen as for Renault, Kansas is the real world of everyday life (although it will be transformed after the vision or revelation of Oz has been assimilated). But Hansen agrees with Dorothy, unlike Renault, that Oz, too, is real. "I realized," she writes, "that Oz only seems unreal if we dismiss the reality of dreams."[35] What makes Dorothy "religious," thinks Hansen, is her persistent belief in Oz and in the joy that is possible even in Kansas. "Dorothy's concern for joy," says Hansen, "is not wishful thinking, not foolishness, but the expression of her sense that joy has a reality, or deeper reality, even than the grayness of Kansas which seems like the 'real world' most of the time to most of us."[36] In short, "Oz is best understood by Dorothy the way we understand dreams, art, literature, therapy: not as a way of escaping Kansas, but as energizing her for Kansas, for the work of bringing joyful possibilities to life there. This integration of Oz and Kansas is Dorothy's task; because of Oz, she is ready now for Kansas to be home. And this integration of the possibility of joy in this world in which we live is also, I believe, the task of the religious life."[37]

For Hansen, in other words, Oz is a kind of liminal experience, a glimpse of the sacred that sends us back into the profane world with the intention of sanctifying it. Hansen also sees *The Wizard* as a critique of power—including religious power. Seeking it, the Witch is destroyed by it. Pretending to have it, the Wizard is exposed as a fraud. Using it to empower others, however, Glinda alone truly understands it. Accordingly, this kind of empowerment is at the heart of what it means to be at home in the world.

In "Waiting for Godoz: A Post-Nasal Deconstruction of *The Wizard of Oz*," David Downing presents another perceptive, though brief, theological analysis. "The 1939 cinematic adaptation of Frank Baum's *The Wizard of Oz*," he writes, "has been called a film classic. It has been called the ultimate children's fantasy. It has been called a mythopoeic milestone. Yet few have recognized the work for what it really is: one of the most devastating exposés of institutional religion ever to reach the screen."[38] Like Renault and many others, Downing assumes that Oz is an unreal reflection of Kansas reality. It is presented as a dream, after all, and dreams are usually assumed to be unreal. "This, then, is the central thesis of the film: that the metaphysical realm posited by religious devotees is nothing more than a projection of the physical realm, a place in which psychic defenses may be revealed and hidden longings fulfilled."[39] Like so many people, he observes, Dorothy is troubled by the inadequacy of the world as it is. She longs for a better world, for "pie in the sky." She succumbs, in other words, to the kind of escapism that, according to Downing, is characteristic of organized religion. Once in Oz, however, she discovers that her fantasy of an ideal world is even more flawed than the reality she had left behind. Almost immediately, she sets off on her "pilgrimage" down the Yellow Brick Road. Joining her on this "Grail-like quest" are three friends who, like Dorothy herself, are troubled by *Angst*, or spiritual emptiness. "The Scarecrow seeks a brain. He goes to the Wizard to find metaphysical certainty, philosophical foundations, a *raison d'être*. The tin man seeks a heart—a transcendent basis for love, a sense of belonging and community. The lion searches for nothing less than, in Paul Tillich's phrase, the Courage to Be."[40]

From the beginning, claims Downing, the experience in Oz is profoundly disillusioning. Even the Munchkins are cynical enough to question the Wizard's existence. According to him, they are agnostics who keep repeating their doubts about supernatural beings who perform signs and wonders: "If ever, oh ever, a Wiz there was...." Downing ignores the fact that the Munchkins have no such doubts when it comes to witches. Nevertheless, he is on safer ground when discussing the Wizard himself. He lives in a "temple" or "cathedral" at the heart of what could be described as a heavenly city. Like the ancient Israelites, the citizens are not allowed to enter the Holy of Holies. In fact, they have never even seen the Wizard. No wonder Dorothy asks them: "Then how do you know he exists?" The question remains unanswered. In spite of all the pomp and pageantry surrounding the Wizard, no evidence of his existence, let alone his power, has been offered. When Dorothy and her friends actually do meet him, however, they find him to be a fraud who is literally projected to larger-than-life dimensions. Mortal though he may be, the Wizard is kind enough and wise enough to help Dorothy's friends. Merely believing in him is enough. "The implication," according to Downing, "is that the religious quest fulfills psychological needs regardless of its actual truth value."[41] Contradicting himself, Downing then observes that if this movie is a deconstruction of organized religion it is not a deconstruction of religion itself. To be sure, the

Wizard is an ordinary person posing as a deity, but this is not true of Glinda. She is a truly supernatural being. Unlike the Wizard, she is not a projection of any earthly character (that is, anyone from Kansas). On the contrary, "Glenda [sic] is always acting, always intervening on Dorothy's behalf. Yet she does so indirectly. She appears according to her own timing, not according to Dorothy's, and she is apparently absent when Dorothy seems most desperately in need of her.[42] What *The Wizard* rejects, according to Downing, is not the existence of God but the manipulation and exploitation characteristic of organized religion. Glinda herself tells Dorothy that dependence on external sources of power is unnecessary. There is much to be said for this interpretation. Unlike Renault's explanation, Downing's is not arcane. It is in keeping with the tendency toward skepticism and the emphasis on self-reliance characteristic of American society. In brief, it makes sense of the massive popularity of this movie. Nevertheless, the appeal of this movie is by no means restricted to "secular humanists."

These theological analyses are noteworthy. Since only one passing reference to religion is made in the movie, and since popular culture is seldom associated with anything profound such as religion, *The Wizard* is usually assumed to be secular. Although it involves some fantastic events and supernatural beings, these take place in the context of a dream; as a result, they are not taken seriously by many except as dramatic devices to capture the imagination of children. In other words, *The Wizard* is usually seen as a fairy tale—a story told to entertain children and possibly help them cope with the emotional problems of growing up. Even so, the situation may be more complicated. I have already suggested that *The Wizard* has taken on vaguely religious overtones. Because it is broadcast annually as a special event, viewers are able to recite the dialogue and sing the songs along with the actors as if they were participants in a festival liturgy. The races, classes, sexes, and generations of which American society consists are thus united by shared experiences and memories. As we have just seen, moreover, several authors also suggest that this movie is not unrelated to religion, be it through inspiration, satire, or both. At the end of my analysis, I propose that it has some specifically mythic properties. Even a superficial examination, however, suggests that *The Wizard* deals at some level with the great problems of human existence such as Origin (Where have we come from?), Destiny (Where are we going?), Home (Where do we belong?), Identity (Who are we in relation to other entities?), and Cosmology (Is the world friendly, hostile, or indifferent to us?). Moreover, its use of fantastic imagery is reminiscent of traditional myths that tell of superhuman beings and supernatural forces irrupting into the world of everyday life. In short, *The Wizard* shows signs of being ambiguously related to both religion (especially, myth) and secularity. But what, precisely, is the relation between religion and secularity? Are they mutually exclusive? Can something be both religious and secular at the same time?

*

Ever since the social sciences were founded, a single model of secularization has reigned supreme. This was summarized by Bryan Wilson in a collection of essays commissioned by The Society for the Scientific Study of Religion as an update to an earlier volume on the subject. "In essence," he writes of secularization, "it is related to a process of transfer of property, power, activities, and both manifest and latent functions, from institutions with a supernaturalist frame of reference to (often new) institutions operating according to empirical, rational, pragmatic criteria."[43] This notion of the increasing marginality of religion is almost always accompanied by two assumptions: that the process always moves in one direction (from religion to secularity) and that the process is irreversible. Many scholars now reject or modify this rigid definition to account for what they observe in the contemporary world. These revisionists recognize, for example, that industrialization, urbanization, and technological advances do not always correlate with a decline in religious institutions; that religion is no longer always "contained" by formal institutions; that a variety of symbol systems may function to create identity and meaning just as traditional religious systems do; and that the rise of countercultural religious movements and evangelical Protestantism in America, Islamic fundamentalism in the Middle East, and liberation theology in the Third World cannot simply be dismissed as irrelevant anachronisms. According to Peter Glasner, the term *secular* has been so misused by social scientists that its meaning has been obscured rather than clarified. In *The Sociology of Secularisation: A Critique of a Concept*, he states explicitly that "most theories of secularisation are really generalisations from limited empirical findings used by social scientists to bolster an implicit ideology of progress."[49] This approach to secularity, he argues, is based on three mistaken assumptions about religion: (1) that there was a time when Western civilization was "really religious" or that the most secular form of culture is modernity (which implies that progress toward the same rational and secular norms can be expected in "developing nations"); (2) that the impact of religion is felt uniformly throughout society; and (3) that religion can be identified with the institutions prevalent in contemporary Western societies (or those institutions at an earlier time). Glasner rejects these generalizations. He notes Roland Robertson's warning against attributing too much importance to the current situation: "Presentism, that posture which tends to claim the uniqueness of the modern period, clouds our judgment as to the long-drawn-out historical unfolding of changes we diagnose in the modern world, and also persuades us that the changes we see are inevitably coming to some early point of termination or fruition."[45] In effect, Glasner finds that the term "secularity" has been used to promote a "social myth," or ideology of progress that cannot be supported by the evidence. According to the prevailing model of secularity, an empirical, rational, and pragmatic orientation inevitably supersedes religious orientations based on the experience of supernatural beings (spirits or deities) and forces. I suggest that we need a more nuanced understanding of the various ways in which religion and secularity are related.[46] Otherwise, there would be no way to account for the overlap that frequently exists.

Communism, for example, is an explicitly antireligious ideology that, nevertheless, has many characteristics of religion. Like Christianity, it is a system of symbols. Moreover, it presents Marx as the founder-hero, Lenin as the faithful disciple, and *Das Kapital* as the authoritative text. These function, as Clifford Geertz would say, by establishing powerful, pervasive, and long-lasting moods (hope or expectancy) and motivations (for the class struggle) based on the communist conception of order: fragmentation in space is transcended when the individual merges with the collectivity. Similarly, fragmentation in time is transcended when past and present reach their ultimate and inevitable goals, the classless utopia of the future. Dialectical materialism gives history meaning, purpose, and direction; consequently, the suffering of individuals and communities can be explained in terms of a more universal order. In fact, basic human problems are all explicable through dialectical materialism. Ignorance (false consciousness), pain (poverty and powerlessness), and evil (bourgeois exploitation) can be accepted because they are not ultimate; on the contrary, they are transient and will inevitably disappear in the post revolutionary utopia. The truth of dialectical materialsim is neither self-evident nor empirically verifiable from an external point of view. Like religion, it is based on belief rather than knowledge; the source of this belief is the authority of Marx himself and his writings. In fact, proto-communist societies have made extensive use of ritual to lend even greater authority to the teachings of Marx and their application by his heirs. Submerging individuals in the collective mass at May Day parades, for instance, or presenting the ubiquitous image of Chairman Mao to them not only expresses the sociocultural system, it also shapes it by providing models to which people may conform. Once people have seen the truth of their own exploitation, once the veil of false-consciousness has been lifted, it is difficult not to see the same forces at work everywhere; with the expectation of similar results, the same logic can be applied to all social, economic, and political problems in all places.

These similarities between communism and religion did not escape the attention of Mircea Eliade. In *The Sacred and the Profane*,[47] he discussed the functional equivalents, which include not only the obvious symbolic parallels (the "proletariat" for the "chosen people" or the "elect" and the "classless society" for the "Messianic Age" or the "Kingdom of God"), but also an ontological one (an absolute end to history for the eschatology of Judaism and Christianity.) In this, he was unlike some other historicist philosophers for whom the tensions of history are inherent in the human condition and, therefore, can never be escaped. Although Eliade does not go on to say (in this particular passage) why communism is still different from Judaism and Christianity, his basic understanding of the sacred makes the difference clear. In Judaism and Christianity, both the primeval past and the eschatological future are ritually appropriated in the present as sacred time. In communism, there is no corresponding provision for the experience of sacred time. Since the eschatological future cannot be experienced in the present through ritual or hierophany, utopia remains a future projection.

But communism can be seen as a functional equivalent to aspects of religion only in societies where it is the established orthodoxy and given public expression. There are examples of the ambiguous relation between secularity and religion closer to home. By its very nature as an immigrant society, America is religiously heterogeneous. Religion means different things to different people. By its constitutional separation of church and state, moreover, it is also an officially secular society. The relation between secularity and religion in this context is somewhat different. Even though many American churches are in the process of institutional decline, for example, there is evidence (to be discussed more fully in the concluding chapter) that most Americans still consider themselves religious. Polls consistently indicate that the vast majority of Americans believe in God and life after death (standard indicators of Christian faith). Besides, the evangelical churches are resurgent. The same is true of traditional Jewish groups such as the Hassidim. New religious movements, some originating in the United States and others in Asia, are also gaining popularity. On the other hand, many Americans are indifferent to religion in any overt or traditional form. They associate religion with Christianity and Christianity with superstition. They accept a scientific description of the physical universe and recognize the legitimacy of no other. They expect medical researchers to find cures for diseases and other scientists to cure the problems created by industrial pollution. They do not turn to faith healers or wonder workers for solutions to such problems.

Between these two extremes, however, are many forms of cultural mediation. Many churches, for example, continue to use sacred symbols and rites inherited from the past but interpret them in radically different ways; they no longer refer to an ontologically distinct realm of experience that could be called "supernatural" or even "superhuman" but to ones that could be, and often are, described in purely sociological or psychological terms. And even though science has become a respectable worldview for many Americans, it may nevertheless be only superficially internalized. Evidence for this can be found not only in the resurgence of traditional forms of religion among highly educated Americans, but also in the popularity of astrology and the occult, in the proliferation of movies and television programs that explore the supernatural through science fiction and in the headlines about "creationists" who challenge scientific assumptions about the origin of the present natural order by using science itself, even if adjusted to serve their purposes, as their chief weapon against "secular humanism." In fact, the situation is even more complex. Two prominent features of American life, Christmas and Memorial Day, illustrate the flexible boundary between religion and secularity in America. The former has an explicitly religious origin (the nativity of Christ) that has been transformed into a midwinter festival in which members of secular society (and even members of non-Christians religious traditions) can participate; the latter has an explicitly secular origin (the Civil War) that has been given explicitly religious expression. (For a fuller discussion of this, see Appendix 3.) *The Wizard*, I suggest, is another form of mediation that illustrates the flexible boundary between religion and secularity, one that is characteristic of American culture in our time.

PROGRAM HIGHLIGHTS
WEEK EIGHT

Tuesday, June 23 at 8 PM
Wednesday, June 24 at 8 PM
RONALD FELDMAN
conducting
Boston Pops Esplanade Orchestra

Overture to *La gazza ladra*	Rossini
Excerpts from *A Midsummer*	
Night's Dream	Mendelssohn
From the Polovtsian Dances	Borodin

Remembering Gatsby:
Foxtrot for Orchestra *Harbison*
Rhapsody in Blue *Gershwin*
JONATHAN FELDMAN
Berlin Bouquet *arr. Mason*
Theme from *The Pink Panther Mancini*
A Salute to the Big Bands
In the Mood *Garland/Miller-Hayman*
Moonlight Serenade *Miller-Hayman*
Sing, Sing, Sing
Prima/Goodman-Hayman

Thursday, June 25 at 8 PM
Friday, June 26 at 8 PM
BILL CONTI *conducting*
Boston Pops Esplanade Orchestra
PROGRAM TO BE ANNOUNCED

Saturday, June 27 at 8 PM
Sunday, June 28 at 7:30 PM
JOHN WILLIAMS *conducting*
Boston Pops Esplanade Orchestra

Celebration Fanfare	Williams
Overture to *Candide*	Bernstein
Suite from *Jane Eyre*	Williams
Richard Rodgers Waltzes	
	arr. Anderson

Concerto for Cello
and Orchestra in C *Haydn*
ALAN STEPANSKY

Hooray for Hollywood! *Whiting-Williams*
Selections from *The Wizard of Oz*
Arlen-Stevens
In the Mood *Garland/Miller-Hayman*
I Love a Parade, from the Cotton Club
Review *Rhythmania* *arr. Hayman*

WEEK NINE

Monday, June 29 at 8 PM
HARRY ELLIS DICKSON
conducting
Boston Pops Esplanade Orchestra

Washington Post, March	Sousa
Poet and Peasant Overture	Suppé
Meditation from *Thaïs*	Massenet
From the *Irish Suite*	Anderson
Concerto No. 5 for violin and	
orchestra in A minor	Vieuxtemps
ZHENG-RONG WANG	

Hey, Look Me Over, from
Wildcat *Coleman-Hayman*
Spring Is Here *arr. Stevens*
Selections from *The Sound*
of Music *Rodgers-Bennett*
Seventy-Six Trombones, from
The Music Man *Willson-Anderson*

Tuesday, June 30 at 8 PM
Wednesday, July 1 at 8 PM
JOHN WILLIAMS *conducting*
Boston Pops Esplanade Orchestra

Liberty Fanfare	Williams
Shaker Hymn from	
Appalachian Spring	Copland

Remembering Gatsby:
Foxtrot for Orchestra *Harbison*
Balloon Sequence and Devil's Dance
from *Witches of Eastwick* *Williams*

Love Is Sweeping the Country
Gershwin-Ramin
The Magic of Walt Disney
arr. Ferguson
The Girl from Ipanema
Jobim-Hollenbeck
Trumpet Blues and Cantabile *arr. May*
Begin the Beguine *Porter-May*
When the Saints
Go Marchin' In *arr. May*

Thursday, July 2 at 8 PM
HARRY ELLIS DICKSON
conducting
Boston Pops Esplanade Orchestra

Washington Post, March	Sousa
Poet and Peasant Overture	Suppé
Meditation from *Thaïs*	Massenet
From the *Irish Suite*	Anderson
Concerto No. 5 for violin and	
orchestra in A minor	Vieuxtemps
ZHENG-RONG WANG	

Hey, Look Me Over, from
Wildcat *Coleman-Hayman*
Spring Is Here *arr. Stevens*
Selections from *The Sound*
of Music *Rodgers-Bennett*
Seventy-Six Trombones, from
The Music Man *Willson-Anderson*

JULY 3, 4, 6, 7, 8, AND 9
CONCERTS IN THE HATCH
SHELL ON THE CHARLES
RIVER ESPLANADE

Friday, July 3 at 8 PM
JOHN WILLIAMS *conducting*
Boston Pops Esplanade Orchestra
A Salute to John Philip Sousa
arr. Williams
Shaker Hymn from
Appalachian Spring *Copland*
The Songs of Stephen Foster
arr. Knight
Bugler's Holiday *Anderson*
The Spirit of '76 *arr. Walker*
JOHNNY CASH

The Star Spangled Banner
Richard Rodgers Waltzes
arr. Anderson
Selections from *The Wizard of Oz*
Arlen-Stevens
Patriotic Sing-Along *arr. Hayman*
"We're Lookin' Good!" *Williams*
Composed for the Special Olympics
in Celebration of the 1987
International Summer Games
Somewhere Out There,
from *An American Tail*
Mann/Horner-Ferguson
MacNamara's Band *Latham-Hayman*

Saturday, July 4 at 8 PM
JOHN WILLIAMS *conducting*
Boston Pops Esplanade Orchestra
A Salute to John Philip Sousa
arr. Williams
Shaker Hymn from
Appalachian Spring *Copland*
The Songs of Stephen Foster
arr. Knight
Bugler's Holiday *Anderson*
The Spirit of '76 *arr. Walker*
JOHNNY CASH

The Star Spangled Banner
Selections from *The Wizard of Oz*
Arlen-Stevens
Patriotic Sing-Along *Hayman*
1812, Ouverture Solennelle
Tchaikovsky
"We're Lookin' Good!" *Williams*
Composed for the Special Olympics
in Celebration of the 1987
International Summer Games
MacNamara's Band *Latham-Hayman*

Monday, July 6 at 8 PM
HARRY ELLIS DICKSON
conducting
Boston Pops Esplanade Orchestra
Entrance of the Guests
from *Tannhäuser* *Wagner*
Overture to *The Barber of Seville*
Rossini
Capriccio Espagnol *Rimsky-Korsakov*

The Star Spangled Banner
Overture to *Die Fledermaus* *Strauss*
Selections from *Fiddler on the Roof*
Bock-Mason
Londonderry Air *Grainger*
Seventy-Six Trombones, from
The Music Man *Willson-Anderson*

Tuesday, July 7 at 8 PM
HARRY ELLIS DICKSON
conducting
Boston Pops Esplanade Orchestra
Rákóczy March from
The Damnation of Faust *Berlioz*
Finlandia *Sibelius*
Movement from Concerto
for piano and orchestra
Khachaturian
SUSAN WORTERS

The Star Spangled Banner
Spring Is Here *arr. Stevens*
Selections from *Gigi* *Loewe-Bennett*
I Love a Parade, from the Cotton Club
Review *Rhythmania* *arr. Hayman*

Wednesday, July 8 at 8 PM
HARRY ELLIS DICKSON
conducting
Boston Pops Esplanade Orchestra
Symphony No. 7 in A major, Op. 92
Beethoven

The Star Spangled Banner
Movement from Concerto No. 1 for
violin and orchestra, Op. 6 *Paganini*
VALI PHILLIPS
Selections from *Girl Crazy*
Gershwin-Anderson

Thursday, July 9 at 8 PM
HARRY ELLIS DICKSON
conducting
Boston Pops Esplanade Orchestra
March Militaire *Schubert*
Symphony No. 7 in B minor, D. 759
"Unfinished" *Schubert*
Prelude to Act III of *Lohengrin Wagner*

The Star Spangled Banner
Emperor Waltzes *Strauss*
Gaîté parisienne suite *Offenbach*
Prayer of Thanksgiving *Valerius*

Baldwin Piano
John Williams and the Boston Pops record
exclusively for Philips Records
Please note that concerts through July 2
take place at Symphony Hall
Programs subject to change

Figure 1

[Permission to reproduce this brochure is granted by the Boston
Symphony Orchestra.]

2 SIGHT AND SOUND

The Wizard begins on a farm in Kansas. Dorothy and her dog, Toto, are running down a dirt road toward the farm where they live with Auntie Em and Uncle Henry. Toto has bitten Miss Gulch and she has threated to take revenge. Unfortunately, Auntie Em is too busy to help Dorothy cope with Miss Gulch. And when the three farmhands—Zeke, Hunk, and Hickory—offer Dorothy advice and support, Auntie Em scolds them for laziness. Then Miss Gulch arrives at the farm with an order from the sheriff authorizing her to take Toto and have him destroyed. Neither Auntie Em nor Uncle Henry can do anything to stop her. As Miss Gulch rides away with Toto, he jumps out of the basket and runs back to Dorothy. Now Dorothy decides that the only solution is to run away from home with Toto.

On the road, she and Toto come across an itinerant charlatan named Professor Marvel. He guesses that the two are running away from home and convinces Dorothy to go back. He does this by sneaking a glimpse of the photograph Dorothy has been carrying in her basket; looking into his crystal ball, he tells Dorothy that he can see a woman falling ill with worry over someone she loves. Deciding that she belongs at home after all, Dorothy immediately sets out for the farm. But a storm begins even as she takes leave of Professor Marvel.

By the time she arrives at the farm, a tornado can be seen sweeping across the prairie. Since the farm community has withdrawn to the cyclone cellar, Dorothy is left to fend for herself. Looking for safety, she runs into her own bedroom. Suddenly, the tornado hits. It knocks the window frame onto her head. After passing out for a few moments, she comes to and looks out the window. In the dream sequence that now begins, she is surprised to find that the whole house has been lifted up into the air by the cyclone. Outside the window, Auntie Em flies by as she sits in her rocking chair knitting. Then the three farmhands fly past in their rowboat. Finally Miss Gulch appears on her bicycle and is suddenly transformed into a

cackling witch on a broomstick. The house then falls to the ground
with a thud. Dorothy walks to the front door. Opening it, she finds
that she is no longer on the farm in Kansas.

Dorothy has arrived in Oz. To be more precise, she has landed in
the Munchkin City. The house falls on top of the Wicked Witch of the
East and kills her. The Munchkins are overjoyed at being delivered
from her tyranny. Now Glinda, the Good Witch of the North, floats
down from the sky in her bubble and proclaims the beginning of a
new era in Oz. At the same time, Dorothy is recognized as a national
heroine. In the middle of the festivities, the Wicked Witch of the
West—an "Ozzified" version of Miss Gulch—appears in a burst of
flame and smoke. She is angry at the death of her sister. But she is
even more upset when Glinda transfers the ruby slippers from the
dead witch's feet to Dorothy's. Since her power does not extend to
the Munchkin City, there is nothing she can do. Before leaving, nevertheless, she threatens Dorothy. And Glinda warns Dorothy that she
will be at the Witch's mercy if she takes off the ruby slippers for even
a moment. Now Dorothy really wants to go back home. Glinda
suggests that she seek help from the Wizard of Oz. That means a
lengthy journey to the Emerald City.

After being escorted by the Munchkins to the edge of town, Dorothy
continues to follow the Yellow Brick Road through fields and
meadows on her way to the Emerald City. Along the way, she meets
three friends. Each of these is an "Ozzified" version of a farmhand
back home in Kansas. One of them is a Scarecrow. Lacking a brain,
the Scarecrow feels very sorry for himself. Dorothy convinces him to
join her in seeking help from the Wizard. Next, she meets a Tin Man.
Lacking a heart, he also feels very sorry for himself. He, too, is easily
convinced to seek out the Wizard. Finally, Dorothy meets a Cowardly
Lion. Lacking courage, he is the laughing stock of the forest.
Although he is afraid to seek help, he is even more afraid to leave
things as they are. Now Dorothy and Toto have three good friends
and one fierce enemy.

Traveling through Oz, the friends encounter a series of problems.
Within sight of the Emerald City, for example, the Witch uses a spell
to prevent them from reaching their destination; the fumes in a field
of poppies put them to sleep. But Glinda rescues them by covering
the flowers with snow. Problems do not cease even inside the
Emerald City. First, they have difficulty getting in to see the Wizard.
When they do have an audience with an "Ozzified" version of Professor
Marvel, he says he will grant their requests on one condition: that
they bring him the Witch's broomstick. Having no other choice, the

friends set out on this dangerous quest.

As they pass through the Haunted Forest, the Wicked Witch sends out her simian "air force." The winged monkeys pick up Dorothy and Toto, leaving the others in a state of disarray. Just after the prisoners are brought to the Witch's Castle, Toto escapes. With Dorothy still in her power, though, the Witch makes plans to take the ruby slippers. This can be done only by killing her. Turning over the hourglass, the Witch tells her that she has not long to live.

In the meantime, Toto has found the friends and led them back to the Witch's Castle. There, they manage to infiltrate the Winkie guards, find Dorothy, and begin their escape. Before they can get away, though, the guards find them. Now the Witch decides to end the matter at once. As she sets fire to the Scarecrow, Dorothy picks up a bucket of water and throws it in his direction. When the water splashes on the Witch, however, she begins to melt. Once she is dead, the guards proclaim Dorothy a heroine just as the Munchkins had done. Now she and her friends can return to the Emerald City and claim their rewards.

When they find themselves, once again, in the Wizard's audience hall, they discover that the Wizard is a fraud. Toto pulls aside a curtain revealing the fact that the Wizard's impressive appearance is nothing more than the image projected by an insignificant little man pulling switches and pushing levers. Their disappointment is short-lived, however, because the man who seems to be a fraud turns out to be a wise man after all. He provides Dorothy's friends with official recognition of their achievements; in this way, their requests are granted. To help Dorothy, however, he must take her back home to Kansas himself. But once Dorothy is in the gondola of his balloon and waiting to take off, Toto suddenly jumps out and runs after a cat. When Dorothy goes to get him back, the balloon takes off without her. Just then, Glinda sails down in her bubble. After Dorothy explains what she has learned from her journey through Oz, Glinda informs her that she has always had the power to go home. But she had to learn that for herself. Now she is ready to go home. She has merely to say "There's no place like home" three times and click her ruby slippers together.

Once Dorothy wakes up in her bed back on the farm, she is convinced that her experiences in Oz were real. Although no one believes her, they are all glad to see her. She is surrounded by those who care about her: Auntie Em and Uncle Henry, Toto, Professor Marvel, and the three farmhands.

*

Even after a single viewing, it becomes clear to everyone that *The*

Wizard consists of three distinct cinematic units: a brief opening unit (set in Kansas), which could be called a prologue; a lengthy middle unit (set in Oz); and a very brief concluding unit (set once more in Kansas), which could be called an epilogue. This cinematic "structure" provides a helpful framework for analysis of the formal properties; it is precisely the use of these that creates this structure. Although it could be argued that using the latter is not legitimate as the basis for a formal analysis because it involves a priori recognition of a cinematic pattern, I argue the reverse: it is precisely the fact that this tripartite structure is so obvious that suggests the usefulness of formal analysis in the first place. In other words, formal analysis is not being used here to establish the *existence* of a tripartite cinematic structure but to discover the ways in which it is *presented.*

Many formal properties used in *The Wizard* could have been selected for systematic study. I have selected seven: dialogue, color, music, mise-en-scène, dramatis personae, space, and time. These are used consistently according to some pattern, or "code."[1] Formal analysis raises questions such as the following. In what way does each formal property differentiate among these three cinematic units? Does a single, generalized, pattern link all of them? If so, what is the relation between this and the narrative pattern (that is, either the plot or the story)? And, ultimately, what is the relation between the patterns of these particular codes and those of American culture as a whole?

*

Normally, people think of dialogue as verbal communication of information. As the vehicles of verbal communication, words are usually considered in their semantic sense. In the days of "silent pictures," verbal information was almost always considered necessary, even though visual communication predominated; at that time, this meant reliance on the printed word (that is, on captions, or "titles"). Even in "talking pictures," the spoken word did not replace visual communication. But words have a phonetic, as well as semantic, aspect. Theoretically, then, dialogue could also be studied as a system of phonemes. In the following pages, however, dialogue is considered from neither point of view. Instead, it is examined as a type of "verbal behavior." The focus of attention is not primarily on the word (or constituent element) itself—considered either phonetically or semantically—but on the kinds of interaction between characters that take place when words are used. A distinction is made between "normal" dialogue (which conforms to patterns of speech familiar in everyday life) and "abnormal" dialogue (which does not and is, therefore, anomalous).

Kansas Prologue: In these sequences, dialogue is generally normal. That is, it is spoken more or less as it is in everyday life. But there is one exception: "Over the Rainbow." This, of course, is *sung* dialogue. Although audiences accept this as normal, such acceptance is possible only as a result of stylistic convention; in everyday life, people do not spontaneously burst into song to express their deepest feelings and thoughts. (It is worth noting that this particular convention was still a recent innovation in 1939. Before the Broadway production of *Showboat* in 1927, and long afterward, songs were included as diversions or interruptions in the dialogue. Very often, they were normalized (or made acceptable by convention) as performances in a play within the larger play. Today, once again, accepted stylistic conventions make "Over the Rainbow" seem "abnormal"). Since "Over the Rainbow" is the only song in the prologue, it must be classified as a formal anomaly. It is not the only one.

Normally, dialogue involves both speech and response. That is, at least one character speaks and at least one other character responds. In the prologue, however, Dorothy speaks not only to other human characters, but also to her dog; Toto, of course, can respond only barking. Once again, this could be called abnormal dialogue. (It may not seem abnormal to pet owners. In a technical sense, though, it is abnormal even when they talk to their dogs, cats, or birds. If dialogue involves the use of language—and I use the word dialogue with that in mind—then communication between pet owners (who use language) and their pets (who do not) is clearly "abnormal.") In one case, Toto does not respond at all. "Over the Rainbow" is generally considered a soliloquy; although technically addressed to Toto—"Do you suppose there is such a place, Toto?" [39]—Dorothy's words are understood to address either herself or the offscreen world of the audience. Either as a song or as a soliloquy, "Over the Rainbow" cannot be considered normal dialogue.

Oz: In these middle sequences, dialogue is used heterogeneously. Sometimes it is normal and sometimes abnormal. The greatest contrast is between the Witch's Castle and the Emerald City.

Emerald City: Here, abnormality is defined primarily in terms of sung dialogue. The major characters are involved in two songs: both "In the Merry Old Land of Oz" and "If I Were King of the Forest" are featured as major production numbers. Nevertheless, there are no passages of nonreciprocal dialogue or any other types of abnormal dialogue.

Witch's Castle: Here, dialogue includes some decidedly abnormal features. Although there is only one passage of sung dialogue (in which the main characters do not participate), it consists of several indistinct phonemes instead of intelligible words. Because it consists of patterned utterances, it must be considered dialogue. Nevertheless, it corresponds to no type of dialogue classified by Seymour Chatman.[2] Dialogue at the Witch's Castle includes another anomaly. In this case, abnormality is defined as nonreciprocal dialogue. The Witch's crystal ball distorts, or perverts, the process of normal, two-way communication. Through it, Dorothy hears the words of Auntie Em: "Dorothy! Dorothy! Where are you? It's me...." But Auntie Em cannot hear Dorothy's words: "I...I'm here in Oz, Auntie Em...Oh, Auntie Em, don't go away! I'm frightened! Come back!" Intercepting the process is the Witch who suddenly appears the way a news flash interrupts a television program: "Auntie Em...Auntie Em, come back! I'll give you Auntie Em, my pretty!"[109]. In short, the Witch's Castle is associated with "abnormal" dialogue.

Yellow Brick Road: Here, dialogue could be described as both normal and abnormal. In the Munchkin City, for example, dialogue is both sung and spoken. Separated by brief passages of spoken dialogue are four songs: Dorothy's "It Really Was No Miracle," Glinda's "Come Out, Come Out, Wherever You Are," the Munchkins' "Ding Dong, the Witch Is Dead" and "You're off to See the Wizard."

Also abnormal is Dorothy's continued practice of speaking to Toto. Upon landing in Oz and taking her first few steps in the Munchkin City, Dorothy utters one of the most famous lines in film history: "Toto, I have a feeling we're not in Kansas anymore; we must be over the rainbow"[53].

In the rural hinterland traversed by the Yellow Brick Road, dialogue is also both normal and abnormal. There is only one song—"If I Only Had a Brain (a Heart; the Nerve)"—but it is repeated twice. Also, the dialogue includes other abnormal elements. In this case, abnormality is defined as nondiegetic (from offscreen). When the Tin Man sings of his need for a heart, he refers to Shakespeare's famous love story: "Picture me a balcony, Above a voice sings low" and a disembodied female voice answers "Wherefore art thou, Romeo?" [74]. And when the friends approach the Emerald City, it is a disembodied chorus singing "You're out of the Woods" that encourages them to push on toward their goal.

Kansas Epilogue: Here, dialogue has been purified of its abnormal features in the prologue. Words are now only spoken, for example, and not sung. And Dorothy speaks only to other human characters (who can respond to her in speech) and not to Toto.

*

The color code refers both to the use of monochromatic or polychromatic film stock and to the patterns in which the latter is used. Today, almost all movies and television shows are seen in color. That has become the norm. Faithful reproduction of natural color is expected, and anything else seems unusual and unnatural—not the way things appear in everyday life. In fact, the current drive toward "colorization" of black-and-white movies is based on the assumption that black-and-white is a barrier for viewers. Black-and-white film is still used for a variety of artistic purposes, to be sure, but greater naturalism is not one of them. Black-and-white is sometimes used to evoke the atmosphere of early movies. This is the case, for instance, in *Zelig* (Woody Allen, 1983), and *Paper Moon* (Peter Bogdanovich, 1973). At other times, sepia-tinted film is used for the same purpose. Examples of this include *Bonnie and Clyde* (Arthur Penn, 1967) and *Butch Cassidy and the Sundance Kid* (George Roy Hill, 1969).

Although the connection between color film and naturalism now seems inevitable, it was not always so. As early as the 1920s and as recently as the 1940s, the situation was somewhat different. Even in those days, color movies (as distinct from those made on tinted monochromatic stock) were not unknown. Color was occasionally used, for instance, to enhance costume dramas set in remote times or exotic places. Examples of this include *Becky Sharp* (Rouben Mamoulian, 1935), *The Garden of Allah* (Richard Boleslawski, 1936), *Gone with the Wind* (Victor Fleming, 1939), and a remake of *Blood and Sand* (Rouben Mamoulian, 1941). More often, color was used for musical extravaganzas. *The Broadway Melody* (Harry Beaumont, 1929), *Rio Rita* (Luther Reed, 1929), *The Hollywood Revue of 1929* (Charles Reisner, 1929), *Show of Shows* (Darryl F. Zanuck, 1929), and *Paramount on Parade* (Dorothy Arzner and others, 1930) all included musical sequences filmed in color. But the color technology of these early musicals was very primitive. Even in the late 1930s, with the invention of three-strip Technicolor, the effect was not entirely naturalistic. Considering the use made of color, though, this was not necessarily a problem. "Musicals were capricious," writes Ethan Mordden, "so the bizarre color scheme only added to their appeal.... Color became so identified with the musicals that when the form ran out of juice in 1930–31, color was given up with relief...."[3] Still, it was revived later in the decade; the association of musicals with color continued with *Ramona* (Henry King, 1936), *Meet Me in St. Louis* (Vincente Minnelli, 1944), and the Rodgers and Hammerstein musicals of the 1950s (when color was still rather unusual in other movie genres). Black-and-white, on the other hand, was often used in the 1930s and 1940s for movies that aimed specifically for naturalistic effects. This is noteworthy in *The Grapes of Wrath* (John Ford, 1940), for example, and *Citizen Kane* (Orson Welles, 1941). In both cases, conscious associations with the newsreels were evoked. In brief, color is not necessarily associated with naturalism, while black-and-white is not necessarily associated with the reverse; the connotations of each really have become very ambiguous.

In 1939, then, the polychromatic sequences in Oz may have seemed "unreal" precisely *because* they were shot in color, and the monochromatic sequences in Kansas may have seemed "real" precisely because they were *not* shot in color. Cinematic conventions have changed in the past fifty years. Would more recent viewers of *The Wizard* not reverse this perception? For various reasons, they may not do so. Although viewers are now more conscious of the "unnatural" quality of monochromatic film and more prepared to accept polychromatic film as "natural," other factors prevent a reversal. The Kansas sequences, for example, were originally printed on sepia-tinted film stock in order to evoke nostalgia for the movie's turn-of-the-century setting (when photographs were usually sepia). Even though many prints no longer have the sepia tinting, black-and-white still evokes the old newsreels. Having considered the use of black-and-white or color film stock, as such, attention can be turned to the particular ways in which both are used in *The Wizard*.

Kansas Prologue: These sequences are monochromatic. That is, things are visible only as gradations in the amount of white, unrefracted light. Until the final frames, no anomaly appears. But when Dorothy opens the front door and enters Oz, viewers briefly see both the monochrome of the prologue and the polychrome of Oz just outside the house. In cinematic terms, of course, this is an anomaly.[4]

Oz: These sequences are polychromatic. Although the multiplicity of colors is very beautiful, it is also the result of fragmentation. That is, colors become visible only when white light is refracted. Here, fragmentation is specifically represented by chromatic contrasts between the Emerald City and the Witch's Castle.

Emerald City: These sequences, of course, are associated with green; in virtually every frame, green is the predominant color.

Witch's Castle: Not quite so obviously, these sequences are associated with red. The Witch herself, for example, is obsessed by the idea of snatching the ruby slippers that had belonged to her sister (the Wicked Witch of the East) and now "belong" to her. In fact, the grains of "sand" in her hourglass are the same red sequins that cover the ruby slippers. Moreover, the poison she concocts in her "lab" is blood red; she uses it to create a field of deadly (red) poppies. That this association has been made can be seen in an advertisement for Sotheby's. Above the text, only the Witch's hat appears. A square of red provides the background on an otherwise white page. Any color might have been chosen to catch the eye, but red *was* chosen. I suggest that this was not entirely coincidental; consciously or unconsciously, a link was made between the Witch and the color red.

Yellow Brick Road: Color is also used to link these chromatic opposites. The Yellow Brick Road is, after all, associated with the color that lies precisely midway between red and green on the color spectrum. In other words, the Road is a chromatic, as well as geographical, mediator.

Kansas Epilogue: These sequences are all monochromatic. This represents a reversion to visual conditions in the prologue—only now there is no anomalous use of color.

*

Film-makers have used music[5] in two basic ways. On the one hand, it is used in the "background" to establish moods. On the other hand, it is used in the "foreground" (as song) either to advance the plot or to articulate feelings and define characters.

Although background music is, in fact, a highly artificial convention (since no one actually hears it in everyday life unless the radio is turned on—and even then it hardly ever corresponds emotionally to what people are saying, thinking, or feeling), the audience can accept it, in the context of movies and television, as part of the "natural order." By 1939, it had become so familiar from both talking and silent movies—the latter were almost always accompanied by orchestra, organ or piano—that it was probably seldom heard as a distinct element in its own right. Indeed, it was not intended to be "heard" at all; it was intended, on the contrary, to draw attention away from itself and toward the verbal and visual elements of the movie. At the same time, musical comedy (spoken dialogue plus songs) had also become a familiar theatrical convention. Nevertheless, as Martin Gottfried[6] points out, songs were seldom integrated into the plot: either they were interludes in the plot or the plot was filler for a musical revue. In 1927, *Showboat* was the first Broadway musical in which songs were integrated into the plot. But few movie musicals followed this innovative pattern. In fact, only three had done so before 1939: *Love Me Tonight* (Rouben Mamoulian, 1932), *Hallelujah, I'm a Bum* (Lewis Milestone, 1933), and *High, Wide and Handsome* (Rouben Mamoulian, 1937). Even the famous Fred Astaire and Ginger Rogers musicals depended on the standard formula in which the songs and dances were entertaining diversions from the plot. As an exception to that pattern, *The Wizard* is important in the history of movie musicals; it links *Showboat* to the later musicals of Rodgers and Hammerstein.

In the Kansas sequences, music creates a naturalistic[7] atmosphere. Just as naturalism in painting is, in fact, "unnatural" (since the objects represented exist in only two of the three dimensions), naturalism in this movie is, in fact, "unnatural" (since members of the audience expect neither to hear music corresponding to their emotions and activities, nor to burst spontaneously into song in their everyday lives). In both cases, though, the "unnatural" is made to seem natural through the use of culturally accepted conventions. (The illusion of three-dimensionality in painting is achieved through the use of perspective; the illusion of normality in this movie is achieved by separating Dorothy and Toto from the other characters when private thoughts are revealed.) In the Oz sequences, however, music adds to the "unnatural" (or theatrical and surrealistic) atmosphere. The music of Oz, in fact, is a parody of grand opera, complete with choruses and ballets in the Munchkin City and Emerald City sequences. From this, it would seem that Kansas is associated with reality (although, as I hope to show, it is an ultimate, not an immediate or local, reality) and Oz with theatrical illusion and artifice (which, as I also hope to show, is a symbolic description of immediate and local, not ultimate, reality).

Kansas Prologue: In these sequences, music is used in ways familiar to American audiences. According to the Hollywood convention accepted in 1939, for instance, music was either confined to the background to evoke moods or brought into the foreground as a diversion. In neither case was it used to advance the plot. Most of the music used in the prologue is confined to the background. But Dorothy's soliloquy, "Over the Rainbow," is anomalous. It reveals her longing for a better world and, therefore, motivates her decision to run away. In effect, background and foreground come together.

But there is a much more jarring musical anomaly. Both the background music and the ballad are "traditional" in style. That is, they are derived from classical music of the nineteenth century. The only really alien musical element is Miss Gulch's theme. Unlike any other musical passage in the prologue, this one is distinctly dissonant. In fact, it is atonal.[8]

Oz: In these sequences, on the contrary, music is heterogeneous. It is systematically used to contrast the familiar and the alien. In the prologue, musical passages are structurally complete because they have beginnings, middles, and endings.[9] In Oz, this pattern breaks down. As a result, music is structurally fragmented. This occurs in at least two forms.

In the first place, concluding bars (or "cadences") are seldom actually heard; almost invariably, the composition is interrupted before it can reach its "natural" conclusion. Musical tension is first built up and then broken by something external to the music itself. Consider these examples: the Munchkin chorus-ballet is suddenly interrupted by the Witch's appearance; the Witch suddenly interrupts Dorothy and her friends as they sing and dance their way down the Yellow Brick Road; then the Lion interrupts their song with a hearty growl; the Witch's sudden appearance in the sky over the Emerald City puts an end to the the chorus below; the sudden closing of a door in the Castle has an identical effect on background music.

But sudden interruptions are not the only form of musical fragmentation in Oz. Bits and pieces of major songs and themes are jumbled up together and scattered everywhere. They are never presented from beginning to end; instead, a few bars are thrown in to suggest a mood or revive a memory. Moreover, these fragments are always distorted in some way. When Dorothy and her friends are walking through the forest on their quest for the Witch's broomstick, for example, the familiar strains of "Over the Rainbow" are heard in the background with atonal modifications. At other times, the same song is rendered alien and disturbing by being played in a minor key. This song returns over and over again in Oz—but only as a distorted, confused fragment. The same is true of a song that had been familiar to Americans since the turn of the century. "In the Shade of the Old Apple Tree" is distorted when it occurs as background music in the orchard sequence. Likewise, Dorothy and her friends fall asleep in the poppy field, a few bars of "Over the Rainbow" convey a sense of nostalgia but also a sense of something gone wrong because the familar melody is now experienced in an alien and threatening context.

Music in Oz also indicates conflict between the familiar musical idiom of America and the alien one of Europe. That is, music not only affirms the "native" American idiom, it also parodies that of Europe. Americans have long associated opera with both Europeans in general and aristocrats in particular (not to mention Americans with aristocratic pretensions). As John D. Shout observes, the conflict between the familiar and the foreign, or the American and the European, has been a motif in many American movies.[10] In *San Francisco* (W. S. Van Dyke, 1936), he notes the gulf between Europe and America, or between the foreign and the familiar, has been symbolically transcended. In *The Wizard*, on the contrary, it has been confirmed, or even widened, throughout the Oz sequences.

Emerald City: Here, Dorothy and her friends are greeted by the soft and welcoming tones of an all-female chorus singing "You're out of the Woods." By 1939, Busby Berkeley (and others) had made the use of female choruses familar to moviegoers. In all cases, these choruses were associated with moods of pleasure. In "I Only Have Eyes for You" from *Dames* (Ray Enright, 1934) and "The Words Are in My Heart" from *Gold Diggers of 1935* (Busby Berkeley, 1935), this takes the form of romance. In "We're in the Money" from *Gold Diggers of 1933* (Mervyn Le Roy, 1933), it takes the form of hope. And in "I'm Young and Healthy" from *Forty-Second Street* (Lloyd Bacon, 1933), it takes the form of sheer frivolity. The use of female choruses, however, was simply the continuation of a tradition begun decades earlier with the chorus lines in cabaret shows and Broadway musical revues. As one historian put it "Ziegfeld glorified them, Berkeley automated them."[11] The point is that this device was characteristic of the American musical idiom familiar to most viewers, and that it evoked strongly positive feelings.

"In the Merry Old Land of Oz" is a production number that, with its chorus girls, might have been part of the Ziegfeld Follies. Unlike the welcoming music in the Munchkin City, this passage is an isolated, self-contained unit; it does not flow into other vocal passages and choruses as in opera. In short, it is very American. In the Lion's song, "If I Were King of the Forest," both American and European elements can be heard, but the latter are reduced to parody. With its exaggeration and its cadenzas (elaborate devices used in grand opera to show off the tenor's virtuosity), it is like an aria; along with all this pretentiousness and pomposity, though, are lyrics derived directly from the musical comedies of Broadway. The Lion (who even speaks with a Brooklynese accent) uses idiosyncratic contractions (such as "compash" for "compassion") in the same way that Ira Gershwin used them (in titles such as "S'wonderful" for George Gershwin's 1927 show, *Funny Face*). In other words, this music is familiar in a distinctly American way.

Witch's Castle: Approaching the Castle, Dorothy's friends are intimidated by the chanting of an all-male chorus of guards. It should be noted here that the guards are all male creatures with lower voices than females—and their voices have been artificially lowered still further.[12] This chant is clearly associated with alien forms of music. Since the Renaissance, Western music has shown a preference in the vocal range for tenors and sopranos (as it has in Italian opera even though castrati have not been used since the eighteenth century). In earlier periods, though, the preferred vocal range had been lower (as in the

Gregorian chant). And in Russia, the ancient liturgical music of the Orthodox Church favored the lower end of the vocal continuum. It was not many centuries after the adoption of Byzantine church music by Russian Orthodoxy that Greek travellers first observed differences between the Russian and Greek manner of singing. What they found particularly strange was the strong preference given to bass voices.[13] That preference has been continued, into modern times, moreover, through opera. Bruce Bohle comments on the preference for basso profondo parts in Russian opera.[14]

The association of the Winkie chant with Russia is evident when it is compared to a Russian folk song that has long been popular in America: "The Song of the Volga Boatmen." Since the chant has no words, but only a sequence of vowels, it is unintelligible. For all intents and purposes, it is in a "foreign language." Nevertheless, the "o-ee-o" of this chant corresponds to the "yo-heave-ho" in English translations of the Russian song.[15] Moreover, the "melodic" structure in one is a precise reversal of the other. Also, both songs make use of the open fifth (a musical form used very seldom in Western music since the seventeenth century but commonly in Russian music). The guards' chant, for example, alternates between the tonic (first) and dominant (fifth) notes of the scale; the mediant (third) note is missing; this makes it impossible to know whether the key is major or minor and gives the composition an eerie quality.

The chant is not only alien, it is threatening. When Dorothy's friends infiltrate their ranks and enter the Castle, a secondary motif is played just above or just below the primary one. But it is played in a different key. This bitonality creates dissonance. And because of its use of woodwind and percussion instruments—to the exclusion of stringed instruments—it has a harsh, brassy, military sound (not unlike the early works of Prokofiev and Shostakovich).

Yellow Brick Road: Traversing Oz, the Yellow Brick Road begins inside the Munchkin City but stops at the gates of the Emerald City. In this mediating region, both American and European elements coexist, but neither predominates. That is, some places along the Yellow Brick Road are musically European, while others are musically American. The Munchkin City itself is European. Its musical idiom is grand opera. Although there are no distinct arias, there are several vocal passages (recitatives) that flow into each other as they do in opera. "Come out, Come out, Wherever You Are," for instance, merges with "It Really Was No Miracle." These, in turn, flow into ballet (the choreographed procession that welcomes Dorothy) and on into choruses of "Ding Dong, the Witch Is Dead," "Follow the Yellow Brick Road," "We're off to See the Wizard."

Beyond the Munchkin City, Dorothy and her friends sing and dance their way along the Yellow Brick Road in a style derived directly from vaudeville (the American musical genre, par excellence, that reached its golden age in the 1920s and 1930s). In this sense, it can be said that "If I Only Had a Brain (a Heart; the Nerve)" is distinctly American (with its limited vocal range; simple, repetitive, rhythm; basic harmonies; simple orchestration; and folklike melody) compared to the elaborate staging, choreography, and orchestration of the "operatic" sequences in the Munchkin City. This song is reminiscent of song-and-dance routines performed in theaters across America in the early part of this century. But the folksy, American atmosphere is introduced even earlier. As Dorothy and Toto take leave of the Munchkins, "You're off to See the Wizard" is briefly interrupted by a few bars of "Turkey in the Straw" (a minstrel song often used in the fiddler's warm-up for square dances).

Another side of the American musical tradition is introduced on the Road. At the beginning (when Dorothy and Toto are just setting out for the Emerald City), there is a brief passage in the background that can be called "Gershwinesque." It is reminiscent, in effect, of the "walking theme" from George Gershwin's symphonic work, *An American in Paris* (1928), and of his later "walking the dog theme" (or "promenade") from the movie, *Shall We Dance* (Mark Sandrich, 1937).

Also worth noting in this context is the American atmosphere created by the apple-tree sequence. Dorothy and the Scarecrow decide to pick some fruit, but the trees have other ideas. When the Scarecrow hints that their apples may be wormy, the trees pelt him and Dorothy with apples—to the (somewhat distorted) tune of "In the Shade of the Old Apple Tree." This popular American song was written in 1905 by Henry Williams and Egbert Van Alstyne; in fact, according to W. A. H. Birnie,[16] it was written with Van Alstyne's boyhood home in mind. But in *The Wizard*, one could argue, it is distorted in two ways. Doubling the first beat has transformed it from a slow waltz to a quick march; this gives it a tense, restless quality unlike that of the original music. Scoring it at the high end of the vocal range, moreover, evokes nostalgia not for the "simple joys of country life" but for childhood itself; the squeaky sound resembles that of a carousel in a playground.

Kansas Epilogue: Once Dorothy returns to Kansas, the conflict between European and American music is eliminated. The musical idiom is familiar, not foreign. It is also homogeneous, not heterogeneous, because the two musical anomalies, or "problems," of the prologue—Dorothy's song and Miss Gulch's theme—have been resolved. The song has become background music, and the atonal theme has been removed altogether. Likewise, the only two units of background music—"Home Sweet Home" and "Over the Rainbow"—flow into each other without interruption. (We must recall that "Home Sweet Home" had become an American folk song by 1939. Although the music was originally written in 1823 by a British composer, Sir Henry Rowley Bishop, the words were written by an American, John Howard Payne. Stephen Foster liked it so much that he wrote many similar songs based on it. Eventually, it became the theme song of Jenny Lind.)[17] This suggests that the songs are linked. In fact, it suggests that "home" really is "over the rainbow." In the prologue, Dorothy longs for happiness "over the rainbow." When she lands in the Munchkin City, she tells Toto: "We must be over the rainbow" (53). But the color code makes it clear that Oz *is* the rainbow. Kansas, on the other hand, is truly *over* the rainbow. Dorothy, in fact, is now both home and over the rainbow. The implications of this will be made clear in Chapter 4. In the meantime, it is worth noting that music and dialogue are now integrated with no separation of one from the other.

*

Borrowed from the theatre, the term "mise-en-scène" is normally used with reference to everything controlled by the director: sets, costumes, props, lighting.

Kansas Prologue: In these sequences, mise-en-scène is used to emphasize the familiar and the American. Most of the sets, props, and costumes would not have been out of place in rural America at any time between the late nineteenth century and the Second World War. Even the farm technology shown would have been familiar as late as 1939. Only the costume of Miss Gulch—which had been fashionable around the turn of the century—is clearly dated; in this respect, it is anomalous.

Oz: In these sequences, on the other hand, mise-en-scène is used to contrast the familiar and the alien. That is, American sets, props, and costumes are contrasted with European—especially Russian—ones.

Emerald City: *Designing Dreams* by David Albrecht[18] and *Screen Deco* by Howard Mandelbaum and Eric Myers[19] are excellent introductions to art deco design and architecture, an extremely influential style in Hollywood during the 1930s. The Emerald City, in fact, is a fantastic variation on the kind of architecture considered avant-garde in 1939. At first glance, it looks like a forest of skyscrapers. Its dynamic verticality (notable in the elevation as seen from the field of poppies, and in the vaulted corridor leading to the Wizard's audience hall), its "streamlined" lighting fixtures and indirect illumination (seen in both corridor and audience hall), its ornamental lettering (which identifies the Wash and Brush Up Company), its glittering, sparkling, highly polished surfaces (seen everywhere), and many other details owe as much to the Exposition internationale des arts décoratifs et industriels modernes (Paris, 1925) and the Century of Progress Exposition (Chicago, 1933-34) as they do to any unique fantasies of William Horning, Cedric Gibbons, or others involved in creating the sets at MGM. Although not all Americans living in 1939 were urbanites, most were aware of the architectural style known as "art deco." It was, after all, the style of some very impressive landmarks such as the Chrysler Building, the Empire State Building, Rockefeller Center, and the Radio City Music Hall. It was the style that prevailed at the New York World's Fair, which opened in that very year. And it was the style favored by set designers for dozens of Hollywood movies such as *Our Modern Maidens* (Jack Conway, 1929), *Palmy Days* (Edward Sutherland, 1931), *Susan Lennox, Her Fall and Rise* (Robert Z. Leonard, 1931), *Trouble in Paradise* (Ernst Lubitsch, 1932), *The Gay Divorcee* (Mark Sandrich, 1934), *After the Thin Man* (W. S. Van Dyke, 1936), *Dodsworth* (William Wyler, 1936), and *Artists and Models* (Raoul Walsh, 1937). To sum up, it was the style of modernity and progress. Since these are major elements in

American identity—a matter to be discussed more fully in
Chapter 4—it seems safe to assume that the Emerald City was
associated with modern America as represented in popular
movies and magazines and reflected in the design of toasters
and radios, if not actually experienced on ocean liners or in
skyscrapers.

Albrecht points out that modernism in architecture did not
originate in the United States. In fact, it flourished in Germany
(Mies Van der Rohe, Walter Gropius, and the Bauhaus), France
(Le Corbusier), and Italy (the Futurists) before becoming popular in the United States. But for many Europeans, modernism
was just one more phase in a long history of stylistic and
cultural change that could be seen in any city. Indeed, modernism was condemned as degenerate during the fascist
periods in Italy (1922-1945) and Germany (1933-1945) and
replaced by new versions of neoclassicism. For many Americans, on the other hand, it corresponded to something inherent
in the national experience: the desire to start over again in a
New World. Whatever the ideological concerns of European (or
even American) architects and designers, many ordinary
Americans recognized art deco as a prominent feature of the
urban landscape and linked to their collective experience as a
new nation.

One of the prominent features of the Emerald City is a
collection of "decorative light wheels"; a similar motif—wheels
and hubcaps—appears on a frieze in the Chrysler Building.
Daniel Boorstin points out that Americans had been fascinated
by speed since the early nineteenth century migrations to the
West.[20] In the twentieth century, speed, cars, and skyscrapers
have all become hallmarks of American cities. Any form of art
or architecture that takes its primary inspiration from
machines—especially cars, trains, ships, dirigibles and airplanes—can be considered characteristically (if not distinctively) American.

Given this art deco aesthetic that romanticized the machine,
it is not surprising to find that technology is a focus of attention in the Wizard's audience hall. In fact, the combination of
technology, streamlined design, bright lighting, and smooth,
shiny surfaces is reminiscent of Hollywood itself. The shimmering Bakelite floor looks as if it had been made for Fred Astaire

and Ginger Rogers. In short, sets for the Emerald City are modern, American, and delightfully glitzy.

The costumes look vaguely futuristic. Some female residents, for example, wear long, flowing, satin gowns with elaborate hats. These are really just exaggerted versions of all the elegant and sophisticated gowns Adrian designed for Hollywood stars such as Joan Crawford and Greta Garbo. Other female residents wear costumes reminiscent of a different American theatrical tradition. Prancing around in their high-heeled shoes, short skirts, and low necklines, attendants at the Wash and Brush Up Company look as if they have just been recruited straight from the Cocoanut Grove or the Ziegfeld Follies.

Lighting at the Emerald City is used very effectively to emphasize modernity: the future anticipated in the present. A future based on scientific discovery and technological progress is associated with rationalism. And rationalism is associated with clarity and light (which is to say, "enlightenment"). As might be expected, then, the Emerald City is first seen in radiant sunshine; shimmering on the horizon, it is like the daydream of a summer afternoon. With the brilliant illumination characteristic of Hollywood at that time (and particularly of MGM), no deep shadows impede visual exploration. Everything can be "known" at a glance. It is, therefore, "familiar."

Witch's Castle: Technology here is primitive. Candles and torches are used instead of electric lights, spears instead of guns, an hourglass instead of a clock. Surfaces, moreover, are coarse and unpolished. Architecturally, the Castle is a maze of twisting staircases and crooked passages. Here, then, the mise-en-scène is alien. It is remote in both time and space. After all, it is a medieval castle complete with turrets, towers, ramparts, and moat with drawbridge and portcullis. Unlike many other styles of period architecture, this one was never "Americanized" despite individual examples of reconstruction and simulation (such as William Randolph Hearst's castle, San Simeon).

For about a hundred years between the eighteenth and nineteenth centuries, Greek Revival architecture was highly favored for both domestic and public architecture in the United States. Since the neoclassical style was associated with the origin of democracy in the ancient world, it was symbolically appropriate as the visual embodiment of a new republic based on Greco-Roman notions of civic virtue. Nevertheless, Gothic Revival architecture was also very popular, throughout the nineteenth century and into the twentieth, for both domestic and public buildings. Examples include the Eastern State Penitentiary in Philadelphia (1829), Stanton Hall in Charlotte City, Virginia (1848), Fonthill in New York City (1848), Lancaster City Jail in Lancaster, Pennsylvania (1851), and the Barracks at the Virginia Military Institution in Lexington, Virginia (1851).[21] Even after its general decline for other purposes, its use in ecclesiastical architecture continued. No matter how drastically adapted according to regional taste and technological innovation, specific elements (such as the pointed arch and stained glass) are still extremely common features of American churches. Though often severely adulterated or trivialized, the Gothic Revival style is clearly a part of the landscape most Americans take for granted; even in 1930, when Grant Wood parodied the moral rectitude and self-righteousness of Midwestern farmers in *American Gothic*, he did so in visual terms that everyone would recognize immediately. Sometimes, however, the style is creatively transformed. A good example of this is the Air Force Academy's chapel near Colorado Springs. Designed by Walter A. Netsch and built by Skidmore, Owings and Merrill in 1962, it is a striking reminder that the old vocabulary has been thoroughly integrated into modern American culture. The chapel is described as follows in an architectural journal: it is "reminiscent of the dominance of the cathedral over a medieval town....Seventeen spires soar in striking fashion over the long horizontals of the other buildings; the glistening, machine-made perfection of their aluminum surfaces and the verticality of their upward-reaching pointedness make appropriate contrasts with the ruggedness of the surrounding Rockies."[22]

But cathedrals are not the only buildings that have come to be associated with the gothic period. The same is true of castles. Although the most characteristic features of castles (the moat with drawbridge and portcullis; the protective walls with ramparts and crenellation) originated several hundred years earlier, these buildings were also built in the age of gothic cathedrals (beginning in the twelfth century). In the nineteenth century, American buildings were sometimes designed with turrets, towers, and battlements. Unlike the medieval cathedral (which became one of the primary symbolic paradigms for American churches) or the classical temple (which became one of the primary symbolic paradigms for American museums, libraries, national monuments, and other public buildings), the medieval castle never became a symbolic paradigm for any type of building. Even though many Americans associated their own religious sentiments with those that inspired the cathedrals of medieval Europe and their own republican ideals with those that inspired the monuments of classical antiquity, they did not associate any particular aspect of American life with medieval feudalism. There was, of course, one exception: the Old South. But even in the Old South (where the social order was self-consciously modeled on feudalism), the planters usually preferred to identify their way of life with the gracious and cultivated ways of contemporary English aristocrats who lived in country houses rather than with the primitive and uncomfortable ways of their ancestors who had lived in castles. In short, the castle was never "Americanized."

Costumes at the Witch's Castle are heavy and anything but sexually revealing. The guards (in their long, heavy coats and massive fur hats) and the Witch (in her long, loose-fitting robe and towering headgear) are covered from head to foot. The guards, moreover, have a distinctly Russian look; their costumes (with flaring coats, fur hats, and spears tipped with stylized eagles) seem to have been borrowed directly from uniforms of the Imperial Cossack Guard or even the Red Army. The Witch herself looks distinctly medieval because her costume (which accentuates tall, thin forms and features a pointed hat with flowing veil) seems to have been borrowed from Flemish and Burgundian paintings of the late fifteenth century.[23] In short, the Witch's Castle is medieval, European, and delightfully "gothic."

Because the only nocturnal scenes in *The Wizard* are at the Witch's Castle, it could be argued that the use of lighting underscores its nightmarish quality (remote, alien, mysterious, and dangerous).

Yellow Brick Road: Here, mise-en-scène is both American and European. With its thatched cottages and cobbled streets, the

Munchkin City is a vaguely Elizabethan village. Female residents romp around in full skirts with laced bodices; male residents are dressed up either as late medieval burghers—with their pointed shoes and multicolored hose—or as early nineteenth-century soldiers from Central Europe (known in Hollywood as "Ruritania"). In general, the merry Munchkins seem to be refugees from one of Bruegel's paintings of peasant life in sixteenth-century Northern Europe.

As soon as Dorothy and Toto leave the Munchkin City, though, the associations of mise-en-scène include American ones. In fact, the journey continues through open countryside not unlike that of the American Midwest with its open vistas, rolling hills, and fields of corn (which is maize, the specifically New World form of corn). The Scarecrow himself is a characteristic feature of rural America. Nevertheless, both the Lion and the Witch are Old World creatures. Then, too, the Yellow Brick Road passes through a haunted forest that conceals a medieval castle. Characteristic, then, of the Yellow Brick Road sequences is a confusing juxtaposition of the familiar (modern America) and the alien (medieval Europe or Russia).

Kansas Epilogue: in the final sequence, we return to the mise-en-scène of the prologue. But the anomaly—Miss Gulch's costume—has been eliminated (since she does not reappear). Moreover, we no longer see any farm machinery. Thus dating and placing the set is more difficult than ever. All we see is a corner of Dorothy's bedroom. In fact, it could be almost anywhere in America at almost any time in the past century.

*

The term "dramatis personae" is, of course, also borrowed from the theater. Here, though, it refers to the characters as formal properties. The debate in literary circles over the relation of character to plot is irrelevant in this formal analysis. Consequently, I have avoided terms such as "actant" (which implies that only plot is of significance) and even "character" (which is often used in connection with psychological categories). In short, the term "dramatis personae" was chosen precisely because it is not associated with Propp, Todorov, Greimas, or any school of literary analysis. Members of the dramatis personae are identified by their traits. Following Chatman, I define "trait" as any characteristic feature that differentiates one individual from another and thus confers a distinctive identity on each.[24] In this case, the traits are biological and moral.

Kansas Prologue: In the opening sequences, all characters are "natural." That is, they are all either human beings or animals. Moreover, all are good except Miss Gulch, the evil antagonist. Since she alone turns into her Ozian counterpart (the Witch) as she flies past Dorothy's window, she is a formal anomaly on two counts: she alone is bad and she alone is other than (or less than) human.

Oz: In these sequences, a number of characters from Kansas reappear in thinly disguised form. Along with some new characters, they can be placed along one continuum between fully human and nonhuman, and along another between good and evil. Dorothy herself, of course, is both good and fully human. And Toto is both good and nonhuman.

> **Emerald City:** This place is associated with the Wizard who reigns over it in name, if not in fact. He is fully human, too—a good but ordinary man "born and bred in the heart of the Western wilderness" (125). But the Emerald City is also associated with Glinda who, in fact, rules it and all of Oz; from here, she sends Dorothy back to Kansas. Glinda could be called "superhuman" since her magical powers are benevolent.

> **Witch's Castle:** This place, on the other hand, is associated with Glinda's evil counterpart: the Wicked Witch of the West. She could be called "subhuman," since her magical powers are malevolent.

> **Yellow Brick Road:** Along the way, Dorothy meets three good friends. They could be called "quasi-human." At any rate, they are humanoids of one kind or another (which is to say, both human and something else). The Cowardly Lion is half man, half animal. The Scarecrow is half man, half vegetable. And the Tin Man is half man, half mineral.[25]

Kansas Epilogue: In the final sequence, all characters revert to their natural state in the prologue—except for the Witch, of course, who does not reappear as Miss Gulch; the formal anomaly is thus eliminated.

*

Another code refers to the cinematic organization of space. By this, I mean the orientation and movement of objects within space. A great deal has been written about the cinematic dependence on illusion and the ways in which illusion may be accepted or rejected by viewers.[26] The debate among film theorists of various schools, however, is not germane to the subject at hand. By definition, all three-dimensional objects—what Chatman calls "existants"[27]—occupy space. Although photographs projected onto a screen are, in fact, two-dimensional, they are accepted by analogy to the familiar world of everyday life as three-dimensional. The spatial code used here, though, refers not to the perception of objects and people but to the organization of space itself—that is, to their orientation and movement within space.

Kansas Prologue: In these sequences, space is organized around a center: Dorothy's bedroom. Movement away from the bedroom always indicates a decrease of emotional intensity, and movement toward it has the opposite effect. This can be seen in two narrative sequences.

In one, Miss Gulch is seen on her bicycle carrying Toto away from the house (and Dorothy's bedroom) in a basket; the mood (reinforced by her dissonant musical motif) is very agitated. As they speed down the road, Toto peeks out of the basket; the mood (reinforced by his playful musical motif) is now much less intense. Then he jumps out of the basket, runs back home, and jumps through the window right into Dorothy's bedroom; the mood, once again, is extremely intense—but in a positive way this time, not a negative one.

In another sequence, Dorothy herself moves away from the house with Toto; the mood along the road is a depressing one. When they reach Professor Marvel, far away from the house, the mood is relatively light-hearted. Then Professor Marvel sees a photograph of Auntie Em standing in front of the house, and tells Dorothy that he can see Auntie Em sinking back onto her bed clutching her heart; this naturally provokes a mood of anxiety in Dorothy. Even as she leaves Professor Marvel, the wind has begun rustling leaves; the mood is becoming more agitated. As she approaches the farm, a tornado can be seen sweeping across the landscape; the mood is even more intense. In the bedroom itself, at the height of the storm, emotional tension is translated directly into physical tension as Dorothy is assaulted by the window frame. A moment later—still in the bedroom—she is horrified to see Miss Gulch riding her bicycle through the air and turn into a witch.

Although space is oriented and organized uniformly, it is somewhat heterogeneous; the bedroom has a special quality absent from other places. This is not a spatial anomaly that needs "correcting," but it should be noted all the same and compared to spatial conditions in the epilogue.

Oz: Here, space is organized around not one center but two *competing* centers: the Emerald City and the Witch's Castle. Each is a possible destination for Dorothy and her friends. Each has a "claim" on her. And each is the "seat" of a witch whose magical powers pervade Oz. Moreover, each has an architectural plan in which the center is protected by a series of gates. There is one major difference between the two however: at the Witch's Castle, attention is focused on getting *out* (away from the center); at the Emerald City, attention is focused on getting *in* (toward the center).

> **Emerald City:** This place is the venue of benevolent power. As the long-sought goal of Dorothy and her friends, it has the same emotional importance as the bedroom back in Kansas. The movement of characters is oriented in terms of this place. Dorothy and her friends cannot simply enter the Emerald City and go straight to see the Wizard. They must negotiate passage through a series of gates. With only minor difficulty—ringing the bell instead of knocking—they manage to enter the city. Entry to the inner sanctum (the Wizard's audience hall) is another matter. First, they must be prepared and made presentable at the Wash and Brush Up Company. Then they approach the next gate; for the second time, they are refused entry by a gatekeeper who says, "Orders are, nobody can see the Great Oz! Not nobody—not nohow!" (94). Taking pity on them when he sees Dorothy in tears, however, the gatekeeper admits them to a long, empty, corridor. In this atmosphere, the Cowardly Lion is nearly overcome by fear and awe. The "antechamber" leads directly into the audience hall itself. There, even the spunky heroine is reduced to fear and trembling; she introduces herself as "Dorothy, the Small and Meek" (100).

> **Witch's Castle:** This place is the venue of malevolent power. As the long-avoided fate of Dorothy and her friends, it also has the emotional importance of the bedroom back in Kansas. The movement of characters is oriented in terms of this place as

well as the Emerald City, but with the opposite goal in mind. As in the Emerald City, the inner chamber of the Witch's Castle is protected (massive wooden doors, patrolled ramparts, and a moat with drawbridge and portcullis). No one enters or leaves on a casual basis. Indeed, the inner chamber serves as a prison for Dorothy and Toto; the aim of sequences shot at the Castle is to get them out safely.

Yellow Brick Road: On the Yellow Brick Road, Dorothy and her friends are constantly moving from one place to another. Places en route—the cornfield, the apple orchard, the field of poppies—are significant not in themselves but in relation to other places. It could be said, then, that while the Yellow Brick Road represents "here," the Munchkin City, Emerald City, and Witch's Castle represent "there." As points of origin and destination, the latter have intrinsic significance—whether positive or negative—and the former does not. (In the larger cinematic context, however, "there" is represented by Kansas.)

The Yellow Brick Road is a venue of both benevolent power (represented by Glinda) and malevolent power (represented by the Witch). Not coincidentally, it is marked by spatial chaos. Dorothy's task on the Yellow Brick Road is to move between "here" and "there," to be sure, but where exactly is "there"? Finding an answer to that question is no easy matter. Glinda gives Dorothy a hint: "It's always best," she says, "to start at the beginning" (63). This, however, turns out to be easier said than done. The Road begins in a swirl of color that reinforces the notion of "center." But it quickly turns into a labyrinth that branches off in all directions without any signs to indicate direction. This motif of spatial chaos is introduced right near the beginning of her journey when Dorothy meets the Scarecrow; neither can remember which way he was pointing. Actually, he had pointed first in one direction, then in the other, and finally in both. Later on, in the Haunted Forest, they come across a directional sign, but it has a very confusing effect. Although it points in one direction and reads "Witch's Castle, one mile," it also "points" in the opposite direction by saying in addition, "I'd turn back if I were you" (103).

Kansas Epilogue: In the epilogue, the bedroom is still the center, but now peripheral space has been "eliminated" (or dramatically reduced in importance) to reveal an underlying homogeneity. This is cinematically expressed by spatial compression: the entire epilogue takes place in one tiny bedroom, even a corner of that bedroom. Although viewers can see through a window into the barnyard and beyond (to peripheral space), all attention is focused on the shallow plane in the immediate foreground. In art historical terms, we have moved from the dynamic restlessness of the Baroque to the static order of the Renaissance; figures are arranged along a shallow plane in the foreground much as they are in Leonardo's "Last Supper." This static arrangement of figures in a shallow foreground was not invented in the Renaissance; it had a long history beginning in the Early Christian period and continuing throughout the Middle Ages. In the stained glass windows of many American churches, this visual tradition has lived on as a widely accepted convention for the representation of events in sacred history (that is, incidents taking place in eternity rather than time).

If emphasis is given in the prologue to movement (passing toward or away from the bedroom), it is now given to repose (being there). Here at the center, there is no visual tension; there is only peace and tranquility. All movement, by the camera as much as by the characters, is reduced to a minimum. The camera, for example, never leaves the bedroom, and hardly moves even within the bedroom. Gradually, the heads of Dorothy and Toto, Auntie Em and Uncle Henry, the three farmhands and Professor Marvel, come together as a complete circle; this geometric form has neither beginning nor end and, therefore, suggests completeness and perfection. When their heads finally block out any view through the window, the sense of being at the heart, or core, of things is palpable. All the same, this only makes clear what was inherent in the prologue. The centrality of the bedroom has been confirmed, not established. Hints of its centrality are given in the prologue, but are only fully realized cinematically in the epilogue.

*

In one sense, time involves the orientation of events in terms of past (beginning, origin) and future (ending, destiny). According to one way of thinking now prevalent in modern Western societies, time flows in only one direction: from past to future. Events occur once and can never be repeated. According to an older way of thinking, a way commonly found in other societies, time can flow in two directions, forward or backward. Events, therefore, can be repeated. The distinction is between what could be called "linear" and "circular" (or between secular and sacred) time. This will be discussed much more fully in Chapter 5. At the moment, these two notions of time will simply be identified as they are presented in *The Wizard*.

Another distinction must be made between external events that involve "doing" (action by one agent on another or on an object) and internal events that involve "being" (thinking or feeling but not acting). I call the former "transitive" and the latter "intransitive." This distinction is not the one made by Chatman between "actions" (in which a character is the subject causing some event to occur) and "happenings" (in which a character is the object of an event).[28] Both transitive and intransitive events, as I use these terms, may be either actions or happenings.

Kansas Prologue: In these sequences, events are almost uniformly transitive. That is, they are about doing rather than being. But one event—Dorothy's soliloquy, the only song—is clearly intransitive. In it, Dorothy reveals her inner state: her reflections on the way things are, could be, or should be. In this sense, it is a temporal anomaly.

Oz: Here, time is intrinsically heterogeneous. Not only are events in all sequences both transitive and intransitive, but time is circular (or reversible) in some sequences and linear (or irreversible) in others.

On the whole, Ozian time is linear and future oriented. (Theoretically, of course, a temporal "line" could point instead toward the past.) The last event (leaving the Emerald City) is a fulfillment of—but not a repetition of or return to—the first event (arriving in the Munchkin City). To put it differently, time in Oz could generally be described in terms of "progress." Dorothy and her friends move along the Yellow Brick Road, define their goals, solve problems, and reach their destination.

Nevertheless, there are also irruptions of the past characteristic of circular time. On the Yellow Brick Road, for example, Dorothy keeps "remembering" Kansas. She tells her new friends (who are, in fact, transmogrifications of the three farmhands she knew back in Kansas): "And it's funny, but I feel as if I'd known you all the time. But I couldn't have, could I?" (76). Then, too, she looks into the Witch's crystal ball and sees Auntie Em calling out to her from the Kansas farmhouse.

In Oz, time is linear and future oriented in connection with immediacy: Dorothy's immediate origin (the Munchkin City) and destiny (the Emerald City). But it is also circular and past oriented in connection with ultimacy: Dorothy's ultimate origin and destiny in Kansas (prologue and epilogue) and the irruptions of Kansas into the Ozian present. In fact, though, the two temporal modes become synonymous because Dorothy's goal in Oz (the future) is nothing other than a return to Kansas (the past); destiny and origin merge.

> **Emerald City:** Here, time is circular because it is to this place that Dorothy returns, not only to Kansas, but to her origin, or past. Destination (Emerald City) becomes point of departure, and the original point of departure (Kansas) becomes ultimate destination. The future leads to the past, the end to the beginning.

> **Witch's Castle:** Here, time is linear. In other words, it is irreversible; the future is cut off from the past. As Dorothy gazes into the crystal ball, the Witch's hideous face suddenly blots out the benign image of Auntie Em (Dorothy's past). The passage of time (as indicated by the hourglass) is a major preoccupation here; it leads relentlessly into the future which, in this case, is death. Not only can there be no return from here to the past (either to Kansas or to the Munchkin City), there can be no continued existence even in the present. Because time can be experienced (in secular Western societies, at any rate) only as past, present, or future, it must be concluded that the Witch's Castle focuses on the latter—even though extinction is a negative future from Dorothy's point of view.

> **Yellow Brick Road:** Here, time is both linear and circular. Since the Road is synonymous with Dorothy's quest, time spent moving along it is linear; it begins in the Munchkin City and ends at the entrance to the Emerald City. Nevertheless, it is circular too, since it is characterized by formal repetition. Most of the time actually spent on the Road involves the successive introductions of Dorothy's new friends; each introduction is really a repetition of the previous ones. Thus, the song "If I Only Had a Brain" is repeated in two slightly modified versions: "If I Only Had a Heart," and "If I Only Had the Nerve." Moreover, Dorothy explicitly acknowledges the possibility that she has met these friends before (in Kansas).

On the Yellow Brick Road, Dorothy and her friends move in time between the beginning and end of their journey. Events in the meantime—meeting each other, evading the Witch, seeking the Wizard—are significant not in themselves but in relation to other events. It could be said, then, that, while the rural Yellow Brick Road represents "now," the urban Yellow Brick Road (including the Munchkin City) represents "then" (before). Representing "then" (after) are the Emerald City and Witch's Castle. As points of origin and destination, the latter have intrinsic significance—whether positive or negative—while the former does not. (In the larger cinematic context, nevertheless, "then"—both before and after—is represented by Kansas.)

Kansas Epilogue: In the epilogue, screen time (plot) corresponds precisely to real time (story); that is, no time elapses *between* shots. The entire segment could have been filmed as a single long take (instead of a sequence of shots edited together). But does this mean that Dorothy's temporal world now conforms to ours or that ours now conforms to hers? If Dorothy were a real person who could walk off the screen and into our world, the former possibility would suggest itself. But Dorothy is not a real person. Viewers know her only to the extent that they can enter her world. And that, after all, is the whole point of watching the movie. In the epilogue, a temporal equation (screen time = real time) gives viewers access to Dorothy's world because no events take place that they do not share. But having gained access, they find that the kind of events taking place on screen are homogeneous to an extent unknown in everyday life off screen. It is, so to speak, another world.

As an intransitive event, "Over the Rainbow" was anomalous in the prologue. Although it has been eliminated as a song, it remains as background music that underscores the "triumph" of intransitive over transitive events. In this final sequence, all transitive events have been eliminated (or drastically reduced in importance) to reveal an underlying unity, or homogeneity. They have become so trivial—Auntie Em tenderly patting Dorothy's head—that they cease to exist for all intents and purposes. The only truly significant event is the intransitive one of being safe, being happy, being loved, being home.

This distinctive reversal—eliminating the anomaly by making everything else conform to it—is interesting because it means that the temporal code is unique. If time is truly the "master code," then the meaning of time in the epilogue is extremely important. This will be discussed much more thoroughly in Chapter 5. In the meantime, it is worth noting that, in purely formal terms, Kansas represents the temporal goal—not the immediate "then" of the Emerald City but the ultimate "then" of the movie itself. Accordingly, it is also the temporal ideal. And it is an ideal that is homogeneously intransitive. It is static. Paradoxically, it is a temporal ideal beyond time or change.

*

From the preceding analysis, a clear pattern emerges. The use of formal properties could be summarized as follows:

Kansas Prologue: Formal properties are used to express cinematic integration, unity, or homogeneity. Every code, however, includes one or two formal "problems," or anomalies—things that do not fit the prevailing pattern.

Oz: Here, on the other hand, formal properties are used to express cinematic confusion, fragmentation, or heterogeneity. But this is done in two ways. On the one hand, formal oppositions are set up between the Emerald City and the Witch's Castle. The relation between them could be described as "either-or." On the other hand, formal mediations are set up along the Yellow Brick Road. Although the Munchkin City, where the Road begins, is in formal opposition to its rural hinterland, which ends at the gates of the Emerald City, both are part of the Yellow Brick Road. As elements of a single cinematic unit, then, their relation could be described as "both-and."

Kansas Epilogue: Finally, unity, integration, and homogeneity are restored. But now those anomalies present in the prologue have been eliminated. Generally speaking, in fact, what we see in the epilogue is just a highly compressed, purified, simplified version of what we have already seen in the prologue.

Although plot has not been treated as a formal property, it is hardly coincidental that the same pattern could be used to describe its use in this movie.

Kansas Prologue: Dorothy is at home on the farm in Kansas. But there is a problem: Miss Gulch comes to take Toto. Feeling isolated and ignored, she runs away with her dog. By the time she returns, though, a storm has begun. Struck by flying debris, she falls into a dream of Oz.

Oz: Dorothy keeps trying to get back to Kansas. And after an eventful journey along the Yellow Brick Road, she does return home.

Kansas Epilogue: Dorothy wakes up in her own room back on the farm. But now she realizes that this is where she belongs. The problem has been resolved; the anomalous Miss Gulch does not reappear in the epilogue.

This correspondence is not surprising. It is through the various formal properties, after all, that the plot is articulated. It remains to be seen how the underlying narrative structure—order violated, order sought, order restored—is related to that of other artifacts or productions of American culture.

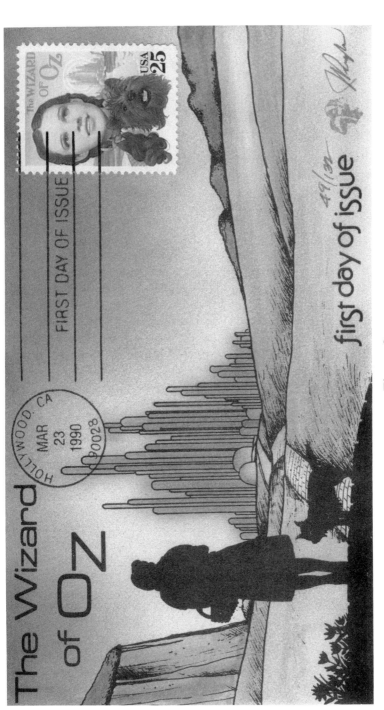

Figure 2

Reproduction of the cacheted first day cover is provided at the courtesy of its producer, Julian Pugh, PUGH CACHETS, P.O. Box 8789, The Woodlands, TX, 77387.

3 HER OWN BACKYARD

Somewhere, over the rainbow, skies are blue, And the dreams that you dare to dream really do come true.

—Dorothy (39)

But it wasn't a dream. It was a place. And you...and you...and you...and you were there!

—Dorothy (131)

The Wizard is explicitly about going home. On several occasions, Dorothy herself makes this very clear. Waking up in her room back home, for instance, she tells Auntie Em that Oz was "a real, truly live place. And I remember that some of it wasn't very nice, but most of it was beautiful. But just the same, all I kept saying to everybody was, 'I want to go home.' And they sent me home" (132). In 1939, after the massive dislocations and migrations caused by the Depression, and with the threat of more to come in another war, the attraction of any movie that emphasized the value of home is not difficult to understand.

The Wizard was by no means the only movie of this period to propagate such a message. *Meet Me in St. Louis* (Vincente Minnelli, 1944) is explicitly about staying home. It is set in St. Louis just after the turn of the century. An otherwise happy family is threatened with a major disruption in their lives when the father is offered a more important job in New York. Just when all arrangements have been made, however, the father realizes how unhappy such a move will make his family and decides to stay in St. Louis after all. Implicitly, however, this movie is "set" forty years later. It was clearly aimed at those who felt threatened by wartime dislocations. Implicitly,

55

then, it is about returning home. Although Judy Garland only hinted at a problem faced by many girls on the home front when she sang "The Boy Next Door," she left little to the imagination when she sang another song that quickly became very popular both on the home front and on the battle front.

> Have yourself a merry little Christmas,
> Let your heart be light;
> Next year all our troubles
> Will be out of sight.
> Have yourself a merry little Christmas,
> Make the yuletide gay; Next year all our troubles
> Will be miles away.
> Once again as in olden days,
> Happy golden days of yore,
> Faithful friends who are dear to us
> Will be near to us once more.
> Someday soon we all will be together
> If the fates allow;
> Until then we'll have to muddle through somehow;
> So have yourself a merry little Christmas now.[1]

Another movie of the same period, *Since You Went Away* (John Cromwell, 1944), is explicitly about returning home. With her husband fighting overseas, a woman tries to keep up morale on the home front by taking an officer from out of town into her home. The officer's grandson falls in love with her daughter but is soon shipped off to war. Although neither he nor the son of a neighbor returns home, the father does. The dominant mood of this very successful movie is set by a title immediately following the opening credits: "This is a story of the Unconquerable Fortress, the American Home... 1943."

I have suggested, however, that "going home" is fundamentally linked, for many Americans, with "growing up." Is there any evidence of this in *The Wizard?* Does Dorothy also grow up? Even though it probably seems fairly obvious to most viewers that she does indeed, it is not quite explicit. To be safe in asserting the implicit presence of "growing up," some reference must be made to established theories of psychological development.

*

Since *The Wizard* is implicitly about maturation, and since most of it consists of a dream sequence, the possibility of using psychoanalysis naturally suggests itself. But is the use of psychoanalytical theory appropriate in nonclinical contexts? There are important differences between real dreams, after all, and the dream-sequences of movies. In the first place, movies are produced by collectivities, not individuals (even when the director is considered an artist). Moreover, movies are produced by people who make conscious choices, not by sleeping or hypnotized patients. Nevertheless, movies and dreams are not utterly dissimilar. There is a reason why Hollywood is so often called a "dream factory."[2] Many years ago, scholars recognized that movies provided more than just casual entertainment for the masses, handsome profits for the studios, and (occasionally) art for the intelligentsia. By now, almost everyone would acknowledge that sitting in a darkened room and becoming absorbed in projected fantasies is a dreamlike experience that should be taken seriously by scholars. This notion has certainly not escaped the attention of film theorists. All would agree that only part of the finished product is the result of conscious planning; much of it, arguably the most significant part, is the result of subconscious "choices" based on personal experience, cultural conditioning, or both. Indeed, this assumption is so widely held in the scholarly world that modern film criticism, for example, would be inconceivable without it.

The relation of movies to dreams has been carefully examined by Christian Metz in *The Imaginary Signifier: Psychoanalysis and the Cinema*. In brief, he suggests that "the filmic state...embodies in a weaker form certain economic conditions of sleep. It remains a variant of the waking state but less remote from sleep than most others."[3] His discussion focuses on three aspects of this relation: knowledge of the subject (that is, the dreamer or the viewer); the difference between perception and hallucination; and the degree to which primary or secondary psychological processes dominate.

By "knowledge of the subject," Metz refers to the extent that the subject is, or is not, aware of reality. Dreamers, for instance, do not know that they are dreaming. Viewers, however, *do* know that they are watching a movie. Only in dreams, then, is the illusion of reality complete; in movies, there is only the impression of reality. The filmic state is conscious, not an unconscious one.

In any event, according to Metz, the gap between these two states can be exaggerated. Sitting in a darkened theater, viewers are immobile, passive, and silent. Under these circumstances, a state of mind not unlike that of sleep is induced. Metz reflects to the filmic state as a "waking sleep." As in dreams, motor activity is reduced to a minimum. Emerging from the darkened room, viewers often seem dazed and, "brutally rejected by the black belly of the cinema into the bright, unkind light of the foyer, sometimes have the bewildered expressions (happy or unhappy) of people waking up."[4] The filmic state, then is a step away from the waking state and toward the dreaming state.

Because they originate in the mind and are therefore independent of external reality, dreams do not involve real perceptions; Metz argues that they can be classified as hallucinations. And because actual images and sounds from the external world are apprehended (as mediated through technology), movies do involve real perceptions. It is precisely because viewers actually receive sensory information from the outside world that a self-contained illusion, or delusion, cannot be complete. The "delusion coefficient," in fact, is higher in dreams for two reasons. In the first place, dreamers "believe" more deeply in what they imagine (being unaware of the external world). On the other hand, what they imagine is "less true" because actual images or sounds from the external world are not involved. In a sense, claims Metz, dreams are always more "satisfactory" than movies. They respond directly and precisely to the wishes or fears of those who imagine them; no collusion with reality (including the fantasies of directors) is necessary or, indeed, possible. "It is like a film which has been 'shot' from beginning to end by the very subject of the wish—also the subject of fear—a singular film by virtue of its censorship and omissions as much as its expressed content, cut to the measure of its only spectator, a...spectator who is also the author and has every reason to be content with it, since one is never so well-served as by oneself."[5]

Movies are not the independent creations of each viewer; on the contrary, they are the creations of others and imposed on viewers. They can never succeed as fully in granting wish-fulfilling fantasies for any individual viewer. Being dependent, to some extent, on the reality principle, the filmic state retains wish fulfillment as its ultimate goal, but moves in that direction along with many difficult and often unpleasant detours. Because of this inherent connection to the external world, complete regression is not possible; that is possible only in the dreaming state when external perceptions are blocked and regressive impressions are thus encouraged. Once again, though, Metz argues that the gulf between the two states can be overemphasized. In the filmic state, a certain amount of regression is still possible. As in the dreaming state, the impression (illusion) of reality and the possibility of emotional satisfaction by way of projection presuppose the beginning of regression. Viewers ascribe reality to the fictional people and events (which are the "signifieds" of a movie) but not to the images or sounds (which are the "signifiers"). To some extent, then, the effect is like that of a dream.

Metz now turns his attention to the content of movies and dreams along with the degrees of "secondarization" (the extent to which revisions are made to primary material welling up from the unconscious). In dreams, primary processes, not secondary ones, dominate. Moreover, the result of such revisions makes sense only in the dreaming state; when recalled in the waking state, they seem incoherent and absurd. Movies, on the other hand, seem much more "logical" or "constructed" than dreams. They are dominated by secondary, not primary, processes. In movies, unlike dreams, unconscious material is mediated, to some extent, and not presented directly. So movies never appear completely spontaneous. This is true even of movies that try to create the impression of incoherent dreams or challenge the normal expectations of the way things are. They are anything but images and and sounds strewn together at random. Consequently, they fail to take on the bizarre, enigmatic absurdity that is the hallmark of dreams.

If a dream actually could be translated to the screen, it would, in fact, be unintelligible. That is, it would be truly unintelligible "and not one of those avant-garde or experimental films which, as the enlightened audience knows, it is appropriate at once to understand and not to understand (not understanding being the better way to understand and too much effort at understanding being the height of misunderstanding, etc.)."[6] Movies of that kind can be classified as a genre. As such, they can be identified by particular patterns or characteristics that produce coherence and therefore some degree of intelligibility. This is why the dream sequences in many movies are generally unbelievable as dreams.

Once again, though, the distance between the two can be overestimated. They are linked at the level of the signifier. In both cases, there are images (or sounds) that cannot be reduced to the categories of logical discourse. In other words, their effect is sui generis (quite apart from any explicit or even implicit meanings attached to them). "The unconscious neither thinks nor discourses," writes Metz; "it figures itself forth in images; conversely, every image remains vulnerable to the attraction...of the primary process and its characteristic modalities of concatenation."[7] Similarly, movies and dreams are linked at the level of the signified. Both involve stories. In movies, the story is narrated either explicitly or implicitly; in dreams, the story emerges from the darkness unformed or deformed by any narrative agency. In both, however, the images are woven together as a succession of characters, events, times, and places.

After discussing some of the specific primary operations that are revised by secondary ones (such as condensation or displacement), Metz concludes by noting that what is presented on screen seems almost as real as a dream for two reasons. Like dreams, movies present viewers with irruptions of primary material worked over by secondary processes. And although viewers are conscious, they are much less conscious than usual. In effect, "a sort of compromise is created, a middle level of wakefulness, itself institutionalized in the classical cinema, where film and spectator succeed in being regulated one by the other and both by an identical or similar degree of secondarisation."[8] Viewers expect to live for a few hours at a lower level of alertness; being at the movies, they have no need for defenses they normally need and can accept what they would reject under different circumstances. They are able in limited but important ways of tolerating unconscious manifestations of primary processes. Clearly, there are many other states of lowered wakefulness (such as those related to the use of alcohol or other drugs), but "among the different regimes of waking, the filmic state is one of those least unlike sleep and dreaming."[9]

In any case, Metz argues that the filmic state can be linked even more closely to that of daydreaming—daydreams being defined as the prolongation and elaboration of more fleeting conscious fantasies —than that of dreaming. Daydreams, therefore, are linked to movies in at least two ways: the relation of both to the dreaming state, and the relation of both to the waking state (or degree of revision by secondary processes). Movies and daydreams are linked to the dreaming state, but without its most characteristic feature: sleep. Both daydreams and movies are conscious activities. Nevertheless, both involve irruptions of unconscious material. In fact, the same features that differentiate movies from dreams link them to daydreams. The relation between primary and secondary revisions, for example, is roughly the same in both cases. Although daydreams are closer to the unconscious than movies, they are nevertheless characterized by the same internal logic characteristic of secondary processes. Like movies, they are organized cinematically as coherent stories or scenes. Daydreams and movies are also linked to the waking state but without its most characteristic feature: activity. Both daydreams and movies are rooted in contemplation and passivity. Moreover, both allow people to rest; they are, therefore, more or less functional equivalents of sleep. In short, there can be no true illusion of reality for either daydreamers or viewers, because the former know they are daydreaming just as the latter know they are watching a movie.

There are basic differences, of course, between movies and daydreams. The former are "material fabrications" in which every detail is chosen (since movies cannot be made without concrete manifestations) while the latter are "mental fabrications" that allow for "blank spaces" or vagueness. But the difference is one of degree alone. The little stories people tell themselves are not very different from the big stories they see on the screen. In relation to dreams, movies are *less* "convincing" (as illusions of reality), but in relation to daydreams, they are equally convincing. Neither movies nor daydreams can provide a perfect illusion of reality; they can provide only a pseudo-belief, or simulation, requiring conscious consent (the "willing suspension of disbelief"). The disadvantage in movies—external imposition of someone else's fantasies—remains. But the advantage of cinematic technology is also a factor worth considering. "Thus the material existence of the filmic images (along with all that issues from it: stronger perception of reality, superiority of perceptual precision and therefore of the power of *incarnation*, etc.) helps recover some advantages that compensate more or less completely for the images' immediately alien origin."[10]

Movies, therefore, can be considered collective daydreams; even if they often emerge from the daydreams of individual directors, they actually function as daydreams for millions of viewers.

> If the film and the daydream are in more direct competition than the film and the dream, if they ceaselessly encroach upon each other, it is because they occur at a point of adaptation to reality—or at a point of regression, to look at it from the other direction—which is nearly the same; it is because they occur at the same *moment* (same moment in ontogeny, same moment in the diurnal cycle): the dream belongs to childhood and the night; the film and the daydream are more adult and belong to the day, but not midday—to the evening, rather.[11]

Metz has established the legitimacy of using psychoanalysis as an interpretive device in film studies because he has located intrinsic features of dreams, daydreams, and other productions of the unconscious. As in daydreams (to say nothing of dreams), unconscious material rises to the surface; if psychoanalysts find it profitable to examine this material in the former case, then why not in the latter? My goal, however, is not to discuss psychoanalysis as an end in itself but to use it as the appropriate means to an end. Since Dorothy's journey through Oz is explicitly presented as a dream, it makes sense to investigate the ways in which it either is or is not like real dreams. Insofar as psychoanalytical theory can be successfully applied—insofar as such an interpretation can be formed that makes sense of what is actually presented on screen and, at the same time, corresponds to established theories of dream analysis—it is a legitimate interpretive approach. The fact that movies are intrinsically dreamlike (or daydreamlike), however, is an additional reason to pursue this line of thinking. In short, my aim is not to equate film and dream, but merely to draw attention to parallels between them. To the extent that movies are like dreams or daydreams—but only to that extent—the methods used to analyze the latter can be applied to the former.

There is no evidence whatsoever to indicate that anyone involved in producing *The Wizard* had the slightest knowledge of, or interest in, either psychology or psychoanalysis. Whatever "insights" can be found in this movie by Freudian or Jungian psychoanalysts, they were probably not placed there by design. Moreover, there is no evidence to suggest that the American people, as a whole, are any different in this respect; if Freudian or Jungian insights are perceived in *The Wizard*, they are probably seldom perceived as such. But I argue here that *The Wizard* is like a collective daydream. In that case, it would not be surprising to find motifs arising from a collective unconscious (either in the general sense of that term or in the more specific sense defined by Jung).

Assuming, then, that a psychoanalytical approach to Dorothy's dream is legitimate, it must be acknowledged that there are two possible functional equivalents for the dreaming patient (or the patient undergoing psychoanalysis): the people who *produced The Wizard*, and the people who *respond* to it. I suggest that just as a psychoanalytical approach to dreams may help explain the subconscious attitudes of individuals, a psychoanalytical approach to movies (as "collective daydreams") may help explain the subconscious attitudes of a nation (including both the people who produced *The Wizard* and those who respond to it). It is true, of course, that the subconscious worlds of those who actually worked on *The Wizard* at MGM are also reflected in its subtext. Had these not corresponded so closely to those of so many other Americans, *The Wizard* would have been just another forgetable movie—that is, a movie of no particular cultural significance—and there would be no point in writing about it. Of interest here is not merely what *The Wizard* says about a few hundred employees of MGM back in 1939, but what it says about a few hundred million Americans over more than fifty years.

*

If it is appropriate to use psychoanalysis as a theoretical device for interpreting movies in general, which is the most appropriate psychoanalytical system to use for this movie in particular? Working within the Freudian tradition, Daniel Dervin suggests that Dorothy does indeed grow up in her dream of Oz. According to him, it represents her passage through the phallic phase of development and is provoked by anxiety over the "primal scene." By this, he refers to an event in the life of a child that is shocking, terrifying, and inexplicable: witnessing sexual intercourse between Mother and Father. Horrified at the thought of being ravished by Father's phallus, Dorothy projects this internal fear onto something in the external world. In this case, it takes the form of a tornado that "may well be a remarkably apt representation of the paternal phallus in its swollen, twisting, penetrating, state which is part of the primal scene."[12] Although Dorothy has her own bedroom in the movie, she shares a one-room house with Auntie Em and Uncle Henry in the book. With this literary background in mind, Dervin assumes that viewers subconsciously understand the cinematic setting as an appropriate one for the primal scene.

In short order, Dorothy is carried off by the "twister" to the Land of Oz; that is, she is carried off by her own anxiety to the land of dreams. There, she symbolically repeats the primal scene trauma in terms of lesser conflicts that are easier to master. By creating an elaborate "family romance," she is able to cope with her fear and undo the damage. By "family romance," Freud referred to the characteristic way children respond to lack of parental concern. In their revision of reality, the present (unloving or unprotecting) parents are humbled or reduced in status (often to adoptive parents), and the "real" parents are idealized. Clearly, Auntie Em and Uncle Henry are not Dorothy's biological parents. In the dream, her imaginary "parents" include a wizard and some witches. All, of course, are far more powerful than Auntie Em and Uncle Henry (both of whom had been exposed as powerless by Miss Gulch with her order from the local sheriff). Creating this family romance, then, is what helps Dorothy "to get back on the yellow brick road of progressive development and come to terms eventually with the male member and its role in procreation."[13]

Dervin also notes that the dream is presented in a way that corresponds to Freud's theory of dream interpretation. The people and objects Dorothy sees floating by her window (fragmentary and distorted recollections of farm life) and the strange new forms taken on by Ozian counterparts of people in Kansas are the day's residue. Regression to the level of dream is achieved through the use of visual imagery. When Dorothy wakes up on the bed and looks through her window, she sees Miss Gulch transformed into a witch flying past on her broomstick; the window is thus transformed into a "dream screen." Along with Dorothy herself, viewers pass through it and into the dreamworld of Oz." By "dream screen," Dervin refers to a receptical—ultimately, in psychoanalytical theory, Mother's breast—onto which children project their wish-fulfilling fantasies.

Regression through dreaming, however, involves more than wish-fulfilling fantasies (such as the family romance); it also involves conflict fantasies. One form of conflict that often leads to that kind of fantasy is ambivalence over Mother. In this case, Auntie Em seems unable to provide Dorothy with the necessary love and support. When Dorothy begs her assistance, for example, this businesslike woman has no time for her. Because wishing harm to Auntie Em is unacceptable in the waking state, it must be repressed. In Dorothy's dream, though, it is expressed by splitting the image of Auntie Em in two. As in so many fairy tales, the "Bad Mother" (that is, the stern, impatient side of Auntie Em) is projected onto a wicked witch. The Wicked Witches of both East and West are killed accidentally; the former is killed when Dorothy's house falls on her, and the latter is killed when the water Dorothy uses to save the Scarecrow splashes on her. This spares Dorothy from any feelings of guilt. According to Dervin, the Witch on her broomstick is a "phallic mother." Although this unnatural figure is frightening enough, it is less frightening than the "enormous and persecuting phalliclike column seen earlier making its way toward Dorothy's house."[14] The "Good Mother" (that is, the loving side of Auntie Em) is projected onto Glinda, Good Witch of the North, Dorothy's fairy godmother. In other words, it is easier—for the moment—to deal with the "witch" (Mother) than the "twister" (Father).

There is a consistent link, according to Dervin, between the Wizard and the storm. When Dorothy and her friends reach the Emerald City, for example, the verticality of its fluted spires dominate the landscape; their serene majesty reminds viewers, in a reassuring context, of the menacing verticality of the tornado. Inside, the Wizard's image is projected in front of what appear to be organ pipes. Accompanied by flashes of lightning and claps of thunder, the image is flanked by billowing flames and puffs of smoke. As the Ozian counterpart of Professor Marvel, adds Dervin, the Wizard is also a "windbag" who uses "windy rhetoric" to create an impression on people. Dervin even suggests that the windstorm which accompanied the phallic funnel is an "instinct storm." By this, he means "the emotional catastrophe of being overwhelmed by instinctual forces."[15] If the storm is connected to the "twister," it is also connected to the phallus (which is, by extension, Father himself).

When Dorothy first encounters the Wizard, he is Oz, The Great and Powerful. He is intimidating, to be sure, but not quite as intimidating as the primal phallus itself. (At the very least, for example, Dorothy is able to talk to him and even make a request.) The time has come for Dorothy to confront the ultimate source of her anxiety. Consequently, the Wizard asks her to bring back the Witch's broomstick (or phallus). Because the first "phallic mother" has been killed by a tornado, her twin sister must be killed by Dorothy herself. When she has done this (albeit accidentally), the phallus can be returned to its proper, paternal owner: the Wizard. In a sense, Oz represents more than a dream; not only does Dorothy engage in fantasies there, she actually works through some of her conflicts.

At this point, according to Dervin, Dorothy has reached a decisive point in her psychological development. She now shifts the focus of her concern from Mother (someone who should not have had a phallus) to Father (someone who should have one). Killing the Witch and giving her broomstick to the Wizard thus initiates Dorothy into the phallic state. This gives her a new sense of power (self-confidence) but also increases her sexual curiosity. In effect, it awakens her oedipal concerns. "When Dorothy lays her broomstick at the base of the Wizard's ominous image, it is a clear measure of her newly acquired sexual knowledge. Putting the phallus where it properly belongs, however, not only disarms the wicked phallic mother but also sets in motion a process that will demythologize the all-powerful Wizard, for he now stands for a merely human organ."[16]

With Toto pulling aside the curtain that surrounds the Wizard, revealing the terrifying image as a projected illusion, Dorothy is once again peeking, symbolically, beneath the blankets of a primal scene. What she finds this time, though, is reassuring. The Wizard, "in his grandiose machinations, functions as an intermediate step between the totally inhuman, persecutory pillar of wind and the altogether human, modestly functioning organ."[17] Observing the cranks and levers and dials operated by the Wizard, Dorothy realizes that "the thing is not supernatural or terrifying at all, but something very natural—at least as natural as adult sexuality."[18] If Dorothy had earlier projected her fear of the phallus onto the "twister," she now finds projection[19] unnecessary. In short, she is growing up.

The Wizard is a fake. He lacks occult power. Still, he does have human power. Dervin says of him that "as owner of the family phallus," he has the power to help his child (that is, Dorothy plus her three friends) in some ways but not in all ways. In other words, he is a real person. As the "missing father," he is benevolent and wise but finite all the same. True to his meteorological associations, he offers to take Dorothy home in his balloon. But when he manages to take off without her, Dorothy discovers that going home is as easy as waking up. And she is ready to do this because she has cleared away all the obstacles in her developmental path. Still, the Wizard has already been very helpful. He has assigned an appropriate task that forced Dorothy to learn. And he has granted the requests of Dorothy's three friends. According to Dervin, they are "dolls" who want to become human (that is, to be capable of intelligence, love, and courage). Since Dorothy participates with the Wizard in "humanizing" them, she symbolically bears his children; she and the Wizard make "babies" out of the "dolls." In this way, Dorothy relives the primal scene. But this time she masters the trauma. "By restoring the father's phallus, i.e. by correctly assigning biological sexual roles and thereby giving up her own phallic wishes, the girl is rewarded by her father with children and an affirmative sense of her own powers of repro-duction. With her own femininity thus safely established, she can relinquish her hold on him and go home to herself."[20] For Dervin, this interpretation is strongly supported by circumstances found in the last sequence. Back in Kansas, "Dorothy awakens on her bed, but now it is sunny outside, and the room is no longer twirled about by the primal scene turmoil. She is surrounded by the pleased faces of the three farmhands who welcome her back to consciousness so eargerly that the emotions virtually transform her bedroom into a maternity setting: she is treated like a proud young mother coming to after a prolonged ordeal; and, in fact, via her dream children, she has given birth to at least a new edition of herself."[21]

Dervin's article is very useful. Here is a Freudian psychoanalyst who sees *The Wizard* in terms of growing up. He refers specifically to "the yellow brick road of progressive development."[22] Elsewhere, he says of Dorothy that "what she really needs—what she must, to a degree, be successful in—is to overcome the obstacles in her developmental path."[23] But Dervin's approach is not without problems. Before discussing these, one more psychoanalytical approach should be examined.

Harvey Greenberg has written an excellent article in which he uses the psychology of personality development to argue that *The Wizard* is about coming of age. For him, therefore, the subtext is addressed to older children. "Dorothy's trip," he writes, "is a marvelous metaphor for the psychological journey every adolescent must make."[24] He takes a nondeterministic approach to psychological development. He does not believe that the structure of personality is frozen in early childhood. Important as the early years are, growth takes place throughout the life cycle. Unlike many Freudians, he places more emphasis on adolescence than infancy or childhood. It is during adolescence that sudden spurts of physical, intellectual and sexual growth take place; these propel youngsters out of the safety and security known hitherto at home. At the same time, though, the repressed conflicts of childhood resurface either to be resolved or to create enduring problems. Adolescents, therefore, are subject to both progressive and regressive tendencies; they are vulnerable to emotional injury but they are also capable of repairing the damage.

One major problem confronting adolescents is how to build new relationships with their parents, relationships not based on utter dependence and the ambivalence that inevitably follows (adulation versus resentment; love versus hatred; need for support versus need for autonomy). Adolescents must learn not only that their parents are fully human (and not terrifying gods or fabulous heroes), but also that they themselves are fully human (and not merely passive recipients of care). In short, teenagers seek a balance between feelings of their own helplessness and their own omnipotence even as they seek a balance between worshipping or imitating their parents and rebelling against them. One way of temporarily resolving ambivalent feelings toward parents is to find substitute parents such as movie stars, sports heroes, mentors, or gang leaders. Heroes replace parents on the pedestal vacated due to the exigencies of everyday life. Attributed to heroes are all the qualities—physical, sexual, intellectual, or spiritual—needed to alleviate a perceived inadequacy of the self. "In other words," writes Greenberg, "everyone wants a Wizard during adolescence, but the wanting will cease when the youngster begins to tap his own unique abilities."[25] Finding surrogate parents also involves a sense of loss, notes Greenberg, because it means giving up some of the intimacy associated with one's own parents. It may also involve giving up the security associated with them because the new heroes may be relatively inaccessible. The void is filled with friends. But it takes time to form satisfying and enduring friendships. Adolescents find it reassuring to know that their real parents are still around to guide them through this difficult transition. They want to know that they can always go home again if necessary. When they must mourn, once again, for a parent already lost, adolescents often cling to an idealized image of the dead parent. This increases the pain of letting go and can impede the process of growing up.

For Greenberg, this is the problem afflicting Dorothy. She is trying desperately to cope with the fact of being an orphan. Neither the book nor the movie explain how Dorothy came to be an orphan. At this point, Greenberg interpolates external material into the film scenario. But if Dervin did so on the basis of Freudian theory (observation of sexual intercourse between the parents), Greenberg does so on the basis of his own experience as a clinician. He suggests that Dorothy's father died first, probably before she was eight, and that this led her to establish an unusually close relationship with her mother. Then her mother also died. This led to severe spiritual and psychological problems. *The Wizard*, as interpreted by Greenberg, shows many signs of desolation over parental loss, especially maternal loss, and extreme anxiety over the potential loss of Auntie Em and Uncle Henry as surrogate parents.

If so, then the problem is not Father (as it is for Dervin) but Mother. In view of this, he explains the paradoxical image of Mother. She is the Good Mother who nourishes and cherishes but also the Bad Mother who sometimes ignores and might even abandon. (Seen from the perspective of adults in religious lore, the Good Mother generates life; the Bad Mother destroys it.) In folk and fairy tales, "the Good Mother is the bounteous fairy godmother, the lovely gossamer queen who makes everything copacetic with a wave of her wand;"[26] "the Bad Mother is the witch who snares the children strayed from home, then enslaves or murders them."[27] As Greenberg and Dervin observe, both Good and Bad Mothers are aspects of the same person. Gradually, children learn that when Mother has other things to do, she is not about to abandon them; but sometimes events occur that compromise their ability to accept this. The death of a mother might well have this effect. Not only do children often blame themselves for a mother's death, they also blame the mother herself for leaving them so exposed and vulnerable. Just when the adolescent Dorothy should be moving away from her (surrogate) parents, her anxiety rises once more over the possibility of losing Auntie Em. (Greenberg notes here that "Em" suggests "M" for Mother.) Dorothy is deeply disturbed in her ambivalence toward Auntie Em. On the one hand, she sees Auntie Em as the Good Mother. On the other hand, she worries that this lady will "turn hard" or die. Along with this fear goes anger. Dorothy is still angry at her real mother for abandoning her. And this anger is projected onto the equally innocent Auntie Em. Being unable to reconcile her conflicting attitudes toward Auntie Em, she projects her rage onto yet another woman. This woman, however, truly deserves to be hated: Miss Gulch, the Wicked Witch of the West. But the solution is only temporary because Dorothy cannot become a mature woman without realizing that grown-ups are neither divine (like Glinda and the Wizard) nor demonic (like the Witch) but fully human. "The drama of Dorothy's search for her authentic, autonomous self is delightfully played out during her adventures in the Land of Oz."[28] Here are the highlights of Greenberg's psychological commentary.

First, the farm is a matriarchy. This supports Greenberg's contention that Dorothy's problem has to do with Mother and feminine identity rather than with Father. Every male character in both Kansas and Oz is presented as weak and damaged in one way or another. The women, on the other hand, are far more capable—for good or for evil. Clearly, Auntie Em rules the roost on the farm. Although the Wizard rules Oz in name, it is Glinda and the other witches who seem to rule in fact. And all three male friends (like their Kansas counterparts) are seriously flawed. Speculating on this, Greenberg suggests that Dorothy's real father may have been equally ineffectual. Even more likely, his death may have come to represent for her a paradigm of masculine failure.

For Greenberg, Toto is an extension of Dorothy. Like her, he is "perky, mischievous, nosing into things that don't concern him, forever *running away* when he should stay put.... Ostensibly, she is worried that Gulch will return to claim her pound of pooch, but actually Toto's escape has given Dorothy the excuse she needed to spread her wings and quit the farm."[29] That is, she is free to seek her own identity separate from that of Auntie Em.

When Dorothy visits Professor Marvel, she explicitly worries that Auntie Em will die: "You don't suppose she could really be sick, do you? Oh! Oh, I've got to go home right away" (47). This idea is reiterated throughout the movie. The Munchkins have been held captive by a Bad Mother (the Wicked Witch of the East). By releasing them from her tyranny, Dorothy herself becomes their Good Mother although their Bad Mother turns up once more as the Wicked Witch of the West. Nevertheless, their obsessive need to verify the demise of their oppressor is another oblique reminder of Dorothy's own preoccupation with her mother's death and Auntie Em's possible death. (After all, they are all characters in Dorothy's dream.) "As coroner," sings one of them, "I must aver I thoroughly examined her, And she's not only merely dead, She's really most sincerely dead" (58). In the Emerald City, Dorothy and her friends are refused access to the Wizard. "Professor Marvel said she was sick," cries Dorothy, "She may be dying, and, and it's all my fault. I'll never forgive myself!" (98). This is the other side of the coin. Dorothy blames herself. When she is hit by the window frame and knocked unconscious, Dorothy is "punished" (in her dream) for running away and abandoning Auntie Em.

While Glinda floats off "by bubble express," Dorothy comments: "My, people come and go so quickly here" (63). Greenberg suggests that she is referring to her own inability to stay put. Dorothy is thus like so many other adolescents who dislike being pinned down physically, emotionally, or intellectually; at this stage, they experience a dramatic surge in the need for exploration and experimentation. If Toto, indeed, is an extension of Dorothy, then restlessness is clearly a theme of major importance. In the prologue, Toto's restlessness motivates the whole story (by causing Dorothy to run away); in Oz, his restlessness causes her to miss the Wizard's flight out of Oz. In any case, Greenberg points out that Dorothy is constantly on the move not only because she wants to avoid the Witch, but also because that is the reverse of her own childish dependence on Auntie Em, her own longing to be safe and secure at home as a "helpless, clinging, unproductive parasite." In cinematic terms, the entire dream is a restless journey along the Yellow Brick Road.

Dorothy meets three friends in Oz. Through them, she deals with her own sense of inadequacy. At this primitive stage in her development, no longer a child but not yet an adult, she finds it difficult to believe that she may actually be smart enough, loving enough, and brave enough to thrive in the adult world. Normally, a girl trying to become independent of Mother would look to Father for support (especially when, as in this case, there are no other women to dilute the intense relationship with Mother). But "there is no Dad for Dorothy, only poignant memories of him, and the surrogate who doesn't really fill the bill. So off she goes with her damaged friends to find the great Pa in the sky, to connect up with the Mighty Wizard and heal her sense of loss."[30] Even so, this is not her primary goal; it is only her way of achieving that goal.

Greenberg makes an interesting observation about the Witch as Bad Mother par excellence. Even the method she uses to prevent Dorothy from reaching the Wizard seems to support her role as the Bad Mother. She conjures up poppies—the source of opium—to lull Dorothy and her friends into fatal passivity (dependence). Glinda, on the other hand, is a Good Mother; she encourages her children to become independent by learning and doing things for themselves.

If any more evidence were needed to support Greenberg's argument, the famous episode in the Witch's Castle would seem to provide it. Dorothy looks into the crystal ball and sees Auntie Em calling out to her. Suddenly, the Witch replaces Em. "See how intimately bound together is [sic] the Good Mother and the Bad: for a brief, nightmarish instant Em and the Witch have fused identities. This scene, I have found, is peculiarly troubling to most children, no doubt because it captures so effectively our archaic terror of the mother's destructive potential."[31]

In general, the Witch's role as Bad Mother is expressed merely as a threat. But one character, the Scarecrow, actually suffers harm to his person. Twice, the Witch tries to incinerate him. On another occasion, she has her flying monkeys literally "destraw" him. It does not take much imagination to see in this scene a symbolic destruction of self (his stuffing) by the titanic power of the Bad Mother.

The traumatic encounter with the Witch is brought to a sudden close when Dorothy accidentally splashes her with water. Greenberg points out the fact that in many science fiction and horror movies, the evil forces are destroyed by absurdly simple devices or by the forces taken for granted in everyday life. Vampires may be destroyed by the rays of a rising sun, the merest glance at a crucifix, or a wooden stake driven through the heart. In *War of the Worlds* (Byron Haskin, 1953), the Martians are destroyed by common bacteria. "We can always end our nightmares just as easily, by waking up and hauling ourselves out of harm's way."[33]

Finally, according to Greenberg, when the Wizard sails off in his balloon without Dorothy, he recreates a painful scene for her. The dream recapitulates the loss of her father when his strength is most needed. But it also emphasizes the fact that he—the Wizard or the father—is only human. His elimination from the scene puts Dorothy back in the hands of Auntie Em. This recapitulates the original scenario of loss and conflict. When Auntie Em reappears, though, it is not as the Bad Mother (who has been outgrown) but as the Good Mother whose humanity Dorothy can now accept.

To do a thorough psychoanalysis of *The Wizard* (or any other movie) would be a massive undertaking. The articles of both Dervin and Greenberg are not only brief though, but seriously flawed: on the one hand, they overemphasize information not provided by the movie itself; on the other hand, they underemphasize some information that is provided. So they cannot account for the remarkable place of this movie in American culture.

Both Dervin and Greenberg depend on nondiegetic information (what is not presented in the movie itself). Dervin, for example, speculates about what might have happened to Dorothy before the plot even begins to unfold. He is quite explicit about the fact that he uses both the book and the movie as primary sources; the book, as he says, "fills in certain details necessary for a coherent psychological analysis."[33] He clearly indicates when evidence comes from one source or the other. In effect, though, he postulates the existence of a third primary source: a combination of book and movie that exists in the minds of viewers. As he says, a primal scene witnessed by Dorothy seems plausible in the book's one-room house—although even then Dervin finds it necessary to explain that Baum was "careful to make the relatives distinctly grey and feeble"[34] to disguise the sexual overtones of his work—but not so plausible in the movie's larger farmhouse (with its separate bedroom for Dorothy). It is true, of course, that viewers always see movies in some cultural context. Many viewers of this one, for instance, may have already read the book; it is quite possible, therefore—though by no means certain—that they subconsciously put the two works together in a way that would support Dervin's theory. Nevertheless, they would almost certainly be confused. Not only is the new information not in the movie, it actually contradicts what is in the movie. Dervin might have tried to solve the problem without resorting to evidence from another source. One could imagine that Dorothy witnessed a primal scene in a single-room house belonging to her biological parents before coming to live in the larger house of her adoptive parents. But this, in fact, would not have solved the larger problem. No evidence from the movie itself supports it. Either way, Dervin's argument is based on speculation. Considering the centrality of a primal scene for his argument, this would seem to be a major flaw.

Greenberg also speculates about Dorothy's dead parents. Although he generally (but not always) resists the temptation to use external sources of information, his entire analysis is focused on a detail that is of no obvious importance in cinematic terms. The fact that Auntie Em and Uncle Henry are Dorothy's adoptive parents is interesting, to be sure, but the importance Greenberg attaches to it is not supported by the movie itself. Dorothy's feelings for them are not significantly different from those of any child for its natural parents. To be methodologically sound, Greenberg would have to show that being an orphan causes her to behave in ways that would be unusual, or unlikely, for other children. He does not do this.

Similarly, both Dervin and Greenberg underestimate the importance of what is actually presented in the movie. It would be difficult to overestimate the importance of the ruby slippers to most viewers. Yet both Dervin and Greenberg virtually ignore them. This seems particularly strange in view of the price they commanded at an auction of MGM props and memorabilia in 1970. Harmetz describes it in great detail.[35] From the auctioneer, David Weisz, she learned that the sale of Dorothy's ruby slippers, in particular, was intensely emotional; it was, he said, "the most exciting moment of the whole auction." They sold (in that particular auction) for $15,000. Even Dorothy's gingham dress went for only $1,000. The Witch's dress went for $350, and her hat for $450. At the same auction, a pair of shoes worn by Elizabeth Taylor sold for $200. Obviously, the ruby slippers had not lost their "magic" after thirty years. But what, precisely, was that magic? According to Harmetz, "The magic had something to do with Judy Garland's clouded death; it had more to do with the ritual appearance of *The Wizard of Oz* each year on television. But it probably had most to do with how visible the slippers are as a talisman—fiercely desirable but useful only to the wearer, capable of keeping one safe in the darkness of the outer world and of bringing one home again without pain or loss of innocence."[36]

But psychoanalysis should be able to provide an even deeper level of insight. One clue is provided by the color of these slippers. Red is commonly associated with fire, blood, and sexuality. Even in a positive context, therefore, an element of danger is present. In American

culture, for instance, red is the color of "stop," or "exit," and of
"communism." As Bruno Bettelheim makes clear in *The Uses of
Enchantment*, the color red is very often found in fairy tales as blood.
When the story is about a girl, this often refers to menstrual blood
and the onset of puberty; examples of this would include *Snow
White*[37] and *The Sleeping Beauty*.[38] It may, on the other hand, refer
to the hymenal blood that ends virginity; an example of this would
be *Cinderella*.[39] In a movie about a young girl whose dream has a
plot that virtually revolves around possession of magical red objects,
it seems safe to suggest that the symbolic reference is to blood, and
very likely to be menstrual blood. Another clue, though, is provided
by the function of these objects.

According to Bettelheim, there is a link between slippers and
sexuality. He discusses the matter in connection with a story that
clearly revolves around a pair of slippers. Her ability to fit into the
glass slipper identifies Cinderella as the Prince's appropriate choice
for marriage. The slippers represent her sexual readiness and desirability. When the sisters try on the slippers, their feet do not fit. In
other words, they are either unfit or unready for marriage. Cinderella
has come of age; she is ready for adult sexuality. The sisters are
adolescents; they are still coping with the problems of puberty
(menstruation). This is why their feet bleed as they try on the
slipper. Unfortunately, Bettelheim does not discuss another fairy tale
that explicitly links "red" and "slippers." In "The Red Shoes," Hans
Christian Andersen shows how sexuality itself (that is, the "red" and
the "slippers") may be associated with danger and even death.
(Because of her inappropriate pride, Karen is unable to remove the
red shoes and is forced to dance until she gets someone to chop off
her feet.) Apparently, red evokes ambivalent feelings: it represents
both promise and peril.

In movies too, red is often used to focus attention on sexuality.
Sometimes, it appears directly in the form of blood. Very often,
though, the reference is less direct. Examples of this would include
the red jacket worn by James Dean in *Rebel without a Cause*
(Nicholas Ray, 1955), the red dress worn by Maureen Stapleton in
Interiors (Woody Allen, 1978), and the red gown worn by Vivien
Leigh in *Gone with the Wind* (Victor Fleming, 1939). Of particular
interest in this context, however, are the red shoes worn by Katharine
Hepburn in *Summertime* (David Lean, 1955). These will be discussed
more fully later on in this chapter.

Even though Dervin does make a passing reference to the onset of menarche, he fails to follow this up with a discussion of the ruby slippers. Greenberg also fails to recognize the importance of the ruby slippers. He mentions them only once as possible "phallic" symbols of interest to "high church" Freudians even though a careful examination of this motif would have supported his own theory about Dorothy's coming of age. To become a woman in physiological terms, girls must begin to menstruate. This begins of its own accord. Symbolically stated, Dorothy does not *seek* the ruby slippers; she *finds* them on her feet when Glinda transfers them, magically, from the feet of a witch. Besides, menstruation ends of its own accord; attempts to interfere with natural processes can have grave consequences. Symbolically stated, once again, Dorothy must learn to wear (or live with) the ruby slippers. "There they are," says Glinda, "and there they'll stay" (61). Later, however, she warns Dorothy: "And never let these ruby slippers off your feet for a moment, or you will be at the mercy of the Wicked Witch of the West" (63). To become a woman in psychological terms, girls must accept the fact of menstruation. In other words, they must understand its "magical power" in connection with marriage and reproduction. When the Witch tells Dorothy, "I'm the only one that knows how to use them. They're of no use to you," Glinda insists that "their magic must be very powerful or she wouldn't want them so badly" (62).

Dramatic changes in her own body can be very frightening to a young girl. It takes time to adjust. At first, she may think of menstruation only as a curse. In Dorothy's case, for instance, the ruby slippers provoke persecution by a witch. Being immured in the Witch's Castle is itself highly symbolic. Dorothy feels trapped in a world of forces she cannot yet understand, let alone control. She is still utterly dependent on help from the outside. This is the low point in her passage through Oz. But the hourglass represents time rapidly running out on this anachronistic state of mind. And by the end of the dream, the mystery has been solved. Now Dorothy is ready to go home. To do so, she has only to recite a "mantra" while clicking the heels of her ruby slippers. It is worth noting carefully that the last objects that viewers see in Oz are the ruby slippers. Dorothy can only return to Kansas by "ritually" acknowledging them. They are that important. When she returns home, Dorothy is ready to participate fully in the adult community because she is able to experience the "magical power" of menstruation as a potential blessing, not a curse.

Having argued very convincingly that Dorothy comes of age in this movie, Greenberg fails to indicate what her "age" might be. In many societies, this would be obvious because biological coming of age (puberty) is followed immediately by cultural coming of age (ritual); that would make Dorothy twelve or thirteen. In modern American society, though, biological and cultural coming of age do not coincide. Because they are separated by many years, puberty does not indicate readiness for marriage and adult responsibilities. The transitional period is called "adolescence." In that case, Dorothy would be a teenager of somewhere between thirteen or fourteen and seventeen or eighteen.

Actually, it would be most helpful to think of her as fourteen or fifteen. This is because the movie, if taken seriously on its own terms, leaves the viewer no choice. Judy Garland was sixteen years old when she played Dorothy. And she looked her age. At first MGM wanted to hire the much younger Shirley Temple, who was ten years old at the time, but negotiations with Twentieth Century Fox failed.[40] To make Garland look younger required some ingenuity on the part of studio technicians; her breasts were concealed with binding cloths.[41] But the result is surprisingly successful: a sexually provocative combination of womanly beauty and childlike innocence. This ambiguous quality has not escaped the attention of many adult viewers (although it was certainly not intended by the studio). In short, viewers are more likely to think of Dorothy as a teenager (in spite of her childlike behavior at times) than as, according to Dervin, a young child.

Greenberg acknowledges that Freudians with a "high church" point of view would claim that Dorothy feels incomplete due to the imagined loss of a penis or that her search for the phallic broomstick represents a repressed wish to take Father away from Mother (the Elektra complex). He does not categorically deny that these elements may be part of Dorothy's mentality, but he wisely observes that "Dorothy's search for a strong, competent, male 'rescuer' seems to stem most potently from the pressure to divest herself of her pathological dependence upon Em-Mother rather than to compete with Em for Henry. Fewer women than Freud imagined actually have fantasies of wanting a penis, but all women—as their male counterparts—seek realized independent lives."[42]

Neither Dervin nor Greenberg is able to explain the massive and enduring popularity of *The Wizard*. Not only does Dervin not do justice to its particularity (depending on information from the book), he trivializes it. Dervin asks us to believe that millions of people are captivated by a subtext about passage through the phallic stage. But this is asking too much. After all, it is not only children below the age of four or five who enjoy this movie. There must be something more in it to retain the love and loyalty of viewers who have long since resolved their phallic and oedipal problems. What does *The Wizard* say to older children or to adults? The answers to such questions cannot be found by adhering strictly to Freudian theory. Even if it could be assumed that many children actually witness their parents in the act of making love and that they find this very distressing—assumptions that, to say the least, are debatable—the continuing popularity of this movie in virtually all segments of the population would remain unexplained. Like Greenberg, I do not want to say that a strict Freudian approach is wrong. I assume that any cultural artifact as popular as this one operates on many levels and addresses many needs. If *The Wizard* "speaks" to both children and adults, why should it not also "speak" to children at different stages of development? But if Dervin is correct, he has discovered only one subtext among several—and by no means the most significant one.

Greenberg, on the other hand, asks us to believe that the subtext which has captured the imagination of millions is about orphanhood. There have always been orphans, but they have always been statistically abnormal. In brief, orphanhood is simply not common enough to explain the universal appeal of this movie. It is true, however, that *anxiety* about parents and orphanhood may well be universal. Consequently, Greenberg's argument can be used quite effectively in this discussion. With only a slight shift of emphasis, Greenberg really could point to a subtext that can address the needs of almost everyone because everyone has been, is, or will be an adolescent. He says hardly anything about Dorothy as an orphan that could not also be said of her as an ordinary adolescent girl—indeed, as an ordinary adolescent of either sex. Even those whose parents are alive must seek new heroes, new models, new friends. Even boys must separate from Mother. Even well-adjusted teenagers must learn about dependence, independence, and interdependence. If Dorothy suffers more acute stress than many other teenagers, she nevertheless suffers from the same kind of stress. It is interesting to speculate on Dorothy's particular biographical journey, but that is hardly necessary to explain the place of this movie in American life. Greenberg's comments on adolescence are in accord with contemporary thought on coming of age as a psychological, social, and cultural phenomenon. Any further implications about orphanhood may be of interest to

clinical psychologists and to orphans but are of little or no importance for the task at hand. In short, whether the dream of Oz
articulates the anxiety of a four-year-old or a fourteen-year-old, *The
Wizard* clearly lends itself to interpretation as a story about the
psychological development of individuals.

*

It seems clear that *The Wizard's* dream sequence can be interpreted psychoanalytically in terms of growing up. Dorothy can be
said to have moved from one stage of development to another, even
though opinions may differ on precisely which stages are involved.
Because the dream is inserted into a larger cinematic unit, however,
it must be interpreted in that context as well. In purely cinematic
terms, then, growing up is linked to going home. *Dorothy grows up in
her dream and, at the same time, goes home to Kansas.* Dervin writes
that at the end of her dream Dorothy can relinquish her hold on the
Wizard and "go home to herself."[43] Still, there is nothing in Freudian
theory to support the idea that growing up is synonymous with going
home or that maturation involves a circular movement (return to
origin). On the contrary, development is seen as a linear process. If
growing up and going home are cinematically linked in *The Wizard*
and other popular movies, it is by no means obvious *why* they are
linked or *why* movies that make such a link should be so *popular.* It
can be assumed, however, that millions of people would hardly
respond so favorably to movies that contradict their own psychological experience. So far, *The Wizard* has been examined psychoanalytically from two Freudian perspectives.[44] Both have provided useful
insights but neither has proven entirely satisfactory. But there is
another psychoanalytical tradition. Freud is famous not only for his
"discovery" of the unconscious but also for his work on early stages
of the life cycle; Carl Gustav Jung is famous not only for his
"discovery" of the collective unconscious but also for his work on
later stages of the life cycle.

Unlike Freud's theories—many of which (though by no means all)
have become part of mainstream psychoanalysis in one form or
another—Jung's theories are usually considered a separate branch of
psychoanalysis (known as "analytical psychology"). Two particular
features of his work—his notion of the collective unconscious and his
assumptions about gender differences—remain controversial. Nevertheless, there are some compelling reasons for examining *The Wizard*
in terms of the Jungian tradition as well as the Freudian. In the first

place, there are some striking parallels between the symbolic motifs in Dorothy's dream and those discussed by Jung in his works on individuation and dream analysis. In some very obvious ways, at any rate, the dream looks as if it might have been used by Jung as a case study. Moreover, there are some striking parallels between the symbolic motifs in Dorothy's dream and those discussed by Jung in his works on the collective unconscious (that is, on myth and folklore) because Jung believed that myths are for communities what dreams are for individuals. Since I argue that *The Wizard* has come to function as a "secular myth" and since *The Wizard* consists mainly of a dream, it makes sense to consider Jung's work. But there is another reason for doing so. Since myth is a characteristic feature of religion, it seems appropriate to include at least one psychoanalytical approach that is not associated with any form of antireligious reductionism (the reduction of religion to a collective neurosis that hides reality, say, or to a collective delusion made obsolete by science). Unlike many other psychoanalysts, Jung believed that religion can play a helpful role in the development of healthy personalities. In addition, he showed how religious traditions (symbol systems as expressed in myth and ritual) can reveal a great deal about the psychic life of both the individual and the collectivity. As a result, he often examined dreams by pointing to parallels in myth and folklore.[45]

According to Jung, individuation (maturation) is a process inherent in human nature. Psychological growth is thus analogous to physiological growth. It consists of two distinct stages. One corresponds to the first half of the life cycle and involves initiation into outer reality (society). This process includes consolidation of the ego (consciousness), differentiation of the main "function" (primary mode of processing information about the world) and "attitude" (primary mode of reacting to the world), development of an appropriate "persona" (the face habitually presented to the external world), and general adaptation of the individual to demands made by the society. The goal of this stage is to become integrated in the life of a community and renew the cycle of life through marriage and reproduction. The other phase corresponds to the second half of the life cycle and involves initiation into inner reality. This process includes acquisition of deeper self-knowledge or bringing to consciousness what had been hidden in the unconscious. The goal is both self-realization and preparation for death. Consequently, it could be summed up as the search for meaning. This second half of the life cycle was of greatest interest to Jung. In fact, when Jung spoke of individuation, he normally had only this second stage in mind.

Although individuation is a spontaneous process, it can be stimulated or intensified by being made conscious. This is the aim of (Jungian) psychoanalysis. Attention is focused on dreams because these consist of symbolic representations of the psychic forces at work. They may either warn of adjustments that must be made if psychic equilibrium is to be restored (in the case of a neurosis) or lead the dreamer on to new levels of insight (in the quest for self-realization). More specifically, individuation is the quest for what Jung calls the "self." By this, he refers to the final "archetype" (symbolic signpost, or milestone) of a series encountered in dreams. Although the particular forms taken by these archetypes vary from one individual to another, each corresponds to more basic, underlying experiences that are common to all people of all times and all places; through symbols, the experiences of individuals are linked to those of the tribe, the nation, and the human race itself.

According to Jung, dreams have a great deal in common with myths. Dreams often reveal more than the concerns of particular individuals, and the interpretation of an individual's dream may be of great interest to others. A dream, says Jung, "will as a rule contain mythological motifs, combinations of ideals or images which can be found in the myths of one's own folk or in those of other races. The dream will then have a collective meaning, a meaning which is the common property of mankind."[46] Moreover, the images found in myths function, on the collective level, in precisely the same way as those in dreams do on the individual (or personal) level. Everything he says about the "social symbol" (used in myth and folklore) Jung also applies to the "individual symbol" (found in dreams). "There are individual psychic products," he writes, "whose symbolic character is so obvious that they at once compel a symbolic interpretation. For the individual they have the same functional significance that the social symbol has for a larger human group."[47] In other words, myths are experienced with the same vividness and unself-consciousness as dreams. Elsewhere, Jung criticizes contemporary scholars for their superficial understanding of myth; this could be corrected, according to him, by applying the insights of psychoanalysis (dream analysis) to myths.

> So far mythologists have always helped themselves out with solar, lunar, meteorological, vegetal, and other ideas of this kind. The fact

that myths are first and foremost psychic phenomena that reveal the nature of the soul is something they have absolutely refused to see until now. Primitive man is not much interested in objective explanations of the obvious, but he has an imperative need—or rather, his unconscious psyche has an irresistible urge—to assimilate all outer sense experiences to inner, psychic events....All the mythologized processes of nature...are in no sense allegories of those objective occurrences; rather they are symbolic expressions of the inner, unconscious drama of the psyche which becomes accessible to man's consciousness by way of projection—that is, mirrored in the events of nature.[48]

Jung even provides the basis for analogies between dream, or myth, and art. Jung's understanding of art does not correspond to that of contemporary Western artists or art critics, but the phenomenon he describes—whatever it be called—does correspond to cultural productions such as popular movies. He questions the primacy of newness, innovation, originality, and persona-based individualism that currently define art in Western societies. It should be noted, however, that Jung does not deny originality to artists. He recognizes that their distinctive insight as individuals allows them to create powerful images. But it is their insight into *universally shared* experiences of the human condition that they express so powerfully, not merely their own personal experiences. It is precisely their effective use of inherited cultural symbols, not idiosyncratic use of private ones, that Jung understands as art. Originality (novelty) is not an end in itself but a means to an end: providing the community with access to collective wisdom passed down in symbolic form from one generation to the next. This is far indeed from "art for art's sake." "The essence of a work of art," writes Jung, "is not to be found in the personal idiosyncrasies that creep into it—indeed, the more there are of them, the less it is a work of art—but in its rising above the personal and speaking from the mind and heart of the artist to the mind and heart of mankind. The personal aspect of art is a limitation and even a vice."[49]

Elsewhere, Jung makes the same point by referring to the relation between art and dream: "Like every true prophet," he writes, "the artist is the unwitting mouthpiece of the psychic secrets of his time and is often as unconscious as a sleep-walker. He supposes that it is he who speaks, but the spirit of the age is his prompter, and whatever this spirit says is proved by its effects."[50] My point here is that

The Wizard should be discussed in terms of myth and dream (which are at the heart of what Jung calls "art") rather than in terms of art as that is generally understood in modern Western societies.

*

The Wizard's dream sequence lends itself very easily to Jungian interpretation. More specifically, the characters Dorothy meets during her dream correspond to the symbolic figures Jung calls "archetypes." In real life, it is unlikely that all of these archetypes would appear in a single dream; they would usually appear in a series of dreams separated from each other by months, years, or even decades. Jung himself was quite explicit about the dangers of relying on scanty evidence even within a single stage of development. "A relative degree of certainty," writes Jung, "is reached only in the interpretation of a series of dreams, where the later dreams correct the mistakes we have made in handling those that went before. Also, the basic ideas and themes can be recognized much better in a dream series."[51]

Nevertheless, it can be argued that Dorothy's dream "telescopes" (or condenses) real time into screen time (just as almost all movies do—with notable exceptions such as *High Noon* [Fred Zinnemann, 1952] in which real time and screen time are identical). In that case, Dorothy's single dream is a symbolic equivalent, in the cinematic economy, of a series of dreams. Moreover, it can be argued that other American movies and television shows are functional equivalents of the dream-series. Indeed, many other American cultural productions reveal similar psychological patterns encoded in symbolic form. The popularity of *The Wizard* has been so massive and so enduring that it can hardly be unique in its depiction of psychological reality; it must correspond to something most Americans "understand" (consciously or unconsciously). In fact, if this movie's depiction of psychological reality were unique (or even idiosyncratic), its place in American culture would be inexplicable.

Because *The Wizard* actually consists primarily of a dream, it is interesting from the perspective of both dream and myth as understood by Jung. At the moment, however, attention will be focused specifically on its dreamlike aspect. The movie clearly distinguishes between two states of mind: conscious and unconscious. This distinction is not a matter of interpretation. On the contrary, it is made explicit in purely cinematic terms. In the prologue, Dorothy is hit on the head, falls onto the bed, and "passes out." This is indicated by the cinematic convention used to indicate sleep, hallucination, intoxication, or any other altered state of consciousness: moving double images. In the epilogue, the same cinematic device is used to indicate a return to the original state of consciousness. Dorothy wakes up in bed surrounded by family and friends—all of whom agree with Auntie Em when she tells Dorothy: "You just had a bad dream" (131). This raises a question in the minds of viewers. But the question is not: Was it a dream or was it real? Clearly, the episode was a dream. And yet Dorothy tells Auntie Em: "No, Auntie Em, this was a real truly live place" (131). The question for viewers is: How real *can* a dream be? The movie itself makes two seemingly contradictory statements: Oz is a dream, and Oz is "real." Viewers are expected to identify with Dorothy (the protagonist) and agree that Oz is *real*, but not to deny the equally strong assertion (made not only by Auntie Em but by the cinematic structure itself) that Oz is a *dream*.

Before discussing the dream itself, however, it is necessary to examine its context: Dorothy's conscious situation in the prologue. That is, an assessment must be made of her ego. The earliest phase of the life cycle is concerned with the development of consciousness or adaptation to the external reality of everyday life. At the same time, though, development of the inner world is also taking place unconsciously. The process of individuation (development of the inner world) begins with a trauma, or shock, that wounds the personality and calls for some response. But the ground may have been prepared by boredom or inner emptiness. In all cases, the problem is not consciously recognized as such; on the contrary, it is projected onto someone or something in the external world. This seems to be the case with Dorothy. Evidently, she has difficulty finding her own place in the scheme of things. She sees herself as isolated and marginal in the farm community; consequently, she also feels alienated. Like so many children in this situation, she decides to run away from home. Nevertheless, her ostensible reason for doing so is to save Toto from Miss Gulch. It is interesting, therefore, that when Professor Marvel says, "They...they don't understand you at home. They don't appreciate you. You want to see other lands, big cities, big mountains, big oceans," he seems to have guessed the deeper, underlying, reasons for her unhappiness. "Why," she replies, "it's just like you could read what was inside of me" (45). The movie thus picks up in a slightly oblique way what the book makes clear from the beginning: Dorothy is bored. Her life seems "gray" and meaningless.[52] She is ready to explore new terrain, geographical and psychological. As Jungian analysts have noted, there are many myths and fairy tales about royal couples who are childless, about demons who keep ships from reaching their destinations, about darkness or famine afflicting the land or—and this is significant here—about monsters who steal the royal treasure. Dorothy's life does indeed seem arid or barren; no wonder she reacts so intensely when a monster (Miss Gulch) steals her treasure (Toto).

Instead of taking Hunk's pragmatic advice on how to avoid trouble—"When you come home, don't go by Miss Gulch's place, then Toto won't get in her garden, and you won't get in no trouble" (36)—she retreats into fantasy and runs away. Professor Marvel helps her realize that she has a more important problem than Miss Gulch; this, too, however, is projected outward as Auntie Em's need for her. Dorothy still imagines that problems can be solved either by running away from home or by running back home. It is not that simple. She is not yet ready to be at home in the world. This is made clear in cinematic terms when a cyclone prevents her from rejoining the farm community. Almost as soon as she enters the bedroom, she becomes unconscious. In her dream, she encounters a series of images (archetypes) that lead her to further growth.

With all this in mind, then, the Oz sequences will be examined in terms of Jung's theory of dreams. The story will be retold as the process of Dorothy's individuation, her encounters with a series of archetypes in the quest for maturity.

*

Although the process of growing up technically begins in Kansas (the waking state) when Dorothy realizes the foolishness of running away, the process of individuation itself actually takes place entirely within Oz (the dreaming state); as I have already noted, her dream telescopes the learning of years into a symbolic span of time. The first archetypal image met in the process of individuation is what Jung calls the "shadow." It represents a dark, shadowy repressed, side of the personality. Usually, this refers to characteristics considered socially unacceptable, flaws people are quite willing to see in others but unable to see in themselves. Theoretically, the shadow could also represent socially desirable qualities; people can choose to live in socially unacceptable ways, after all, and repress those qualities considered desirable. But this is rare. Much more often, it calls attention to the selfishness, pettiness, cowardice, laziness, and other blemishes people try to keep well hidden from both others and themselves.

The Witch, of course, is Dorothy's shadow. She is the first character Dorothy actually meets in her dream; even as the house is being carried off by the cyclone, Dorothy looks out of her window and sees the Witch (whether of East or West) flying by on her broomstick. As the Ozian counterpart of Miss Gulch, the Witch is also the most obviously negative character in the dream. Besides, she is the same sex as Dorothy. "It is particularly in contacts with people of the same sex," writes Marie-Louise von Franz, "that one stumbles over one's own shadow and those of other people. Although we do see the shadow in a person of the opposite sex, we are usually much less annoyed by it and can more easily pardon it."[53]

Dorothy herself is not wicked. But she does have several things in common with the Witch. In the first place, she is not above feelings of aggressive rage. When Miss Gulch comes to take Toto, Dorothy's response, rather than appeasement (which might, possibly, have produced better results) is open hostility—"Ooh, I'll bite you my-self!...you wicked old witch!" (42). On a deeper level, though, it would seem that Dorothy has not resolved her ambivalent feelings toward Auntie Em. Not only does Auntie Em ignore her pleas for help in the opening sequence, but she is the one who actually instructs Dorothy to leave Toto with Miss Gulch. It would not be unusual for a girl in Dorothy's situation to feel resentment. Nor would it be unusual for her to project this negativity (which is unacceptable to the conscious mind) onto someone apart from Mother (or substitute for Mother). Once Dorothy begins dreaming, Miss Gulch becomes resentment or wickedness incarnate: the Witch. This fiend feels intense hostility toward Dorothy for having the ruby slippers. She represents the lengths to which hostility can be taken if it is not consciously acknowledged and understood.

On a still deeper level, the Witch represents Dorothy's sexual immaturity. As we have seen in the preceding discussion of the dream in Freudian terms, the Witch is sexually anomalous. She desperately wants the ruby slippers (representing the menstrual flow that defines femaleness) but has only a broomstick (representing the phallus that defines maleness). Dorothy, on the other hand, has the ruby slippers (without understanding their magical power) but no broomstick (until she gets one for the Wizard). Confronting the Witch, therefore, is what clarifies her sexual identity. Although she acquires a broomstick, she gives it to the Wizard. And although she is tempted to give up her ruby slippers to save Toto, she is unable to do so. As the Witch says, "Those slippers will never come off your feet as long as you're alive" (107). In this sequence, the Witch tries to make Dorothy surrender the ruby slippers to save Toto. In effect, Dorothy's willingness to do so signifies psychological regression. Maturity always involves an acceptance of finitude and mortality. If Toto is an extension of Dorothy herself, this act must represent her refusal to accept a basic fact of the human condition. Sacrificing the ruby slippers is thus synonymous with refusing to grow up. The ruby slippers, however, are not merely symbols of sexual maturity (menstruation). As jewels, ("rubies"), they foreshadow the "emeralds" of Dorothy's final destination in Oz. In fact, they are magic talismans of the kind given to heroes in so many myths and fairy tales. Talismans are objects of power; that is, they give supernatural power to the hero when needed. In myths, the talisman may be the gift of a god; in dreams, it may be a gift of the self. The ruby slippers give Dorothy a hint of her own potential resources; their power derives ultimately not from some external source but from the mature self that is within her.

Encountering the shadow also coincides with conscious recognition of the dreamer's "functional type." By this, Jungians refer to the characteristic way individuals process information about the external world. Two of them are called "rational" functions because they involve judgment, or evaluation. These are thinking (a cognitive activity that distinguishes between true and false) and feeling (an affective activity that distinguishes between pleasure and pain or acceptance and rejection). Because people cannot discern something in both ways at the same time, these are considered mutually exclusive opposites. The other two functions are called "irrational"—a better term would be "nonrational"—because they involve perception but not judgment or evaluation. These are sensation (conscious perception of manifest qualities) and intuition (unconscious perception of inherent, or latent, qualities). They, too, are mutually exclusive opposites. For every individual, one of these functions is dominant, or "superior," while its opposite is undeveloped, or "inferior." The other two are "auxiliary."

In Dorothy's case, feeling seems to be dominant. On the farm—that is, in her waking state—she processes reality according to her feelings of pleasure (being with Toto) or pain (being separated from him). She does not care whether Miss Gulch has a legitimate reason or a legal right to take action when Toto bites her. Nor does she rationally consider ways of preventing encounters between Toto and Miss Gulch. Thinking, therefore, could be considered her "inferior" function. It is part of her "dark side." In short, it is represented by her shadow. To be a mature individual, however, means being able to reclaim these repressed functions. That means "liberating" them in dreams by confronting the shadow figure representing them. If the Witch is indeed Dorothy's shadow, then she must also represent Dorothy's repressed function: thinking. In fact, the Witch does operate on a rational (albeit wicked) basis. Having decided that the ruby slippers are rightfully hers, she is prepared to stop at nothing to achieve her goal. She is just as unbalanced as Dorothy—but in the opposite direction. Her appearance in Dorothy's dream is a warning of what can happen if psychic balance is not restored by bringing repressed material to light. It is surely not by chance that the Witch is robed from head to foot in black, the "color" of shadows.

Similarly, encountering the shadow coincides with conscious recognition of one's "attitudinal type." By this, Jungians mean the habitual way that people respond to the outer world. Extroverts, for example, have a positive relation to the people and objects of the world around them. Introverts, on the other hand, have a negative one. Now when the conscious attitude is one, the unconscious attitude is the other. In other words, the repressed attitude is revealed in dreams. To the extent that Dorothy is poorly adjusted on the farm (in her conscious state), she could be called an *introvert*. She feels isolated, marginal, and alienated. At any rate, she is unable to establish satisfying relationships with anyone in the farm community. In fact, she runs away. The only character who is truly close to her is Toto, and he may be considered a symbol of her own animal instincts. In the unconscious world of dreams, though, Dorothy is quite extroverted. Almost as soon as she lands in Oz, she displays an openness to the world. She looks about her with a sense of wonder. She is eager to learn. She adapts to her new environment. And she is able to establish close friendships. As Dorothy's shadow, on the other hand, the Witch is an extreme introvert. She acknowledges her own isolation. "What an unexpected pleasure," she says sarcastically when Dorothy is brought to her castle, "it's so kind of you to visit me in my loneliness" (107). Her relationship with the guards is based solely on intimidation; when she is killed, they immediately congratulate Dorothy and thank her for delivering them from tyranny. In this case, the Witch represents an exaggeration or distortion of Dorothy's conscious attitude rather than its opposite; she is the shadow not of Dorothy in Kansas but of Dorothy in Oz. But her "message" is characteristic of all shadow figures: a warning that no growth is possible until the "dark side" is explored fully.

*

For boys or men, the next archetypal figure to appear in dreams is the anima; for girls or women, it is the animus. This is what Jung called the "soul image," or "imago." Its function in the psychological system is to help people appropriate (consciously) those qualities said to be characteristic of the opposite sex and repressed in their own. Within every Adam, so to speak, there is an Eve; within every Eve, an Adam. Unlike the shadow, therefore, the animus or anima is always represented by a figure of the opposite sex. And unlike the shadow, the animus is often represented by multiple figures.[54] At the same time, it is very similar to the shadow. Like the shadow, for example, it is made known through projection either onto symbolic figures in dreams (the "inner manifestation") or onto real figures in everyday life (the "outer manifestation"). Like the shadow, it has compensatory relation to consciousness. If the persona (the habitual face, or mask, consciously presented to the outer world) is dominated by one function or attitude, the animus or anima is dominated by its opposite. And like the shadow, the animus or anima may appear in the form of either attack or encouragement. It is less likely than the shadow however, to be represented by negative figures. Failure to learn from a negative encounter means being "possessed" by one's own limitations; failure to learn from a positive encounter means being unable to possess one's own resources.

In Dorothy's dream, three male friends—the Scarecrow, the Tin Man, and the Cowardly Lion—travel with her to the Emerald City seeking fulfillment of needs that are, by symbolic extension, Dorothy's own needs. In effect, they are all qualities Dorothy must incorporate into her own personality at this stage of her development (individuation). And this is precisely what happens. By becoming their friend (assimilating their "message"), Dorothy learns about intelligence (how to live in community by cooperating with others for the common good); feelings (how to express loyalty and love); and courage (how to stand firm in the face of hardship).

The correspondence between Dorothy's friends and the animus figures described by Jung is not perfect, but it is highly suggestive all the same. Together, the three friends constitute Dorothy's animus, a multiple image of the opposite sex. Two of them—the Scarecrow and the Cowardly Lion—represent qualities traditionally ascribed to men: cognitive thinking (intellectuality, or the "logos principle") and physical courage, respectively. But what of the third? What of the Tin

Man? He seems anomalous. Compassion, after all, is stereotypically linked to women, not men. I suggest that the Tin Man functions as an *anima* figure "in drag." Actually, he represents an aspect of the repressed feminine side that boys and men must recognize in themselves; appearing in the context of a girl's dream, however, the anima figure takes on male form. But why should this anomaly have occurred? The point here is not to speculate on the reasoning of those who produced this movie but to explore the "reasoning" of those who respond to it. *The Wizard* could not have achieved such universal popularity if it related exclusively to the female experience. Not coincidentally, this movie consistently emphasizes universality over particularity. In a variety of ways, it seems to invite the interest of people from every segment of American society. The same inclusiveness will be observed shortly in connection with another archetype.

*

When problems related to the animus or anima have been resolved, a new archetypal image, with its associated problem, emerges. For boys or men, it is symbolically represented by the wise old man, which Jung identified with "spirit." In mythology and folklore, he often appears as a sky god, prophet, sage, guru, priest, shaman, magician, or male who presides over initiation into the mysteries of the spirit world (and, therefore, of masculinity and maleness). For girls or women, it is symbolically represented by the great mother, the *magna mater*, whom Jung identified with "nature." In myth and folklore, she often appears as a fertility goddess, priestess, sibyl, sorceress, or female who presides over initiation into the mysteries of the natural order (and, therefore, of femininity and femaleness). In a sense, this archetype continues the work of the animus or anima; the focus of attention now, though, is not the contrasexual but the innermost essence of one's own sex. As usual, there is a hazard. Because these images are so powerful and so attractive, people are apt to identify with them too closely, resulting in self-glorification or megalomania. Only conscious recognition of these figures as archetypal images makes possible freedom from such pathological delusions. We become most truly ourselves by overcoming this last, most powerful, temptation. By implication, this leads to liberation from Father for boys or men, and liberation from Mother for girls or women. Consequently, encountering this archetype makes possible, for the first time, an identity of one's own (in a word, individuality). In view of this, encountering the wise old man or the great mother initiates the final phase of individuation: discovery of self.

Having successfully encountered both the shadow (by killing the Witch) and the animus (by integrating her own personality with those of her friends), Dorothy is ready to meet the next archetype. In this case, it is represented by not one, but two, images. First is the Wizard himself. Nominally, at any rate, he presides over the Emerald City. Surrounded by the pomp of a great "cathedral," complete with "altar," he is the "high priest" of Oz. Then he is revealed as a charlatan by Toto. Looking at the ordinary man behind the curtain, Dorothy exclaims: "Oh, you're a very bad man!" With a sad smile, he replies: "Oh no, my dear. I'm a very good man. I'm just a very bad wizard" (122). In spite of acquiring power and status by encouraging credulity among the Ozians, he uses his power in a benevolent way and in pursuit of justice (saving Oz from the Witch). In fact, like all wise leaders, he discourages dependency by asking those who come to him for help to participate in their own redemption. In Jungian terms, he also discourages pathological identification with his numinosity; Dorothy is in no danger of succumbing to delusions as a result of being in his thrall.

Even though he lacks the kind of power that would send Dorothy back home to Kansas—and she herself has that power—he does have the wisdom to grant the other requests (which are also Dorothy's). One of the most moving scenes shows him delivering the promised goods (that is, insights into human nature and the nature of society). The Scarecrow is "given" his brain along with a brief homily: "Why, anybody can have a brain. That's a very mediocre commodity. Every pusillanimous creature that crawls on the earth, or slinks through slimy seas, has a brain! Back where I come from, we have universities—seats of great learning—where men go to become great thinkers. And when they come out, they think deep thoughts, and with no more brains than you have. But—they have one thing you haven't got—a diploma!" (123). Apparently, this is all one needs to be recognized as intelligent in modern America. Nevertheless, it is only an external token of the true wisdom the Scarecrow has already demonstrated. Likewise, the Cowardly Lion is "given" his courage along with another short sermon. "As for you, my fine friend, you are a victim of disorganized thinking. You are under the unfortunate delusion that simply because you run away from danger you have no courage. You are confusing courage with wisdom. Back where I come from, we

have men who are called heroes. Once a year, they take their forti-
tude out of mothballs and parade it down the main street of the city.
And they have no more courage than you have. But—they have one
thing you haven't got—a medal!" (123). Nonetheless, this, too, is only
an outward symbol of the courage that the Lion has already demonstrated. And finally, the Tin Man is "given" his heart along with still
another kernel of preaching. "As for you, my galvanized friend, you
want a heart. You don't know how lucky you are not to have one.
Hearts will never be practical until they can be made unbreakable. . . .
Back where I come from, there are men who do nothing all day but
good deeds. They are called phil. . .er phil. . .er. . .er. . .good-deed-
doers and their hearts are no bigger than yours. But they have one
thing you haven't got! A testimonial!" (124). Once again, it is only an
external sign of the compassion that the Tin Man has already
demonstrated. It should be noted that although the Wizard does not
present Dorothy with any concrete token (such as a ticket to
Kansas), she benefits from his words as much as her friends because
it is, after all, her own dream. (She has incorporated them all as part
of her own personality; it is her own wisdom, courage, and compassion that the Wizard has formally acknowledged.)

In discussing the previous archetype, I noted that the dream
under discussion is anomalous for presenting both animus and anima
figures. The same anomaly appears once more in this new context
and probably for the same reason. Being female, Dorothy would
encounter a great mother and not a wise old man. But approximately
half the viewers of this movie are male. Since Dorothy is the protagonist, they are asked to identify themselves with her. But because
the movie provides them with an archetypal figure appropriate to
their own needs this is much easier than it would have been otherwise. Even though neither the Tin Man nor the Wizard, according to
Jung, would serve any individuative needs for Dorothy (and the
female viewers), they do for the male viewers. These images are thus
theoretically incorrect, but functionally correct. *The Wizard* could
never have become so popular had it been relevant to only half the
population.

Having said that, discussion can now focus directly on Dorothy's
great mother, Glinda. Dorothy first meets Glinda in the Munchkin
City. At that point, however, she is not yet ready to assimilate the
meaning of an encounter with this archetype; she must first meet her
shadow and animus figures. By the final sequence, though, Dorothy
has successfully done so. She has learned enough to proceed to the

penultimate stage of individuation. Reflecting on everything she has seen and experienced in the dream, she tells Glinda and the friends that "it wasn't enough just to want to see Uncle Henry and Auntie Em. And it's that...if I ever go looking for my heart's desire again, I won't look any further than my own back yard, because if it isn't there, I never really lost it to begin with. Is that right?" Initiating Dorothy into the state of self-realization, Glinda answers: "That's all it is" (128).

As in the case of so many great mothers, Glinda is associated with natural and cosmic forces or universal power. Even the Witch, who is also associated with cosmic forces, has but limited power. In the Munchkin City, only Glinda has no reason to be intimidated by the Witch's sudden appearance; after listening to the latter ranting, she dismisses the whole matter quite flippantly: "Oh, rubbish! You have no power here. Be gone before somebody drops a house on you too!" (62). When Dorothy and her friends are close to death in the poppy field, Glinda's benign countenance appears on the screen; serenely waving her magic wand, she causes snow to fall on the poppies, nullifying the curse's effect. And when she finally appears in the Emerald City, floating down from the heaven in her shimmering sphere, it becomes clear that she, not the Wizard, is ultimately in charge; in relation to her, he is merely a figurehead. It is in the encounter with Glinda, after all, that Dorothy's wish is granted.

In Jungian terms, masculinity is associated with culture and femininity with nature. To grow up (become individuals), therefore, boys must move beyond the domination of their fathers (culture) and girls must move beyond the domination of their mothers (nature); only then can they enter into mature relationships with members of the opposite sex. This is the psychological basis of the hero's quest in myth and folklore. Oedipus, for example, must kill (or transcend) his father to stand as an individual and establish a true relationship with women; it is, however, an incomplete story because this hero establishes an unnatural relationship with a woman (his mother). *The Wizard* presents viewers with a complete story. Before she can go home, Dorothy must "kill" the Wizard; as a man, he is associated with culture and, in this case, specifically with technology. At first, Dorothy thinks of him as a god. When she sees that he is only a man behind his mask (the curtain), she has completed the hero's task (transcending domination by the father and culture). Now she is ready to perform the characteristic task of a girl. Once Dorothy realizes that she does not need Glinda's help but can get back home to Kansas on her own, she has completed the heroine's quest. Here again, *The Wizard's* appeal is universal. Dorothy is both hero and heroine. Both boys and girls are included (through identification) in the cinematic quest for maturity.

*

At this point, the process of individuation is coming to an end. But another problem has arisen. A great deal of unconscious material has been made conscious. With dissolution of the persona (a façade presented to the external world), consciousness no longer dominates the personality; instead, the unconscious dominates. This form of psychic imbalance is no better than the previous one. But balance is restored due to the spontaneous tendency of the unconscious toward equilibrium. The polarization between consciousness and the unconscious is mediated by a final archetype: the self. Realization of the self, of course, is the ultimate goal of individuation. Mature individuals are thus those who have transcended fragmentation or polarization, located the center or united the two psychic elements that have appeared to be in opposition: consciousness and the unconscious. What this amounts to is radical transformation. But the self is not born without travail. Because it takes extraordinary effort to reconcile opposites and achieve this new state of being—in terms of myth or folklore, to win the princess or find the magic talisman— very few people (aside from great religious mystics such as Jesus or the Buddha) actually emerge from the psychic womb. Therefore, a certain enigmatic quality is characteristic of the self; it cannot be adequately described or understood except by those who have experienced enlightenment or discovered the "kingdom within." The archetypal image representing this stage of individuation is what Jung called the "uniting symbol." By this, he meant a symbol that (more than any other) makes possible the *coincidentia oppositorum*, the transformation of opposites into something else that transcends both. It appears when balance between consciousness and the the unconscious is achieved. Since the "message" of this symbol is totality, unity, or wholeness, its image is often an abstract pattern based on formal symmetry (such as a circle or square) rather than a person.

In the movie, the penultimate and ultimate archetypes are encountered almost simultaneously. Both the Wizard and Glinda are "assimilated" at the Emerald City. The Emerald City itself, however, corresponds to Jung's "unifying symbol." It is, of course, explicitly designated as the ultimate goal of Dorothy's quest in Oz. Although it is not a circle or square (as in a mandala), it is a city. As Jung observes, "The city represents a totality, closed in upon itself, a power which cannot be destroyed, which has existed for centuries and will exist for many centuries more. Therefore, the city symbolizes the totality of man, an attitude of wholeness which cannot be dissolved. The city as a synonym for the self, for psychic totality, is an old and well-known image."[55]

Also noteworthy is its color. Green is associated in myth and folklore with vegetation, life, wholeness, and even holiness (as in the green turbans worn by those who have made the pilgrimage to Mecca). As Jung points out, green signifies hope and the future,[56] the Holy Ghost, and therefore, life, procreation, and resurrection.[57] But Dorothy's destination is not merely green, it is emerald green. Emeralds, of course, are stones. Jung notes that the self is often represented by a stone.[58] Like the psychic center, stones are basic (part of the earth itself), eternal (enduring), and still (inert or unchanging). In many traditions, stones are associated with great people or events (the rock used by Jacob as his pillow; monuments at the tombs of saints), as markers of the *axis mundi*, or center of the cosmos (Mount Zion; the Ka'abah's black stone), or as core metaphors (Christ as the "supernatural rock" flowing with life-giving waters; Christ as the rejected keystone; the "lapis," or philosophers' stone, of the alchemists).

Moreover, emeralds are not merely stones; they are crystals, or jewels. For Jung, the jewel is a symbol of renewed life, a harbinger of joy and deliverance. No wonder jewels and precious stones glitter in the celestial light of the heavenly city as described in hymns such as the following:

> With jasper glow thy bulwarks,
> Thy streets with emerald blaze;
> The sardius and the topaz
> Unite in these their rays;
> Thine ageless walls are bounded
> With amethyst unpriced;
>
> Thy saints build up its fabric,
> And the corner-stone is Christ.[59]

As a symbol of the divine, it is also a symbol of the unconscious. Seeing a jewel in a dream, for example, indicates the imminent release of libido (psychic—not necessarily sexual—energy) from the unconscious. According to Jung, "The symbol always says: in some such form as this, a new manifestation of life will become possible, a release from bondage and world-weariness."[60] The geometric patterns of jewels reveal the presence of a "spiritual order" even within the inorganic world; consequently, they stand for the union of opposites: matter and spirit, consciousness and the unconscious. The Emerald City, therefore, is an excellent symbol of the self.

*

As soon as Dorothy has completed the cycle, found her self, she returns home. In purely cinematic terms, the link between growing up and going home could not be more direct or obvious; Dorothy goes back to Kansas as soon as she articulates what she has learned in Oz. Because this link is so clearly emphasized—Dorothy's return to Kansas being dependent on learning something in Oz—it can hardly be dismissed as trivial by anyone trying to understand the movie. And, because the movie has been popular for over fifty years, it can hardly be dismissed as trivial by anyone trying to understand American culture.

As I have already pointed out, nothing in the Freudian tradition can explain this link. For Freud and his many followers, development is a linear process. Individuals go through several stages. They may become fixated at one stage or another, but they do not generally move backward (except in the regression of dreams). And they certainly do not move toward an end that, in some sense, is a recapitulation of the beginning. Freudians would agree that many people *want* to reexperience the past, but these would be classified as neurotics suffering from regressive disorders. From this point of view, the appeal of *The Wizard* could only be seen as evidence of a collective neurosis. This may be true. But Jung offers the possibility of a more charitable explanation for the link between growing up and going home. And this link is closely related to a way of thinking inherent in the religious traditions on which American culture is based.

Although Jung did not consider the idea of return to origin a particularly important element in his theory of individuation, he did allude to it from time to time. It occurs, for instance, in his work on the child archetype. (The process of individuation is dominated by the four archetypes already discussed but also includes a whole range of others.) Since all archetypes have their ultimate source in the collective unconscious, the appearance of a child figure in a dream may represent not only something forgotten in an individual's childhood, but in that of the race itself. On either the individual or the collective level, though, it is a link between past and present. In a dream, the child figure represents something from the past that has been dissociated (through regression) from the present; due to the compensatory function of the unconscious, this material from the past must be confronted in the present. Jung extends the analogy by claiming that

> humanity too, probably always comes into conflict with its childhood conditions, that is, with its original, unconscious, and instinctive state, and that the danger of the kind of conflict which induces the vision of the "child" actually exists. Religious observances, i.e. the retelling and ritual repetition of the mythical event, consequently serve the purpose of bringing the image of childhood, and everything connected with it, again and again before the eyes of the conscious mind so that the link with the original condition may not be broken.[61]

By the same token, though, the child figure is also a link between present and future. Appearances of this archetype in dreams or myths may represent potentiality. The child, as Wordsworth noted long ago, is father of the man. Jung observes that

> the occurrence of the child motif in the psychology of the individual signifies as a rule an anticipation of future developments, even though at first sight it may seem like a retrospective configuration....It is not surprising that so many of the mythological saviours are child gods. This agrees exactly with our experience of the psychology of the individual, which shows that the "child" paves the way for a future change of personality. In the individuation process, it anticipates the figure that comes from the synthesis of conscious and unconscious elements in the personality. It is therefore a symbol which unites the opposites.[62]

The symbols of this archetype "can be expressed by roundness, the circle of sphere, or else by the quaternity as another form of wholeness"[63] and often appear in the dreams of children or even infants. "This observation says much for the *a priori* existence of potential wholeness....But in so far as the individuation process occurs, empirically speaking, as a synthesis, it looks, paradoxically enough, *as if something existent were being put together.*"[64] I have added emphasis here because the notion of *return to origin* is a crucial one in what follows. One of the major differences, then, between a newborn infant and a fully realized self is that the latter has made conscious, through individuation, what was unconscious in the former. Inherent potentiality has been actualized. This can be seen in *The Wizard*. In both prologue and epilogue, the protagonist is Dorothy. Nothing external has changed, but something internal has changed. Dorothy has a new perception of herself and of the world. She is now aware of herself—that is, of her self. To reach that stage, however, she had to learn a great deal. Similarly, the Jungian life cycle begins with what could be called "preconsciousness" (not in the Freudian sense) and concludes with what could be called "superconsciousness." Individuals remain *who* they were at birth or even conception (and not merely as they became after the various traumatic events of infancy), but not *as* they were. They become consciously aware not only of themselves but of their primordial selves.

In view of this, Dorothy's explicit summation of what she had learned in Oz makes perfect sense. "If I ever go looking for my heart's desire again," she tells Glinda, "I won't go looking any further than my own backyard, because if it isn't there, I never really lost it to begin with" (128). *But what is her heart's desire?* At the most obvious level, of course, it is home. Implicitly, though, it is the sense of being "at home" in the world—in a word, maturity. For Jung, maturation is self-realization (realization of the self). In *The Wizard*, maturity is perfectly represented by "home." By definition, after all, home is where people belong, where people feel whole. Dorothy sets out in Oz to find not only her home but her self. *And what is Dorothy's backyard?* In suburban America, backyards are like outdoor attics. Very often, for example, they contain small storage huts for gardening equipment or garages. Despite being close to the house, and thus part of it, the backyard is often ignored. It is considered secondary space. The backyard is used occasionally by adults for sunbathing or entertaining. More often, though, it is used by children for games less confining than those played indoors. Some backyards become overgrown with weeds (unlike front yards which are kept in trim to impress the neighbors). The associations with children (their spontaneous, "instinctive," forms of behavior), with organic forms rising out of the earth (the spontaneity of nature) and with untended or underused space make the backyard an excellent symbol of the unconscious. Dorothy's "backyard" is her own unconscious world. To be fully "at home" means to integrate "backyard" and "house." It means, in short, to explore the unconscious and bring it to consciousness. And this, by definition, is individuation.

Returning now to Dorothy's lesson; what she sought (home or self) had not been truly lost at all because it had always been right in her own backyard (the unconscious) waiting to be discovered in a dream. Going home and growing up are thus, if not synonymous, then at least two ways of expressing the same thing. The circle is complete. It is no wonder, then, that the last frames of the movie show precisely that: a completed circle. Dorothy wakes up on her bed. One by one, family and friends come to see her. Their heads form a circle on the screen. In purely visual terms, the final (or "ultimate") scene represents wholeness, completion, perfection. And yet it is a fulfillment of what was present *ab origine*. Everyone present in this scene was present in the prologue. Dorothy is right back where she started. But she is able to see now what she was unable to see then.

At this point, it should be clear that growing up in *The Wizard* is presented in two ways. When Dorothy comes of age in the Emerald City, she is (symbolically) transformed from child into adult; this, at any rate, is the most obvious conclusion to be drawn from the result of Dorothy's dream journey through Oz. She is clearly able to cope with reality in a new way. But Jung was more interested in the second half of the life cycle. Theoretically, an exceptional individual might discover the self while still relatively young. But (apart from spiritual virtuosi) this would hardly be possible for an adolescent. At one level, then, Dorothy comes of age in the first half of the life cycle; she moves from adolescence into adulthood. At another level, though, she "comes of age" as a fully realized self. The dream of Oz, therefore, telescopes not only the psychic development of the adolescent years, but also that of a lifetime. In both cases, however, growing up is declared to be the equivalent of going home. In the remainder of this chapter, I hope to show that this equivalence is part of the "cultural baggage" carried around by ordinary Americans—not only with reference to the individual, but with reference to the collectivity and the cosmos itself.

Jung's "story" of individuation involves a return to origin. It begins at birth with the unrealized self and concludes (in any case, for those who have gone through analysis) with the realized self. Very few Americans have ever heard of Jung and fewer still have read anything about analytical psychology. But there is evidence that very similar ideas are prevalent in contemporary American culture. This may be due to a popularization of Jung's theory. It may also be due to ideas deeply rooted in the culture that produced the societies of both (Jung's) Switzerland and America. The latter possibility seems

likely because a popularization of Jung's theory would hardly be
possible unless the underlying principles corresponded to ways of
thinking already prevalent in American culture. In *The Hero Within*,
Carol Pearson presents a popular version of Jungian psychology. It is
interesting that she refers over and over again to the specifically
biblical (Judaeo-Christian) notion of return to origin. Passage through
the life cycle involves growth in relation to seven "archetypes": the
Innocent, the Orphan, the Martyr, the Wanderer, the Warrior, and
the Magician. For "heroes" (which is to say, all individuals who seek
growth of this kind) the passage is circular and not linear. In fact,
she writes that everyone ideally makes "three turns around the hero's
wheel."[65] With that in mind, Pearson continually makes statements
such as the following. "Having learned to trust the self," she writes,
"the Magician comes full circle and, like the Innocent, finds that it is
safe to trust."[66] For Pearson, innocence is explicitly linked to paradise.
Referring to the fact that, of all the archetypes under discussion, only
the Innocent is absent from one of her charts, she writes: "When we
live in paradise, there is no need for goals, fears, tasks, work, etc. The
Innocent is both pre- and postheroic."[67] But Pearson refers not only
to paradise in general but also to Eden in particular. "The promise of
a return of the mythic Edenic state is one of the most powerful
forces in human life. Much of what we do—and what we fail to do—
is defined by it. We objectify the earth and each other in a frantic
attempt to remain, or become, safe and secure, cared for, in Eden.
The irony here is that *we can and do return to safety, love, and
abundance but only as a result of taking our journeys.*"[68] Pearson
has thus restated, in the language of pop psychology that is so
prevalent in contemporary America, the link between "going home"
and "growing up" discussed here in connection with *The Wizard*.

Like the seeker described by Pearson, Dorothy must learn about
interdependence (the establishment of a "community" based on
friendship in which individuals cooperate to defeat and even transform evil) before she can return home. Once home, Dorothy realizes
what she had not realized before: that she had always been loved.
Pearson could have used *The Wizard* as a case study when she
discusses

the classic plot in which the hero is an orphan, or is oppressed and
unappreciated in the family, and searches for his or her true home. As
we become more and more who we are, and hence link up with others
with whom we feel a deep connection, we have more, and more satisfy-

ing, intimacy with others. The reward for the hero's inevitably solitary journey, then, is community—community with the self, with other people, and with the natural and spiritual worlds. At the end of the journey, the hero feels and *is* at home in the world.[69]

Pearson never actually refers to *The Wizard*. Nevertheless, this remark and the one that follows make precisely the points I have made about Dorothy:

> Returning to Eden, we are not powerless, childlike dependents, but people who also take responsibility for caring for others and the planet. This return requires interdependency, which necessitates not only the claiming of personal responsibility for the maintenance of our earthly paradise and a trust that some pain and suffering are rightly a part of our Edenic life, but ultimately a childlike attitude of trust and gratitude for all that is given us. This requires a dawning awareness that however painful our lives might have seemed, we always have been held in the palm of God's hand.[70]

Pearson argues here that paradise regained may still involve some suffering. In *The Wizard*, evidence for this is very ambiguous. The "serpent" (Miss Gulch) does not return. All the same, it might be inferred that she remains "out there" and that Dorothy will find some way of coping with her. If so, then the notion of paradise has been somewhat altered in the process of secularization.

*

Through the use of psychoanalysis, it has been possible to interpret *The Wizard* as a coming-of-age story. Dorothy, in other words, represents in psychological terms precisely what she appears to be on the screen in physiological terms: an adolescent girl about to become a young woman. Coming of age, however, is not entirely a private and psychological event. In most societies, it is also a public and social event. To become an adult is to become a responsible member of the community. Considering the need to ensure the continuity of traditional values and lore, it is not surprising that coming of age is almost always marked by elaborate rituals. On these occasions, the transition from childhood to adulthood is not only formally acknowledged but is also made possible in the first place by the transmission of information the initiates will use in their new status as adults.

In *The Ritual Process*, Victor Turner describes the "rite of passage" as a transition from one stable, recognized state (or stage in the life cycle) to another. The passage is marked either by ritual (effecting the transformation), by ceremony (confirming it), or both. During the passage—the ambiguous period "betwixt and between" that defies classification by any of the normal cultural standards and is thus a source of danger and pollution—initiates live in a world utterly different from the one they have just left and from the one they are about to enter. Turner is particularly interested in the actual transition between the two states. Following Arnold Van Gennep's theory outlined in *The Ritual Process*,[71] Turner finds that rituals marking this transition have three distinct phases: separation from society; isolation from society; and reentry, or reintegration, into society. The period of isolation is characterized by "liminality." Several characteristics are worth noting here. First, initiates are usually stripped of status according to age, sex, status, wealth, or power. In this way, all who undergo the rite together are roughly equal (no matter how unequal they will be once the rite is finished). Since they are about to emerge in a radically different form, initiates are often associated with symbols of death and rebirth. They are made "invisible" to the rest of society by means of physical and cultural segregation. They may be given new identities through special names, masks, or other disguises. Submitting to the authority of their instructors meekly and without complaint, their behavior could be described as passive. Finally, they are supplied with new information in this "time out of time" and encouraged to reflect on cultural assumptions about the way things are and how they came to be that way. As Turner puts it: "During the liminal period, neophytes are alternately forced and encouraged to think about their society, the cosmos and the powers that generate and sustain them."[72] In view of these characteristics of liminality, Turner observes, it is not surprising that initiates develop intense friendships and a feeling of group solidarity impossible under normal circumstances. This feeling between people during liminality is what Turner calls "communitas." The fragmentation and multiplicity characteristic of everyday life is broken down. The structures of society (caste; class; hierarchy; social, political, and economic differentiation) are transformed into what Turner calls "antistructure," or radical egalitarianism.

*

Because coming of age as a private and psychological process has already been discussed in great detail, nothing more about it need be said here. Instead, attention may be focused directly on coming of age as a public and social event. The following analogy between Dorothy's experience and a rite of passage can, like the other analogies, be pushed too far. Dorothy's passage through Oz is explicitly called a dream, for instance, and not a ritual. Nevertheless, the parallels are highly suggestive. And I argue that it is precisely this suggestiveness that accounts, in large measure, for the movie's continuing popularity.

In the prologue, Dorothy seems to lack a well-defined "place" in the farm community. Being in the wrong place is most obviously illustrated when she falls into the pig pen. Not only does she run afoul of Miss Gulch (and, by extension, of the sheriff who represents the social order itself), but even Auntie Em accuses her of getting in the way. "Now you just help us out today," she tells Dorothy, "and find yourself a place where you won't get into any trouble" (39). Obviously, Dorothy needs to find a new place in society.

Like other initiates, Dorothy is abruptly, but temporarily, removed from society. In her case, this is caused by something in the natural order (a tornado) rather than something in the cultural order (such as a ritual). But since coming-of-age rites are almost always directly associated with physiological changes (such as puberty), this distinction is more apparent than real.

During her absence in Oz, Dorothy develops intense relationships. Having suffered through one ordeal after another together, the friends do not wish to be separated after the Wizard grants their requests. "Stay with us, then, Dorothy," says the Lion when the Wizard sails off without her, "we all love you." When Glinda tells her how to go home the proper way, Dorothy echoes the sentiment: "It's going to be so hard to say goodbye. I love you all, too." And the Tin Man responds: "Now I know I've got a heart, 'cause it's breaking" (129). Apparently, the friends have developed a real sense of communitas.

Each of Dorothy's friends lacks a skill necessary for effective living within the social order. Or, if they are elements of Dorothy's personality, she herself lacks the ability to integrate their skills in a way that would make her an effective member of society. In short, new insight is needed before a return is possible. The nature of Dorothy's separation from society is explicitly defined as a learning experience that is to demonstrate her worthiness (passing a test by killing the Witch) and her knowledge (the meaning of home). It is interesting that the particular knowledge she has acquired is directly related to propagation of the social and cultural order; every member of a community must believe in the value of "home" (or society). In 1939, with another war about to begin, learning (or reaffirming) this lesson must have seemed particularly urgent to many Americans.

Dorothy's reentry into society is marked by what could be called a "ritual." The girl is asked to recite a "mantra" ("There's no place like home") three times while clicking her ruby slippers together. At the same time, Glinda waves a magic wand over Dorothy's head. This is a cultural counterpart of the natural force (the tornado) that separates Dorothy from society in the first place. But because this ritual involves the ruby slippers (representing menstrual blood), the distinction, once again, is more apparent than real.

Finally, Dorothy's reintegration is overtly acknowledged by family and friends at her bedside. The ritual has been efficacious not only because Dorothy wakes up in her own room, but because she remembers what she has learned and is prepared to use it in her new "state." Although she is physically unchanged, she has been profoundly transformed in other ways. Like initiates in many other societies, she cannot tell anyone about her experiences in the liminal state (in this case, because no one believes her), but she can reaffirm her loyalty to the community.

In 1939, when *The Wizard* was released, teenagers had not yet become a distinct and alienated segment of society. The adolescents romping through Andy Hardy movies of the late 1930s and early 1940s were presented as healthy, happy, and wholesome. That may not have given an accurate picture of all, or even most, American adolescents. But even so, it was the picture that most Americans, including adolescents, found attractive. These were very popular movies. Teenagers wanted to be like Judy Garland and Mickey Rooney. At the very least, they wanted to live in a comfortable, middle-class world with loving mothers and wise fathers. Members of the generation that came of age at that time felt a certain sense of solidarity with parents who were struggling through the Depression and the War; they wanted independence but not separation. For every generation, of course, growing up presents problems; but for that generation, going home presented more urgent problems. The Great Depression led to mass migrations from the land to the cities. Very soon, the Second World War would generate further migrations to defense industries located in or near cities. War itself eventually created an acute preoccupation with home; millions of soldiers overseas longed to return, while their families waited anxiously. It is really no wonder, therefore, to find that movies about coming of age made at this time often feature the aspect of going home by treating it explicitly, while the aspect of growing up may be treated implicitly. This is the case, in *The Wizard*. Dorothy both goes home and grows up. But the former is stated directly; the latter is merely implied.[73]

Why should coming of age be the subject, either explicit or implicit, of massively popular movies? The answer lies partly, I suggest, in the fact that modern American society is notably lacking in public rituals that affirm the process of growing up and give public recognition to those who successfully complete the various stges. One symptom of the widening gulf between teenagers and adults (which has generated a subclass or subculture) is the failure of American society (and most other modern, industrial societies) to provide public, institutionalized ways of easing the transition from childhood to adulthood. (It is true that the Bar Mitzvah still exists for Jews, as does Confirmation for some Christians; nevertheless, these rituals provide, often perfunctory, initiation into *subcultures*, and not into the culture of American society as a whole.) Instead of a formal ritual that is acknowledged by the entire community, there is only a vaguely-defined series of events—such as graduation from high school or college; taking a first job; going to a bar for the first time; going out on a date for the first time; having sex for the first time; getting a driver's license; getting a draft card; or getting married—that mark the transition between childhood and adulthood. In this way, American society is very unlike more traditional societies in which coming of age is considered a public event of great importance for the entire community. As one result, popular movies aimed at young people often explore the subject either directly or indirectly.[74]

THE FAR SIDE By GARY LARSON

"Spiders, scorpions, and insecticides, oh my! . . .
Spiders, scorpions, and insecticides, oh my! . . ."

Figure 3-4

The Far Side cartoons by Gary Larson are reprinted with permission
of Chronicle Features, San Francisco, California.

THE FAR SIDE

By GARY LARSON

"Auntie Em, Auntie Em! . . . There's no place
like home! . . . There's no place like home."

4 THE LAND OF
E PLURIBUS UNUM

And I remember that some of it wasn't very nice...but most of it
was beautiful. But just the same, all I kept saying to everybody was,
"I want to go home!"

—Dorothy (131-132)

Dorothy utters these lines soon after waking up in Kansas. They
reveal her ambivalence over the adventure in Oz. While there, she
made friends and became more sure of herself, it is true, but she was
nevertheless afflicted by anxiety and confusion. Consequently, she
wanted to return home. Before she could do so, however, she had to
grow up (that is, learning how to be at home). A similar link can be
seen between going home and growing up on the collective level: the
nation itself symbolically "goes home" and "grows up." This link is
presented cinematically as a series of symbolic landscapes. Each is
an ecological image, a symbol of the relation between nature and
culture or between the environment and the community. Each of
these ecological images, in turn, is related to a long artistic tradition
ultimately derived from root metaphors that are pervasive in the
religious traditions of America. Not surprisingly, each represents
strongly held beliefs and feelings about what it means to be at home
and, by implication, what it means to be American. Before turning to
The Wizard itself, we must consider more carefully the meaning of
terms such as "landscape" and "home."

*

The word "landscape" is used by people in fields as diverse as
poetry, art, architecture, town planning, geography, history, geology,

and botany. Its ambiguity is almost inevitable. In his introduction to a book on symbolic geography, *The Interpretation of Ordinary Landscapes*, D. W. Meinig differentiates "landscape" from several related words. It is not a synonym for "nature" (since it includes cultural artifacts such as highways and buildings as well as natural features); "scenery" (since it is not defined primarily in normative or aesthetic terms); "environment" (since it exists only for beings who are aware of it and reflect upon it); "place" (since it is a continuous surface rather than a fixed point that can be located on a map); or "geography" (since it cannot be reduced to the abstractions of a map but must be seen and experienced directly). For Meinig, therefore, "landscape" refers to the cultural perspective through which people see and experience the world around them (that is, the ordinary world of everyday life). "We regard all landscapes as symbolic expressions of cultural values, social behavior, and individual actions worked upon particular localities over a span of time. Every landscape is an accumulation, and its study may be undertaken as formal history, methodically defining the making of the landscape from the past to the present. . . . And every landscape is a code and its study may be undertaken as a deciphering of meaning, of cultural and social significance of ordinary but diagnostic features."[1] With this in mind, it could be said that symbolic landscapes are really "codes." Systematic analysis of them, therefore, might be expected to reveal a great deal about the worldview of those who consciously or unconsciously experience them.

Clearly, there is more to a landscape than the land itself; included is an attitude taken toward the land. People may look at the land and see beauty or ugliness, refuge or threat, harmony or conflict, truth or illusion, opportunity or obstacle, the sublime or the pastoral, the sacred or the profane. Very often, an emotional and intellectual investment is made in certain features or regions of the country. These become symbolic landscapes because they represent, in concise visual form, the basic values of an individual or community. In "The Beholding Eye: Ten Versions of the Same Scene," Meinig shows how any landscape can be seen in many different ways depending on how one understands the word "landscape" in the first place. No two people will describe or even experience a particular landscape in the same way. Meinig, in fact, identifies ten ways of interpreting a landscape. Of these, however, only two are of particular importance here because they are hermeneutical keys often used to interpret the kinds of landscape presented in *The Wizard:* these are what he calls "landscape as nature" and "landscape as habitat."

For some people, landscape is seen primarily in terms of "nature." By this, Meinig refers to a perceived polarity between nature and culture. From this perspective, cultural productions (such as buildings, roads, billboards, wayside shrines or railroad tracks) are to be dismissed as trivial and ephemeral in comparison with the awesome, sublime and eternal qualities of nature undefiled by culture. Those who interpret landscape in this way often wish "to remove man from the scene, to restore nature to her primitive condition, to reclothe the hills with the primeval forest, clear off the settlements, heal the wounds and mend the natural fabric to imagine what the area is *really* like."[2] This attitude was very fashionable in eighteenth-century Europe. Romanticism was also very influential in America because it appeared at the very time when the nation came into being and began forming its collective identity. During the nineteenth century, it found perfect expression in the American preoccupation with wilderness and the idealization of pure nature (uncontaminated by human or cultural forces). It gave rise, for example, to the Hudson River school of landscape painting. More recently, it has been expressed in the work of great photographers such as Ansel Adams and conservation groups such as the Sierra Club. "The romantic view," writes Meinig, "is in fact very much alive, usually, perhaps necessarily, expressed as a kind of nostalgia."[3] Unhappily aware of a profound gulf between nature and culture or nature and humanity, romantics wish to return to a primeval paradise in which fragmentation is abolished and unity restored. "There was a time, in the sweet childhood of the human race," writes Garrett Eckbo of this mentality, "when man lived very close to nature...the world of nature and the world of man were synonymous."[4] As I have indicated, the notions of returning to origin and living close to nature are of great importance in *The Wizard.* In the following pages, this will recur very often. For the time being, though, I merely draw attention to the fact that this theme has been linked to the American landscape (and thus to American identity) by a long visual tradition. It is not unreasonable, therefore, to see the landscapes presented in *The Wizard* as cinematic interpretations of the American landscape within that tradition.

For others, landscape is seen primarily as a "habitat." By this, Meinig refers to a perceived unity between nature and culture. Now, as in the beginning, we are at home in the world. "What we see before us," writes Meinig, "is man continuously working at a viable relationship with nature, adapting to major features, altering in productive ways, creating resources out of nature's materials; in short, man domesticating the earth."[5] This is a very optimistic view. Human mistakes are made that corrupt nature, to be sure, but only temporarily; we can learn and nature can heal. There is no inherent opposition or predestined conflict between nature and culture or nature and humanity. This attitude could be called a "prelapsarian" vision in its presentation of undisturbed harmony, "of the earth as the garden of mankind, of man as the steward, the caretaker, the cultivator."[6] Nature, in effect, is fundamentally and dependably benign. When properly understood and used, it provides us with a comfortable and enduring home. Not suprisingly, then, this understanding of landscape was the basis for Jefferson's idealization of yeoman farmers and his vision of the United States as an agrarian republic. Ironically, the same understanding has provided a rationale for massive industrialization and urbanization. Both versions have been celebrated in American art. The former gave rise to a long tradition of pastoral landscape painting that culminated with the regionalist movement. The latter gave rise to art deco and its glorification of speed and progress through technology. And both, I suggest, are represented in *The Wizard*. They will be discussed more fully later.

The crucial factor to be considered here is the relation between attitudes toward nature and attitudes toward home. When landscape is seen primarily in terms of "nature," home is associated with the remote past; to be truly at home in the world means abandoning the cultural order and reverting to a state of primeval innocence and harmony. When landscape is seen primarily in terms of "habitat," home is associated with the present; to be truly at home in the world means using the cultural order to modify the natural order in accordance with human need. But what, precisely, is meant by "home"?

*

In "The Landscape of Home: Myth, Experience, Social Meaning," David Sopher notes the problematic nature of the word itself. In English, "home" has a richness that cannot easily be translated into other languages (except, possibly, for the Germanic ones). Depending on the context, it may refer to house, land, village, city, region, nation, and even planet. Moreover, it transmits the emotional associations of the smallest unit to the largest: feelings of warmth, security, familiarity, order, friendliness, acceptance, and belonging. At the heart of Sopher's work, however, is a distinction between what he calls "domicentric" and "domifugal" orientations. He notes that some societies encourage people to cultivate profound emotional attachments to particular places and others do not.[7] In the nineteenth century, for example, Europeans commonly thought of "vagabond" and "gypsy" as synonyms of "rogue." Those who were homeless by choice—or, in the case of the "Wandering Jew," by curse—were threatening and contemptible. Because society had no emotional hold on them, they could not be trusted. For the same reason, Jews in the Soviet Union have commonly been attacked as "rootless cosmopolitans." It could be argued that American culture is profoundly domicentric; according to Sopher, it is the established orientation. As a result, it exerts tremendous emotional pressure on the behavior of ordinary Americans in everyday life. He cites Vance Packard's warning in *A Nation of Strangers* about the emotional distress caused by American rootlessness. Packard and many others, he observes, use the negative term "rootlessness" to describe migration and mobility: "to be rootless is to be unsound, and, worse, unreliable, unsavory."[8] It is no wonder, then, that one of the most popular American songs is "Home Sweet Home."

Sopher himself opposes the domicentric mentality. He associates it with the evils of nationalism and racism. He also believes it to be false. It is just as logical, after all, to look with contempt on precisely those who remain attached to one particular place because "to be rooted is the property of vegetables. Set against the myths of home and homeland, we find the myths that challenge them, the myth of the voyager, the adventurer, the mythic quest that takes one forth, into and through, the world, not reluctantly but eagerly."[9] These myths, argues Sopher, were produced by domifugal societies. He examines this orientation in several of the world religions. At the heart of these traditions is a longing for transcendence in time and space. As one example, he cites the Christian sense of life as a pilgrimage to the heavenly Jerusalem. To illustrate this point, he cites the "Letter to Diognetus": "They live in their own countries, but only as aliens. They have a share in everything as citizens, and endure everything as foreigners. Every foreign land is their fatherland, and yet for them every fatherland is a foreign land....They busy themselves on earth, but their citizenship is in heaven."[10] The Church, as tradition has it, is to be in the world but not of it. The fact that this attitude has become more or less obsolete since the rise of European nation-states does not invalidate Sopher's observation. The same point can be made about Eastern traditions such as Hinduism and Buddhism; they clearly emphasize the transience not only of life but of perceptions of reality itself.

But Sopher oversimplifies this matter. Many traditions contain both domicentric and domifugal tendencies. He fails to note, for example, that the Hindu yogin and the Buddhist monk are character-istic but hardly typical members of their societies; most Hindus and Buddhists live in agrarian and domicentric villages.[11] If this "domestic pluralism" is characteristic of traditional societies, it is equally true of modern ones. Sopher himself recognizes that the latter are far too complex to be either domicentric or domifugal. With this in mind, he cites the following lines from T. S. Eliot's *Four Quartets:*

> We shall not cease from exploration
> And the end of all our exploring
> Will be to arrive where we started
> And know the place for the first time.[12]

Eliot seems to be affirming both home and the quest; the latter takes people away from home but also returns them home. In other words, people want to make homes but also to leave them. They want to chose not one or the other but both (or at least to accept the tension between home and quest, or between order and freedom). For Americans, I suggest, both home and quest are integrating symbols. They are strongly attracted to images of white picket fences and family farms, but are also strongly attracted to the imagery of "movin' on" down the open road and adventure on the frontier. The idea of quest, after all, is built into American identity at a very basic level: the New World was "discovered" and the United States was "invented." In fact, the American quest was early assimi-lated not only to that of ancient Israel en route to the Promised Land but also to that of the Christian Church en route to the heavenly Jerusalem. The American preoccupation with newness is not merely an accident of history or a perverse national idiosyncracy; it is the secular translation of a hope inspired by religion. It makes no sense, therefore, to speak of American identity without referring to both home and quest. The two are inextricably linked. "Can we not recognize this tension in the fact that a century ago when, just as today, one American in five changed residence within a year and one of the most widely treasured household icons was a plaque or sampler carrying the words 'Home Sweet Home'? Can we not hear the tension in the theme and tone of our folksongs, with their constant plaintive refrain of "movin' on" although the moving that is foreseen often seems as compulsively ritualistic as the South American wanderings of the Apapokuva?"[13] This is precisely the idea symbolically conveyed in *The Wizard*. In the prologue, Dorothy is less than enchanted with conditions on the farm. Consequently, she runs away to seek her fortune elsewhere. Almost immediately, though, she runs back home. In Oz, she keeps trying to find her way home to Kansas. And in the epilogue, she is glad to be back. Nevertheless, she also says of her stay in Oz that "most of it was beautiful." Indeed, she had found that saying goodbye to her friends there was difficult. This kind of ambivalence is characteristic of American society.

But what constitutes home? More precisely, what are the things about home that are either missed or forsaken on the quest? For Sopher, home is represented primarily by people. During an absence from home, travelers remember those who live there more than the house, the fields, or the streets. In fact, he says, home would not be home without the people who give it meaning. Home is "the remembered field of familiar experience, within which particular places stand out as the loci of memorable personal events."[14] In popular movies, for instance, the actual event of coming home is usually signalled by the interaction between characters. One of the most moving sequences of this kind occurs in *The Best Years of Our Lives* (William Wyler, 1946); each returning soldier is greeted in a different way by those who had been close to him before the war. The same is true of Norman Rockwell's famous cover illustration of *The Saturday Evening Post* (26 May 1945): "Private Willie Gillis" returning from overseas. The painting emphasizes the distinct ways in which every individual—mother, father, kid brother, girl-next-door—welcomes him home. Similarly, *The Wizard's* epilogue consists entirely of such interactions. Evidence of the house itself is reduced to a minimum. For Dorothy to come home, she must not only be shown back in her own bed, she must also be shown talking to each of the main characters as they come, one by one, to welcome her. Home is fused with family.

As we have seen, however, home is also associated with landscapes. Any place that is both familiar and distinctive may become a generic symbol of home. A region may be recognized as home by the color of local houses, for example, the shape of local church steeples or the local breed of livestock. Sopher notes a tendency for Americans to

identify home more and more with the national landscape and the
national "family" rather than the local (regional) landscape and the
local (natural) family. In other words, America itself is seen as a
significant place, as home. All Americans understand immediately
what is meant by phrases such as "back East" and "out West." These
are the equivalents of "back inside" or "out front" with reference to
one's own house. Like individuals and families, communities and
nations acknowledge certain features of the landscape as common
symbols of a shared home or homeland. In creating this "mythic
home," the uniqueness of the place is emphasized by accenting distinctive features or modifying features to make them distinctive.
Such actions imply communication within a larger social group and
the existence of conventions making this communication possible in
the first place. Certain specific symbols may thus come to represent
metonymically the totality of a landscape. The cable car in particular
can represent San Francisco in general. Even if the Statue of
Liberty stands in New York harbor, it is primarily a symbol of the
United States and is thus part of the national iconography of home.
A forest of skyscrapers may represent New York City at one level and
America at another. As New York City, of course, it represents the
landscape of home to some Americans; as America itself, however, it
represents the landscape of home to the entire nation. The same is
true of landscapes depicted in *The Wizard.* Kansas, obviously, is a
familiar American landscape. It evokes collective memories of the
frontier. But I argue that Oz, too, is an American landscape thinly
disguised. It is, in fact, a series of American landscapes. And each
evokes collective reflections on such "archetypal" landscapes as the
frontier, the wilderness, and the metropolis.

*

  Having discussed "landscape" and "home," it is necessary to explain
what is meant by a "symbolic" landscape of home. Meinig writes that
"every mature nation has its symbolic landscapes. They are part of
the iconography of nationhood, part of the shared set of ideas and
memories and feelings which bind a people together."[15] This is not an
argument for some kind of quasi-mystical doctrine of *Blut und Boden*
but recognition of the fact that specific images convey specific
messages understood by everyone in the community. The simplest
examples, such as the White House or the Statue of Liberty, are
those associated with major insitutions or events. When people see

pictures of them, it is the nation's history that comes to mind rather than architecture or sculpture. More complex are images that are evocative not as specific landscapes but as specific kinds of landscape. Meinig does not include those, like the Southern Plantation, that are primarily regional rather than national symbols. Instead, he focuses on those that (1) originated in specific regions and periods but (2) have been promoted widely throughout the country in (3) very idealized (simplified or beautified) forms with the result that (4) they have become familiar on sight to all Americans as symbols of community and, more specifically, of home. Three of these—the New England village, the Midwestern small town, and the Southern California suburb—are discussed in detail. Each of these communities, with its distinctive way of life, is associated with a region that has played a critical role in the development of American society. Each has appeared to embody the best, or even the essence, of America itself and thus becomes a model for the nation as a whole. And each continues to have a place in the American imagination as a focus for collective identity. I suggest, however, that several other symbolic landscapes must be considered. I have called these the *Western wilderness, the frontier farm, the Eastern metropolis,* and *the open road.* Each is not only a symbolic landscape corresponding to a particular American way of life and its relation to history—in this way, it has been a focus of American identity—but also an ecological image referring to the relation between nature and culture. In this way, it is related to more universal symbols on which human identity is based. Meinig's symbolic landscapes tell Americans about what it means to be at home. Some of the ones I have identified in *The Wizard* do that, too. But others tell Americans about what it means to be *away* from home. Even so, they are linked to very long and powerful traditions. They cannot be ignored by anyone interested in the symbolic geography of America (which is to say, the formation of collective identity in America). With this in mind, I have examined *The Wizard* as a series of symbolic landscapes. The following discussion begins with Oz and concludes with Kansas.

*

Dorothy's journey through Oz begins at the Munchkin City. Like so many other things in Oz, its name is deceptive. There is evidence to suggest that it is more like a village or small town than a city. It is significant that "boosterism"[16] has been a characteristic feature of provincial American life. Even the tiniest, most transitory hamlets on the frontier often incorporated "city" into their names just as they called their theaters "opera houses" and their inns "grand hotels." In 1971, for example, Valley City, North Dakota, had 8,600 people; Colorado City, Texas, had 6,457; Boulder City, Nevada, had 4,059; Heber City, Utah, had 1,963; Orange City, Iowa, had 1,707; and Elm City, North Carolina, had only 729.[17]

According to Meinig, Americans have idealized a small town that developed from prototypes in Ohio and spread rapidly throughout the Midwest and as far away as Colorado, the Sacramento Valley in California, and even New England. Eventually, it became a symbolic landscape. Unlike an earlier version of the ideal American community, the New England village, the Midwestern small town

> focused not upon the church and village green but upon a street, lined with three or four-storey red-brick business blocks, whose rather ornate fenestrations and cornices reveal their nineteenth-century origins. Above the storefronts and awnings are the offices of lawyers, doctors and dentists, and above these the meeting rooms of the various fraternal orders. A courthouse, set apart on its own block, may be visible, but it is not an essential element, for the great classical columns fronting the stone temple of business proclaim the bank as the real seat of authority. This is Main Street, and parallel with it lies Church Street, not of *the* church, but of churches: Methodist, Presbyterian, Baptist, Episcopalian, and if there are Yankees present, Congregational. Close by it is the academy and perhaps a small denominational college. The residential area begins with big Italianate and Victorian houses on spacious tree-shaded lots and grades out to lesser but still comfortable homes. On the other side of town, below the depot, are the warehouses and small factories. And around it lies a prosperous farming country dotted with handsome farmhouses and big red barns.[18]

This landscape is familiar to all Americans. Not only has it been featured on calendars, posters, Christmas cards, popular prints, and advertisements, it has also provided the mise-en-scène for countless Hollywood movies. Until recently, "Main Street" was visited by tourists on the back lot of Universal Studios; small-town America was filmed over and over again on the same set (with slight modifications for each movie). It has also been the subject of many television shows. "The Twilight Zone" (CBS, 1959–1964) is now considered a classic series. Several episodes involved the longing for a simpler, happier life far from the tensions of urban life in the modern world. In "A Stop at Willoughby,"[19] for example, Gart Williams is an advertising executive commuting to his suburban home after a hard day at the office. Reflecting on the pressures of his job in the big city, he falls asleep and dreams of getting off the train at a restful little town named Willoughby in the year 1880; in his dream, the conductor tells him that this is a place "where a man can slow down to a walk and live his life full measure."[20] Williams then wakes up and gets off the train to call his wife. He tells her that he would like to quit his competitive job and move to a small town. Unfortunately, she is too materialistic to share his longing for the peace and quiet of small-town America and hangs up on him. When he gets off the train once more, he finds himself, miraculously, back in Willoughby where the townsfolk greet him by name. Viewers then learn that a regular commuter on the present-day train had suddenly jumped to his death shouting "Willoughby"; they watch his body being picked up by a hearse from the Willoughby Funeral Home. The implication, of course, is that Williams has now returned to Willoughby for good. That is home. That is where he belongs.[21] According to Marc Zicree, "'A Stop at Willoughby' is one of the most enduring episodes of *The Twilight Zone*. In creating and defining Willoughby, [Rod Serling] stumbled upon an area of universal desire. Virtually all people find themselves in pressure situations at least sometime in their lives, times when they feel ill-equipped to come up to the demands placed upon them. Who at these times wouldn't like to escape to a paradise with no problems or demands?"[22]

Such a paradise was also featured on "The Andy Griffith Show" (CBS, 1960–1968). Some years ago, the cast was reunited for another glimpse of life in the idealized small town of "Mayberry." This is a dream town. For many Americans, it represents the way life should be, the good life. It could even be argued that the show is really about Mayberry itself rather than any of its individual inhabitants. These personifications of a way of life include Andy himself (the sheriff who never carries a gun and has no need to do so), Opie (his wholesome little boy), Aunt Bea (the local earth mother who takes care of them), Barney (Andy's bumbling but lovable deputy), Otis (the town drunk who locks himself in jail every Saturday night and lets himself out every Sunday morning), Floyd (the prissy but good-hearted town barber), Gomer (the unsophisticated but innocent town auto mechanic), and Helen (the local "schoolmarm" who is Andy's girlfriend). All are gentle, friendly, honest, unpretentious, and gen-erally "laid back." They are frequently shown sitting on their front porches in the evening and singing or sitting on Main Street in the afternoon and gossiping. On Sunday mornings, they go to church. On Sunday afternoons, they go fishing. Apparently, the show provides more than just casual entertainment. This is not just another situation comedy. In their review of "Return to Mayberry," Richard Zoglin and John D. Hull note the following: "Even on TV's crowded reunion calendar, *Return to Mayberry* is a special event. *The Andy Griffith Show* was one of the biggest hits of its era (ranking in the Neilsen Top Ten, remarkably, for all of its eight seasons on the air), and continues to have a devoted following in reruns. With good reason. The show was one of TV's most endearing comedies, a graceful blend of homespun morality and small town satire."[23]

The satire, of course, is not that of the big city against the small town but the reverse. The contrast between life in the big city and life in the small town is often made explicit. In one episode, for example a rich young man from the city is arrested for speeding through town in his flashy sports car. Since the local jail closes down every weekend, he must stay with Andy and his family. By the time his lawyer comes from the city to "fix things" with the locals, the young man has been "converted." Instead of being insolent, arrogant, snobbish, and restless, he is polite, friendly, respectful, and—above all—relaxed. It is also worth noting that, although Mayberry is supposed to be in North Carolina, the racial violence and bigotry of some real Southern towns during the early days of the civil rights movement are never shown; this is a fantasy of small town life that could be shared by all (white) Americans. In one episode, Aunt Bea and her friend Clara Edwards write a little song that succinctly expresses the way of life represented by Mayberry:

> My home town is the greatest place I know,
> Where the neighbors I find are gentle and kind
> And the living's easy and slow. . . .
>
> My home town is the only place to be
> Here the worries are small and the kids grow tall
> And strong and healthy and free, its
> My home town, my home town,
> Mayberry, Mayberry

The same fantasy has also been featured in other forms of popular entertainment. Several articles have been written about the fantasy of small-town life expressed by Disneyland (in California) and Disney

World (in Florida).[24] "Main Street USA" is one of the chief attractions at both. Actual conditions in the real small towns of America— conditions that drove millions to seek better lives in the big cities and that were satirized mercilessly by writers such as Sinclair Lewis—are symbolically irrelevant. "Main Street" is a state of mind, not a historical recreation; it is a nostalgic vision of America, not an archaelogical excavation.

The Midwestern small town represents a perfectly balanced way of life, the elusive happy medium. It mediates geographically (between West and East), economically (a commercial center between the agricultural frontier and the industrial cities, or between the surrounding farms and the local factories), socially (with neither extreme wealth nor extreme poverty), and demographically (not too small to be stifling but not too big to prevent intimacy and cohesion). In short, "Main Street is the seat of a business culture of property-minded, law-abiding citizens devoted to 'free-enterprise' and 'social morality,' a community of sober, sensible, practical people. The Chamber of Commerce and the Protestant churches are naturally linked in support of 'progress and improvement.' For many people over many decades of our national life, this is the landscape of 'small town virtues,' the 'backbone of America,' the 'real America.'"[25] The impact of this symbolic landscape, like the others, can be measured by observing the concrete ways in which people modify their surroundings to bring them into conformity with a preexisting model and screen out those elements in the actual landscape that are considered ugly, disturbing, or anachronistic. Even in the nineteenth century, for example, small towns in the Midwest were filled with people who did not "belong" in the idealized vision. Some towns remained white, middle class, and Protestant. But many were populated increasingly by Irish Catholics, poor whites, and "colored folk." Each group created its own landscape (houses, churches, shopping areas, social clubs and taverns, clothing, manners, and so forth). Eventually, the gulf between the real and the ideal became so great that the small town was discredited as a community form. This was reflected in an avalanche of literary denunciations and urban jokes. In spite of what came to be seen as stultifying limitations (indulgence in moralism and self-righteousness accompanied by a preoccupation with respectability, business, and "progress"), it continues to have wide appeal especially to those who live in big cities. To sophisticated urbanites, the scaled-down version of a Missouri town at Disneyland represents something better than what they now call home.

It does not seem unreasonable to suggest that the Munchkin City is symbolically related to the Midwestern small town. Dorothy lands, in what could be called "Main Street, U.S.A." She is welcomed by the mayor and his magistrates on the steps of the town hall. There, she also encounters personifications of local institutions such as the "bank" (local business being represented by the Lollipop Guild), the "theater" (represented by ballerinas of the Lullabye League), the "courthouse" (represented by the coroner and the lawyer), and even the "church" (represented by Glinda on her dais). Moreover, the highway that traverses the countryside (but stops at the gates of the capital city) actually begins at the heart of the Munchkin City; this adds a rural note that mitigates the urban implications of its name. With its childlike inhabitants, protected by their fairy godmother, the Munchkin City is really an embryonic city (which is to say, a small town). It seems to be a happy place for the Munchkins but not for a girl seeking the help of a wizard and menaced by a witch. Dorothy "rejects" the Munchkin City and sets off for the big city, the real city, the Emerald City.

*

To get there, she must follow an established route. Meandering through long stretches of open countryside between its "source" inside the Munchkin City and its "mouth" at the gates of the Emerald City is the Yellow Brick Road. It is, therefore, associated primarily with rural landscapes. In fact, it is associated with three kinds of rural landscape: farmland (the fields of corn), orchards (the apple trees), and meadows (the poppy field). These places are generally attractive. In every case, though, something mars what would otherwise have been a source of happiness. The Scarecrow has been unsuccessful at his job in the cornfield. The apple trees are hostile to those who would enjoy their fruit. And the poppy field is polluted by the Witch's spell. At the end of the road, however, is the Emerald City. It is worth noting here that the journey through Oz recapitulates American history. It begins in the Munchkin City (actually a village or town not unlike those of an earlier America) and concludes in the Emerald City (a large and impressive metropolis not unlike New York or Hollywood). Linking them all is the Yellow Brick Road (a paved highway through the wilderness in both time and space).

Considering the possibility of a fourth term in his set of symbolic landscapes, Meinig mentions the highway as a recent candidate.

Although many Americans have reacted against the stultifying conformity and dullness of suburban life, he notes, the fact remains that they are still moving out to the suburbs and even beyond. Indeed,

> by the mid-1960s, when two cars became the minimum family standard and the engineers had spun a web of superhighways through, around and radiating from every city, "community" was no longer a discrete neighborhood, it was a wide scattering of places bound together by the freeways. The places of sleeping, eating, drinking, relaxing, working and shopping might be fragmented among a dozen points separated by miles from one another. Thus we come to the ineluctable observation that the key landscape symbol in late twentieth-century America is not the home but the highway, and community is not so much a discrete locality as a dispersed social network traced on the landscape by the moving automobile.[26]

It may be, as he suggests, that the car has replaced the house as the most powerful symbol of American values. Through the car, Americans can express their sense of individuality, freedom, status, and even sex appeal.

> It carries us effortlessly to all those amenities and services made familiar and profoundly democratic by the nationwide uniformity of McDonalds, Holiday Inns, and a hundred other franchise operations. We move along a linear landscape, intensely developed strips and open interstate routes made secure and legible by uniform road designs and standardized emblems. And now with citizen band radios, we can communicate directly and anonymously with other individuals, disembodied voices broadcasting at random our craving for contact, as isolated in our steel shells we cruise the monotonous uniformity of our interstate highways.[27]

Although this is the reality, it is not necessarily the ideal. The highways built in the 1950s and 1960s are now crumbling. And the problems associated with them, such as pollution and accidents, can no longer be ignored as minor tribulations. When irate drivers in Los Angeles, "home of the freeway," began shooting at people in passing cars, the situation immediately became front-page news, the subject of jokes and cartoons, even a featured story in news magazines.[28] The attention given to these roving thugs cannot be explained by the actual peril posed to American drivers as a whole or even to those in Los Angeles itself. Public fascination can probably be explained only on a symbolic level. Meinig himself acknowledges that the highway has become a symbol of everything that is wrong in America. The

"atomized dispersal of people living in motorized and electronic connection with their environment and with one another," he writes,
would be a perversion of "community" as that is understood by most
Americans. "Despite its obvious power in fact, despite the great
American phenomenon of the mobile home and the motorized home,
despite the power of the romantic image of the uncommitted, foot-
loose traveler, the Easy Rider drifting from one pad to another, most
Americans would not be comfortable with the highway as the appropriate symbolic landscape for a satisfying concept of community."[29]

When *The Wizard* opened in 1939, however, the highway was still
"innocent." The open road was still a symbolic landscape that meant
freedom and hope, just as it had to the pioneers who set out from
the frontier and crossed the wilderness. This attitude is illustrated in
a painting by Rawlston Crawford. *Overseas Highway* (painted, as it
happens, in 1939) captures the perspective of someone walking, or
riding on a bridge; the pavement leads relentlessly forward to a
vanishing point at the middle of the horizon. The sense of infinite
distance is emphasized by the steel railings that stretch forward on
either side, converging on the horizon. As Dickran Tashjian points
out, "the rhetoric of composition and color obscures the need to
question where Crawford's highway will lead: the open road is one
embodiment of the American Dream."[30]

Just as the open road unifies America, the Yellow Brick Road
unifies Oz. In both cases, moreover, the unification is not only geographical but emotional as well. No matter what perils Dorothy and her
friends encounter along the way, after all, they are free and hopeful
as long as they keep in mind what Glinda and the Munchkins had
repeated so many times in song.:

> Follow the Yellow Brick Road,
> Follow the Yellow Brick Road,
> Follow, follow, follow, follow
> Follow the Yellow Brick Road.
> Follow the Yellow Brick,
> Follow the Yellow Brick,
> Follow the Yellow Brick Road...(64)[31]

It is only when they are *off* the Yellow Brick Road, in fact, that they
are seriously endangered by the Wicked Witch.

Twenty-five years after *The Wizard* was made, the same theme
became the central motif of a very popular television series. On

"Route 66" (CBS, 1960–1964), two young men make their way across the country in search of adventure. Every episode finds Tod and Buz in some new place where they become involved in local problems. Once the heroes have restored order, however, they drive off again down the open road. Twenty-five years later, another popular television series used the same motif. On "Highway to Heaven" (NBC, 1984–1988), two new heroes make their way across the country in search of the wounded and lonely. Every episode finds Mark and Jonathan in some new place where they become involved in local problems. Once they have ensured healing and reconciliation, however, they drive off again down the open road. In both cases, the opening credits are shown against a background of a car moving across the landscape. Despite the ambivalence Americans have come to feel for the open road, it remains a significant symbolic landscape.

*

After a series of adventures, Dorothy and her friends arrive at the Emerald City. But they do not remain there for long. Before their wishes can be granted, says the Wizard, they must first kill the Witch. Without further ado, they set out for the Haunted Forest. Of all the symbolic landscapes presented in *The Wizard*, only this one is completely undesirable. Dominated by the Wicked Witch, the Haunted Forest is filled with sinister beings; their glowing eyes suggest the presence of alien and hostile forces. As Dorothy and her friends begin their journey through this threatening realm, a sign warns them of peril ahead: "I'd turn back if I were you!" (103). Soon enough, their worst fears come to pass and the ferocious winged monkeys swoop down on them. The Haunted Forest, therefore, represents the untamed wilderness. In fact, it represents the Western wilderness, since the Wicked Witch of the West presides over it.[32] The following discussion is based primarily, but not solely, on *Virgin Land*, by Henry Nash Smith and *The Machine in the Garden*, by Leo Marx.

Today, it seems strange that the Western wilderness should have been associated with negativity. We are far more familiar with it as an escape from the dehumanization of industrial civilization; the national parks, for example, are designed at least partly as (temporary) havens for refugees from the urban nightmare. In fact, the wilderness is now associated with a powerful social and political movement represented by organizations such as the Sierra Club and by the environmentalist lobby in Washington. There are, of course, very practical reasons for opposing pollution of the air, water, and land. But the various ecology movements also have another function. When their representatives argue in Congress for measures to promote the recovery of endangered species or to set aside areas for the preservation of wildlife, they are saying something about the symbolic geography of America: if the wilderness were to disappear, then some essential part of American identity would also disappear. Every week, CBS presents "Sunday Morning," a news magazine featuring upbeat stories on contemporary American life. Invariably, the show concludes with about three minutes devoted to the wilderness; during this televised meditation, the camera lingers lovingly on a family of seagulls wheeling above foam-swept rocks on the coast of Oregon, a spray of wildflowers blooming after a sudden shower in New Mexico, or a school of tadpoles swimming near the surface of a crystal stream in Vermont. But the link between wilderness and national identity is not confined to television. A much older American institution, the scouting movement, also promotes enjoyment of the wilderness and wilderness values (such as self-sufficiency, respect for nature, and simplicity) in the context of patriotism.[33]

It was not always so. As a symbolic landscape of America, and as an ecological image of nature without culture (forests, mountains, and deserts that lie beyond the boundaries of civilization), the wilderness has had both positive and negative connotations.[34] The early European explorers and colonists were ambivalent over what they found in the New World. To be sure, they were fascinated by the fact that North America was a virgin land and assumed that it consisted of pure nature, untouched and undefiled by (European) history and civilization. It was a primeval world and its inhabitants were primeval beings (which is to say, they were part of the landscape). But was it a primeval paradise or a primeval hell? In *The Machine in the Garden*, Leo Marx shows that there was no consensus on this matter. The New World was discussed in terms of both garden (positive) and wilderness (negative).

In the sixteenth and seventeenth centuries, what we would now call "wilderness" (untamed, uncultivated, uncharted land) was often called a "garden." Early visitors to Virginia, for instance, described what they found as a luxurient garden. By this, they referred not to colonial horticulture but to nature uncontaminated by history or civilization. They referred, in short, to the benevolent aspect of nature, as such. Not surprisingly, the native inhabitants of this "natural garden" (or "wild garden" as distinct from a "cultivated garden") were idealized as gentle, kind, innocent, faithful, and generally childlike folk; they were, as Jean-Jacques Rousseau put it, "noble savages" living in perfect (even prelapsarian) harmony with the natural order. To many Europeans, the untamed but benign wilderness of North America seemed to be the venue for a new golden age, a chance to start over again. Generations of Americans maintained the vision of their land as a primeval paradise. By the early nineteenth century, in fact, this notion had given rise to what Phillipe de Montebello calls "the first pivotal art movement in this nation's history."[35] He refers to the Hudson River school of landscape painting that persisted, in one form or another, to the end of the century. It was a movement preoccupied by the sublime majesty and transcendence of the American wilderness. The reverential, quasi-mystical, attitude that underlay the Hudson River school was characteristic of the period; it was, in fact, an American version of romanticism; unlike European romanticism, however, it tended to glorify the nation's geography rather than its history.

Until the early nineteenth century, the kind of detachment necessary to contemplate the beauty of nature was seldom possible for Americans; the settlers had been too busy establishing a precarious existence in their villages and on their farms to ponder "the meaning of the land that lay beyond the sunset."[36] After the War of Independence, however, they began to think about their national identity. As Barbara Novak points out, they linked this to distinctive features of the landscape. And the most distinctive feature, at that time, was the prevalence of wilderness. Artists, therefore, realized that they had no need to imitate their European counterparts.[37] For Thomas Cole, Asher B. Durand, and others, the wilderness was temporally ambiguous. On the one hand, it was a primeval paradise that had escaped the ravages of history and civilization. On the other hand, it was a foretaste of the eschatological paradise. No wonder *Newsweek's* review for a major exhibition of the Hudson River school at the Metropolitan Museum of Art in New York is called: "The Search for Paradise Lost: The Hudson River School Saw America as Eden."[38] Even though Cole, according to Oswaldo Roque, "did not spell it out, his discussion of American scenery firmly reasserted the typology established...by Governor Clinton in his address before the American Academy of the Fine Arts. For the artist—the poet as well as the painter—America could either be a primeval wilderness or an arcadian pastoral. In either case, it presented an analogy to the early days of Creation. 'We are still in Eden; the wall that shuts us out of the garden is our own ignorance.'"[39] By the late nineteenth century, though, it had become clear that urbanization and industrialization were threatening the wilderness. Early members of the Hudson River school hoped to inspire reverence and awe for the visible revelation of God but later ones were more practical; they hoped to inspire efforts to save it from the greed and folly of civilization. Referring to a painting by Frederick Edwin Church, John K. Howat writes: "Because of its vividness and strong composition—indeed its gripping theatricality and expressiveness—*Twilight in the Wilderness* stands as an early signpost central to the landscape preservation movement in this century and anticipating the extraordinary popularity of outdoorsmanship, as well as the establishment of our system of national forests and parks."[40]

Even as members of the Hudson River school were becoming famous for their vision of the American wilderness, another painter of the wilderness was living in comparative obscurity. If Edward Hicks had been merely an isolated "primitive" painter, his work would be of no interest here. But since his death in 1849, Hicks has become one of the most popular American artists. It would be very difficult to find a book on American art that does not include an illustration of *The Peaceable Kingdom* in one version or another. "Today," writes John P. Guttenberg, "Hicks's work is widely celebrated as the quintessential expression of the nineteenth-century folk artist."[41] A fervent Quaker, Hicks painted approximately sixty versions of *The Peaceable Kingdom* as visual sermons on the prophecy of Isaiah in which "the wolf shall dwell with the lamb and the leopard shall lie down with the kid."[42] Of interest here is the iconography be used. The presence of wild animals (lions, leopards, bears, and wolves), of course, indicates that the Kingdom is a transformed wilderness. And the presence in the background of figures from local history and features of the local landscape (William Penn signing a treaty with the Indians, for example, or Virginia's Natural Bridge) indicates that the transformation takes place in America. In other words, America itself is the scene of a return to the "wild garden" of Eden, the primeval paradise in which human beings exist in perfect harmony with the natural order. Although his allegorical work was intended mainly as commentary on the conflict between orthodox and "inner light" factions within the Quaker community, it suggests an identification of America with Eden that reaffirms with American traditions dating back to the earliest colonies.

But, as I have said, the word "wilderness" was used at first without the positive connotations of current usage. The early explorers and colonists reserved its use strictly for the negative aspects of untamed nature (since the term "garden" was reserved for positive aspects). Governed by the harsh and primitive laws of nature, many saw it as a dark realm of potential violence and chaos. As in the Bible, which so dominated the imagination of early settlers, the wilderness was seen as hostile and threatening terrain where faith was tested; it was to be endured, not enjoyed. "In this 'hideous wilderness' image of landscape," writes Marx, "the New World is a place of hellish darkness; it arouses the fear of malevolent forces in the cosmos, and of the cannibalistic and bestial traits of man. It is associated with the wild men of medieval legend."[43] The Indians, for example, were seen not as representatives of foreign cultures but as representatives of fallen nature; consequently, they were to be removed from the landscape just as the forests and other natural obstacles were to be cleared away. "This violent image expresses a need to mobilize energy, postpone immediate pleasures, and rehearse the perils and purposes of the community. Life in a garden is relaxed, quiet and sweet...but survival in a howling desert demands action, the unceasing manipulation and mastery of the forces of nature, including, of course, human nature. Colonies established in the desert require aggressive, intellectual, controlled, and well-disciplined people."[44] As Perry Miller shows in his classic study, *Errand into the Wilderness*,[45] no community was more controlled and well-disciplined than the Puritans of New England. Having established themselves in a hostile environment and tamed it, they felt no need to continue the struggle by moving into new areas of wilderness.

By the early nineteenth century, Marx points out, the wilderness was associated not only with savage Indians but also with uncouth, or uncivilized whites who either could not or would not conform to the social standards of settled communities. Speaking for the early American farmers (who made up most of the population), St. John de Crèvecoeur wrote that something terrible happened to Europeans in the dark forests of the frontier. With their lives "regulated by the wildness of the neighborhood," he wrote, they became "ferocious, gloomy, unsociable...no better than carnivorous animals of a superior rank, living on the flesh of wild animals."[46] Eventually, explorers and adventurers such as Daniel Boone were idealized as heroic and romantic figures. But many Americans—especially the farmers—never forgot that those who chose the wilderness had usually been rebels against the social and cultural order that had been established only after a long struggle.

At the end of the twentieth century, the American imagination is still haunted by the wilderness. The prototypical Western wilderness is projected onto a variety of other landscapes. In some cases, the negative aspect predominates. Thus the metropolis is often seen as a threatening and hostile wilderness. The popularity of crime shows on television may indicate a need to assert some sense that the forces of evil and chaos can be overcome by the forces of law and order as they were in the Old West. A more ambiguous wilderness is found in outer space. If "we are not alone," after all, who else is "out there?" When presented as the venue of both good and evil, life and death, outer space is an open, empty, trackless desert waiting to be explored and colonized. This is the astral wilderness of *Star Wars* (George Lucas, 1977) and its sequels, *The Empire Strikes Back* (Irvin Kershner, 1980) and *Return of the Jedi* (Richard Marquand, 1983); in outer space, as in our own world, there is both good and evil, both life force and death force. Sometimes, however, outer space is not seen as the venue of both good and evil; on the contrary, it is seen as the venue of either good *or* evil. In one very evocative movie, *Close Encounters of the Third Kind* (Steven Spielberg, 1977), it is an inviting, welcoming, and reassuring realm inhabited by friendly beings. The same is true in the enormously popular *ET: The Extraterrestrial* (Steven Spielberg, 1982). But in *Alien* (Ridley Scott, 1979) and *Aliens* (James Cameron, 1986), it is a menacing and terrifying realm inhabited by sinister beings. Toy manufacturers have not been slow to exploit public interest in outer space. Their cars and trucks have been redesigned as Walking Astro-Grapplers, Alien Moon Stalkers, Legoland Command Ships, Laser Bolt Vehicles, and Construx Stellar Exploration Units. In short, there is a clear relation between the wilderness of the Old West and that of Outer Space; the latter is an updated version of the former. The traditional "good guys" whose mission is to save civilization from the "bad guys" are now dressed up and marketed as Masters of the Universe. The children of an earlier generation, always on the lookout for Indians or cattle rustlers, carried six-shooters in their holsters; the children of today, always on the lookout for Klingons or other enemy aliens, carry Lazer Tag ray guns in their Star Belts. The link between Old West and Outer Space is sometimes made quite explicit. On March 28, 1989, for example, it was announced on *Entertainment Tonight* that Kenny Rogers is producing a music video (which will eventually be made into a movie) called *Planet Texas;* this combination of country and western music with science fiction is to be about "cowboys from outer space." In effect, the mythic future is not so very different from the mythic past. Out of the American myth has emerged a galactic myth. Indeed, when George Lucas made *Star Wars*, he had the traditional westerns in mind (along with *The Wizard*).[47] It could be argued that the "space operas" of today are the functional equivalents of the older "horse operas." Both indicate an American fascination with wilderness that forms part of the national ethos.

But *The Wizard* has rejected this symbolic landscape. Dorothy is not a conservationist in the Haunted Forest. Nor is she an explorer. She is a refugee from the savagery of a demonic being who incarnates the dark, sinister and threatening face of nature in the wild. The Wicked Witch, ruling this realm from her gloomy castle perched upon a barren crag, is the functional equivalent of Sitting Bull and every other alien tribal chief encountered by white settlers moving West;[48] The Ozian Haunted forest is identified with the American Western wilderness. Evidently, wilderness is understood here, as it was for many of the early settlers, as a primeval hell rather than a primeval garden. There is an obvious reason for this. *The Wizard*, after all, is about going home. And wilderness, by definition, is not home (or not yet home). Once it becomes home, in fact, it ceases to be wilderness; instead, it becomes the frontier of civilization. An American colony on Mars, for instance, would be the American frontier and not the Martian wilderness (although it would be surrounded, of course, by the Martian wilderness). It is worth considering a cliché about the movie westerns. After the bandits have been captured, after the town has been made safe for the preacher and the schoolmarm, the hero rides off into the proverbial sunset (which is to say, the West). He rides away from the frontier farm (settled community life) and further into the Western wilderness; there is no room for him at home. Even at its best, even as the venue of adventure and oppor- tunity and freedom, wilderness is always beyond the horizon. In 1939, after a decade of mass migrations due to the Depression and with war looming in the near future, it may have been necessary for Americans to reaffirm the value of home (emotional roots on the land and in the past). This, at any rate, is clearly indicated in *The Wizard*.

*

While in Oz, Dorothy's goal is to reach the Emerald City. She and her friends, resolutely pursue their course despite the machinations of their implacable foe, the Witch. Even before they set foot inside the capital of Oz for the first time, they are duly impressed by its grandeur. Once inside, they become tourists not unlike country folk who find themselves in midtown Manhattan for the first time. In short, they are awestruck by urban splendor as the Emerald City glitters with hope and opportunity. This impression is confirmed when Dorothy and her friends arrive there for the second time; they are asked to remain and rule Oz. But the Emerald City is not perfect. For one thing, it is not free of fear; flying overhead, the Witch has no trouble in terrifying the locals. Besides, it is ruled over by a "humbug." Most important, however, is one simple fact: the Emerald City is not home. Not even the spectacular capital of Oz can beguile Dorothy into abandoning her wish to be back home in Kansas where she belongs. No sooner does Dorothy return, therefore, than she makes plans to leave. The Emerald City has been an immediate goal; her ultimate goal has always been Kansas. In the same way, Americans flock to their own glittering cities but continue to hanker for the earlier, simpler, ways of rural life, for some place to put down "roots," for home. To the extent that Oz's Emerald City is associated with America's Eastern metropolis, it is also associated with a long-standing tradition of ambivalence toward urban life.

The Eastern metropolis[49] lies at the opposite end of the symbolic spectrum from the Western wilderness. If wilderness is an ecological image representing nature without culture, the city is an ecological image representing culture without nature (even though no actual city could exist entirely cut off from nature). We now think of the wilderness in terms of the American West. Indeed, the Wizard tells Dorothy that he was "born and bred in the heart of the western wilderness" (125). At one time, of course, the American East was wilderness, too. With the arrival of the earliest settlers, however, it was transformed (for Europeans) from wilderness into frontier. Gradually, the frontier was transformed, in turn, into "civilization." Like "wilderness," however, the word "civilization" has both positive and negative connotations. It has been used, for example, to describe both the decadent and oppressive Old World from which European immigrants wanted to escape but also the progressive and exciting New World they wanted to enjoy. To the extent that civilization is considered an advance over more "primitive" forms of existence, the American city is symbolically linked to the root metaphor of Jerusalem (either the Holy City of ancient Israel or the heavenly city of the eschatological Kingdom). But to the extent that civilization is considered oppressive, the American city is symbolically linked to such root metaphors as Babel (fragmentation and chaos), Babylon (exile and alienation), and Rome (decadence and tyranny).

According to Raymond Mohl,[50] early American cities were either commercial or administrative centers. By the mid-nineteenth century, all that was changing. It was the rise of industry that initiated the process of urbanization on a massive scale; at the same time, according to Marx, severe conflict developed between America as "the garden" and America as "the machine." The industrial cities, in any case, attracted not only hapless immigrants from overseas but also discontented rural folk from the hinterland. For the former, cities such as New York often represented refuge from tyranny and poverty in the Old World. But for all of these people, the city—its streets proverbially "paved with gold"—represented opportunity, freedom, and the hope of a better future. By the early twentieth century, American notions of utopia were often projected as fantasies of technologically advanced urban communities. And this was not true only of science fiction novels and movies. A recent exhibition at the Brooklyn Museum, "The Machine Age in America,"[51] showed how the look of everything from cars and ships to teapots and toasters reflected an optimism based on speed, efficiency and technological progress. Robert Hugues observes, interestingly, that industrial design in the 1930s was intended not only to increase efficiency but also to promote a worldview, a weltanschauung; maintaining the long American tradition of faith in progress, during a severe depression, was so vital that it could be taken seriously even when expressed in ways that now seem absurd.

> Was it only fifty years ago? How touching our grandfathers' faith in the future seems, in our day of acid rain, exploding shuttles, decaying inner cities and general creeping dystopia. The mood is epitomized in objects like the male costume of the future dreamed up for *Vogue*—a bearded figure in an immaculate white jumpsuit wearing a circular antenna as a halo on his head, John the Baptist among the insulators. Everything is streamlined, even objects that are screwed down and cannot move, so that America's breathless rush toward Utopia is clearly signified by things like a 1933 Raymond Loewy metal tear-drop desk-mounted pencil sharpener. In the twelve years between the Wall Street Crash and Pearl Harbor, the American imagination seems to have oscillated between two images, the streamline and the breadline—the former promising relief from the latter. And in the maxim of the 1939 New York World's Fair, "See tomorrow—now!" lay the siren syllables of

undeferred gratification that would abolish the constraints of Puritan America while preserving its millenarian fantasies.[52]

And progress came from the city, not from the wilderness or the frontier. As David Albrecht[53] points out, moreover, modern architecture was used with similar connotations in the set designs for Hollywood movies throughout the 1930s. The urban world was presented as glamorous, sophisticated, progressive, and exciting. Very often, in fact, it was presented as a playground for the rich and fortunate who were insulated from drudgery and routine. Even movies that acknowledged urban problems, however, often managed to glorify the city as a world of opportunity for those with talent or ambition. Although poverty and unemployment were openly depicted in *Forty-Second Street* (Lloyd Bacon, 1933) and other "backstage" musicals produced by Warner Brothers, and although such movies often included suggestive references to prostitution, the overall message was that the city represented hope. With good luck and hard work, almost anyone could become a star—and if not a star, then at least an ingenue in the chorus line with a chance either to become a star or to marry one.

Even at their best, though, cities do not necessarily represent home or the ideal community. Consequently, Meinig does not consider it a successor to the Southern California suburb in his set of classic symbolic landscapes.[54] If most Americans live in cities, they often do so with misgivings, even guilt. This is partly because the sophistication and worldliness of urban life has always been associated with the decadent European society rejected in the War of Independence. Americans, in any case, choose to live in cities but continue to dream of Marlboro Country. "Our counter-culture movements," writes James E. Vance, "show the still strong attraction of Arcadia, back to the simple country life, the commune in the woods, ways to drop out of the metropolitan maelstrom."[55] The South Bronx is sometimes described as "bombed out" or even "lunar." But repeated attempts at urban renewal often end in disaster; after only a few years, for example, the Cabrini Green project in Chicago became a dangerous slum. When New York City almost went bankrupt in 1976, due to an influx of the poor on welfare and an exodus of tax-paying businesses, many Americans living elsewhere found the situation in New York, the big city par excellence, either irrelevant or amusing; they opposed the idea of federal grants to save the Big Apple.[56] Residents of almost all American cities, however, have complained about problems such as congestion, pollution, crime, and the destruction of neighborhood communities in favor of office buidings and apartment towers or even parking lots and freeways. And the vision of urban life in the future, the rigidly controlled and aesthetically sterile "environments" proposed by planners and developers, often look like the nightmarish sets for science fiction movies. According to Meinig, Americans are an urbanized people without a satisfying vision, without an effective symbol of what a healthy, happy, urban community would be like.

The antiurban tradition has a long history in the United States. It was Thomas Jefferson's vision of America as a republic of virtuous yeoman farmers, not Alexander Hamilton's vision of America as a land of enterprising merchants and manufacturers, that was first given official approval. This was partly an affirmation of the predominantly rural reality and partly a way of distancing the new nation from Europe; the United States was to be a rural utopia corresponding to the urban dystopia of Europe. Martin Marty points out, moreover, that American Protestantism, which established itself in a predominantly rural America, adjusted with considerable difficulty to the urban environment; the metropolis was identified with temptation and sin.[57] When cities became an important feature of American life, though, the positive traditions of urban life were not strong enough to counteract the negative ones. As Samuel B. Warner puts it, Americans "live in one of the world's most urbanized countries as if it were a wilderness."[58] Urban America, therefore, is a wilderness in the purely negative sense used by the earliest settlers; it is, in short, an "urban jungle."

If Hollywood movies sometimes glorified urban life in the 1930s, they seldom did so in the 1940s. Very few presented the city as an ideal setting for family and communal life; on the contrary, many expressed overt hostility toward the city.[59] The antiurban tradition may have been given its ultimate expression in film noir, a genre associated with the 1940s and early 1950s. Theorists have argued over whether film noir is, in fact, a distinct genre. Nevertheless, they agree that many movies of this period are linked by common features. Emerging from the tradition of gangster movies made in the 1930s and responding to social and political turmoil during the war and its cold-war aftermath, film noir "is contemporaneous, usually urban, and almost always American in setting. The few exceptions involve either urban men in a rural locale or Americans abroad."[60] But film noir conveys a very specific attitude toward the city. The urban world is presented as chaotic (stories of random violence and inno-

cent victims), alienating (glib dialogue), neurotic (characters motivated by murderous obsessions), and thoroughly sinister (deep
shadows, deserted buildings, echoing footsteps). Obviously, this is the
realm of evil. Detectives are as hardened and cynical as the criminals
they pursue. And victims are often as morally dubious as those who
pursue them. Nothing is what it seems to be. According to Foster
Hirsch, an axiom of film noir is that the (urban) world is a dangerous
place.[61] Most Americans are probably familiar with images of traffic
lights flashing as reflections on wet pavement and neon signs flickering over cheap diners or outside the windows of sleazy hotels. Very
often, the city depicted is New York. But in movies based on the
novels of James M. Cain such as *Mildred Pierce* (Michael Curtiz,
1945) or those of Raymond Chandler such as *The Big Sleep* (Howard
Hawks, 1946), it is often Los Angeles. "Los Angeles adds a horizontal
dimension to *film noir*. In place of the monoliths and endless urban
alleyways of the eastern cityscapes, there is a physical and moral
sprawl, a chain of suburbs, full of legal and illegal activities, linked by
wide boulevards and expressways. Chandler saw this and made *The
Big Sleep*, like all his other stories set in Los Angeles, a series of
journeys across a mythical landscape of darkened bungalows, decaying office buildings, and sinister nightspots."[62]

Even San Francisco takes on a sinister quality in *The Maltese
Falcon* (John Huston, 1941). But so could any city. The city itself
seems to become a character as dark as any criminal lurking in the
fog near a waterfront bar or any housewife planning murder in a
suburban living room. According to Hirsch, noir characters "inhabit a
treacherous urban terrain filled with deceiving women and the
promise of money easily and ill-gotten. The city, minatory and
bewitching, is a powerful and inescapable presence in *noir;* but, like
the characters who walk through its mean streets, it, too, comes in
various styles."[63] He identifies three of these styles. At first, cities
were built in studio. They lacked the fullness and density of real
cities. These movies have a generally expressionistic look. "Shown,
most typically, at night, the studio city of darkened rainy streets was
eerily deserted, its pools of shadows pregnant with menace. The
simplified and semi-abstract cityscapes of the studio-made thrillers
provided the appropriate backdrop for stories of entrapment. Films
set in this environment were claustrophobic psychological studies,
stories of obsession and confinement in which the world begins small
and then progressively closes in on the fated protagonists."[64]

After the war, movies were shot more often on location. As a result, they look more realistic. Very often, the camera is used to give the impression of on-the-spot reporting. In other words, these movies emphasize the outward and visible aspects of crime. According to Hirsch, this made them more conservative in outlook. Previously, they had been vaguely subversive in depicting the ordinary world of everyday life going haywire; the relation between guilt and innocence or vice and virtue was subtle and ambiguous. Now, the "good guys" (usually the police or private investigators) were more clearly separated from the "bad guys" (described as "the criminals who hid from the light of day in the bowels of the urban underworld").[65] But location shooting could also have a different effect. By the early 1950s, the city was no longer seen as a neutral background for journalistic accounts of crime; it was shown as a participant in evil. Discussing *The Window* (Ted Tetzlaff, 1949), Hirsch writes that "New York in midsummer is rendered as a wasteland of abandoned buildings, empty lots ringed by fences, and sweltering tenements—an infested environment that seems to be a breeding ground for crime."[66]

Clearly, film noir reveals the profound sense of urban alienation, anxiety, and cynicism that has been prevalent in American society. But why should all this negativity be focused so directly on the city? After all, most Americans have chosen to live in cities. It seems that the long antiurban tradition made this inevitable. For generations, Americans had been accustomed to the idea that the city is the opposite of home; the city is where people do not belong, where family life does not thrive, where community does not flourish. Associated with avaricious bankers, cynical bureaucrats, ruthless industrialists, and sinister mobsters, the metropolis came to be synonymous, for many Americans, with political corruption, moral degeneracy, and personal vice; the city produced nothing but alienation and despair for those condemned to work in its factories and to live in its slums.

Unlike the Western wilderness, the Eastern metropolis cannot be ruled out, by definition, as a symbolic landscape of home. Nevertheless, Americans often find it difficult to think of it in that way. Second and third generation descendents of immigrants often have nostalgic feelings about the homes their ancestors made amid the squalor of tenements and sweatshops (or even about the Old Country that sent them fleeing in terror). And some of them settle in "gentrified" inner city districts.[67] But this does not mean that they consider the city their ultimate goal. For many, it is an immediate goal. Once they have "made it" or "discovered themselves," once they are about to "settle down" with families, it is time to move on to the suburbs or even to some small town within commuting distance.

During the Depression, the nation responded favorably to the idea of urbanization and industrialization as immediate solutions to economic hardship. After the "dust bowl" experience of the early 1930s, many people had no choice but to leave their homes on the land and migrate to cities that promised at least the possibility of a better life. Dianne Pilgrim describes the situation well.

> With the devastating effects of the Depression, existing insecurities dissolved into a general disillusionment. Yet at the same time, this crisis created a national unity of purpose, a need to find a way to assuage the ensuing panic. A feeling emerged that if everyone pulled together, with the help of the machine behind them, a better tommorow could be achieved. From this unity of response developed values, beliefs and symbols that became identified as uniquely American. Streamlining, with its sense of speed, became the symbol of the decade.[68]

No one was more effective in promoting hope than Franklin Delano Roosevelt. Like the President himself, the Wizard keeps up morale in his streamlined and technologically advanced city by a combination of common sense, calculated bravado, and sheer blarney. When the Witch appears in the sky overhead, for example, he tries to reassure the terrified populace (in his guise as doorman): "It's all right! Everything is all right! The Great and Powerful Oz has got matters well in hand—I hope—and so you can all go home! And there's nothing to worry about!" (94). He might well have quoted Roosevelt by adding that "the only thing we have to fear is fear itself."[69] In any event, Americans may also have responded warmly to the idea that the current dislocations were only temporary, that either they or their descendents would one day return to the land, where they belonged. If so, then it could be argued that Oz represents the familiar world of contemporary America and Kansas represents the ideal world of a past and future America.

The capital of Oz appears to be an Eastern metropolis. Its inhabitants are "grown up" and sophisticated. Aesthetically and technologically, it is up to date. And yet, it is not ideal. Although the Wizard's use of technology apparently satisfies the inhabitants, Dorothy finds out that "progress" here is at least partly based on hokum. Things are under control, problems solved, and wishes granted. But Dorothy's wish is to leave the Emerald City. The obvious implication is that even this glittering city, Dorothy's long-sought goal and the most desirable place in all of Oz, is not completely satisying. As I have indicated, this characteristically American ambivalence—wanting the city but also rejecting it—is perfectly expressed in *The Wizard*. From that point of view, nothing has changed in the past fifty years.

*

After their expedition to the Haunted Forest, Dorothy and her friends return to the Emerald City. And from there, Dorothy immediately returns to Kansas. The "preferred" symbolic landscape in *The Wizard* is clearly a farm in Kansas around the turn of the century. Although Dorothy admits, in recalling Oz, that "most of it was beautiful," she goes on to say that "just the same, all I kept saying to everyone was 'I want to go home'" (132). She is truly glad to be back where she belongs. Her last words—the last words of the movie itself—are: "And...oh, Auntie Em, there's no place like home!" (132). Dorothy's home is a farm. She has chosen that over the Emerald City. To the extent that the symbolic landscapes presented in *The Wizard* correspond to those prevalent in American culture—and given the massive and enduring popularity of this movie we have no reason to doubt this—such a preference should indicate something about American identity.

Unlike the Western wilderness, the frontier farm is associated with home. And unlike the Eastern metropolis, it is associated unambiguously with home. In this way, it is like the three symbolic landscapes of home identified by Meinig. On the other hand, it is not merely one of several, one that Meinig inexplicably forgot when establishing his set, but America's symbolic landscape of home par excellence. The New England village, Midwestern small town, and Southern California suburb, after all, are "carried" primarily by sentiment; the frontier farm, however, has been "carried" for 200 years by a culturally dominant worldview known generally as "agrarianism." In the half century before *The Wizard*, agararianism had been given verbal expression as pastoralism, visual expression as regionalism, and political expression as populism. Considering American history, this is not surprising. I suggest that Meinig's three symbolic landscapes are, in fact, all variants of the frontier. By definition, a frontier mediates. The New England village mediates between two forms of wilderness:

the ocean and the forest. Both Midwestern small town and Southern California suburb mediate between country and city, nature and culture. So does the frontier farm. It is primary and the others secondary only because the family farm, isolated on the bleak prairie, is the starkest and most dramatic image of the mediation between nature and culture, between wilderness and civilization.

The frontier farm is not only a frontier community, it is a farm community. Underlying the symbolic landscape of frontier farm is the ecological image[70] of the garden. Lying midway on the symbolic spectrum between wilderness and civilization, the garden is, literally and figuratively, a central ecological image involved in the formation of American identity; it is, avers Marx, the "middle landscape." From the beginning, however, there were two versions of the garden: the natural (or wild) garden and the cultivated garden.

> To depict the new land as a lovely garden is to celebrate an ideal of immediate, joyous fulfillment. It must be admitted, however, that the word "immediate" conceals a crucial ambiguity. How immediate? We may well ask. At times, the garden is used to represent the sufficiency of nature in its original state. Then it conveys an impulse-centered, anarchic or primitivistic view of life. But elsewhere the garden stands for a state of cultivation, hence a less exalted estimate of nature's beneficence. Although important, the line between the two is not sharp. Both the wild and the cultivated versions of garden image embody something of that timeless impulse to cut loose from the constraints of a complex society....To depict America as a garden is to express aspirations still considered utopian—aspirations, that is, toward abundance, leisure, freedom, and a greater harmony of existence.[71]

The wild garden has already been discussed as the benign aspect of wilderness (which, by definition, is not related to the notion of home). Under discussion here is the cultivated garden. After the early nineteenth century, the adventures of hunters and explorers in what Smith calls the "Wild West" had little to do with the social and economic forces actually shaping American life. These forces originated not in the picturesque regions beyond the agricultural frontier but in the domesticated regions behind it. In fact, the imagery of an Agricultural West (cultivated garden) prevailed over that of a Wild West (wild garden or wilderness). Judging from the enormous popularity of westerns (both novels and movies), it seems clear that the former did not replace the latter; the two coexisted. But Smith argues that the former corresponded, for a while, much more closely to historical reality.

With each surge of westward movement, a new community came into being. These communities devoted themselves not to marching forward but to cultivating the earth. They plowed the virgin land and put in crops, and the great Interior Valley was transformed into a garden: for the imagination, the Garden of the World. The image of this vast and constantly growing agricultural society in the interior of the continent became one of the dominant symbols of nineteenth-century American society—a collective representation, a poetic idea...that defined the promise of American life. The master symbol of the garden embraced a cluster of metaphors expressing fecundity, growth, increase and blissful labor in the earth, all centering about the heroic figure of the idealized frontier farmer armed with that supreme agrarian weapon, the sacred plow. Although the idea of the garden of the world was relatively static, resembling an allegorical composition...its role in expressing assumptions and aspirations of a whole society, and the hint of narrative content supplied by the central figure of the Western farmer, gave it much the character of a myth.[72]

Although various versions of this agrarian "myth" had long been familiar in Europe, they took on a specific meaning and importance in connection with the New World. It was assumed that Americans, unlike Europeans, could transform the agrarian vision from nostalgic pastoral fantasies and utopian daydreams into practical reality. After all, there was enough vacant land to be cultivated by everyone, enough emptiness to be filled by anything. Due to growing recognition of what lay beyond the Alleghenies, beyond the Mississippi, it was obvious that America presented the opportunity not only to achieve the agrarian ideal but to do so on a scale so vast that all previous utopian experiments seemed insignificant by comparison; this was to be a major experiment in the transformation of human society. America, in effect, provided the human race with a unique opportunity to start over again. Since identity, by definition, always involves something unique (or distinctive), America's agricultural potential was an obvious source for the development of a new national identity. Not surprisingly, the land soon came to represent much more than the mere production of food.

Even before the Revolution, agrarianism had been influential. The vision of an agricultural paradise gained in importance, however, with the achievement of independence by the United States; this made it possible to translate philosophy directly into plans for a new society. Both Thomas Jefferson and Benjamin Franklin, for example, saw the future of the new republic in agrarian terms (unlike Alexander Hamilton who saw it in terms of commerce and manufacturing). What emerged was a social theory based on the "freehold" concept. The general idea was that free land should be made available to anyone willing to cultivate it. This, in turn, was based on several assumptions. Subsistence agriculture was said to be the only legitimate source of true (spiritual) wealth. Constant contact with the land made "yeoman" farmers not only happy but virtuous as well. This meant that a nation of such farmers would be both happy and virtuous. Farmers, in short, were the ideal citizens. At the very least, encouraging the urban poor—and such people were crowding into American cities even in the early nineteenth century—to migrate westward and settle the land would solve festering social problems in the East. This became the prevailing social and political theory of the new republic. Long before "manifest destiny" became a political slogan in the 1830s, many Americans were convinced that the pioneering farmers would inevitably push the frontier further and further west until the nation had expanded to fill the continent; civilization, they believed, inevitably flowed westward. Eventually, migration to the West was encouraged as an end in itself; settling the wilderness (converting it into a garden, an agricultural frontier) was more important to the new nation than reaching the Pacific and dominating the sea lanes to Asia. Not until the end of the nineteenth century was agrarianism seriously challenged as a political theory; by that time, populism had emerged as an outlet for farmers who had taken agrarianism seriously and were outraged by the social and economic decline of rural America.

Descriptions of the new agricultural territories were frankly, often floridly, utopian. Like the New World itself, the West was seen as a kind of new Promised Land, a new Garden of Eden, a new Beginning. As in the primeval paradise, however, there was a "serpent." Not one but two versions of the agrarian dream of an American paradise flourished side by side in the early nineteenth century. And by mid-century, supporters of the Southern version were prepared for armed conflict with those of an "American" version (the one that developed in the Midwest and eventually became the national version).

Both Southerners and Northerners correctly understood that the vitality of their systems depended on the creation, respectively of new slave or free states. Nevertheless, Southern planters were at a disadvantage. As Smith points out, they were less affected than Northerners by excitement over the new territories. Their vision of agrarianism involved long-established patterns of life in the older slave states along the Atlantic coast. This is why they rejected some of the agrarian doctrines taken for granted elsewhere. They did not agree, for example, that farming, as such, was inherently nobler than other occupations; it was a means to an end, not an end in itself. In fact, it was dirty and undignified. It was suitable only for slaves or poor whites, not for those with intellectual interests and aesthetic sensibilities. The small family farm, they argued, could hardly provide more than subsistence; it certainly could not provide the wealth necessary for an aristocratic way of life. Similarly, they denied that manual labor encouraged political insight and moral virtue; on the contrary, they argued, backbreaking work in the fields from dawn to dusk actually prevented farmers from reading and discussing such matters. The landowning gentry valued leisure over labor.

The South, according to Smith, was also at a disadvantage for another reason. Its version of the garden was inherently less appealing in the West than in the new territories needed by the South to expand the slave system. "The fiction dealing with the plantation system emphasizes the beauty of harmonious social relations in an orderly feudal society. It presupposes generations of settled existence and is inimical to change....Such symbols could not be adapted to the expansion of a society like that of the West, either South or North, where rapidity of change, crudity, bustle, heterogeneity were fundamental traits."[73] So the Southerners would have found it difficult to prevail in the West even if the Civil War had not settled the matter once and for all. They had powerful myths but not ones that encouraged expansion. As Smith points out, the only Southern dream of expansion that had any imaginative depth involved the establishment of a slave empire in Central and South America—not in the Western territories right next door.

The South maintained a vision of itself as a garden paradise reflecting the inherent *order* of both nature and culture. This, of course, corresponded to the aristocratic perspective. Garden imagery in the South, therefore, was expressed in a cluster of symbols associated with the feudal plantation: benevolent and wise masters, charming and accomplished mistresses, devoted and childlike slaves. This group of symbols was so evocative, so thoroughly fused with the warmth and beauty of traditional romances, that they were able to survive the demise of the plantation system itself. Moreover, the Southern garden appealed to Northerners as well as Southerners and to this day is part of the collective imagination. Consider the extraordinary and continuing appeal of *Gone With the Wind*. The two plantations, Tara and Twelve Oaks, are symbols of the Southern garden. Standing at a window overlooking the grounds of Twelve Oaks, Melanie tells Ashley of her love for the way of life it represents: "I love it as more than a house," she sighs, "it's a whole world that wants only to be graceful and beautiful."[74] As the movie makes very plain, this world is "gone with the wind." But, judging from the continuing popularity of *Gone with the Wind*, the value placed on rural life is not. The garden (no matter which version) is what sustains the nation. When Scarlett returns to Tara for the first time, it is not the static, dreamlike world she had known before the war. There are no slaves and no aristocrats in this new garden. In one unforgettable scene (which must have left a profound impression on farmers struggling to stay alive after a decade in the "dust bowl"), Scarlett stands proudly and defiantly in the glowing sunset and proclaims her determination to make the land productive; silhouetted against the heavens, she solemnly vows: "As God is my witness, I'll never be hungry again!"[75] In the final sequence, Scarlett once again dreams of returning to Tara. Realizing that her life in the city, Atlanta, has been a failure, she recalls some words spoken by her father in the first sequence and repeated, slightly modified, by both Ashley and Rhett. Because these are the concluding lines and summarize a major theme, it is worth quoting them here:

Scarlett: What is there to do? What is there that matters?

Father's voice: Do you mean to tell me, Katie Scarlett O'Hara, that Tara doesn't mean anything to you? Why, land's the only thing that matters—it's the only thing that lasts!

Ashley's voice: Something you love better than me, though you may not know it—Tara!

Rhett's voice: It's this from which you get your strength—the red earth of Tara.

Father's voice: Why, land's the only thing that matters—it's the only thing that lasts.

Ashley's voice: Something you love better than me, though you may not know it—Tara!

Rhett's voice: It's this from which you get your strength—the red earth of Tara.

Father's voice: Why, land's the only thing that matters...

Ashley's voice: Something you love better than me...

Rhett's voice: The red earth of Tara...

Father's voice: Tara!

Ashley's voice: Tara!

Rhett's voice: Tara!

Scarlett: Tara! Home! I'll go home—and I'll think of some way to get him back. After all, tomorrow is another day![76]

If *Gone with the Wind* had been popular only in 1939—at the end of the worst depression in American history and years of migration from the farms to the cities—it would be of little interest here. But the American public continues to think of it as one of the best movies ever made because it speaks to them at some deep level. In *Gone with the Wind*, the Southern version of agrarianism survives as a fantasy. But what gives it depth and meaning has been common to all versions of agrarianism: the underlying sense that the land is where people belong, that the land is of enduring and almost transcendent value. Like Dorothy in *The Wizard*, however, Scarlett discovers that going home is impossible without first growing up. As soon as Scarlett realizes her mistakes (failing to appreciate either Melanie's spiritual love or Rhett's erotic love; confusing her own selfish love for Ashley with real love), she also realizes the meaning of Tara. She is ready to go home. And home means the land, the plantation, the garden. This message is emphasized as heavily in *Gone with the Wind* as it is in *The Wizard*. That both movies were made in the same year and that both have in the past few decades become classics can hardly be accidental. The idea of returning to a garden home, whether a Georgia plantation or a Kansas farm, clearly expresses the deepest values and feelings of many Americans, both Southerners and Northerners. In the end, the South was defeated and its version of the garden shared the fate of the wilderness image. Both survive as imaginative devices to express discontent, anxiety or frustration with the present state of affairs. Neither was destroyed. But neither is the basis for public policy.

In *The Wizard*, however, it is the "American" version[77] of the garden, a farm on the agricultural frontier, that represents home. Its supremacy as a social and political ideal continued more than half a century longer than the Southern version. After the Civil War, westward expansion brought settlers from the fertile Mississippi and Ohio valleys of the Midwest to the more arid Great Plains. This region was not obviously a garden. The reality facing settlers included dust, drought, wind, and grasshoppers. The "myth" of the garden, therefore, came face to face with that of the wilderness. Historically, it was inevitable that the former should prevail over the latter; the frontier had been advancing westward ever since the earliest colonists arrived in the New World. At first, though, it seemed to many that this was a world uninhabitable by "civilized man" (that is, by white farmers). Smith points out that even though many believed regions too dry for agriculture could be inhabited by pastoralists with their herds and flocks, they also believed that this way of life was intrinsically unacceptable for settlers from the East. Because this wilderness was a desert, it was associated with other deserts. Just as deserts were inhabited by alien, nomadic tribes (such as the Bedouins of the Middle East and the Tartars of Central Asia), the Great Plains region was inhabited by savage and hostile Indians. And, even if white people could live there, it was believed, the pastoral life imposed on them by the environment would inevitably turn them into brigands menacing the settled, agricultural communities behind the frontier. The conflict between farmers and ranchers with their cowboys has passed into folklore; it was immortalized in a song from *Oklahoma!* (Fred Zinnemann, 1955) called "The Farmer and the Cowman."

In any case, the will to expand into new territory could not be ignored. For settlement of the West to be successful, the wilderness (or desert) metaphor had to be revised or, better still, replaced by the garden metaphor. As settlement moved further and further into the arid region, the garden was projected onto the landscape. Since the crux of the matter was water, imaginative (symbolic) conquest was expressed as the belief that new settlers brought rain with them. What the settlers actually brought with them was irrigation and the practice of dry farming. As a result, they came to believe that the Great Plains could be turned into a garden. The federal government itself actively encouraged this belief. Smith points out that according to a geographical survey begun just after the Civil War, settlement of the region caused an increase in timber due to planting; this, in turn, caused an increase in moisture in the atmosphere and added fertility to the soil. It was in the interest of everyone to propagate the idea that this land could be settled profitably. What they had to do was provide a "scientific" demonstration that rainfall was bound to increase and then reintroduce garden imagery modified for use in the short-grass country. And, in just thirty years, the region was indeed transformed into a garden. If the use of agrarian imagery was contrary to expectations based on geography, it was nevertheless true to patterns discernable in history.

Unlike the explorers of the Wild West, the farmers of the Agricultural West could be integrated into the literary traditions of popular fiction only with difficulty. The problem was public ambivalence. Because they lived in settled communities with families, schools, and churches, farmers represented order and civilization. Those who migrated to the West, however, were also suspected of rebelliousness and primitivism by the more conservative Easterners—especially by New Englanders who had long valued piety, conformity, restraint, and order. Although many Americans felt vague hostility toward urban civilization, they also felt strong desires for the prosperity, security, and comfort it provided. This ambivalence is reflected in nineteenth-century American literature. It is true that the farmer's situation in popular literature rose during the century. At the beginning of the century, farmers were usually depicted as uncouth peasants; by the end of the century, they could be presented as dignified human beings admirable for their endurance and self-reliance. This tendency to glorify farmers continued into the twentieth century. The supreme example of idealization can be seen in John Steinbeck's *The Grapes of Wrath;* the Joad family, representing the "Okies" forced off their land during the Great Depression, is nothing if not heroic in tragedy.

Until the late nineteenth century, garden imagery corresponded roughly to the external (social, economic, or political) and internal (imaginative or symbolic) reality of life for most Americans. Just the same, it became increasingly anachronistic with the rise of urban centers in the Midwest and West. Ironically, this was caused partly by the garden's success. The soil was so productive (when irrigated) and the area under cultivation so vast, that many farmers were no longer content with subsistence farming; they wanted the profits that came from exports. Consequently, they agitated for highways, canals, and railways. The growth of commerce created markets and depots. Cities such as Chicago, Cincinnati, and Louisville sprang up to serve the prosperous hinterland. And with them came the banks, the stockyards, the commodity exchanges, and other institutions characteristic of urban and industrial society back East. Eventually, the city and not the farming community set the tone for life in the West. As cities grew and the transportation system became more complex, the disparity between garden and city widened—just as it had between garden and wilderness at an earlier time. Even by the 1830s, new symbols were needed to interpret the new West that was emerging as a result of forces alien to the agrarian worldview. Of these, the most important was that hallmark of urban civilization: technology. This is what Marx calls "the machine in the garden." Steam power, in particular, made the transition from subsistence to commercial agriculture possible and even inevitable. At the time, this was not immediately apparent to many Americans.

As late as 1862, when the Homestead Act was passed, agrarianism continued to be a major factor in government planning. Many people assumed that this act, which offered free land in the West to anyone willing to move out and farm it, would result in an agricultural paradise. They assumed that by drawing off the surplus population of the urban East (which is to say, the immigrants and the poor), the entire country would benefit. These optimistic assumptions, however, did not make adequate provision for inherent flaws in the system. The government failed, for example, to guard the interests of farmers against the greed and cynicism of land speculators and railroad monopolists. Agrarianism was left behind by the forces at work in American society after the Civil War: technology and big business. "The Homestead Act failed," writes Smith, "because it was incongruous with the Industrial Revolution."[78] In other words, the garden was just as incompatible with the machine as it had been with the wilderness; the corruption of "civilization" had invaded the agricultural frontier and contaminated it. The growing gap between agrarian theory (America as the paradisian garden) and reality (America as an industrial giant) provoked much disillusionment.

> The Western farmer had been told that he was not a peasant but a peer of the realm; that his contribution to society was basic, all others derivative and even parasitic by comparison; that cities were sores on the body politic, and the merchants and bankers and factory owners who lived in them, together with their unfortunate employees, wicked and decadent. He had been told that he was compensated for any austerity in his mode of life by being sheltered against the temptations of luxury and vice, and against the ups and downs of the market. His outstanding characteristic, according to the conventional notion, was his independence, which was understood to be at once economic self-sufficiency and integrity of character.[79]

By the 1890s, this rhetoric was demonstrably false. But the use of garden imagery did not disappear. Hit hard by a depression, the farmers rebelled by establishing the populist movement. This was an activist, explicitly antiurban form of agrarianism. In the 1920s and 1930s, agrarianism was revived once again by writers and painters of the regionalist school. To this day, long after the demise of populism, regionalism, and agrarianism in any form, the garden has continued to function in the imaginative life of the people as an expression of dissatisfaction with the way things are: "When the new economic and technological forces, especially the power of steam working through river boats and locomotives, had done their work, the garden was no longer a garden. But the image of an agricultural paradise in the West, embodying group memories of an earlier, simpler and, it was believed, a happier state of society, long survived as a force in American thought and politics."[80]

Smith does more than merely describe the use of garden imagery. He also evaluates it. He claims that it has been responsible for the political and moral immaturity of Americans. His argument is based on certain assumptions about American notions of both evil and history. Given the subject of this chapter, "growing up" and "going home" as a nation, it is necessary to consider his argument. If America is a garden, and if the garden represents paradise, then America must be paradise. From this syllogism, according to Smith, Americans have argued that

> neither American man nor the American continent contained...any radical defect or principle of evil. But other men and other continents, having no share in the conditions of American virtue and happiness, were by implication unfortunate or wicked. This suggestion was strengthened by the tendency to account for any evil which threatened the garden empire by ascribing it to an alien intrusion. Since evil could not conceivably originate within the walls of the garden, it must by logical necessity come from without, and the normal strategy of defense was to build the walls higher and stop the cracks in them.[81]

It is true that American Christians have been more preoccupied with individual than collective sin. The fact remains, however, that they have been preoccupied with sin. At no time have they imagined themselves immune to sin. Even the notion of collective sin has appeared. Both Southerners and Northerners (albeit for different reasons) considered the Civil War an atoning rite of blood sacrifice. In the South, as Charles Wilson points out, special days of fasting and humiliation were set aside for collective repentance.[82] Although the tendency to blame outsiders for evil is present in the United States (as it probably is in every country), it would be facile to suggest that no other tendencies have also been present. But Smith argues specifically that this tendency is related to the use of garden imagery. I suggest, though, that he has also adopted a facile notion of the garden. It is not inconceivable for evil to originate within the garden if the garden is understood in biblical (as distinct, perhaps from classical) terms. According to the book of Genesis, after all, the primeval paradise *did* contain evil. The serpent existed *within* the garden. The Fall took place *within* Eden. In addition to the primeval garden, however, there is in the Judaeo-Christian tradition of an eschatological garden. It may refer either to Eden or the Kingdom. In the latter, there is no serpent. If America were identified as the eschatological garden, then Smith would be correct. But the evidence for this is unclear. It must be examined in the context of American notions of history.

Smith argues that seeing America as a garden, as a particular form of landscape, elevates the importance of space over time, geography over history. For him, the ability of Americans to participate effectively in history—in my terms, to "grow up"—depends on distance from a static vision such as the garden. It is, he writes "a strangely antihistorical conception, the more so for the utopian overtones that are present in most of its versions. The character of the American empire was defined not by streams of influence out of the past, not by a cultural tradition, nor by its place in a world community, but by a relation between man and nature—or rather, even more narrowly, by American man and the American West."[83] Because the early explorers and settlers in North America found a wilderness, nature without (European) culture, the importance of geography in defining and understanding America has seldom been underestimated. By the end of the nineteenth century, Americans had long been accustomed to thinking of their national experience as having been shaped primarily by the landscape itself and not by social or political institutions brought over from Europe. In the 1840s, for instance, William Gilpin adopted Alexander von Humboldt's theory about the inevitable westward flow of civilization and used it to predict the inevitable westward flow of power and influence within the United States itself. For him, history was predetermined by geography. More specifically, America's glorious destiny and the West's domination of the East were predetermined. The result of this per-

spective was an intense preoccupation with the landscape, its meaning and its symbolism. For all that, the importance of geography in
American self-understanding can be overestimated. It may have been
characteristic of Americans at the time, but it was hardly unique to
them. Romanticism had the same effect all over Europe; in Germany,
it generated a quasi-mystical ideology of *Blut und Boden.* Then, too,
other factors were involved in the formation of American identity.
North America was unique to its early explorers and settlers as
either a wilderness or a garden, but the United States of America
was unique to its early citizens as a new republic. In other words,
Americans have always thought of themselves (that is, of their
identity) as distinctive for reasons related to both geography *and*
history, both nature and culture. By considering only one end of the
continuum, Smith has oversimplified the matter and distorted the
meaning of America as a garden.

There is a great deal of evidence to suggest that Americans today,
at any rate, are concerned with their history. Hardly a town is
without some local museum, historical society, or public monument
devoted to the important people or events of local history. Moreover,
reconstructions of early settlements such as Colonial Williamsburg
are extremely popular. History, however, is about the flow of time.
That includes both past *and* future. Americans have been somewhat
less preoccupied with their past than many other nations, but they
have been much more preoccupied with their future. The American
future, however, is imagined on two levels. The immediate future is
imagined as a utopian city based on technological progress. But the
ultimate future is imagined as an eschatological city or garden. (In
the next chapter, I argue that city and garden are often used interchangeably as root metaphors[84] describing the eschatological paradise.) If anything has made the American view of history distinctive
in the modern world, it has been the impact of millenarian movements. For followers of these, the millenium may have been imminent, but it had certainly not yet arrived. America may have been
seen as the venue of the Kingdom but was by no means synonymous
with it. In fact, it was precisely their insistence on radical transformation that lent such urgency to their revivals and camp meetings. As
J. B. Jackson points out,[85] the impact of millenarianism—in both
premillenarian and postmillenarian forms—can hardly be exaggerated. Even so, Smith fails even to mention the series of "Great
Awakenings" that began in the late eighteenth century and had a
profound impact on American religiosity throughout the nineteenth

century and into the twentieth. It is true that some Americans in recent times have succumbed to a form of "realized eschatology" that comes perilously close to equating the status quo with the Kingdom, but others have been influenced by more traditional forms of "realized eschatology" according to which the Kingdom is present only in some anticipatory or hidden sense for those with eyes to see, as it were, and ears to hear. The use of garden imagery does not necessarily mean that Americans see their nation as an island of timeless perfection in a sea of historical turmoil (no matter how much they would like that); it may mean that they see it as a mediation between the primeval paradise and the eschatological paradise. Whatever others may think of them, I suggest, Americans think of themselves as a people moving between the paradise of primeval origin and that of eschatological destiny. In short, they see themselves as a people in the process of "growing up" and "going home."

Since *The Wizard* is a movie, we should remember that the frontier has evolved historically as a specifically visual symbolic landscape. In the early 1800s, a decisive transformation took place. J. B. Jackson described it brilliantly. Not only did Americans begin to see their landscape in a new way, the landscape itself was renovated accordingly. For Jackson, this was the final and most spectacular attempt ever made at creating a mundane order in harmony with a cosmic order. But the process had begun much earlier. In the middle of the previous century, a cultural revolution had taken shape in America. Its origin lay in two seemingly opposing sources: the revolution in science begun by Isaac Newton and the revolution in religion begun by Jonathan Edwards. The former was based on a rationalistic, even mechanistic, worldview and expressed in terms of mathematics and optics. The latter was based on a dynamic, even fervent, worldview and expressed as evangelical revivalism. Coming together in the decades preceding the War of Independence, they produced a new way of understanding both space and time.

In the seventeenth century, the landscape of Europe was being transformed by a new intellectual order. Newton and Copernicus had provided a new cosmology. And European rulers, realizing the ways in which this cosmology could be used to support their political aspirations, were eager to give it visual expression in their palaces and formal gardens. The most obvious example of this was Versailles where geometrically arranged buildings and gardens converged on the "Sun King's" bedroom. By the end of the next century—at the very time when the United States was emerging as a new nation—it had begun to transform the American landscape as well. In fact, it was in America that the new order was most dramatically and thoroughly expressed. There, "it inspired a society based on the predictable and orderly movements of independent, equal individuals, each occupying a portion of the infinite, undifferentiated space made visible in the National Land Survey of 1785."[86]

The effect could be seen everywhere: gardens, street grids, churches, homes, and even farms. This was most obvious in the layouts designed for Manhattan and Washington in the East. But it was most imposing in the West. Early travelers there commented on the isolation of homes on the frontier and the absence of large towns with their traditional points of reference (such as steeples, taverns, clusters of houses, and passersby). They were deeply aware that space on the frontier was relatively undifferentiated over vast areas. These things, however, were hardly new in the American experience. What was new was the grid layout of the new territory. Land was surveyed, mapped, and sold with geometric precision. In the East, a town might grow up at the intersection of two rivers; in the West, it might grow up at the intersection of two lines on the grid. The full visual impact could not be fully appreciated until the advent of commercial aviation, of course, but anyone could see that straight lines defined the landscape and provided the only visual points of reference. Stretching as far as the eye could see, they suggested space without limit. In effect, they created a landscape of openness to infinity. To the extent that anything associated with infinity is sacred, the frontier was sacred space. As Jackson points out, however, it was sacred in another way as well.

Because the scientific contribution to the American landscape—its rational, pragmatic, rectilinear, and abstract quality—has been widely recognized, there is no need to dwell on it here. The contribution of religion, however, has not yet been as widely recognized. Newton himself was a deeply religious man. He was particularly interested in prophecy and symbolism. For him, God was everywhere. Consequently, it was the state of individuals, not their location, that affected their access to God. This was an idea that anticipated the rise of evangelical religion in the next century. Jackson shows how the Great Awakening, which originated with the preaching of Jonathan Edwards, encouraged Americans to think of the landscape in terms of eternity (as they already had in terms of Eden) and not merely in terms of the physical landscape known to history.

In the early nineteenth century, the colonies were still organized according to traditional (which is to say, medieval Christian) notions of sacred space and time. Space, for example, was organized in centripetal and hierarchical fashion. Seating arrangements at church, plots of land in the graveyard, and positions in civic processions all reflected social status or official rank. Similarly, time was organized into a "fixed sequence of events of increasing sanctity" or "a stately procession of events leading to a dramatic climax."[87] This microcosmic version of the Ptolemaic universe was suddenly shattered by the Great Awakening. Conversion was no longer seen as a gradual, progressive movement; for evangelicals—and they were the most dynamic people in the churches at that time—conversion was a sudden irruption of the Holy Spirit into everyday life. As a result, religion came to be expressed in new ways. The reorganization of spiritual life was in due course reflected in the order of worship. Spontaneity was now expected; no one, therefore, really knew what came next. There were also changes in the notion of sacred space. In fact, the new movement abolished the whole idea that there could be different kinds of space, each with its own level of sanctity. "It decreed that all spaces— whether in the church or elsewhere—were of equal value, undifferentiated and even interchangeable."[88] For traditionalists, of course, this presented several problems. In the first place, it meant that the church, or congregation, was no longer firmly identified with a legally defined and ritually consecrated space. Itinerant preachers, often uninvited, came from beyond the community to conduct new-style worship services. Hierarchical seating arrangements were abandoned. Services were held outdoors or in private houses. And they were held at odd hours. Eventually, sects formed and built new churches far from the established ones, as if dissociating themselves from the old spatial, as well as spiritual, order. By the end of the eighteenth century, then, the new intellectual and spiritual order was being translated into concrete terms throughout the older eastern colonies. In the nineteenth century, though, this was done even more dramatically on the western frontier where older traditions (apart from those of the Indians) had never been firmly established in the first place. The Midwest was characterized by intense individualism, intense otherworldliness, and intense "concern for the significant instant."[89] This was a landscape of itinerant preachers and peddlers of religious tracts. It was a landscape of revivals and camp meetings.[90] It was, in short, the spiritual landscape of millenarians who expected the Rapture at any moment. Just as the frontier's geometrical regularity connoted openness to infinity, therefore, its millenarian expectancy also connoted openness to eternity. In this sense, Jonathan Edwards is to sacred time as Issac Newton is to sacred space.

Jackson links this spiritual restlessness with more mundane (but not unrelated) forms of restlessness. Life on the frontier, he suggests, was characterized primarily by transience. Although he has not made an adequate distinction between wilderness and frontier, he is correct in arguing that wagon trains frequently rolled across the frontier. Nevertheless, their origin was always a city such as St. Louis and their destination was always the wilderness. It is true as well that farmers often pulled up stakes to start over again further west. In doing so, they left the frontier and moved off into what was still wilderness. It is not true, however, that cattle drives were characteristic of life on the frontier; on the contrary, they were characteristic of life in the wilderness. The "cowboys" needed wilderness (unsettled land) for their livestock and were constantly at odds with the frontier farmers whose land was cultivated and, therefore, unavailable for grazing or even passage. Unlike the wilderness, the frontier was, by definition, within the realm of "civilization." But it was the boundary region marking the transition between sophisticated life in the cities or small towns and primitive life in the bush or on the range, between an economy based on commerce or industry and one based on hunting, fishing, or herding. This boundary was not always easy to discern, of course, because what was wilderness one day often became frontier the next. But Jackson's point is not to be dismissed. The frontier was settled—that is, not transient—as a geographical region, but was very transient as a historical episode because it was transformed into "civilization" almost as quickly as wilderness was transformed into frontier. The classic antagonism between farmers and ranchers was almost always settled in favor of the former. To the nation as a whole, they came to represent order, stability, family, and community; they were the American *future* as imagined at a critical moment in the American *past*. At the same time, the antagonism between both of these and the bankers or railroad tycoons spelled the end of frontier life. In the collective memory, the frontier is a happy idyll of rural freedom, independence, closeness to nature, and unlimited possibilities symbolized by the uninterrupted horizon and the immense sky. It could exist only as a transient stage in American history, but it acquired an eternal place in the American imagination. Therefore, it can be understood better in the context of myth than of history.

If communities need myths to serve as foci for collective identity, and if the frontier myth has served the American community well in this capacity, then it is really no wonder that a new frontier myth has been added to the national repertoire. The astral frontier of "Star Trek" (NBC, 1966-1969) has generated what has been called "the most sizable cult in the history of American television."[91] At the beginning of each episode, we are told that explorers on the starship *Enterprise* "boldly go where no man has gone before." The show has recently been revived (substituting gender-inclusive language) both on television as "Star Trek: The Next Generation" and in a series of movies such as *Star Trek: The Motion Picture* (Robert Wise, 1979), *Star Trek II: The Wrath of Khan* (Nicholas Meyer, 1982), *Star Trek III: The Search for Spock* (Leonard Nimoy, 1984), and *Star Trek IV: The Voyage Home* (Leonard Nimoy, 1986). Even after the Challenger disaster, Americans have not abandoned their wish to continue the space program that has already produced hauntingly beautiful photographs from the arid surface of Mars—which looks notably similar to deserts in the wilderness of New Mexico and Arizona—and just beyond the rings of Saturn. The real exploration of outer space has a profound symbolic value in addition to any practical value it may have; planting the American flag on some remote world is a matter of emotional as well as scientific, political, or even military importance. America has always been the New World. From the beginning, therefore, Americans have been explorers of unknown territory.

For Americans, the frontier is also about "starting over again." And this, of course, is what lies at the heart of American identity. The Republic, after all, was founded as a new beginning for the old and tired civilization of Europe. As the basic paradigm for all specifically American attempts to "start over again," the frontier is both the American *future* and the American *past.* Even more important, however, is the link with millenarian expectations of "starting over again." And it could be argued that these, too, lie somewhere near the heart of American identity. The Puritans, for example, established a model of society intended to translate the Reformation (itself an attempt to "start over again") into concrete reality. The frontier, then, has been associated with the future in two senses: mundane and cosmic, immediate and ultimate, spatial and infinite, temporal and eternal. In short, the frontier has been associated with both a historical future and an eschatological one. (The latter is associated in turn, moreover, with the primeval past.) I suggest that "starting over again" refers to both "growing up" and "going home." Paradoxically, then, "quest" (the domifugal motif associated with "growing up") and "home" (the domicentric motif associated with "going home") are linked on the frontier. This is what gives this symbolic landscape its tremendously evocative power. In fact, the official "closing" of the frontier in 1898 may have actually intensified the need to recapture it and reexperience it symbolically (or mythically).

Of interest here is not what the pioneer farmers actually thought and felt about the frontier, but what the nation has thought and felt about it ever since. Because America began as the transformation of wilderness into frontier (and because the frontier had always been settled first by farmers), images of the happy garden, the rural paradise, have always been very popular. When *The Wizard* came out in 1939, however, mass migrations from country to city were still in progress. One year later, *The Grapes of Wrath* (John Ford, 1940) celebrated or eulogized the "Okies" who fled from the "dust bowl" to California. By the following year, millions of Americans were leaving their farms and small towns to work in the burgeoning war plants located in cities. America was rapidly becoming a heavily urbanized and industrialized nation. But the agricultural frontier had been celebrated for so long and was so recent historically that the ideal landscape could still be represented as a farm.

To appreciate the impact of *The Wizard*, we must recall that it celebrates a farm in Kansas. Would a farm in Pennsylvania, Georgia, North Dakota, or California have had the same impact? There is no way of knowing. Every farm is a garden on the ecological frontier; it mediates between wilderness (nature) and civilization (culture). But a Kansas farm is also located on the American frontier; it also mediates between oppositions in both time and space. The settlement of territories such as Kansas had really "taken off" with the proliferation of railways just after the Civil War; this was almost exactly midway between the War of Independence and the present (that is, 1939). Besides, Kansas lies precisely at the geographical center of the country; it is midway between East and West, North and South. This region symbolically transcends time and space, history and geography. It is (to use a metaphor drawn directly from *The Wizard*) the eye of the storm, the calm center around which national life swirls. This landscape belongs to none of the major sources of power. Moreover, it is visually "empty." Consequently, it can be filled with the dreams of all Americans. As "Kansas," the reality of America, a fragmented collection of rival regions, is seen as an ideal unity held together by a shared image of the agricultural frontier. It is fitting, therefore, that the Wizard should have Kansas in mind when he thinks of returning "to the land of E Pluribus Unum." In the decades since 1939, images of the frontier garden have continued to appear in such movie classics as *Oklahoma!* and television shows such as "Little House on the Prairie" (NBC 1974-1982) and even "The Waltons" (CBS 1973-1981).[92]

*

Because the most favored symbolic landscape in *The Wizard* is a frontier farm, the movie overtly supports an agrarian worldview. If agrarianism was still prevalent in 1939, however, it is no longer. And yet *The Wizard* is probably more popular now than it ever was. How can we explain the paradox of a heavily urbanized and industrialized nation continuing to honor agrarian imagery? Why is the frontier farm still a familiar symbolic landscape of America? Why is the garden still a meaningful ecological image? Marx offers a possible explanation. He points out that American identity was shaped in the late nineteenth and early twentieth centuries not by the replacement of garden by city but by the continuing conflict between garden and city. This conflict generates and has been generated by ambivalence. As a mediation between nature and culture, a compromise between the city and the wilderness, the garden perfectly expresses that ambivalence. Being a literary historian, Marx cites evidence from the tradition of pastoralism. Anthropologists use the term "pastoralism" with specific reference to an economy based on animal husbandry; technically speaking, therefore, only those who raise sheep, goats, cattle, or other livestock are pastoralists. Marx, however, uses the term in its more general, literary sense. It refers to a poetic tradition featuring nostalgic fantasies of rustic simplicity and primeval innocence in a bucolic dreamland; whatever the imagery—pastoral or agricultural—the context is always rural. For all intents and purposes, pastoralism is a literary and artistic expression of agrarianism.

The origin of pastoralism as a literary mode is found in the *Eclogues* of Virgil.[93] In the first eclogue, Virgil comments on the problems caused when the Roman government expropriated the property of small landholders to reward military veterans for their services to the state. It is set in the countryside of Arcadia. Two shepherds are introduced. Tityrus has successfully petitioned a friend in Rome for the return of his land. Meliboeus, however, has been evicted. He comes by with his herd and openly envies Tityrus for living a life of ease and tranquility while he, and so many others, have succumbed to exile and impoverishment. Virgil presents us with more than a daydream of bucolic bliss. No sooner does he describe the idyllic landscape of Arcadia (represented by Tityrus) than he alerts readers to the alien and threatening world (represented by Meliboeus) encroaching upon it. From what Meliboeus says,

> we are made aware that the immediate setting, with its tender feeling and contentment, is an oasis. The very principle of natural fecundity is threatened (he has been forced to abandon his newborn kids). What is out there, from the reader's point of view, is a world like the one he inhabits; it contains great cities like Rome, organized power, authority, restraint, suffering, and disorder. We are made to feel that the rural myth is threatened by an incursion of history. The state of mind of Meliboeus—we should call it alienation nowadays—brings a counter-vailing force to bear on the pastoral ideal.[94]

Nevertheless, the whole thrust of the poem is toward a restoration of that pastoral ideal that had been established in the introduction. The eclogue thus brings together nostalgia for a happier time in the past, dismay over problems in the present, and hope for a happier time in the future. Of more immediate concern, however, is the fact that struggle in the present is associated with a conflict between nature and culture. Nature is represented by wilderness (too much nature) and culture by the city (too much culture). Lying happily under his tree and playing his flute, Tityrus enjoys the ideal way of life celebrated by pastoralism: midway between the primitive way forced on poor Meliboeus and the sophisticated way of his friend in Rome. The contrast between the primitive and the pastoral is telling.

> Both seem to originate in a recoil from the pain and responsibility of life in a complex civilization—the familiar impulse to withdraw from the city, locus of power and politics, into nature. The difference is that the primitivist hero keeps going, as it were, so that eventually he locates value as far as possible, in space or time or both, from organized society; the shepherd, on the other hand, seeks a resolution of the conflict between the opposed worlds of nature and art....In the first eclogue, nothing makes the mediating character of the pastoral ideal so clear as the spatial symbolism in which it is expressed. The good place is a lovely green hollow. To arrive at this haven, it is necessary to move away from Rome in the direction of nature. But the centrifugal motion stops far short of unimproved, raw, nature.[95]

For Marx, Virgil has described the prototypical "middle landscape." This is the landscape that symbolically mediates between two equally

undesirable extremes. It is, in fact, a frontier: on one side is civilization (Rome); on the other side is wilderness (marshland). Here,
Tityrus is spared from anxieties associated with the former and
deprivations of the latter. He is free from both the repressive features
of unmediated culture and the chaos of unmediated nature. Plainly,
he has the best of both worlds. In just a few lines, then, Virgil sums
up the benefits to be sought in a pastoral retreat such as Arcadia:
peace, leisure, freedom, and abundance. The key to bucolic bliss is
integration of the individual into the natural environment. Like the
Confucian sages portrayed in Chinese landscape paintings, Tityrus
enjoys a serene partnership with nature; he has no need to dominate
or conquer it.

> In the pastoral economy, nature supplies most of the herdsman's needs
> and, even better, nature does virtually all of the work. A similar accom-
> modation with the landscape is the basis for the herdsman's less
> tangible satisfactions: the woods "echo back" the notes of his pipe. It is
> as if the consciousness of the musician shared a principle of order with
> the landscape and, indeed, the external universe. The echo, a recurrent
> device in pastoral, is another metaphor of reciprocity. It evokes that
> sense of relatedness between man and not-man which lends a metaphy-
> sical aspect to the mode.[96]

In short, Arcadia is characterized by the unity and wholeness
associated with Eden and so many other versions of paradise. Its
popularity in America was inevitable. The European explorers and
colonists were profoundly affected by the landscape of North
America. According to Marx, however, their impressions were not
entirely spontaneous; they were conditioned by expectations based
on the pastoral traditions of Renaissance Europe.

> The pastoral ideal has been used to define the meaning of America
> ever since the age of discovery, and it has not yet lost its hold upon the
> native imagination. The reason is clear enough. The ruling motive of
> the good shepherd, leading figure of the classic Virgillian mode, was to
> withdraw from the great world and begin a new life in a fresh, green,
> landscape. And now here was a virgin continent! Inevitably, the Euro-
> pean mind was dazzled by the prospect. With an unspoiled hemisphere
> in view, it seemed that mankind actually might realize what had been
> thought a poetic fantasy.[97]

But the appeal of pastoral imagery has been used more recently to
ease the transition from a rural and agricultural nation to an urban
and industrial one. More specifically, it has become a bridge between

rural past and urban present, agrarian ideal and industrial reality, garden and machine. According to Marx, however, there are two versions of the pastoral mode. When pastoralism degenerates into escapism and nostalgia,[98] it turns into what he calls "popular and sentimental pastoralism."[99]

> Evidently, it is generated by an urge to withdraw from civilization's growing power and complexity. What is attractive in primitivism is the felicity represented by an image of a natural landscape, a terrain either unspoiled or, if cultivated, rural. Movement toward such a symbolic landscape also may be understood as movement away from an "artificial" world, a world identified with "art," using this word in its broadest sense to mean the disciplined habits of mind, or arts developed by organized communities. In other words, this impulse gives rise to a symbolic motion away from centers of civilization toward their opposite, nature, away from sophistication toward simplicity, or, to introduce the cardinal metaphor of the literary mode, away from the city toward the country. When this impulse is unchecked, the result is a simple-minded wishfulness, a romantic perversion of thought and feeling.[100]

Popular and sentimental pastoralism" may be anachronistic, but, "imaginative and complex pastoralism" is not. It is as relevant in modern America, argues Marx, as it was in ancient Rome. Unlike the popular version, it acknowledges and even focuses attention on the conflict between nature and culture. Just as Virgil commented on policies of the Roman state, American pastoralists have commented on social and economic problems brought on by urbanization and industrialization. Both classical and modern pastoralism not only acknowledge but emphasize the inadequacy of Arcadia as a vision of the ideal and the intervention of reality as a check against bucolic fantasies. Although this mode of pastoralism begins with the need to withdraw from the social and cultural order, it invariably ends with rejection of escapism. Nostalgic reveries in the garden are disrupted or shattered by harsh reminders of the machine. "Most literary works called pastorals—at least those substantial enough to retain our interest—do not finally permit us to come away with anything like the simple, affirmative attitude we adopt toward pleasing rural scenery. In one way or another, if only by virtue of the unmistakable sophistication with which they are composed, these works manage to qualify, or call into question, or bring irony to bear against the illusion of peace and harmony in a green pasture."[101]

Traditionally, the garden has been the symbol of reconciliation between nature (wilderness) and culture (civilization); it is, after all, nature cultivated. Marx correctly points out, however, that the garden has been pushed to the margins of American life. Agribusiness has made the yeoman farmer anachronistic. Technology has made direct contact with the soil unnecessary for the vast majority living in cities. Produce has been contaminated by the chemicals in pesticides and fertilizers. The wilderness itself has been polluted by acid rain and industrial waste. In short, nature and culture are locked in mortal combat; the garden is no longer a symbol of mediation between nature and culture in everyday life. Does that mean it has no symbolic value? For Marx, that is precisely what it means. Although the modern American hero, alienated from an urban and industrial world, "pays tribute to the image of a green landscape, it is likely to be ironic and bitter. The resolutions of our pastoral fables are unsatisfactory because the old symbol of reconciliation is obsolete."[102] But is it? From his normative point of view, Marx can argue that the garden should be obsolete. And many writers agree with him.[103] But from a phenomenological point of view, it would seem that Marx has over-stated his case. The garden is not obsolete. As evidence, I would point not only to the continuing popularity of an ecological symbol (the frontier in theme parks, movies, and television) and to suburban living but also to the growing popularity of gardening itself. In a recent cover story for *Time*, Nancy Gibbs observed that

> suddenly it seems as though all around the country people are going to any length to find their garden: to read about it, visit it and, if at all possible, create it. Mailboxes bulge with gardening catalogs, groceries grow on windowsills, cranes hoist trees onto city rooftops. From coast to coast, nursery owners say their business has doubled. Even baby boomers who did not have the remotest interest in the subject two years ago now rattle off the Latin names of their plants and comb suburban garden stores for just the right style of Japanese weed whipper. Wrestling with the wilderness is an old American sport, turning forests into arbors, fields into farms. Yet this desire to plant something is reaching into places and lives that defy fertility. Throughout the most savage reaches of New York's inner city, community gardeners are transforming burned-out lots into verdant sanctuaries. Across the dry plains of the Midwest, botanists are finding plenty of volunteers to help them reclaim the prairies and replant the wildflowers that belong there.[104]

Most Americans live in cities and depend on their gardens for aesthetic pleasure. But what is the basis for this aesthetic pleasure? Why is it considered aesthetically satisying, even de rigueur, to clutter a small apartment living room with potted plants? Why is it considered aesthetically appropriate to place potted grass, shrubs, vines, and even trees on a terrace thirty floors above the city street? Why, indeed, have the garden-related industries (nurseries to provide the plants; boutiques to provide the tools, equipment, and accessories; specialized periodicals for "serious" gardeners; do-it-yourself books and television shows for novices) become so profitable? And why are Americans from such a variety of backgrounds taking up this hobby?

> Amid so much activity, the stereotypes no longer fit. Through the 1970s, the archetypal gardener was over fifty and had time and money to spare: a smug matron with impeccable calceolarias, an eccentric rosarian, a spinster growing herbs. But now, says the National Gardening Association, 78 percent of America's households garden, and all the recent surveys suggest that the most fervent converts are between thirty and forty-nine and still evenly divided between men and women....The baby boomers get much of the attention because they accounted for half of the record $17.5 billion that was spent last year on things horticultural....The yuppies quickly master the rituals and floral lore, swap compost recipes at dinner parties. Mulching has become elvator talk.[105]

When Gibbs asked people why they spent so much time and energy on their gardens, Oscar de la Renta replied: "You may plan something you will never see yourself....A garden gives you a sense of continuity." Barbara Tuchman observed: "It says that everything is fine in the midst of chaos and bewilderment." Why should it be surprising that people who feel a need to create order and transcend the transience of everyday life in a rapidly changing world would find gardening an ideal hobby? Why should it be surprising to learn that there is an American Bamboo Society and a Cactus and Succulent Society or that 800 books on gardening are currently in print? No wonder Gibbs can report that "garden stores are doing a land-office business in beneficial nematodes, antislug mulch and dozens of bio-organic plant boosters. The ranks of converts grow by the day."[106] Indeed, even the readers of *GQ*, a men's fashion magazine, can be expected to take up the hoe. Noting that "the new world into which Europeans blundered was as close to the Garden of Eden as any place they might have imagined," James Kunstler argues that gardening, far from being a "sissy pastime," is profoundly gratifying: "And when the summer sun rides low on the horizon, and the shadows are long, and I, freshly showered and with a strong drink in hand, stroll among the burgeoning life of my garden, I begin to understand what it means to be happy."[107]

The garden no longer functions as a symbol of the way things are, to be sure, but it may serve as a symbol of the way things once were and the way things may be once again. *The Wizard* contains more than passing references to both garden and machine. All the same, it does not fit neatly into either of Marx's categories. It cannot be identified precisely with the unresolved conflict of "imaginative and complex pastoralism" because it indicates an ultimate return to rural life (represented by the farm in Kansas). On the other hand, it cannot be dismissed as the spurious nostalgia of "popular and sentimental pastoralism" because it overtly acknowledges the competing attraction of urban life (represented by the Emerald City). According to Marx, it must either reject nostalgia for a lost golden age or affirm it. Being a literary historian, his categories represent good art and bad art.[108] If *The Wizard* were in the former category, Dorothy would not return to Kansas; if it were in the latter category, however, Dorothy would not have been so sorry to leave the Emerald City. But what if *The Wizard* is neither good nor bad art? What if, as I have suggested, it is myth (or like myth)? In that case, the imagery representing garden (farm) and machine (city) would form a statement about collective identity (national origin and destiny) not merely to acknowledge paradox and contradiction but to transcend them.

*

Although Marx writes mainly about literature, he occasionally discusses painting. He does so, however, in terms of literary pastoralism. Such is the case in his reflections on Charles Sheeler's *American Landscape* (1930). In this industrial landscape, the natural world has been almost entirely obliterated. Not a blade of grass, not a wisp of cloud, not a speck of dirt can be seen. Lost in the chaos of geometric forms is a solitary man. But Marx points out that the bleakness is softened or "pastoralized." Instead of being the scene of frenzied activity and relentless motion, it is a scene of almost unnatural repose and eerie stillness. In this way, he suggests, Americans have refused to take seriously the reality of industrialization and urbanization. "Even those Americans who acknowledge the facts and understand the fables," he writes, "seem to cling, after their fashion, to the pastoral hope. . . . By superimposing order, peace, and harmony upon our modern chaos, Sheeler represents the anomalous blend of illusion and reality in the American consciousness."[109] This painting does not fit neatly into Marx's categories. Because it acknowledges modernity (ways in which the garden is transformed by the machine), it is more like "imaginative and complex" than "popular and sentimental" pastoralism. In a literal sense, to be sure, the garden disappears. The landscape is no longer an idealized landscape (or "machine"). But because the garden reappears as the underlying pattern, he argues, it is a denial of modernity. It therefore represents the same perverse mentality as "popular and sentimental" pastoralism only in a somewhat more sophisticated modality. On the other hand, neither of these categories really does justice to Sheeler's painting. More important, these categories would prevent Marx from doing justice to *The Wizard.* He has adopted a rigid schema that does not allow him to see the possibility that other modalities of pastoralism may be operating in American culture. A closer look at the history of American painting indicates the existence of at least one other. I refer here to regionalism, a school of art that flourished in the 1930s, and more specifically to Grant Wood, its founder and chief representative. Unlike the creators of "popular and sentimental" pastoralism, Wood acknowleded the machine's presence in the garden. But unlike the creators of "imaginative and complex" pastoralism, he proposed a solution to the conflict between them. This solution was an ultimate one, though, and not an immediate one. It could be realized fully only beyond the flux of time, or history. Wood produced what I call "mythic" pastoralism. Like myth, its point of departure is in a negation of the present: things are not now as they should be. (Cosmogonic myths explain how things came to be as they are; eschatological myths explain how things will be. In some traditions, such as the biblical one, the two merge: things will be at the End as they were in the Beginning.) Sheeler really did pastoralize an industrial landscape; he also created a mythic landscape in which the chaotic transience of everyday life is transformed by the static order of eternity. But he was not directly tied to a tradition of myth. Wood, his contemporary, was. He gave expression to what Smith calls the "myth of the garden." And his work reveals an outlook strikingly similiar to that which can be discerned in *The Wizard.*

Wood was one of the most popular artists of his time. His work was not only familiar (and often despised) by the art world, it was also familiar (and often admired) by the general public. He was, in many ways, the Andrew Wyeth of his generation. Even now, it would be difficult to find a book on American art (to say nothing of American painting) that does not reproduce his best-known work: *American*

Gothic.[110] And Wood's landscape paintings, have been selling well as prints for over half a century. He created a visual lexicon of America, an iconography of the American landscape, that has entered the collective consciousness of the nation. "His idyllic landscapes," according to Wanda M. Corn, "spoke reassuringly of peace and plenty; his figurative paintings made common life in rural and small-town America seem important and worthwhile."[111] For that reason alone (and not because of his stature among either artists or art historians), it is worth noting any visual links between his work and *The Wizard.*

The definitive book on Wood has been written by James Dennis. He explicitly places Wood's landscape paintings in the context of myth. More specifically, he argues that Wood gave visual expression to the "agrarian myth." "Unique in American painting, these inventive idylls can nonetheless be identified with an extended public longing for the bucolic, a longing that has attained mythic proportions in both popular literature and political rhetoric since Thomas Jefferson.... Since colonial times, as the United States was being transformed by the machine from a rural to an urban nation, Americans have persistently envisioned a land of self-sufficiency, a great green garden of farms tended by noble yeomen and their families."[112]

Along with his colleagues, John Steuart Curry and Thomas Hart Benton, Wood was motivated by a desire to create an authentically American form of art. On that basis, they rejected the New York art world that was heavily dependent on European movements and focused attention on the rural landscape of Midwestern America. They rejected not only the foreign but also the modern (which is to say, urbanization and industrialization). In doing so, however, they did not invent a new way of thinking or seeing; on the contrary, they adopted the agrarian traditions that had been part of American life since the colonial period and the populist rhetoric that had appealed to farmers since the late nineteenth century.

American farmers, for several generations a majority of the population, inherited the belief that they had a fundamental and indeed natural right to deferential treatment from all other sectors of society, an attitude supported by a century-old pastoral tradition. A modern equivalent of the classical Arcadian shepherd of Virgilian fame, the noble tiller of the soil, in cultivating God's earth, had acquired free title to his own plot of land in an Edenic garden of the world. Along with this incomparable privilege, went the attributes of the ideal man: total honesty, perfect health, absolute virtue, and permanent happiness.[113]

Agrarian imagery had never coincided perfectly with the reality of everyday life. The gulf between the real and the ideal widened dramatically with the social and economic chaos of the Great Depression, but it had been evident even during the depression of the 1890s. By that time, it was clear that subsistence farmers (glorified for generations as "yeomen") were being replaced by commercial farmers who raised cash crops by applying industrial techniques to agriculture. (In the South, of course, the plantation system had always operated on a commercial basis.) Nevertheless, the symbolic ideal continued to generate political force. As Richard Hofstadter shows,[114] the populists began as a movement of those who saw themselves as innocent victims of the urban and industrial world. Their suffering was due to a conspiracy of Eastern financiers and capitalists. At first, they sought government protection (especially legislation against immigration and impersonal corporate interests). By the turn of the century, twenty years of prosperity had turned farmers into a powerful lobby of technically trained, conservative entrepreneurs; their political activism paid off in terms of federal assistance. Even so, populist resentment persisted. When hard times returned in the 1920s and 1930s, attacks on urban corruption and industrial capitalism emerged once more. Now, though, the attack focused not on specific practices but on the entire urban way of life that rewarded speculation rather than honest labor. It was in this context, Dennis points out, that regionalism developed as an art movement. Wood and his colleagues believed that just as farmers should preserve their agrarian ideals from corruption by the forces of urbanization and industrialization dictated by Eastern bankers and politicans, artists should preserve their authenticity from corruption by the forces of taste and style dictated by Eastern (and even European) academics. Like farmers, artists should be self-reliant; by breaking with the established art world dominated (economically as well as stylistically) by Europe, the regionalists hoped to create a vibrant artistic tradition that expressed the distinctive ethos of America. "In the content as well as the form of his art," writes Dennis, "Grant Wood realized his aspiration of regionalism with national relevance, transcending the bounds of an aesthetic experience to garner the broad-based appeal of a mass-culture myth."[115]

In his landscape paintings, as in his allegorical works,[116] Wood pays homage to the perpetual fecundity of the land. Unlike the peasants who suffer nobly in paintings by Jean-François Millet or even the farmers who struggle heroically against titanic natural forces in those of Curry, the farmers in Wood's paintings placidly and effortlessly dominate the land. In *Spring Turning* (1936) and *Spring in the Country* (1941), for example, we see farmers directing their teams of horses over the low-rising hills as they "turn the sod of flawless fields, slowly cutting a neat and orderly edge between last year's turf and this year's furrow. No harm may come to this luxurious land of soft sounds, diffused sunlight, and quiet shadows as long as the sturdy yeoman retraces his footsteps season by season, turning his hand to the harmonious convergence of nature and man's ability to make rewarding use of it. There is no hint here that any alien force of advancing civilization or any arbitrary act of temperamental nature could tilt this perfect balance."[117]

Wood's attitude toward nature is affirming and even celebratory. Unlike Curry, he usually presents only the benign aspects of nature. In fact, as Corn points out, relations between the human community and nature are intimate in every sense of the word.

> Mingling eroticism with ecstasy, Wood made the relationship between the farmer and mother earth into a Wagnerian love duet. While mother earth is always the principal protagonist, overwhelming the farmer in scale and vitality, she is always loving and benevolent. In Wood's idyllic farmscapes, man lives in complete harmony with nature; he is the earth's caretaker, coaxing her into abundance, bringing coherence and beauty to her surfaces. Wood's way of describing the earth's goodness and fertility is an obvious one; he turned the landscape into a gigantic reclining goddess, anthropomorphizing the contours of fields and hills so that they look like rounded thighs, bulging breasts, and pregnant bellies, all of them swelling and breathing with sexual fullness.[118]

The land has been converted into a verdant garden where human beings are thoroughly at home. We are as far removed from the wilderness as we are in the city itself. Here, though, nature has been pacified and turned into ornamental patterns rather than obliterated and violently distorted. Wood has transformed the fields and meadows of the American Midwest into those of the biblical Eden or the classical Arcadia. They are pervaded by the preternatural stillness and perfection of eternity. This world knows nothing of the hardships involved in tilling the soil (such as clearing the land), the sudden disasters brought on by a capricious nature (droughts, floods, insects, or storms), or the sinister conspiracies promoted by human institutions (mortgages, foreclosures, or fluctuating markets).[119]

Wood's attitude toward culture (modern American civilization) is much more complex. Although he openly affirms tradition, he seems to negate modernity. In most of his mature landscapes (those done after 1930), for example, he makes few, if any, references to technology. Nowhere to be found are factories and smokestacks, railways or tractors. The garden does not seem dominated by the machine.[120] But the mere absence of technology does not mean the absence of modernity itself. As Dennis explains, Wood's landscape paintings include implicit references to the machine. Sometimes, the implied presence of technology is distinctly utopian. Unlike the earliest American farmers who cleared small and irregular patches of land suitable for subsistence farming, modern farmers cleared large and regular fields suitable for commercial farming. The heartland was divided up arbitrarily by surveyors into geometric patterns imposed on the natural forms of hills and rivers. This is what dominates the Woodian landscape. It clearly indicates agriculture on a massive scale made possible only by the advanced technology (mass production), bureaucracy (government funding), and trade (an international market) of an industrialized society.

> Yet tiny figures of farmers with hand plows and teams patiently labor away in the midst of a boundless counterforce of mechanized productivity, almost lost in the enormity of it all. This discrepancy between myth-turned-reality and pure myth occurs in most of Grant Wood's farmscapes, each picture integrating a modern pastoralism with a traditional agrarianism. The agrarian myth presupposes the fixed symbol of a yeoman tending his family farm by hand on a small-scale, subsistence level in complete harmony with his natural environment. But in Wood's pictures, the isolated farmer figures, which recall those noble husbandmen and perform symbolically as a vestige of the agrarian myth, are preserved in an idealized farmscape whose pastoral dimension has acquired a twentieth-century scale through the counterforce of modernization.[121]

Implicitly, if not explicitly, the machine is in the garden and making it thrive. Modernity is present not only in content, however, but also in form. Wood's subject matter may owe nothing to the twentieth century, but his style surely does. It is based on what was then—in the 1930s—the height of modernity. "In evolving a style of artificial geometries, clean surfaces, and relentless patterns," writes Corn, "he was like the Art Deco decorators of his day."[122] This new aesthetic originated in the industrial need to reduce air resistance on surfaces of cars, ships and airplanes but eventually came to glorify the machine by symbolizing speed, efficiency, progress, and modernity itself. In the context of a massive depression, art deco was openly and defiantly utopian. As Dennis point out, however, the simplification and "streamlining" of art deco is also characteristic of Wood's style.

> By 1930, Grant Wood referred to the decorative in his paintings as synonymous with design. At that point, his farm landscapes, built on a superstructure of diagonals, matured as compositions of streamlined forms accented with geometrically patterned textures and rounded details that repeated the dominant contours. Prefiguring the curving hoods and fenders characteristic of automobile styles of the last half of the 1930s, the sloping lines and elongated, sometimes tapered, shapes of Wood's farmscapes, aerodynamic in appearance, confirm an aesthetic analogy between his pictorial process of descriptive abstraction and current industrial design. The visual dynamics of his farmscapes are effortlessly expressive of a machine-driven speed unimaginable to nineteenth-century landscape painters.[123]

Paradoxically, then, Wood used a style based on industrial design to express his vision of the traditional agrarian paradise. Actually, he is the perfect analogue of Sheeler. They have both done precisely the same thing although each starts from the opposite direction. Sheeler has projected the agrarian vision onto an industrial landscape, revealing the garden in the machine; knowingly or unknowingly, Wood has projected the industrial vision onto an agrarian landscape, revealing the machine in the garden.

I have a more specific reason for discussing regionalist versions of the frontier farm. Dennis draws an explicit parallel between *The Wizard* and two of the three regionalist painters: Wood and Curry. "The set designers for the movie version of *The Wizard of Oz* appreciated this in fabricating the film's two landscapes...the real world of Kansas is viewed through a farmyard by Curry, but as Dorothy sets out from the city of the Munchkins on her journey through Oz, the make-believe world into which the yellow brick road travels is a Grant Wood landscape."[124] Dennis illustrates his point about Wood with a still from the movie showing Dorothy as she meets the Scarecrow in a cornfield along the Yellow Brick Road. The neat enclosure with its rows of corn is reminiscent of Wood's *Fertility* (1939). Even more interesting, however, are the decorative patterns formed by patches of flat color; this device is familiar from Woodian landscapes such as *Spring Turning* (1936). There are other visual parallels.

When Dorothy and her friends reach the end of the Yellow Brick Road, they catch their first glimpse of the Emerald City. A forest of green cylinders with domed tops set against the flat Ozian countryside, the Emerald City resembles nothing so much as the far-off sylvan groves in *Fall Plowing* (1931), *Spring Plowing* (1932), or *Arbor Day* (1932). Although there is no evidence to prove that the set designers at MGM actually had Grant Wood in mind when they created Oz, it should be noted that Wood's popularity was then at its height; he and the two other regionalist painters had recently been featured in the Christmas Eve issue of *Time* for 1934.[125] It is difficult to believe that studio artists would have been unfamiliar with the work of a well-known contemporary artist. Documenting stylistic links, however, is not the purpose of this book. It is enough to indicate that in both cases the American landscape has been interpreted and transformed in much the same way. This suggests that there was, at the very least, a common visual idiom shared by Grant Wood and the set designers at MGM. Much more important for the purpose at hand, though, it suggests that this was based on cultural traditions familiar to the American public at large.

Dennis claims not only that Oz is a Grant Wood landscape but also that Kansas is a John Steuart Curry landscape. The parallel seems clear enough in a painting such as *Tornado over Kansas* (1929). Only ten years later, a very similar scene was enacted on the back lot of MGM: Auntie Em, Uncle Henry, and the farmhands rush toward the storm cellar as a tornado sweeps toward them across the fields. It was no accident that Curry chose this kind of scene to paint. He was more influenced than Wood by the Southern Agrarians (a group of writers who opposed urbanization and industrialization). The Southern Agrarians argued that subsistence agriculture provided an escape from the drudgery of factories and the horrors of slums, but they did not argue that rural life was characterized by bucolic serenity. Nature was not necessarily benign; on the contrary, it was often terrifying and always mysterious. For them, nature was still "sublime" in the sense of nineteenth-century romanticism. It might even express the will of a wrathful or indifferent God. Instead of urging an unrelenting and possibly self-destructive war of exploitation against nature, they urged people to respect nature's awesome grandeur. Consequently, they opposed the standardization inherent in technology and industry; they wanted to divest people of the illusion that nature could be controlled through practical reason or empirical knowledge. In short, they wanted a return to the land and a primal relationship with nature. Unlike Wood, who emphasized the eternal context of human existence in a bucolic environment, Curry emphasized the finite context of human existence in a capricious one. For him, nature was dramatic more often than it was placid. But is this what *The Wizard* actually says about Kansas?

Dennis is correct, I think, in suggesting a general correspondence (intentional or not) between *The Wizard* and regionalist painting. But this analogy can be taken too far. The cinematic patterns revealed through formal analysis do not support a neat identification of Kansas with Curry and Oz with Wood. It is true that the Kansas prologue looks like the world described by Curry, but the Kansas epilogue "corrects" this impression. The tornado and everything associated with it have disappeared. Still, there is a clear continuity between the former and latter versions of Kansas. To suggest, then, that the works of Curry can be used as a hermeneutical key for understanding Kansas is to miss the specific form of closure that gives the movie its semantic context. It is similarly true that the Ozian landscape looks like the world described by Wood, but a closer examination of conditions in Oz corrects this impression. It is a land of confusion, fragmentation, anxiety, and alienation. Moreover, it is a land that has been starkly polarized by good and evil. Wood's Iowa, on the other hand, is a realm of order, unity, security, and happiness; the polarization between good (rural and agrarian America) and evil (urban and industrial America) has been resolved, albeit implicitly. Both Oz and Iowa look like fantasies. But the similarity ends there. The former is a disguised view of everyday life in America's present; the latter is a mythic vision of America's future.[126] In fairness to Dennis, it must be acknowledged that his analogy was made mainly on the basis of stylistic similarities. The value of examining Grant Wood here, though is based not on the possibility that a precise parallel can be drawn between his works and the cinematic structure of *The Wizard* but on the possibility that more general parallel can be drawn between the cultural traditions that underlie Wood's paintings and those that underlie *The Wizard*. In both cases, there is a mythic sense that America's ultimate destiny ("growing up") will be a return to the conditions of its ultimate origin ("going home"). And in both cases, the agrarian version of this myth has provided appropriate imagery. America not only begins as a frontier community building a garden in the wilderness, it also reaches its destiny as a garden of the world. In other words, there is no ultimate future for an urban or industrial America; the nation will "outgrow" its ugly and oppressive cities with their factories and slums, their banks and stock markets, and return to a state of balance and harmony with nature. For some, this has meant abandoning urban (or suburban) desolation along with industrial technology and setting up rural communes based on the self-sufficiency of subsistence farming. For others, it has remained a dream to be fulfilled in the remote future—at the end of time, as it were, or history—and experienced now only in the imagination.

*

To sum up, it would seem that *The Wizard* has been popular at least partly because it has allowed Americans to have their cake and eat it, too. When it first came out, this movie supported the progressive, urban utopianism that supplied themes and visual motifs for both the Chicago World's Fair of 1933-1934 ("The Century of Progress") and the New York World's Fair of 1939-1940 ("The World of Tomorrow"). At the same time, it supported the traditional, rural utopianism of the agrarian, or populist, worldview. The immediate solution to poverty and despair lay in the development of cities and factories. But the ultimate solution lay in a return to the bucolic paradise envisioned by Jefferson, Franklin, and other founders of the republic (possibly through the application of industrial technology to agriculture itself). If so, the nation would be moving from paradise, through history, and back to paradise. That, of course, is a mythic (circular rather than linear) notion of time. To the extent that Americans affirm this "myth of the eternal return" and to the extent that *The Wizard* provides symbolic support for it, this movie can be said to function as a "secular myth." This says, in effect, that for Americans to "grow up" as a nation (to realize their ultimate destiny as a garden paradise) they must also "go home" (recapture their innocence in the original garden paradise).

Figure 5-6

Doonesbury Copyright 1987 and 1988 G. B. Trudeau. Reprinted with permission of Universal Press Syndicate. All rights reserved.

5 THE SWEET VALES OF EDEN

And the Lord God planted a garden in Eden in the East; and there he put the man which he had formed. And out of the ground the Lord God made to grow every tree that is pleasant to the sight and good for food, the tree of life also in the midst of the garden, and the tree of knowledge of good and evil.

—Gen. 2:7-9

Then he showed me the river of the water of life, bright as crystal, flowing from the throne of God and of the Lamb through the middle of the street of the city; also, on either side of the river, the tree of life with its twelve kinds of fruit, yielding its fruit each month, and the leaves of the tree were for the healing of nations.

—Rev. 22:1

There is only one explicit reference to religion in *The Wizard*. After Dorothy screams at Miss Gulch for coming to destroy Toto, Auntie Em begins to express her own feelings: "For twenty-three years I've been dying to tell you what I think of you! And now...well, being a Christian woman I can't say it" (43). Although this line is a trivial one in purely cinematic terms—it does nothing to advance the plot and only a little to define the character of Auntie Em—it is nevertheless suggestive of the cultural environment in which this movie is understood. Just as the United States is officially secular but implicitly religious (since most of its citizens consider themselves religious), I suggest that this movie is explicitly secular but implicitly religious because its popularity depends on the familiarity of viewers with ways of thinking derived, no matter how remotely, from traditional forms of (Judaism or) Christianity. Explicitly, *The Wizard* is

179

about Dorothy's passage from Kansas, through Oz (growing up), and back to Kansas (going home). Discussing the psychology of individuals, I explained that this link between coming of age (growing up) and returning to origin (going home) may have deep roots in the unconscious development of individuals. They pass from (unrealized) self, through the life cycle (growing up), and back to (realized, or individuated) self. Following this, I suggested that this pattern can also be discerned on the collective level. The nation passes from utopia, through history ("growing up"), and back to utopia ("going home"). History is thus a passage from the agrarian order and harmony of antebellum America, through history, and back to the agrarian order and harmony of millenial America. Likewise, the cosmos itself passes from eternity, through time ("growing up") and back to eternity ("going home"). In other words, our relation to the cosmos is experienced as a passage from paradise (Eden), through history (exile), and back to paradise (Eden). Because religion has played a fundamental role in shaping the American identity, I also argue that this is the paradigm on which the other two are based, the "type" to which the "antitypes" correspond. To be sure, the paradise sought by Christians, including American Christians, is not always represented by a heavenly garden (Eden); it is also represented by a celestial city (Jerusalem). Even so, the difference between these two images of paradise is more apparent than real. In fact, they are often used not only interchangeably but even simultaneously. Ultimate destiny is understood by many Americans, in short, as a return to ultimate origins. Consequently, "growing up" is linked even on a cosmic level to "going home." This accounts (partially, at any rate) for the remarkable success of *The Wizard*. Evidence for this, in fact, is provided by the paradisian imagery of devotional works in use during the 1920s and 1930s. Before turning to these primary sources, however, it will be necessary to provide an introduction to the cosmology implicit in these works and, more specifically, to the ways in which American Christians have understood the "cosmic frontier" between time and eternity (death), between the present world and the world beyond (paradise).

*

When Carl Sagan used the word "cosmos" as a title for his 1980 television series on the Public Broadcasting System, he referred to the observable universe that can be explored through science and technology. But "cosmos" and "observable universe" are not necessarily synonymous. In books such as *The Sacred and the Profane* and *The Myth of the Eternal Return*, for example, Mircea Eliade uses the former in referring to the known and inhabitable universe established by the gods, as distinct from the unknown and uninhabitable chaos surrounding it. The familiar world is the cosmos. The alien world beyond is chaos, inhabited by ghosts, demons, or foreigners. Cosmos and chaos are ontological opposites. As Eliade points out, though, every inhabited, organized space (cosmos) was once uninhabited and disorganized (chaos). It became "cosmicized" when the gods created it; "creation" means bringing cosmos out of chaos. This cosmos in which the community lives has been the setting of divine acts in the primeval past and continues to be the setting of divine acts in the present. Although the world can be experienced as either sacred or profane, the latter is always open to the former; irruptions from the sacred plane into the profane are not only possible (as kratophanies, hierophanies, or theophanies) but *repeatable* (through myth and ritual). During these sacred times, people are released from the tyranny of (profane) time and become witnesses to, even participants in, cosmogonic events. For Eliade, then, the religious and cosmogonic become virtually synonymous. "The sacred reveals absolute reality," he writes, "and at the same time makes orientation possible; hence it founds the world in the sense that it fixes the limits and establishes the order of the world."[1]

In spatial terms, the cosmos always has a sacred center where creation is said to have begun. This is the *axis mundi*, a sacred mountain, city, temple, or palace that is the meeting place of heaven, earth, and hell. Because people experience sacred space, they are able to "found the world" (establish and maintain the cultural and social order). When the sacred is revealed, the real is unveiled. Oriented toward the source of reality, organized human existence becomes possible. But the center is not merely a point of orientation in the midst of what would otherwise be chaos; it is also a window in the wall that normally separates sacred from profane, heaven and earth (or even hell and earth). At the center, it is possible to pass from one ontological plane to another. Once again, however, the sacred plane (in this case, sacred space) is identified with the primeval and cosmogonic realm. Consequently, "every spatial hierophany or consecration of a space is equivalent to a cosmogony. The first conclusion we might draw would be: the world becomes apprehensible as world, as cosmos, in the measure in which it reveals itself as a sacred world."[2] A good example of sacred space is provided by

Mount Zion, the site of Jerusalem. For Jews, it is of central importance as the location of the Temple, meeting ground between heaven
and earth, God and Israel. For Christians, it is identified with Eden;
the new Adam is crucified on the very spot where the old Adam was
buried. For Muslims, it is the place from which the Prophet ascended
on his night journey to the heavens. It is, in short, an *axis mundi*.

In temporal terms, argues Eliade, the cosmos is organized as a
sacred cycle in which cosmogonic events are reexperienced periodically through the ritual reenactment of myths. Now this is what he
calls the "myth of the eternal return." All religious traditions, he
argues, are said to have been founded by gods or mythical ancestors.
"Man only repeats the act of creation; his religious calendar com-
memorates, in the space of a year, all the cosmogonic phases which
took place *ab origine*. In fact, the liturgical, or sacred year ceaselessly
repeats the Creation; man is contemporary with the cosmogony and
with the anthropogony because ritual projects him into the mythical
epoch of the beginning."[3]

Both spatially and temporally, the cosmos is a sacred archetype,
the basic paradigm of reality itself. To be real (have meaning), anything that exists in space (the city, the temple or palace, the human
body itself as an *imago mundi*) and anything that exists in time (the
rite of passage or the festival as a return to conditions *in illo
tempore*) must be a symbolic repetition of its sacred prototype.[4]
Moreover, the cosmos is a living organism. The secular universe is
mute, opaque, inert, or indifferent, but the sacred universe is not; it
calls out to *homo religiosus;* it "wants to say something." In fact, the
gods reveal themselves to people through the cosmic forces permeat-
ing the natural order. Since men and women themselves are part of
the cosmos, it follows that they are also microcosms. The same
sanctity that pervades the former inhabits the latter. "It follows,"
writes Eliade, "that [human] life is homologized to cosmic life; as a
divine work, the cosmos becomes the paradigmatic image of human
existence."[5] It also follows that chaos, the opposite of cosmos, must
be shunned; disorder is precisely what threatens both the natural
and cultural order. Without sacred models, human existence would
be meaningless and, indeed, impossible.

Here, "cosmos" is used with a number of the same implications. By
"cosmos," I mean not the observable universe but the sacred universe.
The cosmic frontier, for example, is a sacred cosmological prototype
of *all* frontiers. In this sense, the cosmos includes not only the stars
and comets that can be observed through a telescope or the spores

and cells that can be observed through a microscope, but also the heavens, hells, and purgatories that can be experienced through meditations, rituals, or visions of transcendent reality. A cosmology, in this sense, is like an "icon" in the theological sense of that word: a sacred picture of the universe or a picture of the sacred universe. Derived from a religious tradition, it is understood primarily in terms of myth and experienced primarily through ritual.

But the cosmic level of interpretation is actually not distinct from the individual and collective levels; it includes both. In Judaism, for example, paradise is associated not only with a "new heaven and a new earth," but also with the restoration of Israel in this world and personal salvation in the world to come. All are modalities, as it were, of a single cosmology. Under discussion here is not only how Americans understand the life cycle or how they understand history, but how they understand time itself—that is, the relation of both to eternity. On the collective level, a link with eternity is provided by the notion of America as a frontier. The American frontier is now located somewhere in the depths of outer space.[6] At first, however, it was located somewhere in the agricultural "West." The frontier is an image of the American future that became central to American identity at a critical moment in the American past. This blending of past and future in itself suggests eternity and, by definition, is beyond both. As the eschatological nation (explicitly for millenarians and implicitly for many others), America is a *cosmic frontier.* So far, however, only individuals have crossed this frontier. On the individual level, of course, a link with eternity is provided by the notion of death as a frontier of the life cycle. Just as birth is the boundary between whatever precedes it and life, death is the boundary between life and whatever follows it. For many American (Jews and) Christians, death is rebirth into a new form of existence beyond time and space. It is, in short, the cosmic frontier par excellence.

Stated briefly (at this point in the discussion), most Americans believe, say they believe, or would like to believe that they have souls, spiritual entities that are separated from their bodies at death and continue to exist forever in some transcendent dimension. Moreover, they believe that this transcendent dimension can (for the righteous, at any rate) be identified as paradise. Finally, they believe that paradise can be described either as a city (the eschatological Jerusalem) or a garden (the primeval Eden) or both. The specific aim here, though is not to point out these obvious features of popular religion in America, but to show how these may be translated into secular terms by the popular culture of America. Of particular interest here is the secular translation of the belief in paradise as a return to Eden.

*

The cosmological foundations for American notions of paradise can be traced back to the biblical tradition but not to a single idea or a single period. Biblical notions of life after death,[7] for instance, evolved in response to a variety of needs and with the resources of at least two traditions. One focused on resurrection of the dead. Although it came to be characteristic of the biblical worldview, it replaced an earlier biblical tradition in which the dead were thought to be permanently extinguished (either disintegrating in the grave or continuing to exist in a shadowy realm known as *sheol*). Gradually, in response to the undeserved suffering of individuals, Jews came to expect God's justice to prevail after death if not in life; the dead would be physically resurrected. At first, this applied to a few righteous individuals. Then it was extended to include all the righteous as a group. Finally, it came to include both the righteous and the unrighteous; all would be raised, judged, and appropriately punished or rewarded in the Messianic Age. The notion of resurrection, of course, was originally based on a "materialistic" conception of the hereafter. The individual was thought to consist of physical and spiritual elements permanently linked in one way or another—the precise way has always been a matter of speculation—so that the somatic particularity of each individual (no matter how glorified or dematerialized) survived the apparent decomposition of death. To the extent that resurrection was assumed to involve conditions not experienced in everyday life (such as bodies rising from their graves), it was associated with the eschatological future (judgment and the establishment of God's Kingdom or the Messianic Age). But to the extent that resurrection was believed to involve events that could be experienced in everyday life (such as conversion or rebirth), it was associated with the immediate present. According to this specifically Christian refinement, resurrection was a more "spiritual" affair. With the physical resurrection of Christ, a new eon had replaced the old; the decisive eschatological event was no longer a future event but one that had already taken place. For individuals who had appropriated the death and resurrection of Christ through faith, the future life (that is, true or eternal life) was a proleptic reality. It could be experienced immediately, but only in a partial, anticipatory, way; it would be experienced fully only in the future. In any case, the fate of the physical body was no longer a matter of great concern. This came close to a Greek tradition that focused on immortality of the soul (a spiritual entity that exists both before and after the finite body that houses it during the life cycle). Nonetheless, it was distinguished from the Greek idea by a belief in the continuing particularity of the soul, its association with a specific incarnate individual, and by the belief that its fate depended on divine grace rather than on any inherent indestructibilty.

On the basis, the notion of immortality entered the Judaeo-Christian tradition. It can be found for example, in midrashic literature; souls, according to one account, are created by God in the Beginning, stored in Eden until sent by God to enter the bodies of newly conceived individuals, and returned to Eden after they die.[8] Like Jews themselves, Christians have oscillated between the Hebraic idea that the dead remain dormant until the end of history when they are raised, judged, and rewarded or punished and the Greek idea that the dead enter immediately into some blessed state. Although most Christians have accepted the idea of a last judgment and resurrection of the dead, they have also accepted the idea of communion of the saints (according to which, in some traditions, the dead may continue their relationship with the living by acting as intercessors with Christ).

Considering the heterogeneous origins of Jewish and Christian beliefs about life after death, it is not surprising that divergent traditions about paradise itself developed over the centuries. Since the historical evolution of ideas about paradise is notoriously complex and, in any case, beyond the scope of this book, I present here only those features that have been either characteristic or problematic during the past 2,000 years.[9] Unless otherwise indicated, I rely on the work of Frank and Fritzie Manuel for this purpose. In their article for *Daedalus*, "Sketch for a Natural History of Paradise," they begin by noting the importance, even the centrality, of paradise in the Western imagination.

> A revealing way to examine the psychic life of Judeo-Christian civilization would be to study it as a paradise cult, isolated fantasies about another world as they found expression in sacred texts, in commentaries upon them, and in their secular adaptation. . . . In visions of paradise terrestrial and celestial, men have been disclosing their innermost desires, whether they thrust them backward into the past, projected them forward into the future on earth, or raised them beyond

the bounds of this sphere. As in dreams, men displaced themselves in time and space and compressed their manifold wishes into an all-embracing metaphor.[10]

Given the centrality of paradise (more specifically, return to paradise) in my analysis of *The Wizard*, it is worth noting that Harry Levin goes even further in a similar article for *Encounter*. For him, the notion of paradise is endemic not only in Western civilization; but also in human culture, as such. Since it is impossible to prove that anything is universal, I will not debate the point. Nevertheless, Levin is probably justified in writing that the notion of paradise is extremely common cross culturally.

> The radiance, the fragrance, the balmy climate, the spontaneous bounty, the twittering birds, all those lawns and terraces and fountains, those pavilions of so little else except crystal and jasper, that continual music in the background, the fruit so available and uniformly delicious that Eve grew fatally bored with it, the colorful verdure and kindly animals varying only with flora and fauna known to the describer—there can hardly be another theme, among the universals of folklore, that has been sounded for so long and so widely with such a modicum of variation.[11]

On the other hand, Levin says elsewhere in this article that the human fascination with hell is even deeper; commentaries on Dante's *Inferno*, therefore, greatly outnumber those on his *Paradiso*. It may be that some religious traditions have stressed the damnation of sinners more than the salvation of the elect.[12] The most immediate concern, then, would be to avoid the former and not to dream of the latter. It may also be that narrative interest in paradise is inherently limited because "all paradisiacal visions take place in a static world," as Levin writes, "in a time that is out of time, an everlasting spring or unending youth."[13] Eternity, by definition, is timelessness; it precludes change and development (which is to say, plot). Be that as it may, it seems clear that the vision of a world free from the suffering of this one—but overflowing with its joys—is, if not universal, then at least extremely common. In Western societies, at any rate, it has a very long history. Jews and Christians have traditionally used both garden and city as images of paradise. But the notion of paradise may have developed before the rise of urban civilizations. In that case, the garden would be, if not "the Ur-myth of mankind," then at least part of a very ancient mythological scenario. "The garden...is central to the human condition because it sustains a personal relation with the universe; it embraces man's adaptation to nature and nature's adaptation to man; it domesticates for him what would otherwise be an alien environment."[14] It is not difficult to understand why the image of a garden would be so attractive to desert nomads in the ancient Near East; those who lived in a sunbaked wilderness had good reason to dream of a land flowing with milk and honey. It is somewhat more difficult to explain why people living under very different circumstances have continued to find in the same image inspiration for their fantasies of transcendent happiness.

The "evolution of paradise" can be studied in terms of several modalities. The first may be identified as myth. From the beginning, paradise has been an ambiguous, but evocative, concept that stimulated the imagination. In the formative stages of both rabbinic Judaism and early Christianity, however, myth was crystallized, even rigidified into doctrine; at the same time, however, orthodoxy was challenged by mystical[15] visions that strayed far from the established theologies. By the late Middle Ages, the idea of paradise was transformed yet again. Now it was no longer the subject of contemplation and speculation; it inspired revolutionary movements in both Judaism and Christianity. Still later, in the eighteenth and nineteenth centuries, the notion of paradise was transformed into utopia; as such, it was a major feature in secular literature as well as the inspiration of political movements. The myth of paradise may be traced to two sources. The Greek tradition begins with Hesiod's *Works and Days*. The author writes of five races in descending order of excellence. For the golden race, life was serene and happy. They knew no pain, no grief, no violence, no fear, no labor (but also no sexual activity). The golden race, however, lived in the mythic past. For Hesiod, history was a process of slow decline. The present was grim and the future could inspire only melancholy. Hesiod's work passed through several Greek and Roman mutations in which it was harmonized with changing religious and philosophical attitudes. Eventually, it was reduced to a matter-of-fact account of origins in which myth and history were indistinguishable. At some point, Hesiod's five races were transformed into four ages. And the golden race became the golden age. Largely through Ovid's *Metamorphoses*, the idea of a lost golden age was bequeathed to the Renaissance. All the same, more than nostalgia may be involved in the myth of a lost paradise.

The other mythic strand in Western notions of paradise is the Hebraic one. Although much of the imagery of Eden may be derived from ancient Near Eastern myths,[16] scholars now agree that the biblical tradition has transformed it. Whatever the origins of this tradition, however, it is noteworthy that it became thoroughly assimilated into the biblical tradition. Over a period of 3,000 years, the two or three lines in Genesis that describe the primeval Garden have inspired a vast number of commentaries and fantasies. The word "paradise" does not occur in the Hebrew Bible; in its Greek form, it first appears in the Septuagint as a translation of *gan eden*. From there, its usage spread among both Greek and Latin Christians. The word "paradise" does not occur in the Talmud either. The Talmud recognizes four temporal divisions: Eden; this world *(ha-olam ha-zeh)*; the Messianic Age; and the world to come *(ha-olam ha-ba)*. The last, in turn, is usually identified either with a heavenly Eden or with a heavenly Jerusalem; sometimes, however, it is identified with the Messianic Age. Usually, the Talmud contrasts this world and the world to come, but confusion is caused by the notion of a Messianic Age. Is it worldly or otherworldly? Then, too, there is an ambiguous relation between paradise in the world to come and paradise in the Garden of Eden. Is the former a return to the latter? Doctrines of prefiguration were developed to account for the affinity between them. Partly in response to Christian interest in messianic theology, the rabbis were reluctant to discuss the matter; there was a distinct tendency to minimize distinctions between this world and the Messianic Age. They did, however, allow a radical distinction between both of these and the world to come. In popular midrashic literature, the world to come is characterized by the study of Torah but also by sensual pleasure and the radiance of gold and gems. The imagery of light is common to both the Beginning and the End. Paradise in the world to come has distinctly Edenic overtones.

Together, these two mythic traditions generate a paradoxical combination of nostalgia and hope. "The stage scenery of the human imagination can readily be shoved about," write the Manuels, "and the same props reassembled in different sequences. Many Western thinkers have joined the notion of a primitive golden age with a promise that the happy epoch now vanished will be reborn."[17] In fact, the idea of rebirth seems to be inherent in many forms of this myth. Generally speaking, paradise is associated with feminine imagery. In some cases, it is an island. In psychoanalytical terms, the human foetus is also an island. The primeval world of a "desert island" (one of the most popular contemporary symbols of paradise), therefore, is a very appropriate image of that primordial paradise, the womb. If so, no wonder maternal symbols are prevalent in the imagery of most paradises. The garden itself, of course, is associated with female fertility and fecundity. It could be argued, then, that paradise is associated with the womb and that returning to the former is associated with returning to the latter. There is a danger of reductionism here. The notion of paradise cannot be written off as an atavistic or neurotic desire for union with Mother. Still, the link between paradise and birth or rebirth cannot be denied. The whole notion of paradise is associated with a primal event in the human life cycle. If an explanation is required for the continued power of the garden as a symbol for paradise long after nomadic life in the desert was left behind, this link must be taken seriously.

During this same formative period, it became common to use allegory as a hermeneutical device. Thus, for Philo of Alexandria, the fruit of the Garden represented the virtues of the soul and tending the Garden represented observing the commandments. The use of allegory, however, was common among both Jews and Christians. In this case, Eden became the type corresponding to the antitype of a future paradise in the world to come.[18] That, in turn, led to further speculation among those with gnostic tendencies and contemplation among mystics. The rise of apocalypticism during this period is associated with a number of scholarly problems. To what extent, for example, was it a break with earlier biblical traditions? It could be argued that apocalypticism, whatever its origins in the biblical tradition, represented a parting of the ways in Judaism. Moving in one direction were those who preferred to fix theological speculation in doctrine and law; moving in the other direction were those who either could not or would not limit their imagination in response to the mysterious. The latter developed a tradition that, though never condemned by the orthodox, was considered with suspicion by them and marginalized as far as possible. Apocalyptic scenarios characteristically begin with the oppression of Israel in the present, continue with a titanic struggle, and conclude with visions of a Messianic Age following the holocaust. The new age is an earthly paradise in which the enemies of Israel have been permanently removed from Jerusalem. There is peace not only for Israel but for all nations. In fact, sin itself has been banished along with the demons. The same scenario is present in the source of all later forms of Christian millenarianism: the Apocalypse of St. John (that is, the book of Revelation). In this version, Christ triumphs over the Antichrist. For millenarians, the seven days of creation are types corresponding to the antitypes of seven millennia; the seventh millennium is the functional equivalent of the Messianic Age in Judaism. But is the millennium to be taken literally or allegorically? And is the seventh millennium an other-worldly paradise or a terrestrial one?

Following St. Augustine, the Church upheld the otherworldly view. Paradise was a spiritual realm in which there would be perfect harmony between body and soul. Although inhabitants would have all their organs, those now necessary for such practical purposes as eating and reproducing would no longer be used; existence in paradise would be devoted exclusively to the contemplation and praise of God. Living at a time of persecution, Tertullian added the idea that martyrs would be taken directly to paradise, but others would have to wait in some preliminary state until the end of days and the last judgment. Centuries later, St. Thomas Aquinas upheld a similar view. The millenarians, on the other hand, upheld the alternative one. They sought a terrestrial paradise. From time to time, they tried to establish paradise on earth. Although all were attempts at renewal, they differed in their understanding of what renewal implied. For some, it meant that something radically new would be born—and they often used the imagery of reurning to the womb—while for others, it meant merely renovating the old or restoring what the ancients had always intended.

During the Middle Ages, the "alternative" tradition of mysticism also flourished. In Judaism, the kabbalists speculated about the mystical meanings underlying scripture. They were particularly interested in the cosmological implications of Genesis. In these theosophical systems, there was a plurality of "worlds" (dimensions of reality represented as microcosms) and creations. Not only did Jewish mystics use meditation to enter the paradisian world of the Garden, they also devised rituals by means of which they could control the cosmic forces flowing through all "worlds." Heterodox Christians also proposed new cosmologies. Abbot Joachim, for example, suggested a temporal hierarchy of three ages: that of the Father, that of the Son, and that of the Holy Ghost. Because the latter was to be a terrestrial paradise, however, he relativized the position of Christ and the Church.

Views of this kind were especially popular among those who were unhappy with the present political and ecclesiastical order. For them, visions of paradise were often catalysts for either revolt or adventure. In Judaism, the search for paradise led from mystical speculation and theurgic practices to messianic movements. Some of these, such as the one led by Shabbetai Zvi in the seventeenth century, had masses of followers eager to end their collective struggle through history. In Christianity, the preoccupation with paradise led to both a resurgence of millenarianism and the voyages of discovery that brought the Middle Ages to a close.

The Church could not deny that Eden was a real place. "Immemorially," writes Levin, "the Garden of Eden had been the navel of the earth, the centre of the cosmos, beyond the dawn."[19] But where, precisely, was it? Only one of the four rivers said to have their origin there, the Euphrates, could still be identified by the same name; the others were identified as the Tigris, the Nile, even the Ganges. Consequently, speculative geographers shifted the location of Eden from Asia to Africa, the Americas, the North Pole, the stratosphere, and even the Moon. But the early explorers often thought about the location of Eden in more practical terms; they actually tried to find it. When Columbus reached the mouth of the Orinoco in 1498, he quickly noticed that the water seemed to be flowing from a very high place. Moreover, he noticed that the river had four tributaries, and that the region was favored with gold and gems. Since Eden was said to be the highest point on earth (and had thus survived the Flood), the source of four rivers, and studded with gold and gems, he was convinced that he was really approaching the terrestrial paradise itself. Accordingly, he revised his earlier picture of the earth; it was no longer a perfect sphere. Instead, it was pear-shaped; the newly discovered terrain sat on the globe like the breast of a woman, with paradise corresponding to the nipple. Moreover, early visitors to America, as I have already noted, had been conditioned by a tradition that linked paradise and the primitive.[20] This was true, for example, of the search for Prester John's mythical realm. Between the sixteenth and eighteenth centuries, this way of thinking became dominant. It was best expressed by Rousseau's notion of the "noble savage." Even missionaries sometimes saw the American Indians as inhabitants of a terrestrial paradise or survivors of a lost golden age. As soon as America was economically developed, the search for Eden and its noble savages took European refugees from civilization to the South Seas. Nevertheless, it is important to remember that the exotic dream of an earthly paradise, primitive and innocent, did not originate with the secular utopias of the seventeenth and eighteenth centuries. By the time America was being explored, the quest for a terrestrial paradise had been saturated with religious imagery for centuries; the fascination with the exotic, in other words, was not something peculiar to the seventeenth and eighteenth centuries. Even the demand for a consummation of paradise here and now had its origin in religious tradition. Movements of the late Middle Ages called for radical social and political change. And as Norman Cohn has pointed out in *The Pursuit of the Millennium*,[21] religious notions of a terrestrial paradise underlay them. There was a pattern. The charismatic leader was identified as a prophet. The coming conflict was identified as one between Christ and the Antichrist. On the side of the latter were the rich, the powerful, the clergy, or the Jews. A day of reckoning would be followed by universal recognition of the good emperor, the mystic leader, or Christ and the inauguration of paradise on earth.

Although Greek traditions of a lost golden age were often used in the utopian writings of the Renaissance and later periods, the Hebraic tradition of paradise was by no means lost. The former, in fact, was often denigrated either as an imitation or prefiguration of the latter. Beginning with Thomas More's *Utopia*, though, and continuing into the eighteenth century, the "myth" of paradise was gradually secularized. In works from this period, classical imagery predominated, but its spiritual underpinning continued to be religious (that is, biblical) in origin. When religious belief itself declined, however, traditional notions of paradise were often replaced with self-conscious, deliberately fabricated utopias. Even in these, vestiges of the traditional paradise can be discerned. Very few of these utopian works have failed to deal in some way with problems traditionally associated with Eden, the Messianic Age or an otherworldly paradise. There are, of course, some important differences. Utopia is created by human beings, not by God. And it is located in this world, not in some other one. The fate of utopian visions in a modern, secular context has not been encouraging. In many science fiction books and movies, futuristic societies use technology in the service of tyranny; the focus on utopia is transformed into a focus on dystopia. Even so, the idea of paradise is not yet extinct. "There is still a paradise in the collective unconscious of the West, a rich repository with myriad interconnections available to those who write fantasies or organize movements. The emotional potency of these images derives from aspects of the myth that reanimate deep-rooted psychic experiences and may kindle a hope for rebirth, for another chance. The myth, religious or secular, serves a purpose in the psychic economy, for it makes possible the continuance of living in the unease of civilization."[22]

On several occasions, the Manuels refer to the historical prevalence of this dual nature of paradise (past and future). "But the unique contemporary predicament of Western civilization, with its frantic demand for paradise *now*, can be understood only against the shadowy background of those two other paradises 'in the beginning' and 'in the world to come' whose images grow ever dimmer. The question remains: Can paradise be anything but ephemeral when two of the three paradises—the past and the future—that composed the triune have vanished and paradise has to be compressed into the fleeting present?"[23] They are merely stating their own opinion here, of course. Be that as it may, the publication of such an opinion is itself not without interest in this context. Echoing the writings of Eliade, they continue by suggesting that the idea of returning to paradise is so deeply engrained that it is unlikely to disappear altogether; it is more likely, instead, to reappear in disguise. "But if paradise was born of that mystical union between mother and child, is it not man's fate to oscillate forever between a longing for the return of that state and disillusion when it finally arrives? The flux and reflux of belief in paradise then becomes a part of the order itself, and do what you may, destroy its traditional religious functions, abolish Eden and the world to come, paradise will reappear in a new place."[24]

Clearly, the various ideas discussed here have not come together as a single, homogeneous, tradition. Aside from the fact that the notion of paradise has always been taken literally by some and allegorically by others, it has continually provoked debate over at least two questions. First, is paradise to be worldly (terrestrial) or otherworldly (heavenly)? Second, is paradise (either terrestrial or heavenly) to be experienced in the immediate future (just after death or even during the life cycle itself) or in the remote future (at the end of history)? These questions have never been answered definitively because Jews and Christians have, by and large, refused to choose one possibility over the other in either case. Instead, they have chosen to retain both possibilities, applying one or the other depending on the circumstances. It would seem, therefore, that they cannot avoid contradicting themselves when discussing paradise. But contradictions may be more apparent than real. For the dead, after all, mundane categories of time (past, present, and future) need not apply; beyond the cosmic frontier of death may be eternity. It is thus quite possible to accept both ideas: the dead will be resurrected in the (possibly remote) future of this world, but may also enter the paradise of a transcendent world immediately. Consequently, paradise may be both wordly (following history) and otherworldly (following death). In any case, these ideas have coexisted since biblical times.

Both Judaism and Christianity have found ways of accommodating the needs of individuals. In the memorial liturgy recited by Jews on festivals—not, as the Manuels claim, at funerals—this is made clear: "May God remember the soul of my father (or mother)...who has passed into his (or her) eternal rest. I pledge charity in his (or her) behalf and pray that his (or her) soul be kept among the immortal souls of Abraham, Isaac, Jacob, Sarah, Rebekah, Rachel, Leah, and all the righteous men and women in paradise."[25] The Hebrew term used for paradise in this prayer is *gan eden*, the Garden of Eden. Ultimate destiny, therefore, is seen as a return to ultimate origin, the eschatological future is thus a return to the primeval past. Furthermore, the same sort of accommodation has taken place in Christianity and is assumed by many, if not most participants in the popular Christianity of the United States. In fact, I suggest, similar assumptions are made even by those not directly involved with religious communities. Levin writes, for example, that "everyone goes back to the ancestral sources in his own fashion, reenacting the myth of our common progenitor Seth, retracing the footsteps of our ultimate parents down a green path to their proscribed abode, yearning for the days when man lived in primordial innocence with the beasts and near to God, close to the tree of life and uncontaminated by the tree of knowledge."[26] The beliefs of popular religion, in any case, may or may not be consistent with those of theologians or even with those articulated in the sacred texts. This is partially explained by the fact that the sacred texts themselves do not present a thoroughly consistent point of view. But intellectual consistency is not a defining element of religion. The inconsistencies that trouble theologians and scholars may not trouble everyone else. To put it differently, the inconsistencies that trouble people at study may not trouble them at worship.

*

There is yet another problem to be encountered in any study of paradise. In *The Architecture of Paradise*, William McClung discusses the relation between primeval garden and heavenly city as images of paradise. He does so, however, by examining the relation of literature and architecture to both. "The paradises between which the iron age of history is a parenthesis are a garden without a building and a building enclosing a garden. One, conspicuously unprotected, is lost or displaced beyond reach; the other, a fortress, is accessible only at the apocalypse. Both are dwelling places for the body as well as the spirit, and in recommending themselves to us as models, they propose different kinds of bliss, physical and spiritual."[27]

The heavenly city, of course, is identified with the eschatological Jerusalem described in the book of Revelation. It is represented in art as a fortified enclosure, usually a palace within which the arts and sciences are brought to perfection. Architecture is thus intended to represent an idealization of urban life. An impression of glittering splendor is evoked by the monumental scale, sophisticated plans, brilliant surfaces (often plated with gold and encrusted with jewels) and symbolic or ideal proportions (often expressed by the multiplication of parts) of celestial temples and palaces. In such a setting, the mood is one of ecstasy and celebration. "The wall was built of jasper, while the city was pure gold, clear as glass. The foundations of the wall of the city were adorned with every jewel; the first was jasper, the second sapphire, the third agate, the fourth emerald. . . . And the twelve gates were twelve pearls, each of the gates made of a single pearl, and the street of the city was pure gold, transparent as glass."[28] The celestial city described in this passage from the Apocalypse— which is, not incidentally, the book that concludes the Christian Bible—lies ahead in the ultimate future. Consequently, it is the source of all utopian imagery.

The celestial garden, on the other hand, looks back to the primeval past described in the book of Genesis. It is nostalgic. Like the myth of a lost golden age, moreover, it exemplifies an Arcadian or pastoral tradition that rejects the vice and degeneracy of urban civilization. Paradise is characterized by the absence of war, pain, grief, and hardship. It is a world of serenity and repose made possible by the benevolence and plenitude of nature itself; the role played by culture is minimal, to say the least. If any architecture appears in these gardens, it is very primitive. Even in georgic literature (a specifically agrarian variation of this genre that must, therefore, tolerate at least some crafts or technologies), buildings are justified only if they can be identified with a pristine way of life (which is to say, if they are products of "natural" building materials and methods of construction).

But there is a mediating image of paradise that combines elements of both Eden and Jerusalem. Like the former, it is a verdant landscape filled with fragrant blossoms and shady groves. Like the latter, though, it is also equipped with grottos, pavilions, fountains, and other refinements of civilization. Unlike either, however, it is a terrestrial paradise associated, no matter how vaguely, with the present. This mediating image may take two forms. The *hortus deliciarum* is a garden of sensual delight. This combination of horticultural and architectural models has appeared in both secular and sacred works. Its image of a delightful but hidden park provides a visual background for both religious and erotic allegories. It is both exquisite and remote. On the whole, it gratifies a human desire for the fabulous rather than for the transcendent. By the Renaissance, this version of Eden lost even its claim to being a seeker's ultimate destination; it became in secular literature a metaphor describing states of mind or morality through which heroes pass on the way to their real goals.[29] The *hortus conclusus* is the walled garden. It has similar literary functions but, being based more directly on the garden in Song of Songs, is more evocative. The protective wall surrounding Eden is a condition of its survival in a postlapsarian world. Within the wall is the realm of grace, or redeemed nature; outside the wall is the realm of law, unredeemed nature. But the walled garden is also the goal of romantic quest. For McClung, the power of this image depends more on the fact that it is walled than the fact that it is a garden. If paradise is the venue of fulfillment, and if enclosed places are seen as the most fulfilled, it would follow that enclosed gardens are, by definition, paradisian whether the fulfillment reached within is spiritual or sexual. In either case, however, the terrestrial paradise is both a survival of the primeval one and a foretaste of the eschatological one. Summarizing his typology, McClung writes that "to the extent that Paradise is of the past, it is arcadian and open, the epitome of that nature of which it is a small part; to the extent that it is imagined to survive into the present (but in some obscure or inaccessible or forbidden spot), it is a secret garden, walled or otherwise barred against man; to the extent that Paradise signifies the Paradise to come, it is urban and conspicuously fortified."[30]

In short, McClung argues that Eden and Jerusalem have been two opposing paradigms of paradise; that Eden is a paradigm of the primeval paradise (with emphasis on the memory of loss) and Jerusalem a paradigm of the eschatological paradise (with emphasis on the hope of recovery); that the history of both literature and architecture reflects a movement away from Eden (a backward-looking vision of open and easy relations with nature) toward Jerusalem (a forward-looking vision of more structured relations with nature); and that literary and architectural attempts at synthesis, or reconciliation, have been made by transforming the idea of "garden." McClung focuses attention on the evolution of celestial architecture as either imagined in words or materialized in stone. At the same time, he discusses the tradition of hostility toward celestial architecture and its version of paradise. Corresponding to the classical moralists who condemned luxury, ostentation, and pretentiousness in architecture are modernist architects who condemn the "dishonest" use of form to disguise function. In addition, McClung argues that the celestial city, the New Jerusalem, is not merely an alternative to the Garden of Eden as an image of paradise to come and that the two are not merely interchangeable versions of the same thing. To say that, according to him, would be to ignore "the revision of Eden's typological role in the final state of assimilation to and within an urban framework."[31] This last point is problematic.

A dichotomous relation between Eden and Jerusalem, however, would not make much difference for the topic at hand. The point here is that the cosmic cycle begins and ends in paradise, not that it begins and ends in precisely the same paradise. In fact, it is apparent that paradise lost and paradise regained are different in at least one important way: the serpent in the former is absent in the latter (just as Miss Gulch in the prologue of *The Wizard* is absent from the epilogue.) To put this in more sophisticated theological terms, there is a difference between the unfallen world of Eden and the saved world of Jerusalem. However that may be, McClung overstates his case when he writes about "the inadequacy of a conception so wide-spread that I shall document it by one instance, a conception that the city of New Jerusalem is merely an 'accepted alternative' to the Garden of Eden as the model for the paradise to come and that garden and city are 'interchangeable figures.'"[32]

McClung acknowledges no ambiguity in the word "garden" itself. He seems to assume that it refers only to (the positive aspect of) wilderness. But, historically, the same word has been used to mean both "wild garden" and "cultivated garden." The latter, of course, does not negate culture; on the contrary, it represents the perfect balance between nature and culture. The confluence of urban and rural, architectural and horticultural, motifs describing the eschatological paradise need not be considered contradictory. In that case, Eden and Jerusalem may indeed be alternative versions of paradise. More specifically, in fact, they *are* often used interchangeably and even simultaneously.

McClung argues that the garden is merely a vestigial element in the eschatological paradise. "The uncertain status of the garden in history reflects the failure of an arcadian or pastoral model of beatific existence within the context of a purged and renewed heaven and earth; the survival of Eden depends, therefore, upon whatever accommodation can be reached with the city. To survive, in fact, Eden must become a garden-city."[33] The reverse, however, could also be argued. Despite the power an image of the celestial city must have for an urban society, the fact that a garden must be incorporated testifies to the enduring need of people to *affirm* their rural origins. To survive as an adequate image of paradise, the city must reach some accommodation with the garden. McClung, however, uses his own flawed argument on a number of occasions. Although cloister gardens are conventionally assumed to represent the primeval garden, for example, he argues that they actually represent the eschatological city "which is in like manner foursquare, planted and irrigated." This type of garden reveals a synthesis of horticultural and urban elements. But which takes priority, he asks, and which is assimilated? "Arguably, when one is perceived as the figure, the other becomes the ground, and vice versa without resolution. But although many...have felt that nature is compromised by artifice, I know of no objection to architecture adorned by a garden."[34] This argument, too, can be turned around: if nature is more vulnerable, after all, it may also be more valuable. A rural landscape without buildings is acceptable but an urban landscape without trees is not. From the evidence produced by McClung himself, it would seem that images of an eschatological paradise can glorify the city only if their urban character is mitigated, or compromised, by the presence of a garden. This is because the city, unlike the garden, represents an imbalance between nature and culture; without restoring the balance, at least symbolically, the city is intolerable. The evidence from American popular culture, as I have indicated, strongly suggests that the city's triumph over the garden is considered a frightening prospect—and anything but paradisian. The relation between Eden and Jerusalem is too ambiguous for the priority of one over the other to be decided by aesthetic considerations of this kind.

As a scholar in the field of literature, McClung has relied on the literary images of paradise found in the work of such luminaries as Virgil, Ovid, Augustine, Isidore of Seville, Dante, Milton, Marvell, Spenser, and Bunyan. Aside from scattered references to Henry David Thoreau and some concluding comments on Frank Lloyd Wright, he has very little to say about paradise as understood by the intellectual leaders of the United States. And he has nothing at all to say about paradise as understood by ordinary Americans. At issue here, though, are notions of paradise that are consciously expressed or unconsciously revealed in the popular culture of modern America.

*

It is impossible, of course, to know precisely what thoughts flow through the minds of people as they watch *The Wizard*. To some extent, therefore, any discussion of the reasons for its popularity must remain speculative. The task here, though, is not to get inside the minds of either those individuals who produced it or those who have responded to it, but to examine the cultural matrix of both. Given its popularity, *The Wizard* must express a way of thinking that profoundly reflects that of many Americans. So far, this phenomenon has been observed on two levels: commonly held notions about the process of growing up both on the individual and collective levels and commonly held beliefs about the cosmos itself. These ideas would be found on a third level; they would be reflected in American religiosity—and more specifically, in popular American religiosity. In examining this possibility, I rely not on treatises or sermons, but on popular hymns. The former are written by religious leaders; they may or may not reflect the beliefs of laypeople. The latter may be written either by learned theologians or by devout laypeople; sung in churches week after week, from early childhood to old age, they come both to shape and express popular piety in distinctive ways.

The hymns used here as primary sources were not selected at random. An authoritative list is provided by Katharine Diehl in *Hymns and Tunes*.[35] Seventy-eight of the more important collections are indexed. Many were prepared for use by specific denominations (such as the Methodist, Baptist, Lutheran, Episcopalian, Reformed, or Roman Catholic churches), others for use by communities bound together more informally (such as those loosely termed "evangelical"), and still others for use by specific groups of people (such as students or soldiers). An extensive study of all these would have been both impossible and unnecessary, however, since my aim is to show that *The Wizard* reflects a worldview supported by popular forms of Christianity—not that it reflects a worldview common to all forms of Christianity or even that it reflects a worldview presented consistently within any particular Christian tradition. It is thus appropriate to select hymn books representing the major Christian traditions (defined in terms of either size or influence) and refrain from considering those of more isolated or less influential communities such as the Moravians or the Mennonites. Still, I found it necessary to add hymn books representing the black and revivalist traditions because these have played a fundamental role in shaping American spirituality. My scope is further limited by period. Since *The Wizard* was produced in 1939, I have selected hymn books that were in use during (approximately) the previous twenty years.

To include relevant information, I have found it necessary to modify the standard format for notes. Most hymns were written years, even centuries, before these particular collections were edited and published for use in churches; with this in mind, I have added the dates of each author (whenever possible). I have not included this information in the text itself because this book is about the function of these hymns in America during the interwar period, not in their original *Sitz im Leben*. At the end of each note, I have added two other units of information. Since the terminology of hymns is often ambiguous—*home*, for example, can refer either to home in this world or to home in a transcendent world—I have included the category of each hymn (whenever possible) in brackets; the word "home" in a hymn from the section called "Last Things," for example, is more likely to be understood as a reference to the latter than to the former. Finally, I have added a reference to the number of collections in which the hymn cited appears. What follows is not based on statistics; the verses quoted merely illustrate the fact that certain beliefs or motifs were familiar to those who were members of, or influenced by, the churches that were culturally dominant at a certain period in American history. Even if a hymn appears in only one collection, it is worth noting. Nevertheless, many of them appear in so many—forty or fifty in some cases—that this fact cannot be ignored.

Close examination of these hymns indicates the widespread notion of a cosmic life cycle. By this, I mean a life cycle in two phases: life in this world (the terrestrial phase) is fulfilled in heaven, or paradise (the celestial phase).[36] What follows is a study of each, in turn, as it is evoked through the imagery of popular hymns. Although several motifs are associated particularly with either the former or the latter, it should be noted that they are thoroughly interrelated; each is implied by the others and often many of them appear in the same hymns together.

* *

The first phase of the cosmic life cycle is terrestrial. As H. Richard Niebuhr makes clear in *Christ and Culture*[37] there have always been several quite different Christian attitudes toward the social and cultural order of this world. Some of them could be called "life affirming" and others "life denying." Still others could be considered mediations between these two extremes. Very often, these divergent traditions are discussed in terms of the Church being "in" or "of" this world. The task here is neither to trace the origin and evolution of these traditions nor to evaluate them theologically, but merely to isolate one of them to establish a link between popular religion and popular culture in modern America. Before doing so, we must return to the question of Dorothy's dream and what its presentation suggests about the world's ontological status.

The Oz sequences in *The Wizard* may be viewed, paradoxically, as a representation of both dream and everyday life. The movie explicitly states that Dorothy's experience of Oz is a dream. Nevertheless, this does not mean that it must be interpreted as a mere fantasy (which is to say, something "unreal"). The truth is that Oz can be seen in many ways as a (partly satirical) comment on the way life *is* in the waking state (which is to say, in the real world). In that case, however, what can be said of Kansas? That, after all, is where Dorothy wakes up from her dream. The answer to this question may be found in the religious notion that life in this world is a dreamlike prelude to eternal life in some transcendent world. This does not necessarily involve the assumption that this world as such, is "unreal." It may suggest merely that conditions in this world normally prevent people from seeing an underlying reality. "For now we see in a mirror dimly," writes St. Paul, "but then face to face. Now I know in part; then I shall understand fully, even as I have been fully understood."[38] This longing to see Christ face to face is echoed in many hymns.

> Only faintly now I see Him,
> With the darkling veil between,
> But a blessed day is coming,
> When His glory shall be seen.[39]

If life is like a dream, then reality may be perceived but only in a distorted or veiled form. Echoes of this notion can be found even in secular culture. One has only to think, for example, of the traditional round song familiar to small children throughout the English-speaking world:

> Row, row, row your boat
> Gently down the stream,
> Merrily, merrily, merrily, merrily,
> Life is but a dream.

But there is no need to rely on miscellaneous bits of folklore whose meaning is seldom, if ever, seriously considered. The link between life in this world and dreams has been made explicitly in a number of hymns whose content is often taken very seriously indeed. Several, in fact, link life in this world to both dream and stream.

> Swiftly thus our fleeting days
> Bear us down life's rapid stream;
> Upward, Lord, our spirits raise;
> All below is but a dream.[40]

> Time, like an ever-rolling stream
> Bears all its sons away;
> They fly forgotton, as a dream
> Dies at the opening day.[41]

> Some day, I know, in yonder realms of glory
> I and the friend I found while on the way
> Shall speak of that new life and tell the story
> Of this old life, dimmed like a dream by day.[42]

In these hymns, the emphasis is on the ephemeral nature of both dreams and life in this world. Other hymns suggest that it is not only the transience caused by natural finitude that makes life dreamlike, but also the illusions fostered by earthly ambitions. The problem lies not in idle fantasies, as such, but in dangerously distorted notions of the way things truly are.

> Like flow'rs of the field they perish,
> The works of men decay,
> The power and pomp of nations
> Shall pass like a dream away.[43]

> Nothing between my soul and the Savior
> Naught of this world's delusive dreams:

> I have renounced all sinful pleasure,
> Jesus is mine; there's nothing between.[44]

In some cases, life as it is experienced in this world is presented in hymns not merely as a dream but as a nightmare.

> Age after age their tragic empires rise,
> Built while they dream, and in that dreaming weep.[45]

Not all hymns, to be sure, accept the notion that life is like a dream (to say nothing of a nightmare). At least one openly denies it.

> We are not here to play, to dream, to drift,
> We have hard work to do and loads to lift.[46]

Nevertheless, this analogy between life and dream has been part of American popular religion. And it was part of the cultural background in which *The Wizard* was made. I suggest that widespread familiarity with this notion accounts at least partly for the appeal of the movie. To what would otherwise be an ordinary story about the private dreamworld of a little girl, it adds the richness and depth of traditional notions of life and death.

When Dorothy "falls asleep" in Kansas, she dreams of Oz. The first thing she says on awakening in the Munchkin City is "Toto, I have a feeling we're not in Kansas anymore" (53). From the beginning of her sojourn in Oz, then, Dorothy's sense of not being at home—even though the house itself has landed there—is of paramount importance. In fact, her desire to return home motivates her throughout Oz. A similar sense of not being at home in this world, and of longing to be at home, is explicitly stated in many hymns.

> O cease, my wand'ring soul,
> On restless wing to roam;
> All this wide world, to either pole
> Hath not for thee a home.[47]

> I am a stranger here, within a foreign land;
> My home is far away, upon a golden strand.[48]

To be sure, many hymns suggest that Christians can be at home even in this world if "home" is defined as being in the presence of God, or in a state of Grace.

> Anywhere with Jesus, I can go to sleep,
> When the dark'ning shadows round me creep;
> Knowing I shall waken, never more to roam,
> Anywhere with Jesus will be home, sweet home.[49]

Nevertheless, even the presence of God is often understood as a home away from home rather than home itself. It may be a foretaste of the true home, a refuge in a world that would otherwise be intolerable.

> Beneath the cross of Jesus
> I fain would take my stand,
> The shadow of a mighty rock
> Within a weary land;
> A home within the wilderness,
> A rest upon the way,
> From the burning of the noon-tide heat,
> And the burden of the day.[50]

It should be recalled here that Dorothy does not land up in Oz of her own volition. She is brought there, against her will, by forces beyond her control. When Christians sing about being strangers in a foreign land, the same thing is often implied: Christians live in this world as exiles from another world. Not all Christians share this view, of course, but many do. Given the story of Adam and Eve, this is hardly surprising. According to Scripture, the first humans were also the first exiles; the story explicitly refers to the banishment of Adam (and Eve) from Eden and into the world as we know it. "There-fore the Lord God sent him forth from the garden of Eden, to till the ground from which he was taken. He drove out the man; and at the east of the garden of Eden he placed the cherubim, and a flaming sword which turned every way, to guard the way to the tree of life."[51]

Many hymns are equally explicit about the fate of their descen-dents. Most of these express simple longing for the end of exile (that is, the return home).

> Far from my hoe, how long, dear Lord,
> Before my exile endeth?[52]

> Long thy exiles have been pining,
> Far from rest, and home, and thee:

> But, in heavenly vesture shining,
> Soon they shall thy glory see;[53]

Eventually, the exile will end. Home will be restored. This hope alone, according to many hymns, mitigates despair over conditions in the immediate present.

A tent or a cottage, why should I care?
They're building a palace for me over there;
Tho' exiled from home, yet still I may sing:
All glory to God, I'm a child of the King.[54]

In the hope of that immortal crown,
I now the cross sustain;
And gladly wander up and down,
And smile at toil and pain:
I suffer out my threescore years,
Till my deliv'rer come,
And wipe away his servant's tears,
And take his exile home.[55]

Though in a foreign land,
We are not far from home;
And nearer to our house above
We every moment come.[56]

Other hymns, however, suggest that the possibilities for happiness in this world of exile are virtually nonexistent; the only hope is to escape as soon as possible.

O home of fadeless splendor,
Of flow'rs that bear no thorn,
Where they shall dwell as children
Who here as exiles mourn.[57]

Like the ancient Israelites who had to pass through the wilderness on their way back to the Promised Land and, like the early Americans who had to tame the wilderness on their way to becoming a great nation, Dorothy must pass through a wilderness before she can reach her destination. Indeed, Oz contains a Haunted Forest that recalls the untamed forests of early America (when wilderness was threatening "civilization" and was not yet a refuge from it). By the late nineteenth century, though, the forests had long since ceased to be obstacles in the path of progress. Instead, the arid western region of the Great

Plains—what eventually became the "dust bowl"—was most threatening. Since the biblical wilderness was also a desert, it is not surprising
to find this image featured prominently in hymns about life in
exile.

> Guide me, O Thou great Jehovah,
> Pilgrim through this barren land.[58]

> I'm but a stranger here,
> Heav'n is my home;
> Earth is a desert drear,
> Heav'n is my home.[59]

> No tranquil joys on earth I know,
> No peaceful, shelt'ring dome;
> This world's a wilderness of woe,
> This world is not my home.[60]

Be that as it may, life may flourish even in the desert because there
are oases for those who know where to look for them. The following
verse was included in a hymn intended to close worship services; the
congregation is sent out into the wilderness with fresh hope:

> Let us each, Thy love possessing,
> Triumph in redeeming grace.
> Oh, refresh us, Oh refresh us,
> Travelling thro' this wilderness.[61]

Both visually and musically, the Yellow Brick Road is a major
motif in *The Wizard*. In fact, it is a unifying element. By following the
Yellow Brick Road, Dorothy moves not only between the Munchkin
City and the Emerald City, from beginning to end of the dream, but
also from Oz to Kansas. Similarly, Christians follow a path through
the exile, or wilderness, of this life.

> And through the dark, its echoes sweetly ringing,
> The music of the Gospel leads us home.[62]

In fact, "road," "path," and "way" are commonly used as metaphors
for "tradition" in general; more specifically, they may refer to the
Gospel, the Church, faith, or Christ. Moreover, verbs are often used to

emphasize the idea of moving, or being led, toward a transcendent goal.

> Lead us, O Father, in the paths of peace:
> Without Thy guiding hand we go astray,
> And doubts appall, and sorrows still increase;
> Lead us through Christ, the true and living Way.[63]

> Make me to walk in Thy commands;
> 'Tis a delightful road.[64]

If life in this world is truly an exile in the wilderness, then it follows that life is about "movin' on." As I have already noted, this is an extremely common motif in American popular culture. The same is true of American popular religion. Hymn books are filled with references to "walking," "travelling," "sojourning" and "wayfaring."

> I looked to Jesus, and I found
> In Him my Star, my Sun;
> And in that light of life I'll walk,
> Till traveling days are done.[65]

> I am a poor wayfaring stranger,
> While traveling thro' this world below;
> There is no sickness, toil, nor danger
> In that bright world to which I go.[66]

> Lead us on our journey,
> Be thyself the way
> Through our earthly darkness
> To the heav'nly day.[67]

A number of hymns refer to "wandering," or "roaming." The context always makes it clear, however, that for Christians, this journey has a specific destination (which means, in effect, that "wandering" and "roaming," which imply aimlessness, are not to be taken at face value).

> O spread Thy covering wings around
> Till all our wanderings cease,

And at our Father's loved abode
Our souls arrive in peace.[68]

I'm going there to meet my father,
I'm going there no more to roam;
I am just going over Jordan,
I am just going over home.[69]

Given the popularity of literary classics such as *The Pilgrim's Progress* by John Bunyan, it is not surprising to find that many hymns present the Christian life more specifically in terms of a quest, a pilgrimage.

Soon shall close thy earthly mission;
Soon shall pass thy pilgrim days;

Hope shall change to glad fruition,
Faith to sight, and pray'r to praise.[70]

Just as Dorothy's quest begins in Oz and concludes in Kansas, the Christian pilgrimage begins in this world and concludes in the next. Consequently, pilgrimage hymns emphasize both the transience of earthly life and the eternity of heavenly life. Once again, there is no need to rely on inference. This motif appears explicitly in so many hymns that a brief sampling here will be enough to illustrate my point.

Sometimes, the mood is one of desperation. In hymns of this kind, the need for escape as soon as possible is paramount. The road, of course, is fraught with perils both seen and unseen. And these are not merely inherent in "the way things are." They may also be the results of a diabolical conspiracy. The following verse, for example, might well summarize Dorothy's situation in Oz.

I walk in danger all the way.
The tho't shall never leave me
That Satan, who has marked his prey,
Is plotting to deceive me.
This Foe with hidden snares
May seize me unawares
If e'er I fail to watch and pray.
I walk in danger all the way.[71]

Like Satan, the Wicked Witch designates Dorothy as her target, makes elaborate plans to deceive her and finally captures her. Indeed, Dorothy "prays" for help by calling out to the image of Auntie Em in the crystal ball.

> My days are gliding swiftly by,
> And I, a pilgrim stranger,
> Would not detain them as they fly,
> Those hours of toil and danger.[72]

More often, however, the mood is one of excitement. Compare, for example, the preceding verse with the following one.

> Who shall give us strength and courage,
> Patience, hope, and wisdom too,
> That we may, as cheerful pilgrims,
> Still our journey here pursue?[73]

*

If the cosmic life cycle begins with birth into this world (or with spiritual rebirth following conversion), its second phase begins with death and entry into the heavenly world. It may therefore be called the "celestial phase."

> Despair not, O heart, in thy sorrow,
> But hope from God's promises borrow,
> Beware, in thy sorrow, of sinning,
> For death is of life the beginning.[74]

This of course, has been a very common belief in the Christian world. Although no longer maintained by some theologians, it remains strong at the level of popular religiosity; this, at any rate, is revealed by the statistics. A study conducted in 1980 indicated that 71 percent of the American public claimed belief in life after death in heaven (although only 53 percent claimed belief in hell).[75] A study conducted in 1988 showed that 87 percent believe in heaven, 86 percent in eternal life, and 76 percent in hell.[76]

Dorothy's dream of Oz ends when she wakes up. In this case, going home is virtually synonymous with waking up (even though it is also the result of growing up). If life itself is a dream, then it follows that death means ending the dream, or "waking up" from it (providing, of course, that it is preceded by some form of spiritual "growing up" such as repentance or conversion). This is precisely what is indicated in many hymns. It is hardly surprising that "waking up" is a popular phrase in American devotional works. Among the most significant events in American religious history were the "awakenings" that began in the 1740s with the Great Awakening. The topic under discussion here, however, is neither conversion nor repentance but "immortality."

Earlier, I suggested a cultural link (no matter how indirect) between a well-known children's round song and the idea of life as a dream. Sometimes, the link is taken a step further. One hymn, for example, indicates not only that life is a dream, but also that death is the stream that must be crossed to "wake up" from it. It is interesting to compare this with the song.

> Row, row, row your boat
> Gently down the stream,
> Merrily, merrily, merrily, merrily,
> Life is but a dream.

> When ends life's transient dream,
> When death's cold, sullen stream
> Shall o'er me roll,
> Blest saviour, then, in love,
> Fear and distress remove;
> O bear me safe above,
> A ransomed soul.[77]

The idea of "waking up" may be either implicit or explicit. Sometimes, it is implied by the use of nocturnal and diurnal imagery.

> Life's dream is past,
> All its sin and sadness;
> Brightly at last
> Dawns a day of gladness.[78]

At other times, however, the idea of "waking up" beyond the grave is made quite explicit. In the following verse, for example, it is linked to the pilgrimage motif.

> Onward, therefore, pilgrim brothers,
> Onward, with the cross our aid;

> Bear its shame, and fight its battle,
> Till we rest beneath its shade;
> Soon shall come the great awaking,
> Soon the rending of the tomb,
> The scattering of all shadows
> And the end of toil and gloom.[79]

When Dorothy wakes up at home in Kansas, the background music is from "Home Sweet Home." This secular song had been popular for many years. Sigmund Speth notes that "With 'Home, Sweet Home' another landmark is reached in the history of America's popular music,"[80] even though the tune was written by an Englishman, Sir Henry Bishop. Because its key phrase, "there's no place like home," is also a key phrase in *The Wizard* (being the final words spoken) and because the tune flows directly into "Over the Rainbow," it is worth commenting on the origin and history of "Home, Sweet Home." Maymie Krythe devotes a chapter to it in her *Sampler of American Songs*. The words for what eventually became something like an American folksong were written in 1823 by John Howard Payne for his opera, *Clari or, The Maid of Milan*. Although Payne wrote many other songs, his fame rested on this one alone. And he became exceedingly famous for it. Over thirty years after his death in 1852, Payne's body was taken from Tunis, where he had served as the American consul, and given a quasi-state funeral in Washington. "Home, Sweet Home" achieved a durable place in popular music. During the Civil War, for example, it was sung by both Union and Confederate troops—occasionally together. It became the "theme song" of Jenny Lind[81] just as "Over the Rainbow" became the theme song of her counterpart, Judy Garland, seventy-five years later. In fact, "Home, Sweet Home" has been more than a popular song; it has been included as a hymn in at least three collections!

> 'Mid pleasures and palaces though we may roam,
> Be it ever so humble, there's no place like home.
> A charm from the skies seems to hallow us there,
> Which, seek thro' the world is ne'er met with elsewhere.
>
> I gaze on the moon as I tread the drear wild,
> And feel that my mother now thinks of her child,
> As she looks on that moon from our own cottage door,
> Thro' the woodbine whose fragrance shall cheer me no more.
>
> An exile from home, splendor dazzles in vain,
> Or give me my lowly thatched cottage again,

The birds singing gaily, that came at my call,
Give me them, and that peace of mind dearer than all.

Home, home, sweet home,
There's no place like home,
O there's no place like home.[82]

The key phrase, of course, is "home sweet home." It has been used not only in samplers to decorate homes but in many hymns as well.

In the glory land with Jesus on the throne,
I'll live on, yes, I'll live on;
Thro' eternal ages singing, home, sweet home;[83]

'Mid scenes of confusion and creature complaints
How sweet to the soul is communion with the saints!
To find at the banquet of mercy there's room,
And feel in the presence of Jesus at home.
Home! Home! sweet, sweet home!
Prepare for me, dear Saviour, for glory, my home.[84]

Without a bar of separation, "Home Sweet Home" flows into "Over the Rainbow" in the epilogue of *The Wizard*. Although the latter is not sung in the epilogue itself, the words are familiar from the prologue.

Somewhere, over the rainbow,
Way up high,
There's a land that I heard of
Once in a lullaby.

Somewhere over the rainbow,
Skies are blue,
And the dreams that you dare to
Dream really do come true.

Someday I'll wish upon a star
And wake up where the clouds are far
Behind me,
Where troubles melt like lemon drops,
Away above the chimney tops,
That's where you'll find me.

> Somewhere, over the rainbow,
> Bluebirds fly,
> Birds fly over the rainbow,
> Why, then—oh why can't I?
>
> If happy little bluebirds fly
> Beyond the rainbow,
> Why, oh why, can't I? (39-40).[85]

The connection between "Home Sweet Home" and "Over the Rainbow" is clear: home is not here but there, not now but then. As Dorothy herself says, it is "behind the moon, beyond the rain" (39). The same sentiment can be observed in many hymns.

> There's a home for little children
> Above the bright blue sky,
> Where Jesus reigns in glory,
> A home of peace and joy.[86]
>
> Still out of the deepest abyss
> Of trouble, I mournfully cry;
> And pine to recover my peace,
> And see my Redeemer, and die.
> I cannot, I cannot forbear
> These passionate longings for home.[87]

Just as the final destination of Dorothy is home, the final destination of Christian pilgrims, according to many of these hymns, is home. Like "waking up" and several other motifs, "home" may imply repentance or conversion.

> Jesus is tenderly calling thee home—
> Calling today, calling today;
> Why from the sunshine of love wilt thou roam
> Farther and farther away?[88]

The meaning of "home" is particularly ambiguous in black spirituals dating from the period of slavery. Although very few of these can be found in hymnals published during the 1920s and 1930s (even in those used by black churches), John Lovell makes it clear in *Black Song* that overt references to a heavenly home beyond the grave

were often understood as covert references to a terrestrial home
beyond the Mason-Dixon line. He gives the following as examples:

> Swing low, sweet chariot,
> Comin' for to carry me home[89]

> An' I will die in de fiel'
> I'm on my journey home[90]

The hope of crossing the Jordan River, which separated the wilderness from Canaan, could also be understood, for example, as hope of
crossing the Ohio River, which separated the slave states from the
free states.[91] To what extent this political double-entendre continued
after the Civil War is difficult to determine. Nevertheless, the spirituals
are filled with references to a heavenly "home" that is not here but
"over there." For the slaves, no plantation could be understood as
home. This was not only because the slave cabins were generally
squalid; even the most adequate material conditions were marked by
extreme transience because slaves were bought and sold according
to social and economic forces utterly beyond their control.[92]

Most often, however, "home" refers to an otherworldly paradise. It
may, for example, refer to the ultimate destiny of the community (or
its faithful members). In such cases, it is the millenarian tradition
associated with eschatological resurrection that supplies the imagery.

> We wait for Thee; soon Thou wilt come,
> The time is swiftly nearing;
> In this we also do rejoice,
> And long for Thine appearing,
> O bliss 'twill be when Thee we see,
> Homeward Thy people bringing,
> With transport and with singing![93]

> When Thou, my righteous Judge, shalt come
> To take Thy ransomed people home,
> Shall I among them stand?[94]

More often, though, "home" clearly refers to the ultimate fate of
individuals following death. Although the cosmic life cycle could be
discussed on both collective and individual levels, then, evidence

from these hymn books suggests that personal mortality, the ultimate
fate of individuals, is of primary concern for most Americans.

> I'll soon be at home over there,
> For the end of my journey I see;
> Many dear to my heart, over there,
> Are watching and waiting for me.[95]

> Heavenward still, when life shall close,
> Death to my true home shall guide me:[96]

> I know of a sleep in Jesus' name,
> A rest from all toil and sorrow;
> Earth folds in her arms my weary frame
> And shelters it till the morrow;
> My soul is at home with God in heav'n,
> Her sorrows are past and over.[97]

Lovell also points out that the spirituals placed emphasis on reunion
with loved ones after death, possibly because the slaves, even in life,
were so often separated by being sold.[98]

Hymns about reaching home in eternity extend the "road" imagery
discussed earlier. Home is the end of the road, the goal of the
pilgrimage.

> It is not death to die,
> To leave this weary road,
> And midst the brotherhood on high
> To be at home with God.[99]

> Here in the body pent,
> Absent from him I roam,
> Yet nightly pitch my moving tent
> A day's march nearer home.[100]

By far the most common use of "home," however, is with specific
reference to paradise itself. Given the fact that most Americans by
far—81 percent in 1988—claim belief in a future reunion of loved
ones separated by death, it is not surprising that this is one of the
most important features of paradise, or heaven.

My Saviour is now over there,
There my kindred and friends are at rest;
Then away from my sorrow and care,
Let me fly to the land of the blest.

I'll soon be at home over there,
For the end of my journey I see;
Many dear to my heart, over there,
Are watching and waiting for me.[101]

I know a home of joy eternal,
Where all the pilgrim hosts shall meet
In radiancy and bliss complete
Around the Christ in realms supernal.
From east and west, from ev'ry zone,
They gather there before the throne,
At home in joy eternal.[102]

And precisely where is paradise? Traditional imagery usually refers either to the primeval garden or to the eschatological city (or to both). It is derived, in other words, from either Eden or Jerusalem. Christian Scripture begins in the former (Genesis) and ends in the latter (Revelation). Although the iconography differs, the state of being that is described does not. In either form, paradise exists in eternity, beyond the flux of history. They are, therefore, functional equivalents. Still, each is related to the iconography of *The Wizard* in a slightly different way. And it is this difference between "Eden" and "Jerusalem" that may account for the popularity of *The Wizard*.

No one familiar with the imagery of Revelation can fail to see a distant reflection of its cosmic splendor in the Emerald City. Apart from the chromatic domination of one gem, its glossy surfaces and dazzling architecture are reminiscent of the heavenly Jerusalem as described in both scripture and hymnody.

With jasper glow thy bulwarks,
Thy streets with em'ralds blaze;
The sardius and the topaz
Unite in thee their rays;
Thine ageless walls are bonded
With amethyst unpriced;

The saints build up thy fabric,
The cornerstone is Christ.[103]

On the other hand, the celestial city is not only identified as a realm of splendor and happiness beyond compare. Very often, it is also identified as home. Sometimes, this is done implicitly.

> Now, in the meanwhile, with hearts raised on high,
> We for that country must yearn and must sigh,
> Seeking Jerusalem, dear native land,
> Through our long exile on Babylon's strand.[104]

Since a "native land" is where people (or at least their ancestors) were born, Jerusalem is, by implication, the original home. But Jerusalem is also identified as home quite explicitly.

> Far o'er yon horizon
> Rise the city tow'rs,
> Where our God abideth;
> That fair home is ours;
> Flash the streets with jasper,
> Shine the gates with gold;
> Flows the glad'ning river,
> Shedding joys untold,
> Thither, onward thither,
> In the Spirit's might:
> Pilgrims to your country,
> Forward into light![105]

> In the bright eternal city
> Death can never, never come!
> In His own good time He'll call us
> From our rest to home, sweet home.[106]

As we have seen, the garden (either wild or cultivated) took precedence over the metropolis as a vision of American destiny. Agrarianism was a major cultural (and even political) force long after power had shifted from the country to the city. In popular religion, however, urban imagery retained its hold on the American imagination. Here, then, is a discrepancy between the composite picture of paradise presented by the hymns and the one presented symbolically in *The Wizard*. If the entire story had taken place in Oz, then the Emerald City would have been Dorothy's ultimate destination and could thus be associated (no matter how indirectly) with an antitype of the heavenly Jerusalem. But the image of a celestial metropolis is relativized by the addition of a prologue and epilogue set on a farm in Kansas. The Emerald City is Dorothy's *penultimate*, not her ultimate goal. As such, it is more like the utopias that, as McClung points out, have usually been secularized versions of the heavenly Jerusalem. In the 1920s and 1930s, the metropolis was often seen as the realm of progress. This was a time when the agrarian dream was becoming socially and economically anachronistic, after all, and the industrial city seemed to be the only source of hope for many people. The Emerald City not only looks like an art deco fantasy of utopia, albeit a caricatured version, it even contains specific references to both technology (the Wizard's projection booth) and capitalism (the Wash and Brush Up Company).

Dorothy's ultimate goal, however, is not the city but the country. Although *The Wizard* has not succumbed to the antiurban tradition, it has not abandoned the agrarian tradition either. Kansas cannot be identified with a terrestrial paradise. It is too far away. In fact, it is "over the rainbow." To the extent that Kansas represents an order of being qualitatively different from that of Oz, it can be identified as an image of paradise derived from the rural vision of Eden.

The discrepancy between popular culture (the movie) and popular religion (the hymns) can be exaggerated. In the first place, rural imagery is often included in hymns about the heavenly city. Because the same thing happens in Revelation itself, this is hardly surprising. The two versions of paradise are not mutually exclusive.

> Thy gardens and thy goodly walks
> Continually are green,
> Where grow such sweet and pleasant flow'rs
> As nowhere else are seen.
> Right thro' thy streets, with silver sound,
> The living waters flow,
> And on the banks on either side,
> The trees of life do grow.[107]

If the agrarian paradise is not quite as common in hymns as the urban one, moreover, it is by no means ignored. Like most of the other images discussed here, Eden may appear in hymns either implicitly or explicitly. Some hymns, for example, merely suggest a garden.

> Paradise, Paradise,
> Fairest truths delight our eyes;

Where thy verdant trees are planted,
Bliss beyond all dreams is granted:
Take us, Lord, to Paradise,
Take us, Lord, to Paradise.[108]

There pure life-giving streams o'erflow
The sower's garden-ground;
And faith and hope fair blossoms show,
And fruits of love abound.[109]

Other hymns, however, are more direct. They refer explicitly to the Garden of Eden as the paradise to come.

Beautiful valley of Eden,
Home of the pure and blest,
How often amid the wild billows
I dream of thy rest, sweet rest![110]

In the better land,
In that sunny land,
In that Eden land, safe by and by;[111]

Although the urban vision of paradise has always been attractive, it has also been problematic. On the one hand, it corresponded to the immediate needs of a community becoming more and more dependent on cities for solutions to economic problems. By the 1920s, the agrarian dream was being successfully challenged by an urban and industrial dream. As a result, it was not difficult to "translate" the imagery of a heavenly Jerusalem into that of world's fairs and architectural utopias. But for those condemned to endure the dehumanizing aspects of life in real industrial cities, it made sense to believe that the ultimate future would be not merely an improved version of this situation but something radically different.

The soul-starved mountain highlands,
The need of countryside,
The city's creeping darkness,
Where sin and fear abide,
Shall see the marching thousands
That come from far and near:
America, America,
We bring our lives to thee.[112]

In short, the urban paradise was rapidly secularized (relativized) while the rural paradise retained its cosmic (otherworldly) status. All the same, Eden is presented, like Jerusalem, as home.

> Oh, the dear ones in glory,
> how they beckon me to come,
> And our parting at the river I recall;
> To the sweet vales of Eden
> They will sing my welcome home;
> But I long to meet my saviour first of all.[113]

Going home is not necessarily *returning* home. Usually, it is true, home implies origin. Home, in other words, is normally where people (or their ancestors) were born. Going home, therefore, *implies* returning home. The implication, though, is not a logical necessity. Being at home may be a goal for the future rather than a memory of the past (or reality of the present); the search for home may be the search for something not previously experienced. The synoptic gospels themselves do not support an equation of home with origin; the story of Jesus actually begins at a Bethlehem inn, not at the home of his family in Nazareth. The fourth gospel, however, indicates that the Christ originated in Heaven ("In the beginning was the Word, and the Word was with God, and the Word was God. He was in the beginning with God"[114]), lived temporarily on earth as Jesus of Nazareth ("And the Word became flesh and dwelt among us"[115]), and then returned home to Heaven ("I am ascending to my Father and your Father, to my God and your God"[116]). This Johannine pattern, it seems, is implicit in *The Wizard*. Dorothy could make a new home for herself in Oz, after all, but prefers to go back to her old home in Kansas. Moreover, the structure of the movie emphasizes the idea of return. It need not have done so; the same story could have been told differently. Had the prologue in Kansas been dropped, the final return to Kansas in the epilogue would have been a mere explanatory device tacked on to an otherwise independent cinematic unit (Oz). By beginning the movie in Kansas, Oz becomes a parenthesis within the cinematic context of Kansas. The idea of return, therefore, is stressed both narratively and cinematically. The same Johannine pattern is expressed more or less directly in many of the hymns I have examined.

> When from flesh the spirit freed
> Hastens homeward to return,

> Mortals cry, "A man is dead!"
> Angels sing, "A child is born!"[117]

> With my lamp well trimmed and burning,
> Swift to hear and slow to roam,
> Watching for Thy glad returning
> To restore me to my home.[118]

Some hymns, it is true, refer to Heaven as *God's* home; Christians are invited to live there but not because they started out there. The following verses provide an interesting contrast.

> Wherein as Christians we may live
> Or die in peace that Thou canst give,
> To rise again when Thou shalt come
> And enter Thine eternal home.[119]

> Let us, like these good shepherds, then employ
> Our grateful voices to proclaim the joy;
> Trace we the Babe, who hath retrieved our loss,
> From his poor manger to his bitter cross;

> Treading his steps, assisted by his grace,
> Till man's first heav'nly state again takes place.[120]

Most of these hymns make it clear that the home to which Christian pilgrims are drawn is, in some sense, both destiny and origin. It is implied, for example, by the use of terms such as "homeland," "native land," or "fatherland" with reference to paradise. These are all designations of origin; those who do not come from there as individuals do so as members of a collectivity (family or ancestors).

> Rise, my soul, and stretch thy wings,
> Thy better portion trace;
> Rise from transitory things
> Toward heaven, thy native place:[121]

> Immanuel! God with us!
> This is our final sigh
> When our last hour comes on us
> And death's dark vale is nigh.

'Tis then His love enfolds us
And takes us by the hand
To lead us safely homeward
To our true Fatherland.

My loved ones in the Homeland
Are waiting me to come,
Where neither death nor sorrow
Invades their holy home;
O dear, dear native Country!
O rest and peace above!
Christ bring us to the Homeland
Of Thy redeeming love;[122]

The biblical "homeland" is first described as the Promised Land. Abraham and Sarah did not originate there, but it became home for them and the community they founded. It was the home to which their descendents returned after centuries of absence in Egypt. It was the home to which the Jews returned after seventy years of exile in Babylon. And it is the home (whether terrestrial or heavenly) to which many Jews and Christians hope to return in the future.

Heavenward still our pathway tends;
Here on earth we are but strangers,
Till our road in Canaan ends,
Safely past this wild of dangers;
Here we but as pilgrims rove,
For our home is there above.[123]

While on this sad earth we stay,
We must here as pilgrims wander.
Through the desert we must roam,
Till we Canaan reach, our home.[124]

The mere use of agrarian imagery connotes both the Promised Land and Eden. Consequently, references to either must also connote the idea of return home (that is, return to the origin of the community and the origin of the cosmos itself).

Rejoicing now in earnest hope,
I stand, and from the mountain top

See all the land below:
Rivers of milk and honey rise,
And all the fruits of paradise
In endless plenty grow.[125]

Unlike Jerusalem, Eden is not only home, it is the *original* home. Any reference to Eden as a future home is, by implication, also a reference to returning home.

The limitations imposed by finitude may generate the desire to experience higher, deeper, or altered states of consciousness. Most traditions have provided "religious technologies" (such as meditation techniques or hallucinogenic drugs) for use toward this end by mystics and shamans. But they have also enabled ordinary people to share the experience—even if only for brief periods in highly controlled settings. Sacramental rituals, by definition, provide access to a dimension of reality beyond the flux of time, a glimpse of the gods and spirits in some primeval or eschatological realm that would otherwise be inaccessible. For Roman Catholics, the Last Supper can be reexperienced through transubstantiation. For the Eastern Orthodox, the Messianic Banquet can be "preexperienced" at the same time. In most Protestant churches, the eucharist is understood as a symbolic event, not an actual event; communion is a present-day ritual recalling a past event rather than a replay of the past event itself. Although this is much closer to the secular notion of linear time (in which time is irreversible), it is still related to the notion of mythic time because events in the primeval past or eschatological future still provide a normative orientation in time. If only on the cognitive level, time or history is still "punctuated" by eternity (to use the term of Abraham Joshua Heschel).[126]

Even Americans whose religious traditions do not emphasize sacramental ritual are familiar with the temporal framework on which they are based.

Lord Jesus, Light of Paradise,
Shine on me my life long,
In all earth's din cause me to hear
Faint fragments of that song.[122]

Let me with my heart today,
Holy, holy, holy, singing,

Rapt awhile from earth away,
All my soul to Thee upspringing,
Have a foretaste inly given
How they worship Thee in Heaven.[128]

Lord, give us such a faith as this;
And then, whate'er may come,
We'll taste e'en now the hallowed bliss
Of an eternal home.[129]

Although the last verse is from a Lutheran collection, the other two are from collections of the Reformed tradition that moved much further from the Roman Catholic doctrine of transubstantiation. There is evidence to suggest that the notion of mythic time has survived in the modern, secular world. While Dorothy makes her way through Oz, at any rate, she is by no means cut off from that other world, Kansas. Not only does she witness Auntie Em calling out to her through the Witch's crystal ball, but she is dimly aware that her three new friends, are in fact, old friends from the farm.

*

The Judaeo-Christian tradition has made Americans familiar with the notion of life in this world as a dream; this world is real, to be sure, but not as real as the paradisian world into which we "wake up" after death. Because the Oz sequences take place in Dorothy's dream, it is logical to conclude that Oz, not Kansas, represents life as we know it in this world. For most Americans, that has included religion. We should therefore expect to find cinematic parallels in the Oz sequences to a notion that lies at the heart of traditional forms of religious life: the notion that we can glimpse eternity within time or paradise within history (that is, either before death or before the end of history). The sacraments in older forms of Christianity (along with their functional equivalents in Judaism and other traditions) are not merely pedagogical devices designed to propagate theological or ethical precepts. Nor are they merely formalized reminiscences of historical events. These rituals (along with their corresponding myths) make it possible to participate in primordial events (such as the resurrection of Christ, his founding of the Christian community, and re-creation of the cosmos) that took place *in illo tempore*, as Eliade puts it, and continue to take place in sacred time and space. In short, they reveal the sacred that normally lies hidden within the profane. Many features of *The Wizard* suggest familiarity with (if not belief in) this worldview.

In *The Wizard*, there are two interrelated worlds: Kansas and Oz. They correspond, I suggest, to the two interrelated dimensions of reality noted earlier: the sacred and the profane. To put it another way, what Kansas is to Oz the sacred is to the profane. The sacred is normally identified with the harmony, order, and perfection of The Beginning, or paradise. But, in the prologue, Kansas includes disharmony, disorder, and imperfection. How, then, can it be discussed in terms of sacred time? Kansas, I suggest, should be understood as paradise in the same sense as Eden itself. In Genesis, Eden is first described in explicitly paradisian terms: "And out of the ground the Lord made to grow every tree that is pleasant to the sight and good for food."[130] This brief passage provides a backdrop for the Fall. In *The Wizard*, the paradisian aspect of Kansas is implicit rather than explicit. When Professor Marvel tells Dorothy that he can see the farm in his crystal ball, she immediately remembers the happiness and security she had always known there. Although the prologue actually begins with events leading directly to Dorothy's "fall" and "expulsion" (her inability to cope with Miss Gulch), therefore, these events may be seen as part of the transition from Kansas to Oz (just as the Fall itself is the transition from eternity to history) and not as inherent features of life in Kansas. If Kansas—implicitly in the prologue and explicitly in the epilogue—corresponds to paradise, then it also corresponds to eternity, or sacred time. Being dialectically related to the profane, the sacred is experienced within and through the profane. Similarly, Kansas is experienced by Dorothy while still in Oz. Throughout her sojourn there, Dorothy meets characters familiar from Kansas. In fact, she remarks on this both in Oz ("And it's funny, but I feel as if I'd known you all the time") and back home in Kansas ("And you...and you...and you...and you were there"). This mingling of the sacred (Kansas) and the profane (Oz) has a somewhat ritualistic quality. The same event (Dorothy meeting someone she "knows" from Kansas) takes place three times. Each time, it is accompanied by music and dance. And in each case, the songs and steps are variations on a common theme. In the midst of Oz, at any rate, Kansas is accessible. But it is accessible only imperfectly (Dorothy is unable to identify the Kansas counterparts of her new friends precisely) and temporarily (she soon forgets about them in view of more urgent problems). The same is true in religion. While still in this world, Jews cannot dwell too long on the Sabbath and Christians cannot tarry too long at the Eucharist. But these rituals provide at least a foretaste of what is to come, a preview within time, or history, of eternity.

The meeting of sacred and profane is represented much more dramatically in one scene at the Witch's Castle. Peering into the crystal ball, Dorothy has a "vision" of Auntie Em. Terribly anxious about Dorothy, she calls out for her lost child. Dorothy can hear Auntie Em but cannot be heard *by* Auntie Em; communication is frustrated. To make matters worse, the Witch violates even this pathetic attempt to stay in contact with Kansas. It is she, not Auntie Em, who hears Dorothy. Responding with a sinister cackle, her leering face blocks out the benign image of Auntie Em. Dorothy's "vision" does not correspond to the definition of a ritual, but it does correspond to another feature of the relation between sacred and profane. Although human communities can organize life around sacred places (such as holy cities or pilgrimage churches) and sacred times (rituals or festivals), they cannot control the sacred. According to Eliade, the sacred may be experienced on a regular basis (through myth and ritual), but it may also manifest itself suddenly and spontaneously (through hierophanies, theophanies, or kratophanies). This is precisely what happens over and over again in Oz. The Good Witch of the North (Glinda) and the Wicked Witch of the West have agendas of their own. Sometimes, for example, the former responds directly to pleas for help; at other times, she appears or disappears without warning or time for preparation. The latter always appears and disappears without warning or time for preparation.

As supernatural beings, the two witches are implicitly linked to two modalities of the sacred that have long been recognized (on the popular level if not always on the elite level) in Judaism and Christianity: the divine and the satanic.[131] The cosmic forces represented by these two characters apparently correspond to traditional notions of angels and demons respectively. Both are identified with fire, it is true, but angels are identified more specifically with light and demons with flame or smoke. Both are also identified with air, but angels are associated with the sky or clouds and demons with wind or storms. In *The Wizard*, both witches travel by air but aboard different "carriers." The Good Witch takes off and lands gently in a silvery bubble accompanied by the tinkle of a glockenspiel; the Wicked Witch takes off and lands violently in a ball of flame and smoke accompanied by claps of thunder.

Sacred space is defined partly as the source and center of sacred power. Religious people are thus spatially oriented. Jews see themselves in relation to Jerusalem, for example, and Muslims in relation to Mecca. Because sacred beings may be either divine or satanic, we may expect the places associated with them to reflect these modalities. The Emerald City (where Glinda, not the Wizard, seems to be firmly in control) is the venue of benevolent power and life; the Witch's Castle is the venue of malevolent power and death. If the Emerald City is associated with integration and harmony (since this is where Dorothy and her friends are officially welcomed as members of the community), the Witch's Castle is associated with disintegration and disharmony (since this is where Dorothy is separated from her friends—and where the Witch disintegrates as a result of her wickedness). Dorothy and her friends are spatially oriented in relation to both. As much as they seek the former, they avoid the latter. It is worth examining each of these places in more detail at this point.

The Emerald City is clearly an art deco structure. As such, it bears unmistakable associations with modernity. And modernity, in turn, is generally associated with technology, progress, and secularity. Nonetheless, its formal features (considered separately and not as part of a stylistic package) bear unmistakable associations with the temples and shrines of religious architecture throughout the world. This is true especially of its elevation (seen at a distance from the field of poppies). It has the verticality, massiveness and grandeur of a gothic cathedral or a Babylonian ziggurat. In fact, it calls to mind the prototypes of all such religious structures. Isolated against a low horizon, it is the sacred mountain—the Zion or Fuji of Oz. Being green,[132] moreover, it is also the cosmic tree. Both represent the *axis mundi* linking heaven and earth. Considering that the Emerald City is Dorothy's final goal, the culmination of her journey in Oz, it is worth noting that its plan, too, is strikingly similar to those of temples, churches, and other sacred buildings—particularly those associated with pilgrimage routes. Characteristic of these buildings is a succession of gates separating courts that increase in sanctity toward the center. Like Gentile visitors to the ancient Temple in Jerusalem, Dorothy and her friends find it difficult to make their way to the "holy of holies." They manage to enter the city proper with only minor difficulties at the gate. Entry to the inner sanctum is another matter. At first, they are told to go away. Then the gatekeeper relents, admitting them to a long and distinctly numinous corridor. Now fear, not external authority, hinders their progress.

Still, they emerge from this awesome corridor—a vaulted pastiche of the naves in Cistercian abbeys—and find themselves in a grand audience hall. Confronted by the Wizard's august presence, they fall to the ground in terror as if they have encountered what Rudolf Otto called the *mysterium tremendum et fascinans.* Just below the exalted visage of Oz, the Great and Powerful, they find an altar, candles or incense burners (flames) and what appear to be organ pipes. These visual motifs are all familiar features of modern American churches. At the heart of the Emerald City, in short, is a church or temple. It is not unreasonable, therefore, to see a symbolic connection here between the Emerald City and the goal of a pilgrimage route or even the *axis mundi.*

If it is an *axis mundi,* it is only one of two in *The Wizard.* This would not surprise Eliade. He has often pointed out that the *axis mundi* links earth not only to heaven but also to hell. The Emerald City is an artificial mountain; the Witch's Castle is set upon a mountain. This identifies it as an *axis mundi.* And just as access to the Emerald City's "holy of holies" is restricted by heavily guarded doors, or gates, the same is true of the Witch's Castle. In most ways, however, the latter is as different from the former as the Wicked Witch of the West is different from the Good Witch of the North. I have already pointed out many differences in Chapter 2. But two are worth noting here. One is the presence of fire. This is an extremely common symbol of the sacred. As at the Emerald City, fire is a prominent motif at the Witch's Castle. But instead of inspiring awe by suggesting the presence of a divine being at the altar, it provokes terror by suggesting the presence of a satanic being lurking in the shadows. It is with fire from her blazing broom that the Witch intends to kill the Scarecrow. She herself has been heavily identified with fire; almost every one of her appearances is marked by a burst of flame and smoke. The eerie glow of leaping flames, of course, is conventionally associated with the lakes of burning brimstone in hell. Also worth noting here is the use of light. The Witch's Castle is seen only at night (a time of chaos when the ghosts of the dead haunt the living and the eyes of the living are closed in sleep). The Emerald City, on the other hand, is seen either under brilliant illumination or in broad daylight (a time of order when the ghosts return to their graves and eyes are open once more to the light of consciousness).

According to many religious traditions, the world of everyday life is characterized by ambiguity. It is the realm of both good and evil, both order and chaos, both divine and satanic forces. But there is a way to pass safely through the life cycle's terrestrial phase: religious tradition. Very often, the journey between this world and the next, birth and death, origin and destiny, is described as a road or path. Along the way, it is possible to catch a glimpse of whatever transcends the confusion of everyday life. And at the end (in the West, at any rate) is paradise, eternal life or some other form of transmundane existence. Religious seekers, therefore, follow terrestrial pilgrimage routes to holy cities or sacred shrines where visions of the celestial, or ultimate pilgrimage are clearest. And ordinary people follow along, as well as they can, in their footsteps. The Yellow Brick Road is not only the open road to freedom, it is also the Way to inner harmony, mystical union or, at the very least, a better life in the world to come.

If my analogy between *The Wizard* and Judaeo-Christian notions of sacred and profane is correct, life in this world is represented by Oz—and, more specifically, by the Yellow Brick Road that traverses it from one end to the other. It is characterized by the search for order in the midst of chaos. Consequently, it is also characterized by pilgrimage through chaos (the Haunted Forest) to the source of life, holiness, and order (the Emerald City) by staying safely on the path (following the Yellow Brick Road) and avoiding the source of death, sin, and chaos (the Witch's Castle). Along the way, we may encounter divine or satanic beings (Glinda or the Witch). Having completed the terrestrial phase of our journey, the celestial phase begins; we are ready for the return to paradise (Kansas).

As I have already suggested, Kansas is not only the beginning of the movie, it is the Beginning. It is the world as it was *in illo tempore*. The biblical Eden is paradise. But within paradise is a serpent. It is within paradise, therefore, that Adam and Eve fall from grace. Kansas is not immediately revealed as paradise. The movie begins (in the prologue) not with Dorothy's "prelapsarian" life in Kansas but with her "fall" and "expulsion." This is because Kansas is always seen through Dorothy's eyes; if she is unable to "see" truly in the prologue she is able to do so after returning from Oz in the epilogue. Consequently, Kansas is not only the end of the movie, it is also the End. It is the world as it will be at the *eschaton*.[133] In the prologue, Dorothy is forced by a serpentine tornado to leave home. Otherwise, she could not have reached the level of maturity necessary to understand the meaning of being at home with her family, being at home in the world at large and (by implication) being at home with God. In the epilogue, she is ready to take her proper place at

home, in the world and (by implication) with God. The main difference is to be found not in Kansas but in Dorothy herself. In the
epilogue, unlike the prologue, she has "eyes to see and ears to hear."

Ultimately, then, *The Wizard* is a statement of faith not only in the
individual and the nation but in the cosmic matrix of both. Despite
the perils, despite the lapses into chaos, life in this world is worth
living because there is an underlying order that can be experienced
partly now (in everyday life) and fully then (in another life beyond
the flux of time and space). And what was true of America in 1939 is
true also of America today. (For evidence of this in American popular
culture, see Appendix 4.)

*

American notions of both the individual and the collective life
cycles are based on deeply rooted notions of a cosmic life cycle. The
individual grows up by going home (and vice versa). The nation
"grows up" by "going home" (and vice versa). The soul "grows up" by
"going home" (and vice versa). Evidently, there is a pattern here. All
three, in fact, are linked by a biblical paradigm of "growing up"
through history (informed by Torah or Gospel) and "going home" to
Eden. Usually this link is made implicitly. But sometimes it is made
quite explicitly. It seems appropriate, therefore, to conclude by
examining the symbolic mechanism that makes these links possible
and even likely.

According to traditional forms of both Judaism and Christianity, it
is not only the individual soul that returns to its origin in eternity;
the same thing is true of the community and, by implication, the
cosmos itself. The latter, unlike the former, is clearly indicated in
Scripture. In *The Great Code*, Northrop Frye discusses the typological
way of thinking that has traditionally been characteristic of Judaism
and Christianity.

> Typology is a figure of speech that moves in time. The type exists in the
> past and the antitype in the present, or the type exists in the present
> and the antitype in the future. What typology really is as a mode of
> thought, what it both assumes and leads to, is a theory of history, or
> more accurately of historical process: an assumption that there is some
> meaning and point to history, and that sooner or later some event or
> events will occur which will indicate what that meaning or point is,
> and so become an antitype of what has happened previously.[134]

The basic story, spanning the entire corpus of the Christian canon, from Genesis to Revelation, begins in paradise and ends in paradise. The Garden of Eden represents the world as it once was: a realm of pristine beauty, harmony, and perfection. It is untainted, undefiled, unpolluted. But something goes wrong. The inhabitants, Adam and Eve, fail to understand who they are and where they are. They make a mistake and pay for it by being thrown out of the garden and into the wilderness. The world they enter is the world as we know it now. It is the ordinary, everyday world of finitude, fragmentation, alienation and imperfection. It is the world of profane time and space. But God has not abandoned the human race. Through various covenants (the first one being with Noah), we are shown how to transcend the ravages of history, how to maintain the relationship with God that was once so much more intimate and direct. At the end of history, we can expect some final cataclysm, or apocalypse, which will be followed by a new and everlasting order of perfection. In Revelation, it is described as a heavenly city that, nevertheless, contains the tree of life identified with the primeval garden. The underlying assumption of return to paradise found in scripture has been summarized by Frye.

> There are two levels of nature: the lower one, expressed in God's contract with Noah, presupposes a nature to be dominated and exploited by man; the higher one, expressed in an earlier contract with Adam in Paradise, is the nature to which man essentially belongs, and the Eden story prefigures the redemption which takes him back to this level. On the way from the lower level to the higher one we meet the images of the world of work, the pastoral, agricultural, and urban imagery that suggest a nature transformed into a humanly intelligible shape. The Bible's structure of imagery, then, contains, among other things, the imagery of sheep and pasture, the imagery of harvest and vintage, the imagery of cities and temples, all contained in and infused by the oasis imagery of trees and water that suggests a higher mode of life altogether.[135]

Unlike our ancestors, we will have learned from our journey through history; we will know how to live at peace among ourselves and in harmony with God. This macromyth is the "type" corresponding to numerous micromyths that are its "antitypes."

One of these begins in the land of Canaan during the patriarchal period. Life is not quite as idyllic as it was in Eden. Nevertheless, it is remembered as a kind of golden age, a new beginning. It was, after all, the origin of Israel just as Eden was the origin of the human race. Eventually, the Children of Israel must leave home because of famine.

In at least one midrashic source,[136] the famine that precipitates the migration to Egypt (like any other famine) is not seen as a freak of nature, an accident, but as a divine act. It is a punishment. It is a kind of "fall." In any case, the Children of Israel enter a world of slavery in Egypt. This is followed by wandering through the wilderness (first the sea and then the desert). As in the macromyth, however, God maintains contact with them through a new covenant given at Mount Sinai. Through the Ten Commandments, the Israelites have continuing access to holiness and truth. Toward the end of the story, some decisive battles must be won against the Canaanite inhabitants of the Promised Land. Finally, they are back home. But, before long, problems emerge again and a new cycle begins.

This micromyth begins with the rise of the First Temple. It represents direct and immediate access to the *shekhinah* (divine presence). Gradually, the situation deteriorates due to royal infidelity and sinfulness (which, by extension, includes that of the people). Disaster strikes with the arrival of Nebuchadnezzar and the resulting exile. God's presence, however, is mediated in a new way; the origin of the synagogue as a (not quite perfect) replacement for the Temple can be traced to the needs of an exiled people. According to the general pattern established in the macromyth, a major battle takes place; in this case, it is between the Persians and the Babylonians. With a Persian victory, Cyrus (an agent of God) sends the Jews back home. Once again, though, problems soon emerge and a new cycle begins.

After the Temple is restored, the situation deteriorates once more until (according to one Jewish tradition) collective guilt makes the people unfit to dwell in the holy land. After their defeat by Rome, the Jews adjust to the idea of an exile coextensive with history itself. In other words, it will come to an end but only with the end of time, as such. In the meantime, Torah living (as understood by the rabbis) mediates holiness and truth. After an apocalyptic event of one kind or another, the Messianic Age will mean a return to (among other things) the immediacy of God's presence in Temple worship. The goal of history is thus a new beginning, a collective return to origin. This story, of course, represents the merging of "antitype" and "type," of micromyth and macromyth.

The early Christians, observes Frye, continued the tradition of typological thinking that had been characteristic of the prophets. That is, they added new symbolic layers to the prophetic vision. "That vision...had two levels: the level of the present moment and the level above it. The latter is both that of the original identity sym-

bolized by the garden of Eden (along with, as we shall see, the
Promised Land and the Temple), and the ultimate identity symbolized
by the return to these things after the 'Day of the Lord' and the
restoring of Israel. Jesus' teaching centers on the conception of a
present spiritual kingdom that includes all these upper-level images,
and on earth he is thought of as living simultaneously in it and
among us."[137]

For the early Christians, the merging of time and eternity takes
place (proleptically, at any rate) within history. The primeval garden
is restored with Christ living intimately among his followers just as
Adam and Eve lived with God in Eden. In spite of the many conflicts
recorded in the gospels, this period is remembered by the tradition
as one of unparalleled sanctity. But there is a serpent in this garden,
too. Christ is betrayed.[138] This leads to the crucifixion, which, in turn,
leads to a new, less exalted, era. Just as diaspora history has meant
terror and alienation for Jews, church history has involved the
increasing fragmentation of heresies, schisms, and religious wars.[139]
Still, the apostles and their descendents have not been left without
consolation. Just as Torah provides Jews with access to eternity, the
sacraments do for Christians. And just as Jews reexperience Eden
and preview the Messianic Age on the Sabbath, Christians reexperience the Last Supper and preview the Messianic Banquet at the
Eucharist. At the end of time, a final battle, this time against the
Antichrist, will be won. At that point, we will have come full circle; in
the Kingdom, we will have returned to the Beginning when Christ
lived among his followers.

As Frye keeps pointing out, however, this story is only the ultimate
version, for Christians, of a story that is repeated over and over
again throughout Scripture. He observes, for example, that "This
Kingdom of God is an idealized world, metaphorically identical...with
the spiritual Garden of Eden and the Promised Land, including the
future Promised Land of the restored Israel and the New Testament
apocalypse."[140] Elsewhere, he writes that "the garden of Eden, the
Promised Land, Jerusalem, and Mount Zion are interchangeable
synonyms for the home of the soul, and, in Christian imagery, they
are all identical, in their 'spiritual' form...with the Kingdom of God
spoken of by Jesus."[141]

Given these religious traditions, it is easy to see why early
Americans saw their own history in typological terms. That is, they
saw their own communal story as one more in a long series of
antitypes beginning within scripture itself. In *Righteous Empire*,

Martin Marty discusses the emergence of identity in Protestant America. For the earliest settlers, Providence was the driving force behind history. Providence had inspired the Reformation. Providence had led the pilgrims on their "errand into the wilderness" and established their "city set upon a hill." For a later generation, Providence had blessed the national struggle for freedom from a corrupt England. In fact, Providence was routinely invoked by leaders such as Jefferson, Franklin, Washington, and Lincoln until well into the nineteenth century. Providence did not refer to random change. It referred, on the contrary, to change in relation to a goal. God had a goal. Consequently, the nation under God had one too. More specifically, its mission was to be the new Israel. For some, indeed, America was to be "a kind of public and semi-political counterpart to the religious ideal of the Kingdom of God."[142] Many scholars have commented on the tendency of Americans to see themselves, their land and their history in redemptive terms. The first generation of Americans (that is, the first generation after independence) was very secular; only 5 or 10 percent of the population was affiliated with a religious institution or community. But the next generation was very different. "A strong sense of place was fused with their sense of mission and destiny. As had their fathers before them, they regularly resorted to scriptural imagery to define themselves. In the colonial era the image of the wilderness prevailed. Now the familiar term was 'the Promised Land,' and they were the Israelites who were called to conquer it."[143] The identification of America with Israel was made not only by orthodox Protestants but by the often unorthodox literati as well. Though far from being a conventional Protestant, for example, Herman Melville could write the following: "We Americans are the peculiar, chosen people—the Israel of our time; we bear the ark of liberties of the world."[144]

Typological thinking about America, however, is no longer expressed solely in theological terms. By the eighteenth century, many Protestants were reinterpreting their tradition in deist, or quasi-deist, terms; for them, Providence was a vague force that guided the destiny of the nation. And by the late nineteenth century, the term was sometimes dropped altogether. It was replaced by a secular term. "Progress," writes Marty, "became the high intellectual drama for Protestants in much of the second century of their life in the United States."[145] Inherent in the idea of Progress, however, is a linear notion of time. Destiny is seen as something other than, better than, origin. I would argue that this was only one "translation" of Providence into secular terms. The other involves a circular notion of time. Destiny is seen as a return or a series of returns to origin. In both cases, history is seen in teleological terms. But the *telos* of the former is very different from that of the latter. In a paradoxical way, Americans would like to embrace both. They want to affirm the notion of Progress represented by the Emerald City. At the same time, they want to affirm the notion of Return represented by Kansas. Because the latter is given preferred status in *The Wizard*, it is worth noting some of the characteristically American antitypes of the biblical type (that is, the macromyth of return to paradise). Both focus on nostalgia for a lost golden age. This golden age may be located in the earliest days of America or in a world that vanished only "the day before yesterday." In all cases, though, the idyllic dream is shattered. There is always a serpent in the garden. Something always goes wrong. Within this general framework, we can discern at least two distinct traditions. One of them emphasizes the freedom of that lost golden age. The other emphasizes its order. In other words, each can be traced back to the biblical notion of Eden but each selects a slightly different aspect as its central motif.

One story opens in the Old West. This new beginning is a withdrawal from the corrupting and confining civilization of the East. The frontier opens up new possibilities of freedom. But civilization eventually catches up with the lone hero on horseback. This is the fall from a primeval paradise of empty plains and thundering herds. Unlike Adam and Eve, however, the hero is not banished from paradise; on the contrary, paradise is invaded and overrun. The present finds America with its "wild garden" vanishing due to urbanization, industrialization, and the inevitable consequences of both: overcrowding and pollution. Through environmentalism (with its national parks) and populism (based on hardy individualism and independence) and the productions of popular culture (such as "Frontierland" theme parks or western novels and movies) Americans retain a vision of the way things should be. Will they ever return to a primeval frontier? Possibly, but not to the same one. The newest frontier of all transcends America itself (except insofar as the heroes, who represent the human race, are still Americans). This is the frontier of outer space, known to aficionados of "Star Trek" as "the final frontier." It, too, has a primeval quality. After all, the very fabric of our planet comes from the stars. Not only is outer space our origin, it is also our destiny. The story begins, as it does in *2001: A Space Odyssey* (Stanley Kubrick, 1968), somewhere in the void at some time in the remote past. Earth is infused from beyond with the makings of life and, eventually, of civilization. The latter, of course is a major source of conflict. In our time, this serpent has left us with (among many other problems) the deadly competition, in space as elsewhere, between the United States and the Soviet Union. Through science, though, we are still in touch with the mysterious, numinous emptiness and beauty of galaxies far from our own troublesome world. The final trial, or apocalypse, may include a nuclear war that renders earth uninhabitable. In any case, the story often concludes with the establishment of new colonies in space. This completes the circle. The notion of primeval harmony has also survived in various forms of American folklore. In "horse operas," the frontier represents a new beginning for the individual: someone who cannot cope with the complexities and restrictions of industrial civilization. In "space operas," however, we are closer to the idea that began in New England: the frontier as a new beginning for the entire community (in this case, the human race).

Another kind of nostalgia seems to operate in American fantasies of the Old South. Being an agrarian world, it, too, represents harmony in nature. The appeal, however, is not to the natural freedom of life in the wilderness but to the natural order of life in the garden. It is the inherent order of society, based on the inherent order of nature itself, that is most evocative. The Old South, after all, represents an aristocratic vision of society; everything and everyone has a pre-ordained, even primordial status and role. This is a static world in which harmony results from acceptance of a timeless and natural hierarchy binding everyone in a web of mutual obligation. The story begins in the antebellum South. After a bitter struggle, the relentless forces of history overtake this arcadian world of order and beauty. This brings about what is generally considered America's official loss of innocence (the "fall" from grace). As in the Old West, the inhabitants of paradise are not banished; Dixie is invaded and occupied. In the present, contact with the dream may be maintained through such political ideologies as racism or nativism along with the fantasies of popular culture (such as *Gone with the Wind*). As for the final trial that presages the return to arcadia, war, once again, seems the most likely scenario; order can be restored only after the ultimate in disorder, which is war. As in the Old West, the "return" will not be to a past historically recreated (such as a plantation system based on slavery) but to a world founded on similar notions of order and harmony (such as those espoused by some fundamentalist communities). Somehow, America will be renewed as a paradise.

Even though such fantasies of empty frontiers and bucolic landscapes may have little or nothing to do with the actual course of
American history, they are still very real responses to that history.
Industrialization, it is true, may have actually begun decades before
the Civil War, but that event is usually taken as the symbolic
beginning of "modern" American history. It is the coming of age; it is
the ordeal that initiates America into the openly cynical and corrupt
civilization to which earlier generations had believed themselves
immune. After that, urban blight and industrial expansion completed
the transformation of an isolated, rural, and verdant Peaceable
Kingdom to a polluted, crowded, noisy, and corrupt Naked City. But
hope remains for a return to order and harmony. Without such a
hope, without "secular myths" to articulate visions of the future,
there could be no meaning in the present.

From the preceding, it is clear that the individual, collective and
cosmic levels of identity are profoundly interrelated. We cannot discuss the celestial phase of the life cycle of the soul without discussing
its terrestrial phase. Nor can we refer to either without referring as
well to the life cycle of the nation. All are modalities of a symbolic
structure that has been assumed by (Jews and) Christians for many
centuries. In that case, it is not unreasonable to suggest that a movie
about an individual who grows up and goes home is linked, subconsciously if not consciously, to those other stories of growing up
and going home. Although *The Wizard* explicitly says nothing about
religion, it implicitly restates the religious worldview that has
shaped American culture and provides, even today, the symbolic
matrix of American life.[146] By affirming the traditional notion of
return to origin (paradise), it gives mythic expression to the deepest
hopes of the American people—religious and secular, young and old,
male and female, rich and poor, black and white, eastern and western.
Movies of this kind are not only nostalgic recollections of the past or
naive affirmations of the present; they are also profound statements
of faith in the future.

Figure 7

©1988, Washington Post Writers Group. Reprinted with permission.

6 CONCLUSION

All things considered, *The Wizard* is in many ways a religious or quasi-religious phenomenon. It is, however, a movie. And movies are not normally studied as religious phenomena. They are usually studied as either sociological or aesthetic phenomena. (A fuller discussion can be found in Appendix 1.) From the former perspective, movies are of interest primarily as the products of an industry and for what they reveal about the relation between those who produce them and those who "consume" them. Generally speaking, this school of thought is represented by Marxist theories of hegemony. The popular movies characteristic of mass culture, they argue, reproduce the power of the ruling class by propagating false consciousness; this renders the working class unable to understand its own reality (exploitation) and challenge it. In "Hegemony and Mass Culture: A Semiotic Approach," M. Gottdiener has proposed another theory. He argues that subclasses and subcultures often "transfunctionalize" popular culture; that is, they assign new meanings to suit their own needs. These may even contradict those intended by the producers. Gottdiener is thus able to take mass culture seriously instead of dismissing it as evidence of a conspiracy. Unfortunately, though, he has only modified the hegemony theory and not challenged it. For him, the issue is still primarily one of class struggle. He shows how popular culture can be used by subclasses or subcultures to subvert the intention of the ruling class, to be sure, but cannot explain why a movie like *The Wizard* is so popular across the lines of class, race, sex, religion, and region. Far from promoting the interests of one group over another, it promotes the integration of all in a unified society. Gottdiener's theory may be very useful in connection with other movies (especially those associated with "cults" appealing to members of alienated groups defined by age, social class, or some other criterion), but it is not very useful in connection with this one (a "cult" including virtually all Americans).

The other major way of studying film is in terms of art. The problem here is that the definition of art prevalent in the contemporary Western world is not very helpful when discussing movies such as *The Wizard*. In *The Transformation of the Avant-Garde*, Diana Crane points out that art is now associated primarily with innovation and provocation. Artists stand back from their cultural environment, often as alienated or marginal figures, and challenge the aesthetic, social, economic, or political status quo. Their aim is to generate new ways of thinking, feeling, or perceiving the world. Consequently, they are most often explicitly hostile to tradition—not merely to this or that tradition but to the whole idea of tradition. *The Wizard*, however, clearly supports a traditional way of life; after all, it is about returning home. Evaluated in terms of the avant-garde, it could be classified only as bad art. It is well to remember, however, that the avant-garde notion of art is by no means the only one. In *Art in Primitive Societies*,[1] Richard Anderson points out that in most societies art is understood in a very different way, even the opposite way. It is almost always used to support and propagate the commonly shared values of society. Far from being alienated or marginalizd, artists are usually well-integrated members of society who happen to have a particular skill that they are expected to use in the service of the entire community. The function of art varies from one society to another. It may be used to pass on vital information about the environment from one generation to the next, for example, or to flaunt the wealth and prestige of an important clan. Whatever else it does, though, art is normally used in the service of religion. It gives tangible expression to myths and provides objects to be used in ritual.

*

More than one scholar has already considered the possibility that popular movies (and, indeed, popular culture in general) may be closely related to myth and ritual. In *The TV Ritual: Worship at the Video Altar*, Gregor Goethals[2] discusses television as the source of icon and ritual in contemporary America; everything he says about television, however, applies equally to film. The main argument is that, by providing Americans with a rich source of icons[3] and rituals, television has become a substitute for religion. Goethals makes a distinction (albeit a blurred one at times) between religion and secularity. Television is not religion as such, but it is very much like religion.[4] The two are linked by function (mediating both the sacred and the cultural order) and process (the use of visual images and ritual) but are usually distinguished by content (the presence or absence of references to supernatural beings). Goethals argues that modern cultural productions may be extremely successful in mediating the sacred or something very much like it. Nothing in his work suggests that his use of words such as "transcendent," "sacred," or "sacramental" in connection with television are meant to be taken metaphorically. He has adopted a positive view of the relation between religion and modernity.

Although Goethals discusses television in terms of both ritual and icon, the latter is more germane to this particular discussion. In most societies, he explains, visual images constitute the major medium of public expression; they project a worldview. Since images are drawn from myth or scripture, sources that form the heritage of an entire community, they promote social and cultural integration. It is through these images, by and large, that we learn how things came to be as they are and how we fit into the scheme of things as individuals. In short, they represent the world as an orderly and meaningful place. Amid the confusion of everyday life, we see ourselves as participants in a larger chain of events in which coherence prevails. Icons are the concrete visual expression of a symbolic order in time and space that makes sense of life. They not only depict the primeval origin and eschatological destiny described in myth, they also offer answers to questions about life in the present. We learn to cope with moral problems, for example, by reflecting on the mythic activities of exemplary figures. Icons articulate virtues and vices by showing archetypal heroes and their foes being rewarded and punished. Value systems differ from one society to another but all presuppose the need to ask questions about the conduct expected of ordinary people in daily life, and all provide answers to such questions through the use of role models.

Traditional religious icons, however, have some characteristics not found in the modern secular ones. For traditional icons, the source of imagery is sacred scripture or folklore; there is no fixed tradition on which modern ones can draw. Then, too, traditional icons are usually produced in accordance with prescribed rituals; modern ones are produced in accordance with the law of economic return. Moreover, traditional icons are experienced in special places or at special times set aside for their use or contemplation; modern ones are not (which is why television schedules change so frequently). Both traditional and electronic icons, he notes, make visible an invisible core of meaning and value. In many ways, television is the primary icon maker of American society. Because the function of icons is to articulate and shape beliefs through images, Goethals sees no reason why this cannot be done as effectively by secular images as by religious ones. Indeed, he argues, as the functional equivalent of religion, television has succeeded brilliantly.

Goethals identifies three basic preoccupations of American television: community (family, neighborhood, city or nation), nature, and technology. The images presented in various genres, he argues, are used to explore these. But this is no recent innovation dating from the rise of television; it has been a feature of American art and folklore from the beginning. One type, images of the family, will illustrate what Goethals is saying. The visual representation of family life has been a constant feature of American culture from the early family portraits in oils to contemporary family snapshots, from Currier and Ives prints to Norman Rockwell's covers for *The Saturday Evening Post*, from Ozzie and Harriet to Archie and Edith, from the Ricardos to the Waltons. Although portrayals of family life in contemporary situation comedies on television are different in some ways from earlier portrayals, the use of this image to comment on America itself has remained constant. To know what American identity is all about is to know what American family life is all about. The family provides a symbolic system, in other words, that can be shaped to accommodate a wide diversity of characters, attitudes, moral principles, or social and economic conditions. At the same time, it is the most easily understood world because it is part of everyone's life. In the family context, everyone learns about basic human relationships (such as love, trust, respect, fidelity, or the struggle for independence); the basic sources of human suffering (betrayal, separation, poverty); the basic role models (father, mother, son, daughter, brother, sister); and attitudes toward possessions, vocations, social status, and the various economic and political institutions. All family shows on television offer viewers the possibility of analyzing social norms. But since television images are so intimate and so compellingly lifelike, people are usually unaware of the symbolic nature of these images. Occasionally, a member of some television family becomes a cultural hero or heroine. Mary Richards, on *The Mary Tyler Moore Show* became an exemplary figure. Ambitious but anxious young women responded to a key line in the show's theme song: "You're gonna make it after all." Occasionally, some member of the television family becomes an antihero. Archie Bunker, on *All in the Family*, helped people live with the fear and ignorance that is part of life for everyone. Thus, the American television family functions as an icon, according to Goethals, because it meets at least two basic criteria: it propagates the cultural order (since each episode shows the family struggling to transform the way things are into the way things should be) and it provides contact with culturally significant archetypes (the career woman; the bigot).

Two other institutions have traditionally been associated with the propagation of visual images: the churches and the arts. Because the latter has already been discussed, I will comment briefly on the former.[5] *The Book of Common Prayer* defines a sacrament as "an outward and visible sign of an inward and spiritual grace."[6] The idea that human beings are innately sacramental beings is central to Goethals. He seems to understand sacramentality (the "inward and spiritual grace" mediated by television) in terms of deep feelings about the way things are; what is innate, according to Goethals, is the need for visual images that convey truths about the natural or cultural order. Although they cannot perform the complex analytical functions of verbal signs, visual images have an unparalleled power to evoke deep feelings. In view of this, it is striking that the ecclesiastical world, like the art world itself, has abandoned its traditional task of providing the public images necessary to sustain society. Goethals traces this state of affairs to the rise of Protestantism (which is to say, the dominant religious tradition in America). As he understands it, Protestantism has devalued the visual image, as such, and substituted the word as the only legitimate mediator of truth. (In fact, as he points out, it has also devalued ritual and elevated more cognitive forms of religious expression and experience such as the sermon).[7] If Goethals is correct in his claim that images (and rituals) are basic human needs, then the spectacular success of television is hardly surprising. By default, the churches have lost their monopoly on the images that transform human lives. The implication is clear: "Theologies and faiths that confine their expression to the word, written or spoken, and to music, have issued an invitation to secular culture to minister to the sacramental needs of people. Secular culture is popular not because it is secular but perhaps because it is sacramental."[8] By now, it is television, not organized religion, that has become the primary purveyor of public images in America. "Television," writes Goethals, "has woven a web of myths, furnishing the rhythms, the visual extravaganzas and pseudo-liturgical seasons that break up the ordinariness of our lives."[9] It provides access to larger imagined worlds and offers the thrill of vicarious human adventure; one reason for the decline of some (though not all) religious institutions in America may be that nothing competes with television in doing this. "Through what forms are religious traditions currently communicating the really great adventure? Until they can quicken the sensations of risk and challenge that animate the last nineteen seconds of a championship playoff with goal to go, the illusions of culture will continue to satisfy our need for belonging and wonder. Until institutional religion can excite the serious play of the soul and evoke the fullness of human passion, television will nurture our illusions of heroism and self-transcendence."[10] By "illusion," Goethals does not mean delusion, error, deception, or unreality; he means the kind of imaginative play that is part of being human. In this, he follows the argument put forward by Johan Huizinga in *Homo Ludens*.[11]

This discussion of television as the source of American icons has indicated that the mere production of visual images accessible to the entire community may link popular culture and religion. But *The Wizard* is more than a very beguiling series of visual images; it is also a story, and it would be unwise to underestimate the importance of its narrative content. The whole idea of an icon, however, suggests an even more helpful model. Icons, after all, have served mainly to give visual expression to *myths*.

*

The nature of myth is still subject to scholarly debate.[12] From the many possible theories,[13] I have selected three. Unlike most, these explicitly discuss the relation between the stories of traditional societies (such as myths or folktales) and those of modern societies (such as movies). One of the first scholars to do this was Mircea Eliade. Of particular interest here is his notion of *homo religiosus;* everyone, as a member of the human race, has specifically religious needs. Since myth is the primary expression of religion, it follows that myth in some form exists in all societies. To be sure, most of his work deals with the great cosmogonic myths of what he calls "archaic religion." But Eliade was not unaware of the link between traditional myths and modern movies. Some brief comments on his notion of the "fallen myth" will be useful at this point in the discussion.

When traditional myths are marginalized by modern societies

along with the institutions of organized religion, according to Eliade, they survive in fragmented, distorted, and confused forms. They are little more than tattered remnants, weakened and degraded expressions that only partially satisfy the needs of *homo religiosus*. The process of degeneration, however, did not begin with the advent of modernity. At a much earlier stage, myths about the cosmogonic acts of the gods turned into folktales about the exemplary deeds of heroes and founders; these were then turned into more trivial stories about the activities of ordinary people. The latter, so characteristic of movies and television programs, are what Eliade calls "fallen myths." Even though he would probably recognize mythic properties in *The Wizard*, he would have to argue that such a myth is not "the real thing" and that it cannot function effectively in mediating the sacred. Consequently, he would be unable to explain its extraordinary appeal over more than fifty years. Given the powerful response to movies such as *The Wizard*, I suggest that a more helpful term would be "risen tale." Movies of this kind show evidence of reversing the process of degeneration, of moving back toward folktale and even myth proper.

Eliade discusses myth in virtually all of his books. Considering the topic under discussion, however, his remarks in *Myth and Reality* are of particular importance. According to him, myths are stories—not ideas or propositions, but stories—with specific characteristics. First, they are cosmic in scope. Myths recount acts of the "supernaturals." Because these events are primordial (beyond history), the characters are divine beings and not mortals. From this, it follows that myths convey profound meaning. The meaning they convey, in other words, is absolute, ultimate, or sacred. Furthermore, the meaning is foundational because myths are about origins; they are cosmogonic. They relate events connected with the simultaneous creation of cosmos, tradition, and community. For these reasons, myths are told only in connection with special events (sacred time) and in special places (sacred space). Second, myths represent efficacious paradigms. They not only relate how the world came to be as it is but also provide a way of sustaining the world as it is. By reenacting cosmogonic events in ritual, the cosmic forces on which all life depends are periodically renewed. This is true, moreover, on both macrocosmic and microcosmic levels. No significant human activity (such as art and work) or institution (such as marriage or war) is without a sacred model described in myth. To be fully alive, to be truly human, even to be completely real, men and women must recreate the prototype by imitating the deities who caused them to be in the first place. Third, myths provide a release from the profane world of everyday life and access to the sacred realm of the gods. Without such access, without periodic renewal through telling the myth and enacting it in ritual, the community would be cut off from the vitality that sustains it. Myth and ritual, in other words, are two sides of the same sacred coin. Myths are associated with irruptions of sacred power (kratophanies), beings (hierophanies), or divinities (theophanies) into the world of everyday life (profane time). These may occur spontaneously, but they also occur on a regular basis. When myths are recited and reenacted during sacred festivals, time is abolished and primordial, cosmogonic events are reexperienced. For Eliade, there is a basic human need to keep going back to the way things were in the Beginning, to start over again; time is thus reversible, or cyclical, since these primordial events are repeated over and over again. Only in modern (secular) societies has the notion of linear time (in which the past can never be repeated and the future never foreseen) been introduced.

The Wizard does not seem to be a myth in this sense. It seems more like a traditional folktale. Myths are cosmic (being cosmogonic stories in which the characters are all divine beings); folktales are mundane (being amusing or edifying stories in which the characters are human heroes, tricksters, or even animals). The gulf between myth and tale is narrower in traditional societies (especially oral or folk societies) than in modern (complex and literate) societies. Myth, in the former, may be blended with tale. Although Eliade acknowledges that tales are more mundane than myths in content, he also writes that

> it is not always true that the tale shows a "desacralization" of the mythical world. It would be more correct to speak of a camouflaging of mythical motifs and characters; instead of "desacralization," it would be better to say "rank-loss of the sacred." For...there is no solution of continuity between the scenarios of myths, sagas, and folk tales. Moreover, if the Gods no longer appear under their real names in the tales, their actions can still be distinguished in the figures of the hero's protectors, enemies, and companions. They are camouflaged—or, if you will, "fallen"—but they continue to perform their function.[14]

So myths are the prototypical sacred stories and tales are derived from them. They are less sacred; it is in this sense that they are "fallen." By this, however, Eliade does not mean that tales have no legitimate and even necessary role to play. He means only that they describe the way things are, and even how things came to be as they are, at a more mundane level. There is no great gulf, therefore, that necessarily separates myth from tale. In folk societies, the status of each may be very ambiguous. Moreover, a story that functions as a myth in one community may function as a tale in a neighboring one. In fact, the same ambiguity may operate even within a single community. This is true not only of folk societies but even of more complex traditional societies such as India or medieval Europe. In modern societies, however, there is a much greater gulf between traditional myths and contemporary (secular) stories. The sacred is not dead, according to Eliade, but it is no longer apprehended directly on the conscious level. "A religion is always lived...in several tonalities; but between these different planes of experience there are equivalence and homologation. The equivalence persists even after the 'banalization' of religious experience, after the (apparent) desacralization of the world....But today religious behavior and the structures of the sacred—divine figures, exemplary acts, etc.—are found again at the deepest levels of the psyche, in the 'unconscious' on the planes of dream and imagination."[15]

In other words, religion may be associated with the productions of secular culture (such as novels, movies, or television shows). Though not explicitly religious, they still have a deep affinity for religion. At this point, Eliade touches on a problem of immediate concern in this discussion.

> Though in the West the tale has long since become a literature of diversion (for children and peasants) or of escape (for city dwellers), it still presents the structure of an infinitely serious and responsible adventure, for in the last analysis it is reducible to an initiatory scenario: again and again, we find initiatory ordeals (battles with the monster, apparently insurmountable obstacles, riddles to be solved, impossible tasks, etc.), the descent to Hades or the ascent to Heaven (or—what amounts to the same thing—death and resurrection), marrying the princess. It is true...that the tale always comes to a happy conclusion. But its content proper refers to a terrifyingly serious reality: initiation, that is, passing by way of a symbolic death and resurrection, from ignorance and immaturity to the spiritual age of the adult.[16]

It seems clear that initiation is a major theme of *The Wizard*. This would not surprise Eliade. For him, modern tales (stories told in urban, industrial, and technologically advanced societies) have merely

"fallen" even further from the ancient mythic prototypes than folktales (stories told in more traditional societies). Eliade sees a continuous decline from myth to folktale to modern tale. What survives
of myth in modern tales is merely a vestigial narrative structure that
can no longer provide direct (conscious) access to the sacred.
Experienced at the conscious level, the remnants of mythic imagery
in modern tales are trivial and ephemeral. Experienced at the subconscious level, however, they retain at least some of their power. If
they cannot provide initiation into the sacred realm of divine beings,
they can at least provide initiation into the mundane realm of
exemplary mortals.

> We could almost say that the tale repeats, on another plane, and by
> other means, the exemplary initiation scenario. The tale takes up and
> continues "initiation" on the level of the imaginary. If it represents an
> amusement or an escape, it does so only for the banalized conscious-
> ness, and particularly that of modern man; in the deep psyche, initia-
> tion scenarios preserve their seriousness, and continue to transmit
> their messages, to produce mutations. All unwittingly, and indeed
> believing that he is merely amusing himself or escaping, the man of the
> modern societies still benefits from the imaginary initiation supplied by
> the tale....This point of view will surprise only those who regard
> initiation as a type of behavior peculiar to the man of the traditional
> societies. Today we are beginning to realize that what is called "initia-
> tion" coexists with the human condition, that every existence is made
> up of an unbroken series of "ordeals," "deaths," and "resurrections"
> whatever be the terms that modern language uses to express these
> originally religious experiences.[17]

For Eliade, as I have said, myths are the prototypical expression
of religion. Although folktales deal with exemplary mortals instead of
gods and goddesses, they retain the structure of sacred stories and
have much in common with myths. To the extent that modern
societies are secular, they have no cosmogonic myths to provide a
source for their tales. The latter are so divorced from their mythic
prototypes that the connection is no longer recognized consciously.
To the extent that modern people still respond to the sacred (that is,
to the extent that they are still representatives of what Eliade calls
homo religiosus and not truly secular), they can do so only by
subconsciously absorbing whatever mythic properties survive (such
as the motif of initiation or patterns of time derived from the
Judaeo-Christian tradition). This they can do at the movies. Eliade
does not suggest that movies are the only survivals of myth. He

suggests, in fact, that vestiges of myth can also be found in psycho-analysis, the arts, and secular ideologies. Psychoanalysis, for example, preserves the pattern of initiation so central to both myth and ritual. Patients are asked to make a dangerous voyage into their inner selves. By doing so, they can relive their own past and reexperience traumatic events. This is morphologically similar to the descent into hell found in so many folktales; the initiate enters the realm of ghosts and monsters, gives battle and, in some sense, "dies" before being "resurrected" in the end. Just as the mythic hero reenters the world at a new stage in the life cycle, so the patient reenters the world at a new stage of maturity and health. Psychoanalysis demystifies the sacred world of inner being to discover the true (original) significance of human behavior. But, says Eliade, there is also a need to work in reverse. Modern people

> have to "demystify" the apparently profane worlds and languages of literature, plastic arts, and cinema in order to disclose their "sacred" elements, although it is, of course, an ignored, camouflaged, or degraded "sacred." In a desacralized world such as ours, the "sacred" is always present and active chiefly in the imaginary universes. But imaginative experiences are part of the total human being, no less important than his diurnal experiences. This means that the nostalgia for initiatory trials and scenarios, nostalgia deciphered in so many literary and plastic works, reveals modern man's longing for a total and definitive renewal, for a *renovatio* capable of radically changing his existence.[18]

Eliade's work is helpful because it suggests a link between myths, folktales, modern tales, and movies. Although I agree with much of what he says, I disagree with his rather negative evaluation of modern tales (movies). Many, no doubt, do fit his description. On the other hand, it would be a mistake to assume that all of them can be trivialized as "fallen myths" that can hardly meet religious needs. *The Wizard* does not conform ostensibly to Eliade's notion of a myth; instead, on first glance, it corresponds closely to his notion of a tale. It is about an individual who comes of age (or is initiated into the adult world): Dorothy "dies" (by falling asleep), is severely tested (on her quest through a strange and hostile land), and is "resurrected" (by waking up). Since these motifs are all found in traditional tales, *The Wizard* could be called a folk tale or a "fallen myth." But its place in American culture indicates that this analysis would be inade-quate. *The Wizard* appeals strongly to Americans not only as individuals but also as a nation. Its function cannot be dismissed as mere diversion or escapism (although it may also function in these ways). Nor can its popularity be dismissed as ephemeral now that more than fifty years have passed since its original release. *The Wizard* has not only some characteristics of a folktale or a "fallen myth," but also those of a "risen tale" (a story that has the form of a tale but has begun to take on the functions of a myth). If so, then the regressive process described by Eliade is here reversed; *The Wizard* represents not the final stage in the degeneration of myth, but the first stage in its regeneration.

Despite Eliade's notion that the movies of contemporary societies are "survivals" from earlier myths (or perhaps because of it), scholars in the field of religious studies have not adapted their techniques or broadened their interests accordingly.[19] The field of religious studies is well-equipped to analyze myth. But even though some scholars in the field see religion as a human phenomenon that is sui generis, they seldom venture beyond the traditional texts of organized religion in general and the "world religions" in particular. Anthropologists, on the other hand, are interested in contemporary societies (as distinct from those that can be known only through archaeology). From the beginning, however, their field was defined by the study of contemporary societies that are oral and rural, while sociology was defined in terms of contemporary societies that are literate and urban. And myth was taken to be characteristic of those studied by anthropologists, not sociologists. Even Claude Lévi-Strauss, who argued that myth is a universal mode of human thought, refused to extend the scope of structural analysis to include the stories told in literate societies such as ancient Israel (to say nothing of modern America). In short, this traditional emphasis on oral, rural cultures and on religion as a more or less autonomous cultural system has not encouraged the study of myths in relation to movies.

With the trend toward interdisciplinary studies, however, scholars have begun to take seriously the mythic elements in the cultural productions of modern (literate, urban, and technological) societies. In *Mythologies*,[20] Roland Barthes discussed a variety of seemingly trivial and banal phenomena (such as wrestling, striptease, and jet travel) as mythic forms expressing the underlying organizing principles of French culture. For him, though, myth was an insidious form of linguistic skullduggery that systematically obscured truth. But academic hostility toward popular culture is no longer unquestioned. A graduate program in popular culture has been established at Ohio's Bowling Green State University. It is interesting to note that a number of scholars are now writing specifically about the relation between

popular culture and myth. Several schools of thought can be identified. According to the dominant one, myth reflects culture. The productions of popular culture, therefore, support and propagate the
beliefs and values of American culture. Because no culture can do
without order and continuity, they play an important, even necessary
role. Nevertheless, these scholars present only one aspect of popular
culture's importance. According to an even more recent school of
thought, myths not only reflect culture, they also generate and shape
it.

The first approach is represented by M. Darrol Bryant. In "Cinema,
Religion, and Popular Culture," he focuses attention specifically on
movies. These are linked to religion, he argues, precisely because they
are technological artifacts; and technology, in American culture, has
spiritual aims. This requires some explanation. The rise of experimental science did not destroy the theurgic aspirations of the
alchemists; on the contrary, the new worldview focused on an idea of
infinite progress that provided the basis of industrialization and
captured the imagination of the nineteenth century. Science and
technology continue the millenarian dreams of the alchemists, only
in secular terms, because both scientists and alchemists have sought
to improve, master and transform nature. In other words, both
alchemy and science-technology have not only practical aims but
soteriological ones as well. They are thus analogous. Film is a characteristic product of technological civilization. Like alchemy, it
conquers or negates time: whatever it records lives forever. It achieves
what the alchemists always dreamed of achieving: immortality. Or, to
put it another way, it transforms base metals (the ones used in the
production of film itself) into the precious metal of the "silver screen."
Not only are the movies themselves immortal but the culture is also
immortalized; the contents of culture (people, objects, symbols,
ideologies) are lifted beyond the flux of daily life. "In the camera,
then, we have confirmed the popular belief that the everyday world
we endure, itself shaped by technological civilization, is capable of
achieving its noble but hidden dream: the transmutation and deification of the world."[21]

Just as the arts of other cultures (such as the ritual objects
associated with hunting or with agriculture) give visible form to the
deep relationships between the community and the sacred powers
that live in animals and plants, film is a popular art that represents
the deepest aspirations of American culture. "Consequently," writes
Bryant, "I propose that we approach film as a response to the

ambition of a technological civilization to discover the alchemical formula that could wed the machine to the transmutation of nature and the deification of human culture. In a word, as we sit and watch a film, we are participating in a central ritual of our technological civilization."[22]

Because of the unrivalled ability of film to record, reproduce, and represent the natural order, viewers are easily led to believe in the reality of what is seen on the movie screen. Consequently, they may easily be transformed by movies. They immediately recognize the kind of people, places, and events known from everyday life. They identify themselves with the characters portrayed. In fact, they vicariously participate in what is going on in the movie, becoming part of its time and space. And this, claims Bryant, is exactly what icons have always done. Far from being merely ornaments, educational devices or—as Eliade would argue—superficial forms of entertainment, they are channels that allow viewers to make contact with a mythical world. Bryant emphasizes the fact that icons in premodern Europe provided public images that pervaded the consciousness of everyone. "Is it not on the screen," he asks, "that we discover both new and familiar images of humanity that call forth in the viewer an expanded sense of what is possible? desirable? and worthy of emulating?"[23]

Ever since the Enlightenment, it has been common for intellectuals to claim that religion is anachronistic and that cultic forms are unnecessary to sustain civilization. But has the cultus of Western civilization really disappeared or has it merely been transformed in some way? This is the question that provoked Bryant's paper. "My concern is to overcome a false dichotomy between 'religious' and 'secular' cultures. All cultures are dependent on cultic forms, even our own technological culture. The difference between a 'religious' and a 'secular' culture is that a religious culture seeks to mediate a transcendent order, whereas a secular culture has no referent beyond itself and consequently worships itself. Thus, the basis of cultural life becomes power rather than transcendence, and the cultic forms of secular culture become self-reflection."[24]

Given the technological ability to represent the imaginative world of a society realistically, movies and television shows are the primary propagators of myth in modern societies. On that basis Bryant presents his major thesis: that film is a form of popular religion. "As a popular form of the religious life, movies do what we have always asked of popular religion, namely that they provide us with archetypal forms of humanity—heroic figures—and instruct us in the basic values and myths of our society. As we watch the characters and follow the drama on the screen, we are instructed in the values and myths of our culture and given models on which to pattern our lifes."[25]

Due to its unique properties, then, film presents the cultural vision of order through fantasy while, at the same time, maintaining the illusion of reality. Of all the "arts," film is best-equipped to sustain and nourish the aspirations of a technological civilization because it is in the movie theaters that people meet their cultural heroes and are instructed in the appropriate ways to think and act. Viewers are thus able to participate, as their ancestors did, in the lives of powerful beings who overcome chaos. Like their mythic counterparts in other cultures, movie heroes are often technological adepts; that is, they use skills (mastery of techniques) to cope with whatever difficulties confront them. Heroes may be masters who manipulate the techniques of violence, for example, or masters who manipulate the techniques of love. The point is, they demonstrate the victory of order over chaos and confusion, control over impotence. Ordinary people may or may not be able to imitate these heroes, but they can nevertheless affirm the values of their culture and believe in its ability to overcome chaos and achieve order. In fact, movies work so well because most people cannot actually be like their heroes. They can imitate general mannerisms and social skills, but they cannot hope to achieve perpetual and perfect mastery of all situations in daily life. If they could, movies would merely be pedagogical devices; they would be useful but also superficial in their ability to stimulate the imagination or warm the heart. Like the people who tell myths about gods and heroes, ordinary people in modern societies also hunger for a world in which they are more competent or more in control than they are most of the time. Movies satisfy this hunger, according to Bryant, by providing heroes who are the equivalents of the mythical heroes of other societies.

> Consequently, the world of the cinema provides us, in the realm of popular culture, with a magically transformed and ordered world where the discontinuity between desire and reality is overcome. In the movies, boy gets girl, the lawman gets his man, the mistreated get revenge. In film, intimate and harmonious contact with elemental powers that order things is re-established; the human world is brought into line with the forces that rule our lives. We can thus see in the popular response to cinema a desire to reconnect the ordinary world with a more magical realm.[26]

Movies present viewers with an orderly cosmos. It is not only orderly, however, it is also unified. Visual images, dialogue, and music are orchestrated to form a complete whole with a beginning, a middle, and an ending. This completion, wholeness, or perfection is juxtaposed in the minds of viewers to the fragmented world familiar in everyday life. That world is presented in the movie, to be sure, but rearranged and corrected according to some pattern. "Greatness is evident," writes Bryant, "when a film discloses an order of being that lies behind it, yet manifests itself in the world of everyday. . . . It is in that transformation of the familiar as well as in the disclosure of the familiar that we are led to see with greater insight."[27] Bryant, then, is less concerned with the specific content of symbols than he is with the process by which they are presented. Sitting in a darkened theater, cut off in time and space from the humdrum routine of everyday life, people experience something not unlike (though not synonymous with) sacred time and space as understood by Eliade.

That the movies express our primordial longing for interaction with the gods and goddesses, observes Bryant, is evident from the vocabulary associated with actors and actresses (as distinct from the exemplary figures they portray). They are known as "stars" and "idols." Their images are both literally and figuratively "larger than life." For all intents and purposes, they are superhuman beings. Although we sometimes see in movie stars grander, nobler, or more tragic versions of ourselves (as in the case of James Dean who inspired what has been called a "cult" following his accidental death at the age of twenty-four), we identify ourselves more often with the characters portrayed than with those who portray them. The latter are expected to live apart from the social conventions, even the moral conventions of society. Popular magazines dwell on the details of their private lives; the more fantastic the better. "Through the popular mind," writes Bryant, "runs an ambivalence toward film personalities that characterizes a relationship between mere mortals and semi-gods."[28] And this reinforces our own need, as ordinary mortals, to live securely within the boundaries of conventional morality while, at the same time, transcending those boundaries vicariously. For Bryant, then, film is extremely close to religion.

Most scholars assume that the function of popular culture is to reflect the established values of society. At least one anthropologist, Lee Drummond, strongly disagrees. He emphasizes the cultural generativity of myth and argues that most scholars writing about popular culture in relation to myth do not go far enough in appreciating the cultural significance either of myth itself or of its functional equivalents in the modern world. They present only one side of the relation between culture and its various forms of expression because they see the latter as epiphenomena that merely reflect a preexistent and autonomous culture, the things people already think and feel. Myths, according to that view, are nothing more than charters that legitimate the social and cultural order. Scholars who look at popular culture from that perspective, he argues, are different from those who are hostile to popular culture only in arguing that this function is legitimate and necessary instead of being irrelevant or sinister. For Drummond, however, culture (including popular culture) is not a static belief system; on the contrary, transformation is always taking place. But this does not occur in some autonomous realm called "culture," which then spins off multiple and nearly identical expressions called "popular culture." Movies do, of course, reflect the larger culture; if they did not, if they presented nothing familiar to viewers, they would be unintelligible (as is often the case with avant-garde art). Nevertheless, movies also generate culture and shape it. They are actively involved in the process. And this is true not only of the art films produced by elite culture but also of the entertainment movies produced by popular culture. In view of this, the rigid distinction between high and low culture, between elite and popular culture, is becoming anachronistic. The difference, according to Drummond, is quantitative rather than qualitative. Popular movies, for example, are accessible to far more people than art films. Both, however, do much the same thing for their respective viewers. They may not only mirror widely held assumptions but also raise questions about the way things are, should be, or could be. Even though art films (according to the avant-garde definition of art) challenge the values of a dominant society, they still affirm those of the patrons themselves. In the same way, it is true that popular movies affirm the established values of society; nevertheless, they may also challenge them. This is the case in *The Wizard;* satire is used to deflate the smugness and pomposity of contemporary America but also to reaffirm the youthful energy and homespun authenticity of an earlier America.

Drummond is more specific about the cultural generativity of myths and, by extension, movies. Myths, he argues, are basically about human identity. They are metaphorical ways of defining and redefining what it means to be human. Is there an essential difference between human beings and animals or between human beings and machines? What is the relation between our own community and the alien ones all around us? How do we live between the friendly and hostile forces of the universe? Only by asking questions such as these can human beings identify themselves to themselves. Moreover, it is a neverending process; there are no answers that correspond to givens of either nature or history. Because human identity is never finally resolved, myth is never obsolete. The fact that we participate in myth, that we engage in the process of forming identity by sitting in a darkened theater instead of at church or in a sacred grove is less important than is often imagined.

In "Movies and Myth: Theoretical Skirmishes," Drummond's criticism of prevailing approaches to myth extends to those based on materialism. From the materialistic point of view (such as that of the hegemonists discussed earlier), myth is an insidious cloak that hides the true social, economic, and political order; myth is a lens that systematically distorts reality to cover up the aims of elite groups. Myths are studied, then, primarily to unmask the ways in which they perpetuate injustice and inequality. The problem with this approach is that it assumes the prior existence of social inequality, which is then expressed in legitimating myths. Elite members of society demand the "best" food, for example. But desirability is

> not simply given in the nature of things, nor does it follow from a convenient principle like the "law" of supply and demand. If that were true, then...we would "naturally" value the scarce organs of food animals—its [sic] heart, brains, tongue, and liver—over its more abundant steaks and roasts. Desirability is the effect, and not the cause, of a system of shared understandings about the nature of human life and the entities—plants, animals, machines, and inanimate objects— utilized by humans. That system of shared understandings is culture. Before a materialist logic can hope to produce meaningful statements, therefore, it is first necessary to identify elements of culture and the order or disorder of their arrangement.[29]

For Drummond, then, culture is something dynamic. It is always coming into being because the known world is always coming into being. The natural order, paradoxically, is a cultural construct because nature is only known through culture. "It is precisely at this point that myth re-enters the picture, for the organization of culture—the system of meanings that are central to a notion of human identity—is the problematic of myth. Why there are powerful and powerless, why one food is inherently better than another, how beauty differs from ugliness, all these questions are the stuff of myth."[30]

In American culture, the stuff of popular movies is akin to myth. Like myths, popular movies are fundamentally about human identity; apart from all else, they are metaphorical ways of defining what it means to be human.

Myth is a prominent force in the world precisely because human identity and creativity were not self-evident, fixed aspects of existence, from the earliest hominid days. If the divisions of the world into plant and animal species, human groups, and types of material productions were naturalistic...then there would have been absolutely no need for the development of classificatory thought, and hence no need for the intelligence we are accustomed to call "human." The first hominids would have sorted out themselves and their surroundings once and for all, assimilated the given order of things, and settled into a social life that varied only in response to the environment and other random factors. That people are still sorting out their lives attests to the intrinsically unfinished nature of culture and the mythic processes which fuel it.[31]

But Drummond suggests that movies are like myths in another way, too. They are partially independent of both their creators and their audiences. George Lucas has said several times that he made *Star Wars* purely and simply as escapist entertainment, and many people have experienced it in just that way. But things are more complicated for anthropologists. "The question," writes Drummond, "is whether they are escaping from something or to an underlying reality—a Dreamtime—that is only intuitively sensed in ordinary time. I think that they are doing the latter and, moreover, that what really packs them in is a movie's resonance with irreducible problems, dilemmas, tensions in human life. Movies do not avoid contradiction: they revel in it."[32]

In a collection of essays edited by Hervé Varenne, *Symbolizing America*,[33] Drummond has written at some length about the series of James Bond movies. These explore human identity in relation to machines, he argues, just as it has always been explored in relation to animals in the totemistic myths of primal cultures. But Bond is not only an isolated figure who is part man and part machine. He is also an agent working for the British government. As such, he represents the ambiguous relation between the individual and the state. By raising questions about human identity, by generating new ways of thinking about human identity, the Bond movies function as myths. With its witches and magic, *The Wizard*, at first glance, seems merely to reiterate traditional clichés. On closer examination, however, things are much more complicated. *The Wizard* does indeed reflect American traditions, but it does more than that. It also makes an original contribution to the search for collective identity in modern America. Far from being a mere passive reflection of American culture, in other words, it is also an active participant in the creation of American culture. Conrad Phillip Kottack, another anthropologist, makes the same point as Drummond. In "Social-Science Fiction," he points out that *Star Wars*, like *The Wizard*, is both reflective and generative. "For the anthropologist, the 'creativity' of any work of art lies in how successfully it brings together cultural themes, motifs, symbols, and meanings that are familiar and significant to the natives. *Star Wars* summarizes and synthesizes the experiences that millions of Americans have shared during the past half century. Like myths, fairy tales, and 'new' religions, the film is significant not because it is new, but because it is both old and new—a novel and meaningful blend of preexisting themes."[34] This is true of *The Wizard* in at least two ways. Each of these is related to the specific conditions of life in the United States between the Great Depression and the Second World War. More specifically, each explores the meaning of American identity in relation to threats posed by both technology and hostile foreign powers.

By 1939, the United States had become an industrial giant. Not even a decade of economic disasters could hide the fact that the machine had come to stay. Indeed, Margaret Bourke-White illustrated the first cover story for *Life* with a photograph of the Fort Peck Dam in Montana.[35] And it was clear that the American ability to mass produce airplanes and weapons would be a decisive factor in the war then looming on the horizon. But Americans had never thought of themselves as an industrial nation. In only one or two generations, the United States had been transformed from a predominantly rural and agricultural nation to a predominantly urban and industrial one. It should come as no surprise, therefore, that a massively popular movie such as *The Wizard* comments, albeit in symbolic form, on this very problem. Dorothy's immediate goal is the Emerald City (the metropolis, industry, high technology, modernity, and progress) but her ultimate goal is Kansas (the frontier, agriculture, low technology, tradition, and stasis). What is distinctive about *The Wizard* is that instead of affirming one and condemning the other, it affirms both. It does not present a radical statement, to be sure, but it does not present a reactionary one either. It was (and may still be) necessary for Americans to hold these two perspectives in tension. If the enduring popularity of *The Wizard* is taken seriously, this ambiguous solution has been a very successful response to the problem of collective identity in a rapidly changing world. The problem of identity in relation to the machine is also raised by the Wizard himself. He uses technology as a facade to hide his own ineptitude. Pulling the curtain aside, Toto exposes the mystique of technology—and this was the very mystique that produced and sustained the dream factory of Hollywood itself—as an illusion. The Wizard, moreover, has not mastered even the most primitive technology. Sailing off in his balloon without Dorothy, he says: "I can't come back! I don't know how it works!" (127). He may be a bad wizard, Dorothy discovers, but he is a good man. Other characters are more ambiguous in their relation to the human race. The three friends Dorothy meets are humanoids representing a continuum between animal and machine. The Tin Man is not merely an animated tin can; he is, more or less, a robot. He is an earlier incarnation of C3PO from *Star Wars*. Significantly, his particular lack is a heart. The problem he represents, then, is the use of technology without compassion. But this problem is solved. He receives (or discovers) his heart. As one member of the Emerald City's ruling triumvirate (following the Wizards' departure), he testifies to the faith of Americans, despite anxiety, in the beneficent possibilities of their burgeoning technological civilization.

Then, too, it was becoming increasingly obvious by 1939 that another war would soon engulf the world. Even though isolationism was still a powerful political force in the United States (for various reasons including xenophobia, the lingering effects of the Monroe Doctrine, and the natural desire of parents to prevent their sons from being destroyed in another foreign war), Americans were already emotionally involved in the European struggle. Before Pearl Harbor, the Japanese were not perceived as a major threat; the Nazis were. Despite some residual antisemitism, Americans supported Britain and her allies, not Germany. In short, American identity was informed by attitudes toward opposing forces in the larger world. There was a line between "us" and "them." And that can be seen in *The Wizard.*

Conflict between the forces of evil and death (represented by the Wicked Witch) and the forces of life and goodness (represented by Glinda) is obviously a major narrative element. Given the political situation in 1939, we would expect the Witch to be associated, consciously or unconsciously, with Hitler. In fact, as viewers must have recognized, her squadrons of winged monkeys resemble the squadrons of dive-bombers sent by Hitler to Spain during its Civil War. On the other hand, I have argued that the Witch herself is associated with things Russian (costumes, settings, music). She is not only "black" (death), she is also "red" (blood, fire, danger, "stop," and communism). We should remember that Russia has always been seen by Western Europeans as remote, alien, primitive, and barbaric. Even the form of Christianity found there seemed suspiciously pagan (especially to Protestants). With the gradual growth of democracy in the West, moreover, czarist tyranny became a symbol of evil. Peter Filene[36] points out that, by the early twentieth century, even the massacre of Jews in state-sponsored pogroms could evoke a public outcry in Western countries.[37] In the foreword to a recent history of Russia, Edwin Reischauer discusses the emotional gulf separating that country more specifically from the United States. He observes that

> no part of the Western world is more alien to Americans than is Russia. Russia stems culturally from the Byzantine area of southeastern Europe, while the United States is an offshoot of the British Isles in the extreme northwest. Russia grew up on the defenceless North European plain, swept by invading hordes and conquerors; the United States, across the Atlantic Ocean, where it found no dangerous rivals. No two countries within the bounds of Western civilization could have had more dissimilar histories or developed more divergent attitudes toward the outside world and the problems of their own societies....At times, small bands of zealots have looked on the Soviet Union as the promised land of the future. Much more prevelant have been feelings of deep distrust, fear, hatred, and even revulsion.[38]

The book's author, Robert Daniels, makes the same point in his discussion of American attitudes toward Russians since the Revolution. "Russia," he writes, "has always been an abstraction for Americans. Before the Revolution it was a dim and backward wasteland; afterward, an embodiment of cosmic destructiveness. Only for a few Americans did Russia become a distant utopia; for many, it was a terrifying revelation of evil; for most, it was an inchoate menace to their national existence."[39] Most Americans were soon disabused of the idea that the Russians would create a democracy along the lines of their own. They came to believe that the new Soviet Union was even more sinister and threatening than the regime it had replaced.[40] Of particular importance was the atheistic nature of the state.[41] Some American Protestants, it is true, admired the Soviet experiment and tried to disbelieve news of atrocities; they were soon accused of hoping that persecution of the Orthodox Church would mean new mission fields for themselves. With the Wall Street Crash and near collapse of American capitalism, anxiety was greatly exacerbated. No American could look on with complacency at events in the Soviet Union. "Soviet Russia was suffering from a shortage of workers in her drive to meet the ambitious schedule of the Five-Year Plan: the United States, meanwhile, had no Plan and millions of unemployed....The New World was suddenly an old, decadent, economy exactly fulfilling the dooming prophecies of Marxian dogma, preached now by a 'new civilization' whose success was astounding the world."[42]

Given this general attitude, it is not surprising that Hollywood movies have often depicted Russians as alien, hostile, and threatening. In fact, observes Robert Fyne, it was necessary to make a deliberate effort to reverse this cinematic convention during the Second World War when Stalin became an ally (thus negating his earlier nonaggression pact with Hitler).

> Since the U.S. and the Soviet Union were now brothers-in-arms, this new, and strange, alliance had to be solidified on the screen. Immediately Hollywood took its call to colors. Overnight, new scripts were hacked out and unusual ideas developed. Even the American President...instructed Jack Warner to make propaganda films depicting the amity between the two former adversaries....What followed for the next five years was a collection of pro-Soviet films (many of them ludicrous), where the bravery and suffering of Comrade Ivan oozed out in every frame while the Communist leader, our new friend Uncle Joe, almost reached the level of apotheosis as he fought...the Nazi beasts.[43]

This situation did not last long. Although negative feelings toward Germany were quickly replaced by sympathy for its people starving in defeat, positive feelings toward Russia were just as quickly replaced by fear of its empire expanding in victory. Thomas R. Maddux points out that Americans in both the prewar and postwar periods tended to emphasize the similarities rather than the differences between Nazi Germany and the Soviet Union; both were menacing totalitarian regimes.[44] I suggest, therefore, that the Witch was associated primarily with Stalin and Russia (but, by implication, with any foreign dictator).

If so, then it would not be unreasonable to suggest that the Wizard was associated with Roosevelt. Like the Wizard, the President was far from being in complete control of things. He arrived in Washington as a savior; he was proclaimed the one man who could get America moving again. He told the people that a way to end the Depression would be found by trial and error. In fact, he had no more real control over the economy (that is, the ship of state) than the Wizard had over his balloon. Neither Roosevelt nor anyone else really knew how to rescue the economy. But like the Wizard, he did know something about the emotional needs of his people. He certainly kept public morale higher than it might have been. Although he was often accused of ruling the nation through bravado and sheer blarney, he may well have held things together by a combination of shrewd insight (reminding people that they had nothing to fear but fear itself) and genuine compassion (realizing—and many at the time did not—that the government had a moral responsibility to provide people either with jobs or with food and dollars). Whether Roosevelt was reading comic strips over the radio during a newspaper strike or delivering his "fireside chats" during the war, he was seen as far more than a public official; he was seen as a benevolent father. The Wizard is a benevolent father too. As such, he actually hands power over to Dorothy's three friends. This may reflect the populist tradition in American politics. The nation will get back on its feet if power is given back to ordinary people with enduring values (such as common sense, compassion, and courage). Likewise, what America needs is not a larger bureaucracy (such as the Munchkin City with its unctuous officials) but good will and hard work.

As a response to threats from outside, this polarization between "us" and "them" in *The Wizard* could hardly be called innovative. Within this traditional perspective, however, is one element that could certainly be called innovative: once the Witch is killed, her menacing hordes cheer Dorothy for liberating them. It was not the "people" who were evil but their leader. Tyranny has not merely been defeated, it has been transformed. The result is not occupation (continuing fear and hatred) but reconciliation. Here again, *The Wizard* presents Americans with a "both-and" solution rather than an "either-or" solution. In the near future, to be sure, conflict is inevitable; in the more distant future, healing is possible. The immediate goal is to prepare for war; the long-term goal is to integrate the United States in a postwar world.

Because the preceding chapters have emphasized the reflective aspects of *The Wizard* (its ways of mediating traditional notions of individual, collective, and cosmic identity), these observations on its generative aspects are noteworthy. Successful myths respond or adapt to the immediate needs of people. And myths—either their forms or their interpretations—have always changed to meet new needs. In *The Wizard*, we find a number of traditional stories (about the individual, collective, and cosmic "life cycles") converging in ways that add up to fresh insight on disturbing issues of the present (that is, from the 1930s to the 1990s and possibly beyond).

*

The Wizard has come to function in many ways as a myth. Unlike traditional myths, though, it is not linked in any overt way to religion. In view of this, it could be called a "secular myth." To understand why Americans would want or need a "secular myth" in the first place, it is necessary to consider the peculiar position of religion in American life. Prior to the 1930s, there were no scientific studies of American religiosity. Nevertheless, European visitors, such as Alexis de Tocqueville, remarked on the vigorous religious life that character- ized the new nation.[45] Based on their accounts, George Gallup writes: "While the data available indicate that the level of church membership was far lower in the nineteenth century and the first decades of the current century than it is today, it is probably safe to assume that the vast majority of Americans were "believers."[46] During the past fifty years, however, many studies of American attitudes toward religion have been done. In a recent issue of the *Gallup Report* devoted exclusively to religion, conclusions are drawn about American religiosity from studies conducted between 1935 and 1985.[47] Looking back over fifty years, Gallup isolates several patterns that seem to be characteristically American. First, there is a yawning gulf between belief and commitment. Moreover, there is a glaring lack of religious knowledge. And American faith tends to be superficial (although there is some evidence that this may be changing). Consequently, organized religion has failed to "make a difference in society." Most important here, however, is the widespread popularity of religion; most Americans continue to identify themselves as religious people (which is to say, they claim a belief in God and the importance of religion in their lives). In this last sense, nothing has changed over the decades despite periods during which the insitutions of organized religion have declined. Looking ahead, Gallup includes the following trends (among others): a continuing focus on the individual instead of the community; an "intensive spiritual search" and desire for inward growth; a continuing rejection of ecclesiastical authority; and a proliferation of religious movements to answer spiritual needs.

According to Kenneth Briggs, these trends are already in evidence. The religion editor of the *New York Times* reports that America's return to prayer is by no means superficial. "From the burgeoning retreat houses and spiritual centers of various faiths," he writes, "the message is the same: a prayer revival is the most powerful, least-documented development within modern American religion today."[48] For Briggs, the current longing for in-depth prayer and meditation indicates a new phase of the "born again" movement of the 1970s. If the earlier phase was characterized by outward revivalism and dramatic conversion experiences, the more recent one is characterized by inward awakening and deepening of faith. No wonder that religious life is now focused not on the congregation but on the individual, and the primary religious functionary is no longer the charismatic preacher but the intuitive spiritual director who guides each pilgrim on a solitary quest for holiness (the immediacy of God's presence in everyday life). At the heart of all this is an urge to transcend the superficial sense of prayer as a "hotline" to God in time of crisis or a vehicle for wish fulfillment.

Briggs reports that there are approximately 600 retreat houses, and that these are often booked years in advance. From this, he concludes that the phenomenon should not be dismissed. Moreover, the people who participate in these retreats are drawn from a broad spectrum of the population. They include both Evangelical Protestants and Charismatic Catholics. Even Reform Jews, long known for their movement away from traditional practices considered incompatible with scientific modernity, have been calling attention to Jewish forms of prayer and spirituality. Both Jewish and Christian seekers are now more likely to shift through the spiritual resources of their own traditions—the Desert Fathers and Eastern Orthodox mystics, for example, or the Hassidic masters—than they once were. In short, "contemplative prayer, once thought to be the speciality of monks or cloistered nuns, has been adapted in easy steps for common usage. A life of action is no longer regarded as antithetical to a life of prayer."[49] The comments of Briggs are not based on a scientific survey. Their importance lies in the mere fact that they appear in the *New York Times Magazine* and are therefore considered likely to interest the general public.

Religious profundity, of course, cannot be measured by any questionnaire. Religion itself is far more complex than any statistics on belief or church attendance could possibly indicate. After all, people attend church for many reasons. And beliefs are often abstractions that are taken for granted and have little or no impact on everyday life. Not surprisingly, therefore, some observers (especially theologians) are very skeptical about surveys of religiosity. As Briggs points out, they often argue that much of what passes for "new spirituality" is just trendy nonsense designed to promote self-fulfillment or even hygiene rather than attentiveness to the will of God. It is not my intention to assess the quality of American spirituality. It may be theologically sophisticated or naive, profound or shallow. What matters here, though, is only that Americans *consider themselves* religious, not secular.

Significantly, there are some features of American life (for a discussion of these, see Appendix 3) that indicate a complex relation between religion and secularity. This is due partly to the ambivalence of individuals; it is due mainly, however, to the ambiguity of their situation. As a people, Americans are not secular (indifferent to religion), but as a republic, the United States of America is officially secular (without an established church). After more than 200 years, the conflict generated by this paradox remains unresolved. In "The Myth of Religious Neutrality by Separation in Education,"[50] David Leitch discusses the constitutional confusion resulting from the separation of church and state under the First Amendment: "Congress shall make no law respecting an establishment of religion, or prohibit the free exercise thereof." The first clause (known as the "establishment clause") was designed to promote freedom of choice for individuals in matters of belief. These provisions were included not because the framers of the Constitution were indifferent or hostile to religion, but because a unified nation could not be formed out of thirteen colonies—each of which, aside from Rhode Island and Pennsylvania, had its own established church—in any other way. Pluralism, then, not secularism made the separation necessary in the first place. Then, too, the founders were primarily concerned about the possible intrusion of government into religion, not of religion into government. But separating church and state is easier said than done. The boundaries of each remain ambiguous. Although Thomas Jefferson's metaphor—a "wall of separation"—has been used in attempts to interpret the First Amendment, its precise meaning has never been clear. It has never prevented general references to God and Providence in presidential addresses. Nor has it prevented Americans, since the 1950s, from referring to "one nation under God" as they pledge allegiance to the flag. Nor has it prevented the words "in God we trust" from being engraved on American coins. It has, however, been the subject of many cases brought before the Supreme Court.[51]

The fact that controversy has not died down after more than 200

years indicates at least two things of importance in this discussion:
Americans are not, by and large, secular (indifferent to religion), and
have not yet adjusted to the paradox of private religiosity and public
secularity (separation of church and state). Movies such as *The
Wizard*, I suggest, are one way of mediating the gulf. They are what I
call "secular myths." Before examining this notion in more detail,
though, it is important to consider a much more direct and
obvious form of mediation between public secularity and private
religiosity.

*

The paradox of a people who consider themselves religious but
want a secular state has generated attempts to create a replacement
for the national churches of other countries (such as the Church of
England). In what has become a famous essay, "Civil Religion in
America," Robert Bellah suggests that this replacement has taken the
form of a "civil religion."[52] The phenomenon he describes is evidence
of a widely perceived need to bridge the gulf between religion and
secularity. According to Bellah, civil religion exists as a kind of
umbrella tradition that draws on Judaeo-Christian motifs but also
transcends both Judaism and Christianity. Referring to some Christian
theologians and to the earlier theory of Will Herberg, Bellah writes
that "while some have argued that Christianity is the national faith,
and others that church and synagogue celebrate only the generalized
religion of 'The American Way of Life,' few have realized that there
actually exists alongside of it rather clearly differentiated from the
churches an elaborate and well-institutionalized civil religion in
America."[53] Bellah believes that the American civil religion is expressed in public ritual. He notes that references to God are very often
found in the inaugural addresses of presidents and other solemn
occasions of public life—but seldom in the working messages presented to Congress. This does not mean that these formal statements
are trivial; on the contrary, they are indicative of deep-seated convictions that are not always made explicit in everyday life. References to
God in presidential speeches never refer to specifically Christian
notions of God. They never mention Jesus or any of the churches. It
could be argued that this indicates a vestigial place of religion in
American life, that the forms of religion are preserved but emptied of
content. For Bellah, however, these generalized references reveal the
adjustment made necessary by the Constitution. The separation of
church and state guarantees freedom of religion, but it also segregates

the private sphere of religion from the public sphere of politics. Nevertheless, this has not been interpreted as a denial of the religious dimension of political life.

> Although matters of personal religious belief, worship, and association are considered to be strictly private affairs, there are, at the same time, certain common elements of religious orientation that the great majority of Americans share. These have played a crucial role in the development of American institutions and still provide a religious dimension for the fabric of American life, including the political sphere. This public religious dimension is expressed in a set of beliefs, symbols, and rituals that I am calling the American civil religion.[54]

Far from being trivial (mere forms), according to Bellah, this civil religion is vital to the nation. When American presidents swear allegiance to the Constitution, they do so before both the people and God. Their obligation extends, therefore, not only to the people, but also to God. Sovereignty explicitly rests with the people; ultimate sovereignty rests both implicitly and, at times, explicitly with God. In other words, the will of the people is not, in itself, the ultimate criterion of right and wrong; there is a higher authority by which the people (and government) will be judged. For Bellah, this gives the civil religion a "prophetic voice" in American public life. It may therefore call into question any policy pursued by the state—even one supported by a majority of the people. It may even, according to Bellah, provide the legitimation for revolution. Not only is any form of political absolutism challenged, but a goal for the political process is provided: to carry out God's will on earth. This, of course, is a notion characteristic of American thought since the days of Puritan New England. Americans, claims Bellah, have always understood their destiny in terms of mission, both individual and collective. On this matter, if nothing else, most of the Americans who identify themselves as religious seem to agree.

The term "civil religion" was not invented by Bellah. He has taken it from *The Social Contract* by Jean-Jacques Rousseau. Although it was not used by those who wrote the Constitution, Bellah argues that they had very similar ideas in mind when they established the republic. For Rousseau and many other political philosophers in the late eighteenth century, some symbolic system was necessary to support the social and political order. It did not have to be Christian, but it did have to articulate the existence of God, encourage belief in a life to come with rewards for virtue and punishment for vice, and prevent religious intolerance. Apart from these doctrines, religion was considered a private matter of interest only to individuals. The founders of the republic were not mystics. But, as Bellah points out, even pragmatic men such as Benjamin Franklin and George Washington wrote of the need for some form of religion in public life; in fact, he claims, religion—the idea of God, at any rate—played a constitutive role in the thinking of early American statesmen.

The contents of American civil religion are derived from Christianity, according to Bellah, but only selectively. The civil religion is not itself a form of Christianity. On the other hand, it is not a form of deism either. God is actively interested in history and has a special concern for America. In fact, the analogy with biblical history has often been quite explicit. The Old World of Europe was linked symbolically to Egypt, while the New World of America was linked symbolically to the Promised Land. God actually led the people to establish a new social order that would be a light to the nations.

If the collectivity is itself the "sacred," as suggested by Emile Durkheim, then the beliefs, symbols, and rituals developed in the early years of the American republic can well be called a "religion." Because most Americans at the time were Christian, it seems unlikely that the lack of specifically Christian references in the civil religion was intended to spare the feelings of a few non-Christians. Apparently, Bellah avers, it reflected the private as well as the public views of those who framed the Constitution. The need, as they saw it, was not for a "religion in general" based on political expediency (since most of the original colonies had established churches of their own), but for a specifically American civil religion. As Bellah points out, this civil religion may have referred only vaguely and indirectly to Christianity, but it referred very specifically and directly to America. "Precisely because of this specificity," he writes, "the civil religion was saved from empty formalism and served as a genuine vehicle of national religious self-understanding."[55] At the same time, the civil religion was not intended as a replacement for Christianity; the two were mutually compatible, not mutually contradictory. As citizens, Americans were free to believe and practice any or no religion; as public officials, though, they could operate only under the rubrics of the civil religion. The solution has been very effective.[56] It originated in a cultural and historical setting dominated by Protestantism and the Enlightenment but has endured in spite of massive social and cultural changes.

The first major challenge faced by the civil religion was also the first major challenge faced by the state itself. During the antebellum period, the focus was on the Revolution. This was seen as the final act of an Exodus from tyranny in Europe. The Declaration of Independence and the Constitution came to function as sacred scripture. And George Washington became an icon functionally equivalent to Moses who led his people out of bondage into freedom. The Civil War, however, required a major adjustment in national self-understanding. It was the time of trial. For Abraham Lincoln, much more was involved than saving the Union. The War was a divine judgment on the nation. The man who never joined a church publicly proclaimed in his second inaugural address that slavery and the war should be seen in an ultimate perspective. After his death, Lincoln himself became a major symbol in the civil religion. "With the Civil War," writes Bellah, "a new theme of death, sacrifice, and rebirth enters the civil religion. It is symbolized in the life and death of Lincoln. Nowhere is it stated more vividly than in the Gettysburg Address, itself part of the Lincolnian 'New Testament' among the civil scriptures."[57]

Following Robert Lowell, Bellah notes the repeated use of birth (initiation) imagery in the Gettysburg Address: "these honored dead" are said to have "brought forth," "conceived," and "created" a "new birth of freedom." According to Lowell, this speech was a sacramental act. In it, Lincoln symbolically died just as the soldiers had really died—and just as he himself would soon really die. Not only did he give the field of battle a significance it had previously lacked, he also joined Jefferson's ideals of freedom and equality to the Christian notions of sacrificial death and rebirth. Bellah believes, with Lowell, that the Gettysburg Address is nonsectarian (accessible to everyone) in spite of its obvious derivation from Christianity. "The earlier symbols of the civil religion had been Hebraic without being in any specific sense Jewish. The Gettysburg symbolism ("those who have given their lives, that the nation might live") is Christian without having anything to do with the Christian church."[58] Apparently, a symbolic equation between Lincoln and Jesus was made very early. Lincoln's former law partner, for example, not only referred to Lincoln as having been tested in the "fiery furnace" to purify him, but also as "the noblest and loveliest character since Jesus Christ" and "God's chosen one." So Lincoln, "our martyred president," was linked to the war dead, "those who gave their last full measure of devotion," and the theme of sacrifice was indelibly written into the symbolism of America's civil religion. It has been given both physical expression in public monuments and national cemeteries as well as verbal expression in the speeches and rituals associated with Memorial Day and Veterans Day.

> Just as Thanksgiving Day, which...was securely institutionalized as an annual national holiday only under the presidency of Lincoln, serves to integrate the family into the civil religion, so Memorial Day has acted to integrate the local community into the national cult. Together with the less overtly religious Fourth of July and the more minor celebrations of Veterans' Day and the birthdays of Washington and Lincoln, these two holidays provide an annual ritual calendar for the civil religion. The public school system serves as a particularly important context for the cultic expression of the civil rituals.[59]

Bellah observes that one major problem faced by advocates of the American civil religion involves defining its central symbol. In the eighteenth century, virtually all inhabitants of European descent understood the word "God" in roughly the same way. And few, if any, actually denied the existence of God. Today, though, the meaning of this word is far from clear. There is no formal creed in the American civil religion. Consequently, it was possible to elect a Roman Catholic president. It might even be possible to elect a Jewish president. But, asks Bellah, would it be possible to elect an atheist? Would someone who refused to use the word "God" be acceptable as president? If such a basic idea could no longer be taken for granted, then the civil religion would no longer be able to unify the nation (much less give it meaning and purpose). Writing in 1967, of course, Bellah could not have forseen the continuing power of religious belief in America. It seems that the theological crisis of the 1960s afflicted only a small segment of the population; since then, Americans have reported some difficulty with organized religion but (apart from Marxists, some Buddhists, some members of the academic community—and some theologians!) not with belief in God.

At the deepest level, the success of *The Wizard* is due to its function in American society as a secular myth. More specifically, I suggest that it functions very much like the civil religion. As all people do, Americans want to have their cake and eat it, too. They want to maintain the political benefits of a secular state but also to nourish a spiritual identity based on religious tradition. Not all Americans can agree on the doctrinal articulation of that spiritual identity. Even so, virtually all of them can enjoy popular myths (such as *The Wizard*) and participate in public rituals (such as Memorial Day) that, though explicitly secular (or only vaguely theistic), implicitly express Judaeo-Christian ways of thinking that form the basis not only of the churches themselves but of the nation as a whole.

*

In the introduction, some questions were posed. What is it about *The Wizard* that transcends the boundaries separating races, classes, sexes, generations, and regions? Why has this movie been so massively and enduringly popular? There are many ways of explaining this phenomenon. For one thing, *The Wizard* is a superbly crafted production. Then, too, it incorporates features that bind viewers together in spite of demographic differences. Jungian analysis indicates that boys as well as girls can identify with Dorothy in her efforts to grow up and go home. Likewise, I have also noted that this movie is set in the heart of the country both geographically (Kansas) and historically (the frontier). Not surprisingly, Americans from every region can identify with Dorothy in her desire to go home. It could even be argued that the appeal of this movie crosses racial (or other socio-economic) lines because, in addition to its universal themes of growing up and going home, the four major characters are "racially" varied: a white girl, a tin man, a talking lion, and a dancing scarecrow. The image of this foursome skipping down the open road, arm in arm, may well be associated, consciously or subconsciously, with a harmoniously integrated society. It should also be said that most Americans have watched *The Wizard* on television every year as they were growing up. Watching it again, as adults, is a nostalgic link with their childhood. Moreover, it is an experience they can share with their own children. And, for those who are familiar with the unhappy life of Judy Garland in the years following her portrayal of Dorothy, there is another dimension to this nostalgic experience. Garland's touching rendition of "Over the Rainbow," her theme song in later years, is a perpetual reminder that the innocence and promise of youth are vulnerable to cynicism and despair. At the same time, it is a perpetual reminder of the need to believe in the possibility of renewed innocence and promise.

Nostalgia is often condemned by those who consider themselves enlightened, progressive or radical. For them, it only undermines the effort to mobilize popular support for social, economic, or political change. Basking in the warm glow of fond memories, they insist, is a distortion of the past at best and a form of anesthesia at worst. Instead of passively daydreaming about the good old days, people should be actively involved in planning for the new age. According to Fred Davis, however, this analysis misrepresents the nature and function of nostalgia. Far from contributing to reaction, he argues in *Yearning for Yesterday*, nostalgia actually facilitates change by placing it within a familiar context. Change is rendered less threatening by seeing it as a repetition of earlier changes; if those could be survived, so can more recent ones. Moreover, "collective nostalgia acts to restore, at least temporarily, a sense of sociohistoric continuity with respect to that which has verged on being rendered discontinuous. And this period, when the nostalgic reaction waxes strong, may afford just enough time for the change to be assimilated into the institutional machinery of a society (e.g. into the realms of law, politics, religion, and education) as it could not at first and, were it left wholly up to purely *private* feeling, might not for some time thereafter."[60]

At a time of massive dislocations, according to Davis, it is not suprising that American society is undergoing a wave of nostalgia. As evidence, he points to the popularity of revivals from earlier periods in both the fashion and entertainment industries.[61] If nostalgia mitigates the disruptive effects of rapid change at the collective level, moreover, it also does so at the individual level. Nostalgia, according to Davis, is an emotion that helps people cope with periods of great stress due to major transitions in the life cycle. More specifically, it reasserts continuity and identity in the face of discontinuity and loss of identity. Far from being merely a way of escaping from reality, nostalgia is a healthy way of appropriating reality. By focusing attention on personal success in meeting earlier crises, for example, we reinforce the hope that current problems will also be resolved. If so, then it would surely make sense to find that nostalgia for adolescence is particular strong among those entering middle age.[62] "But while the gestalt inversion of an adorned past...and of an anxious present...may constitute...the psychological essence of *all* nostalgia, it seems that for Western man the transition from adolescence serves, at the mythic level at least, as the prototypical frame for nostalgia for the remainder of life. It is almost as if the depth and drama of the transition were such as to institutionalize adolescence in the personality as a more or less permanent and infinitely recoverable subject for nostalgic exercise."[63]

Apart from moralistic or ideological denunciations, very little has been written about nostalgia with the exception of this phenomenological study by Davis. It is a useful corrective, to be sure, but no less reductionistic. He argues that nostalgia can have a socially and politically useful function. Nostalgia is good, not bad. I suggest, however, that nostalgia, like fantasy of any other kind, is neither good nor bad in itself; in one form or another, it is just part of the human experience and requires no legitimation.

According to Eliade, nostalgia is virtually a defining element of the human race (which is to say, of *homo religiosus*). For him, nostalgia operates ultimately on the cosmic level. At the heart of all religious experience, he observes, is a "myth of the eternal return," a desire to reexperience primordial events that took (or take) place *in illo tempore.*

> The repetition of archetypes shows the paradoxical wish to achieve an ideal form (the archetype) in the very framework of human existence, to be in time without reaping its disadvantages, without the inability to 'put the clock back.' Let me point out that this is no 'spiritual' attitude which deprecates life on earth and all that goes with it in favor of a 'spirituality' of detachment from the world. On the contrary, what may be called the 'nostalgia for eternity' proves that man longs for a concrete paradise, and believes that such a paradise can be won *here*, on earth, and *now*, in the present moment. In this sense, it would seem that the ancient myths and rites connected with sacred time and space may be traceable back to so many nostalgic memories of an 'earthly paradise,' and some sort of 'realizable' eternity to which man still thinks he may have access.[64]

No wonder *The Wizard* is so massively and enduringly popular. It gives brilliant expression, on all three levels, to an emotion that can be exploited by entrepreneurs, trivialized by reviewers, attacked by moralists and ideologues, or legitimated by sociologists and psychologists, but not suppressed.

In times of increasing mobility and rapid social change, many people assume that happiness means excitement and adventure. Since everyday life is generally a humdrum affair, they dream, like Dorothy, of finding what they seek "somewhere over the rainbow." When Dorothy lands in Oz, she assumes that she has found the land of her dreams. Then she realizes that Oz, though colorful, beautiful, and fascinating, is also fragmented, illusory, and confusing. Oz is not a paradise somewhere over the rainbow; it is more like the rainbow itself. Dorothy's task is to seek the proverbial pot of gold at the end of the rainbow. To do this, she follows the "golden" path in the middle of its spectrum. By the time she reaches the end of the rainbow, Dorothy knows how to use what is in the pot. After clicking the heels of her ruby slippers, she returns to Kansas "in just two seconds." So, as she wakes up back in her own bed, both Dorothy herself and the background music make it very clear that "home sweet home" lies "over the rainbow."

NOW YOU DON'T HAVE TO BE A WIZARD TO GET PERFECT PICTURES.

Imagine if you were afraid of photography, like the cowardly lion, yet your first roll of film turned out perfectly!

Imagine if you knew nothing about photography, like the scarecrow, yet your pictures were beautiful!

That's what Minolta's 35mm Autofocus Compacts can do for you. They're so completely automatic they do everything but buy the film.

The incredible Minolta Talker actually talks you into great pictures with three handy voice reminders.

And with the brilliant Minolta Freedom II you'll never have to make another photo decision. It even sets the DX film speed for you. And it's the most affordable Minolta Autofocus you can buy.

With both cameras, you just pop in the film and start shooting. Minolta's film-handling systems load, advance and rewind the film all automatically. And both have built-in flash systems to give you more light where you need it.

So join the wizard of autofocus technology and, like Dorothy, you can have wonderful memories.

With the easy-to-use Minolta Autofocus Compacts, you'll never worry about getting great pictures again.

Be certain that the valuable Minolta one year U.S.A limited warranty is packaged with your products. For more information, see your Minolta dealer or write: Minolta Corporation, 101 Williams Drive, Ramsey, N.J. 07446. In Canada: Minolta Canada, Inc., Ontario. © 1985 Minolta Corporation.

TALKER

FREEDOM II

© 1985 MGM/UA Entertainment Co.
"The Wizard of Oz" characters.

ONLY FROM THE MIND OF MINOLTA

MINOLTA

Figure 8

[Permission to reproduce this advertisement is granted by the Minolta Corporation.]

APPENDIX 1
METHODOLOGICAL NOTES

Normally, movies are studied in one of two ways: either in terms of sociology (film as industry) or in terms of aesthetics (film as art). Neither of these approaches was adequate for a discussion of *The Wizard*. Nevertheless, I will discuss them briefly to provide a theoretical background for my own work.

It is no longer considered unusual for scholars to study popular culture, but usually it is either dismissed as aesthetically worthless or attacked as politically reactionary. M. Gottdiener has developed a theory of mass culture[1] that is more flexible and sophisticated than most. My purpose in discussing his work in this book is to introduce some of the problems involved in studying mass culture, to indicate why new approaches are still needed, and to suggest that a distinctive contribution can be made by scholars in the field of religious studies. Gottdiener is dissatisfied with the prevalent theory of mass culture: hegemony. According to Antonio Gramsci's refinement of earlier Marxist theory, the ruling class maintains its privilege not only through economic power but also through cultural domination. Through the mass entertainment industries that propagate class-specific perceptions of reality, the "ideology" of the ruling class (that is, its beliefs, values, and attitudes) saturates all aspects of everyday life and thus "reproduces," or perpetuates, the status quo. In short, it generates either "false consciousness" (based on illusion instead of reality) or "contradictory consciousness" (based on confusion and fragmentation instead of clarity and coherence) when assimilated by the masses. "In particular," writes Gottdiener, "according to hegemony theory, the abilities of the working class to think reflexively and to analyze the social and individual conditions of everyday life have been short-circuited by this consciousness industry."[2] For those who belong to this school of thought, then, mass culture is "bad," not only in aesthetic terms but also in political and moral terms. Gottdiener, however, writes that this theory is flawed by reductionism.

> By asserting that class consciousness is controlled in the interests of the bourgeoisie through the mediation of mass culture, hegemonists assume the unity of all thought and beg the more essential theoretical question concerning the constitutive nature of the human subject. Consciousness itself can never be controlled in the manner suggested by this theory because it implies the existence of a homogeneous human subject who has been produced by modernity and whose mental state has a reflexive thought capacity that is indistinguishable from either consciousness or even subconsciousness. At its core, therefore, the assertion of consciousness control commits the fallacy of idealism...that implies that the mental activity of individuals can be separated so easily from the material conditions of their existence that consciousness can be "false."[3]

The hegemonists fail to distinguish between ideology and consciousness. The former is an imaginary construct propagated by the state or by the ruling class; the latter is a complex organization of perceptions experienced by individuals. Only when the study of ideology is separated from that of individual consciousness, notes Gottdiener, will scholars be free to examine the social processes associated with imaginary constructs (ideology) and their relation to mass culture, on the one hand, and to individuals, on the other. Although he acknowledges that institutions (such as the schools, churches and mass media) propagate ideology, Gottdiener denies that an industry can produce consciousness itself. "Consequently," he writes, "the control of ideology in society is a much more volatile and contingent process than hegemonists suggest."[4]

Like most other theorists, Gottdiener stresses the importance of the political struggle among what could be called "taste cultures" whose preferences will provide society with its symbols, values, and worldview. Although Marxists seldom underestimate the power brought to this struggle by the ruling class, he suggests, they often underestimate the ability of the masses to resist. For Gottdiener, the notion that the masses are anesthetized by false consciousness is untenable. He points out that objects (cultural productions such as movies) can mean different things to different people under different circumstances, and that these meanings are not necessarily predetermined by the ruling class. "Control of the parameters involved in the possible interpretations of events may lead to the reproduction of ruling class ideology in mass culture, but it is not guaranteed to produce false consciousness. Therefore, ideological domination of the mass culture industries is also not guaranteed to control or even affect the audience's behavior."[5]

Gottdiener's emphasis on the possibility of cultural resistance makes his theory unusual in contemporary (American) scholarship. He writes that meaning is always created in the context of social groups. Mass cultural productions, therefore, are given meaning in the contexts of particular communities. Some communities are hostile to the worldview presented by these productions of the larger society. Such communities resist cultural domination. Therefore, community life has "relative autonomy" in terms of the social, economic, and political forces at work in society as a whole. The impact of popular culture, then, must be examined in this context. Even though the production of meaning is often dominated by the mass entertainment industries (which is to say, the larger society, or ruling class), enough freedom remains for the production of meaning independent of both the logic of exchange value and the dominant cultural values.

Having located problems in the hegemony theory, Gottdiener develops his own theory of mass culture. This involves three-way relations among cultural objects, the institutions that produce and distribute them, and the people who use them. According to Gottdiener, many scholars select one of these three elements for emphasis at the expense of the other two. He refers, for instance, to those who focus primarily on the object; this is the case in aesthetic comparisons between the productions of elite culture and those of mass culture. Equally inadequate, from his point of view, is an over-emphasis on users, those who borrow the tools of market research to examine the sociological and psychological effects of mass culture while ignoring the objects themselves and those who produce them. Similarly, he rejects an overemphasis on the producers. According to that school of thought, the key factor in mass culture is the bureaucratic nature of mass entertainment industries; this leads scholars to dismiss the users as a passive and undifferentiated mass. Following Roland Barthes, Gottdiener takes a semiotic approach. In his early works, Barthes tended to reduce all objects to signs. For Gottdiener, this was based on a "linguistic fallacy": since all languages consist of words, all systems of signs must be languages. Later on, Barthes abandoned this "translinguistic" approach. He no longer emphasized the objects themselves, but the discourse about them. Although objects of clothing become signs, for example, they only do so in the context of fashion (the discourse about clothing as distinct from anything intrinsic to the actual pieces of clothing) propagated by an industry; they form a code used to manipulate the public into buying products. Consequently, Gottdiener understands mass culture as a discourse about objects.

From Martin Krampen, Gottdiener takes the notion of "transfunctionalization." By this, he means a process in which the original, primary meaning of an object is superseded by new, secondary meanings. Because transfunctionalization involves the behavior of producers as well as users of objects, all three of the elements identified as central by Gottdiener are integral parts of a unified system. The process of transfunctionalization (or semiosis) takes place in three stages; each involves the relations between two of the three elements.

The first stage involves a relation between producer and user. Objects are produced for their exchange value (profit) but are bought for their use value (function). Since the aims of producers and users do not coincide, some way of bringing them together must be found. Through advertising, exchange value is transfunctionalized into use value. That is, consumers are convinced that products have symbolic value, often related to status, in addition to their ostensible functional value. Since negotiation is necessary (and since not all advertising campaigns are successful), Gottdiener concludes that domination of users by producers is by no means automatic.

The second stage involves a relation between user and object. Objects can also be transfunctionalized by users. This stage involves the creation of new meanings unintended by the producers. Referring specifically to the work of Luis Plascencia, Gottdiener notes that Chicanos modify their cars to reflect the taste and values of their own subculture—even though this may actually render the cars impractical for the purpose of transportation. Although mass culture theorists in the United States have generally neglected this phenomenon, such has not been the case everywhere. Gottdiener discusses studies on the use of popular music by alienated British subcultures such as the Teddy Boys, Skinheads, Rastafarians, and Mods. These youth subcultures use popular music in ways unintended by the music industry—and often in opposition to the aims of that industry.

The third stage involves a relation between producer and user. Cultural objects can be recycled once more by the producers. Objects that have already been transfunctionalized by particular groups or subcultures are reprocessed; they then become raw material for new productions by the mass culture industries. If British punk rockers transfunctionalize objects of mass culture (provide them with secondary meanings to suit their own needs), the producers of mass culture eliminate the context of radical alienation, trivialize the objects and market them once more as innocuous objects accessible to the general public; the punk style generated by a marginal sub-culture is thus sanitized as "new wave" for the dominant culture with its interest in "new" consumer products.

Attention must be devoted to Gottdiener's theory because it is one of the few that do not begin with an a priori assumption that mass cultural productions are either inherently worthless or inherently destructive. He has opened up an interesting possibility not often recognized by American scholars: that the social context of mass entertainment—and not necessarily either the productions themselves or those who produce them—generates meaning. From this, it follows that users are not a passive, undifferentiated mass but are active participants in the creation of culture. And from this, it follows that mass entertainment may sometimes be understood in ways appropriate to the needs of users. Nevertheless, Gottdiener's work is not quite as innovative as it seems. He has slightly modified the hegemony theory, it is true, but he has not challenged it. He has not suggested that the model of hegemony is seriously flawed (or even that it is one model among many) but merely that hegemony is not always achieved. Although he acknowledges that consciousness cannot be perfectly manipulated and controlled and more is involved in mass entertainment than the mere propagation of ruling class ideology, he nonetheless succumbs to a very similar form of reductionism. His criticism of hegemony theory notwithstanding, Gottdiener maintains the belief that class struggle is the major, if not the sole, issue at stake in the creation of meaning through mass entertainment. As a result, he admits that mass entertainment is sometimes transfunc-tionalized by a subculture to serve its own needs as a class—that is, in opposition to other classes—but he does not suggest even the possibility that the meaning of mass cultural productions may also be generated for other reasons or in other social contexts. Nor does he discuss the fact that no society, by definition, can exist without some sense of common identity based on beliefs shared by everyone because they transcend social, economic, and political divisions. It is useful to consider his use of terminology with this in mind.

For Gottdiener, the term "producer" refers specifically to the indus-tries that manufacture objects of mass culture (such as movies). A sociologist, he is interested in producers as a class. But the people who write the scripts, design the sets, compose the music, choreograph the dances, point the cameras, direct the scenes, and act the roles are not representatives of a single class; their interests, values, and taste may or may not coincide with those of the industrialists and financiers who market the finished product. It seems naive to assume that this social and cultural diversity is not reflected in their work and, therefore, need not be considered in a discussion of the "producers." Moreover, Gottdiener's use of this term is reductionistic. There is an industrial aspect of mass entertainment, it is true, but there are also other aspects worthy of consideration. Even in the days of the Hollywood studio system, the people whose creativity actually produced the movies were not merely cogs in an industrial machine. Not once does Gottdiener raise the question of art and its ambiguous relation to mass entertainment. I do not want to suggest that mass culture can be discussed adequately in purely aesthetic terms. In fact, I argue that aesthetic categories would be distinctly unhelpful in discussing *The Wizard* and movies like it. But my aim is very limited; I am studying the function of one particular type of movie. Gottdiener's aim is much more comprehensive; he is proposing a general theory of mass culture. And he has failed to account for a significant aspect of it.

Similarly, Gottdiener's employment of the term "user"[6] is somewhat limited. To be sure, he acknowledges that members of the audience cannot be reduced to the status of passive victims. But he sees only one way for them to create meaning of their own: subcultural resistance to the dominant culture. I do not want to reject this possibility. It could be argued, indeed, that the hippies of the 1960s transfunctionalized *The Wizard* by selecting aspects of it that supported their own worldview. Such aspects would have included the social satire associated with the Wizard himself. As an authority figure, he is plainly a humbug, a satirical portrait in keeping with the rejection of established authority emphasized by the hippie movement. In addition, however, the Wizard could have been seen as a countercultural wise man who was only pretending to be an authority figure. His advice to Dorothy's friends includes satirical attacks on the smugness, self-righteousness, and pretentiousness of American life. Finally, the hippies could have identified their own psychedelic experiences with Dorothy's surrealistic dream of Oz. Nevertheless, the popularity of this movie has by no means been confined to cultural minorities seeking a distinctive identity in opposition to that of the larger society. On the contrary, *The Wizard* is notable precisely for the universality of its appeal. To follow Gottdiener's argument, this would be due to an extraordinary coincidence: dozens of subcultures trans-functionalizing *The Wizard* to suit their own particular—but neces-sarily divergent and often conflicting—needs. This would be a very cumbersome explanation. Gottdiener's theory does not allow for the possibility that something about movies of this kind functions to unify, rather than fragment, the community. Indeed, its association with the nation as such (illustrated by its role in the Boston Pops concert on Independence Day) clearly indicates this. Besides, not all subcultures are based on alienation from or hostility toward the larger community. Most ethnic and religious subcultures, for example, take extreme pride in their patriotism. For members of these com-munities, a movie that affirms American identity would be welcomed precisely because it allows them, as members of minority groups, to feel part of the nation as a whole. The hippies may well have trans-functionalized *The Wizard* to suit their own needs. That hardly explains the massive and enduring popularity of the movie (though it may be part of the explanation). The question raised here is not why *The Wizard* appeals to this or that group of Americans, but why it appeals to Americans in general. I suggest that it represents a world-view that is neither imposed by a producer class on a class of hapless users nor one that has been transfunctionalized by an alienated subculture but one so consistent with that of the nation as a whole that the passage of over fifty years marked by profound social change has not diminished it as a representation of meaning.

Gottdiener uses the word "object" to describe the result of a cul-tural process. Occasionally, he reminds his readers that objects may involve people and events.[7] Because he thinks of users primarily as consumers, however, he also thinks of cultural objects primarily as commodities. Although economic transactions do take place (both literally and figuratively) in connection with mass entertainment, and although he makes intelligent comments on the social and political implications of these transactions, he does not do justice to the richness and complexity of at least some mass cultural objects. Con-sumers, after all, own commodities; viewers of a movie do not. For the latter, the subject-object duality breaks down; they "lose them-selves" in the world presented on screen. Is "commodity" the best model for discussions of this kind? Must we assume that the produc-tion of meaning can be explained adequately according to a model based on the production, distribution and consumption of merchan-dise? In the case of movies, at any rate, it is at least worth considering the possibility of using other models. One of these is art.

*

Like the various forms of art, movies may be (and often are) studied as the imaginative creations of individuals or small groups of individuals; it is assumed that their nature and function correspond very closely to those of novels and plays, for instance, or possibly paintings. In many cases, this is probably so. Nevertheless, I suggest that this model is not adequate in every case. Despite the fact that film has long been established as a legitimate form of art and despite the fact that the trademark displayed on the opening title of every MGM release includes the words *ars gratia artis*—art for art's sake having long been a rallying cry for at least one wing of the avant-garde—no one would seriously argue that *The Wizard of Oz* is art. According to current definitions of art, it could be seen only as "bad art." This is because "good art" is now considered virtually synonymous with avant-garde art. In *The Transformation of the Avant-Garde*, Diana Crane notes that the term "avant-garde" was first used in France during the early nineteenth century. It appeared as a result of the fragmentation caused by industrialization. Before the mid-nineteenth century, European artists served the ruling class, an elite whose values they expressed and usually shared. Some groups of artists became socially and politically entrenched. "Those who were excluded," writes Crane, "developed an ideology of their own that justified their commitment to aesthetic innovation and liberal political views....By the early twentieth century, when the role appears to have reached its full development, it was characterized by its alienation from the rest of society and particularly by its opposition to bourgeois culture."[8] She argues that the avant-garde has always had a dual role in the art world. On the one hand, avant-garde artists have seen themselves as aesthetic innovators who challenge visual traditions; on the other hand, they have seen themselves as prophetic innovators who challenge social or political traditions.

The term "avant-garde" implies a cohesive group of artists who have a strong commitment to iconoclastic values and who reject both popular culture and middle-class life-style. According to the prototype, these artists differ from artists who produce popular art in the content of their works, the social backgrounds of the audience that appreciates them, and the nature of the organizations in which these works are displayed and sold. Often esoteric, avant-garde art is purchased by a relatively small group of admirers who possess or have access to the expertise necessary to evaluate it.[9]

There is no universally accepted theory of the avant-garde. According to Crane, however, every new (avant-garde) art movement redefines some conventional notion of what art is, has been, or should be. She locates three contexts in which redefinition takes place. Art movements are generally considered avant-garde in their approach to aesthetic content if they (1) redefine artistic conventions, (2) utilize new artistic tools and techniques, or (3) redefine the nature of art objects including the range of objects that can be considered art. Movements that foster the revival of earlier aesthetic conventions are unlikely to be considered avant-garde even if they do so in new contexts. In addition, art movements are usually considered avant-garde in their approach to social content if they (1) incorporate social and political values that are critical of (or at least different from) those that are dominant, (2) redefine the relation between elite and popular culture, or (3) adopt critical attitudes toward artistic institutions themselves. Finally, art movements are normally considered avant-garde in their approach to the production and distribution of art if they (1) redefine the social context of production in terms of the appropriate critics, role models, and audiences; (2) redefine the organizational context of production, display, and distribution of art; or (3) redefine the artist's role, or the extent to which the artist participates, in other social institutions (such as education, religion, and politics).

Crane's intention is not to define "avant-garde" from a normative perspective but to show how it is defined by various segments of the (artistic) community. True, the term "avant-garde" may be used in a variety of ways, but all have one thing in common: the avant-garde is always defined in *opposition* to something else. It tries to provoke viewers by forcing them to think or feel something new and different. It challenges or attacks what are perceived as established norms. This is not suprising when the military origin of the term is recalled.

Art is associated not only with the avant-garde, however, but also with "high culture." Although she acknowledges that the latter can be defined in several ways, and that the boundaries between it and popular culture have been questioned by scholars such as Herbert Gans, Crane writes that "the concept of the avant-garde is central to the sociology of art because it is a major element in the definition of high culture."[10] Even though her argument is that the distinction between high culture (including avant-garde art) and popular culture is now breaking down, Crane also asserts the legitimacy of such a distinction (which is to say, the assumption that this distinction is made or has been made). Following Gans, she writes that high culture is always associated with works based on aesthetic tradition. This may refer to traditions that have long been established; these are represented by "classical" works or "old masters." But it may also refer to new traditions that are struggling to gain acceptance; these are represented by avant-garde works of a highly esoteric nature that focus attention on the solutions to technical aesthetic problems. Like J. G. Cawelti, Crane defines popular culture in terms of aesthetic formulas or standardized procedures for creating an aesthetic effect. Elite and popular culture, however, also appeal to different segments of the population. High culture is accessible to the middle and upper-middle classes. It is created by individuals and distributed by small or highly specialized organizations (such as galleries or museums) that serve primarily those classes. Popular culture, on the other hand, is corporately produced and distributed by industrial means to a mass audience. Crane argues against those who say that there are no inherent differences between these two "taste cultures." According to them, cultural productions are one or the other depending on the social circumstances in which they are produced, presented, and "consumed" or on the historical and sociological environment of the critic. "These authors would like to eliminate the distinction between the two types of culture," writes Crane, "but since high culture is often created in a distinctive context, one that grants greater autonomy to the artist than to the creator of popular culture...this argument is difficult to make."[11] Note that she does not call the creators of popular culture "artists."

Crane agrees with those who believe that the gulf between elite and popular culture is eroding. She does not agree, however, that this is happening because the aesthetic tradition underlying elite culture is exhausted. She explains this phenomenon in sociological rather than aesthetic terms. For her, the avant-garde is in decline because the art world has been transformed into big business and artists have become highly successful entrepreneurs with a heavy stake in the perpetuation of middle-class values (such as the importance of prestige) and institutions (such as the museums, galleries, universities, and critics). These institutions depend on government and corporate grants. Their orientation toward the public has led them to seek larger audiences in order to legitimate their use of funds. This, in turn, gives artists an incentive to create works that will be accessible to larger segments of the public.

No one today, as Crane points out, lives completely within the realm of either elite or popular culture. People are exposed to a continuous barrage of visual images through the press, film, television, and other visual arts. These images are culled, moreover, from sources that are both familiar and remote (in time or space). And they are continually being recombined to create new or apparently new meanings. Unlike those who claim that cultural productions serve the needs primarily of those who control social institutions, Crane writes that "contemporary society can be viewed as an arena of conflicting and shifting definitions of reality in which various actors compete with one another to impose their interpretation of events."[12] So it is possible to maintain that mass cultural productions are continually recycled with new interpretations depending on circumstances. Here, once again, is Gottdiener's argument. Her theory of the avant-garde corresponds to his theory of an alienated subculture that creates new meanings through transfunctionalization. This is obviously true in the case of pop art (which deliberately selected the mass-produced objects of everyday life—such as Andy Warhol's soup cans—for transfunctionalization); this is not the case, though, of movements such as abstract expressionism or minimalism (which deliberately avoided any familiar reference points).

In effect, Crane argues that the avant-garde (in New York City, at any rate) has become a "moyen-garde." If so, then "art" is no longer synonymous with "avant-garde." The very fact that such an argument must be made, however, suggests the point I am trying to make: that the equation between art and avant-garde has been prevalent. It has been assumed that art is primarily the self-expression of individuals and does not, therefore, express the values and sentiments of society as a whole (as distinct from the members of an intellectual subculture). Consequently, those artists who do become very popular with the public at large are suspect in the art world. Andrew Wyeth has been accused of being an "illustrator" instead of an artist.[13] Recent movements (such as pop art) may be challenging the "traditional" (avant-garde) definition of art, but, paradoxically, they are being very avant-garde in doing so. My point here is that the avant-garde definition of art has been dominant for so long in our society that most people consciously or unconsciously accept it—even if this means admitting that art is inaccessible to them!

The polarization between elite and popular culture is still very widespread. In a recent edition of "Sunday Today,"[14] for example, one segment was devoted to "Culture." By this was meant elite or high culture. It was explicitly opposed to popular culture. Throughout the broadcast, elite culture was identified with "serious" culture and "the arts." Art was described as the "pure expression" of cultural values (with the suggestion of "art for art's sake") but also as the "uncompromising vision" (which suggests the "prophetic" side of avant-gardism). On several occasions, it was implied that popular culture was a threat to "serious" culture; the latter had to be protected from the former. But the premise of this broadcast was that the longstanding gulf between the two was breaking down. On the one hand, "serious" culture can be, should be, and is being made more accessible to ordinary people. On the other hand, it was noted that artistic institutions such as symphony orchestras that are funded by the public must consider the wishes of those who support them. In the concluding sequence of this show, an orchestra in the town of Marshall, Montana, played "Over the Rainbow" from *The Wizard!*

It is unnecessary to assume that "art" and "avant-garde" have ever been perfectly or completely synonymous. Some movements are generally acknowledged to have produced art even though they are not recognized as avant-garde schools. American regionalist painters of the 1930s fall into this category. Because of their emphasis on naturalism in the aesthetic (stylistic) realm, they are usually classified as members of a conservative movement. Nevertheless, these artists conformed to certain very general criteria central to the avant-garde. In the first place, they strove to make original, unique contributions as individuals. Indeed, the works of Grant Wood can hardly be mistaken for those of anyone else; even though they are representational works and, therefore, much more accessible to the general public than works of pure abstraction, his paintings are highly stylized in a way that calls attention to Wood's own distinctive personality as much as to the cultural traditions he tried to represent. Moreover, Wood and the other regionalists saw themselves as opponents of both the dominant artistic movements and social trends of their time. Populists often see themselves as radicals but are not often seen that way by others. Whatever the social content of their work, the regionalists are not considered avant-garde because they adopted styles based on the tradition of realism or naturalism. But they are also acknowledged, albeit grudgingly, as important American artists. Even those working outside the avant-garde may be considered artists, therefore, as long as they conform to at least one criterion that has been prevalent since the Renaissance and is the sine qua non of the avant-garde: the originality of each individual artist or, in a word, innovation.

It is true that MGM was very innovative in its use of technology for *The Wizard*. Such innovation, however, necessarily remains hidden from viewers. Some viewers may have been impressed by technical virtuosity, but awareness of technical innovation behind the special effects has probably not been a major factor in the movie's appeal to most viewers. (Even fewer would be impressed today, of course, after decades of technological advances in the movie industry.) Although *The Wizard* responded to some of the problems of modern American life in innovative ways, it did not do so by rejecting traditional beliefs—such as the importance of cultural stability and continuity—that are very widespread among Americans. If it affirmed a modern worldview associated with progress, it also (and more deeply) affirmed a worldview closely associated (consciously or unconsciously) with that of both the populists and the regionalists of the 1930s. Unlike the paintings of Grant Wood and his colleagues, however, *The Wizard* was not produced by an individual whose unique style permeates the work. In fact, it was created by an even wider variety of people—including four directors and ten screenwriters—than most other productions of the Hollywood studio system. In short, *The Wizard* is marked neither by the individuality of its creator nor by the revolutionary nature of its content. Not only can it not be classified as avant-garde art, it cannot truly be classified as art even in the slightly looser sense that admits the regionalist painters. But if the model of art as currently understood in our society is inadequate to understand the function of movies, it may be useful to consider the model of art as understood in other societies or even at other times in our own.

There are some movies, of course, that can be, and should be, discussed in terms of art (that is, the avant-garde). In fact, they are generally known as "art films." In this category are the works of *"auteurs"* such as Ingmar Bergman and Michelangelo Antonioni who see themselves as artists whose proper role is to challenge established social and aesthetic coventions. They conform, in other words, to the avant-garde notion of artists. But not all movies are created by *"auteurs."* If *The Wizard* were not so pervasively and persistently popular, it could be dismissed as an example of "bad art." Given its remarkable durability as a part of American life, though, that explanation seems facile. But if it does not function as "good art," how *does* it function? One possible solution is to broaden the definition of art. Defining it in terms of the avant-garde, after all, is by no means universal. On the contrary, it is a distinctive (and possibly unique) feature of contemporary Western societies according to a cross-cultural study: *Art in Primitive Societies*, by Richard Anderson.

As an anthropologist, Anderson is interested primarily in the art of primal societies.[15] "Those things are considered to be art," he writes, "which are made by humans in any visual medium and whose production requires a relatively high degree of skill on the part of their maker, skill being measured, whenever possible, according to the standards traditionally used in the maker's society."[16] Defined in this very general way, art is a universal phenomenon. But the specific ways in which art is understood vary greatly from one society to another. In some ways, Western art—including avant-garde art—is similar to that of primal societies. Because the task here, though, is to broaden the definition of art (that is, to show how the avant-garde definition is a very limited one), only the differences need be discussed.

By definition, primal societies are small-scale ones that cannot support much specialization. Artists live with everyone else and, much of the time, also work with everyone else. Accordingly, they are integral parts of society. They share the same worldview as everyone else. Their particular skills notwithstanding, artists seldom adopt beliefs or forms of behavior radically different from those of the community at large. "In direct contrast to the often-heard stereotype of the contemporary Western artist, with a bohemian life style and eccentric beliefs, the artist in primitive societies is usually a well-integrated member of his or her group.... In such a setting, it is virtually impossible for the artist *not* to be highly integrated into the social system—either as an 'unknown' whose skills go unrecognized, or as an eccentric who relishes the life of self-imposed alienation."[17]

Modern societies, by contrast, support a great deal of specialization. Not only are artists full-time specialists, but the art world includes many other specialists: art dealers, art curators, art educators, the producers and sellers of art materials—and even art forgers. With all these specialists in mind, it is easy to understand why artists are able to live within a relatively small subculture. They can limit their social circles to other artists, dealers, critics, and patrons. Not surprisingly, artists in modern societies tend to be isolated from their society rather than integrated within it. Ever since the romantic period, artists have been stereotyped as rebels or even as neurotics, but this has not always been so. Before the romantic period, artists were usually respectable and ambitious participants in the elite society of their patrons. There were a few mavericks such as Caravaggio, Rembrandt, and (possibly) Bosch. But there were many more socially prominent artists such as Rubens, Titian, Van Dyke, Velazquez, and Reynolds (all of whom were members of the aristocracy). Anderson examines the relation between social structures and particular stylistic forms and concludes that art provides a "map" of the society in which both artists and their public live. The correspondence between map and reality is not always perfectly accurate, "but insofar as there *is* a correspondence, art must be seen as a conservative, rather than innovative, expression of culture. Art gives legitimacy to the traditional way of doing (or thinking about) things, providing a tangible support for the *status quo*. Or, if it does point to a currently unrealized ideal, its goal is a traditional one, not a revolutionary vision for a future that is radically different from the present."[18] When anthropologists such as Anderson refer to the "conservative" nature of art or to its support of the *"status quo,"* they do so in descriptive, not normative terms; the negative connotation these words have acquired among many Western thinkers are not implied here. Indeed, Anderson suggests that no society could exist, as such, without some degree of order, continuity, and cohesion. Communities differ only in the degree to which these are considered desirable. Stability is not preserved automatically. It must be continually maintained in the face of individual needs that threaten traditional ways. These are therefore encoded, propagated to the community and preserved for future generations. This, argues Anderson, is one of the most common functions of art.

Following Emile Durkheim, A. R. Radcliffe-Brown, and Talcott Parsons, Anderson suggests that living in any society inevitably involves a modicum of uniformity in belief and behavior. Through various institutions, individuals come to accept, to a greater or lesser extent, the goals, attitudes, and ways of living that are in harmony with those of others. These institutions include law, religion, kinship, language—and art. Anderson illustrates this with examples of art being used to encourage respect for law and order (among the Mano and Gio tribes of northeastern Liberia), to establish authority and legitimacy (among the Andaman Islanders), to enhance status (among the Ashanti of southern Ghana) and to teach ethical principles (among the Lega of central Africa). In these cases, art is used explicitly as an agency of social control; in other cases, though, this

can be done implicitly because artistic styles reflect beliefs so fundamental that calling attention to them in the first place is unnecessary.
As Anderson points out, however,

> The notion that art may help maintain the *status quo* is a conclusion
> that goes contrary to many of our own preconceptions about art. For
> most of us in the twentieth century western world, artists are first and
> foremost innovators—bohemians and visionaries who would rather
> improve or renovate their social milieu than produce works that
> support the *status quo*. But such a characterization of our own art
> community would be in error; and, more, importantly, ours is only one
> of the thousands of societies that inhabit the earth. Because *our* art
> often seems anti-establishmentarian we cannot safely assume that art
> is thus everywhere.[19]

Although some other societies acknowledge and even approve of
innovation in art, the degree to which it is valued in our society may
be unique. In primal societies, art is often used to preserve and pass
on vital information about the environment, the way of life or the
spirit world; even when innovation is valued, it cannot be allowed to
threaten tradition itself. Change is inevitable, of course, and universal.
In our society, though, change is linked to purposeful innovation and
defined as "progress." And this has actually become a defining element
of modernity—including modern art; avant-gardism is based precisely
on the notion of attacking tradition. To sum up, change, or innovation, has become an end in itself. A "derived" work is, by definition,
an inferior one.

What it all boils down to, according to Anderson, is a radically
different relationship between artists and the communities they
address through art. In primal societies, art is typically public in
nature. Not only does it communicate specific messages, it also becomes a medium of communication for the entire community. And
the message communicated remains intelligible across both time and
space.

> The artist in primitive societies may—and typically does—call upon a
> whole repertoire of symbols (or icons) that are readily recognized by
> large sectors of the audience. By contrast, western artists have come to
> rely in greater or lesser degree upon images from their own vision of
> the world, making art that is highly personal and idiosyncratic. Perhaps
> more important than the change from a reliance on public symbols to
> an increased use of private ones is the shift in ideology that has
> accompanied the change: Western artists are not necessarily obliged to
> make their works understandable to nonartists; if others fail to under-

stand an artist's works it can be argued that the problem is not the artist's but, if anyone's, the viewer's.[24]

To some extent, the use of private symbols can be traced to a preoccupation with personal self-expression at the expense of communal self-expression, but, in many cases, another factor is involved. As Crane has observed, one form of avant-garde art is based on the idea of "art for art's sake." Art exists, in other words, as an end in itself. And artists who see themselves as aesthetic innovators legitimate their work on its own (formal) terms, not in terms of social or political goals. Nonetheless, even these artists are seldom actually indifferent to the response of viewers. To be sure, they reject their didactic role of propagating a worldview (either the established one or their own), but they do aim to undermine any worldview that is accepted uncritically. The aim of their art is to shock the sensibilities, alter the visual perception, or challenge the assumptions of viewers. It is often with this idea in mind, that viewers are not expected to understand art. To do so would be to rely on superficial notions of order and clarity instead of acknowledging the underlying ambiguities and paradoxes of reality. On the contrary, viewers are expected *not* to understand. Under these circumstances, art becomes the functional equivalent of the Zen *koan* or the parable as understood by John Dominic Crossan (while movies and other productions of popular culture become the functional equivalent of what he understood as myth).[21] In any case, Anderson correctly points out that primal societies seldom (if ever) prefer the private expression of individual artists to the public expression of the collectivity; even esoteric art in more complex traditional societies (such as Islam or India) is based on coherent systems of symbols that are accessible to initiates from one generation to the next.

The prevalence of abstract forms is often cited as a hallmark of modern art. Be that as it may, the situation is somewhat more complex. Abstraction, as such, is indeed characteristic of modern art but not only of modern art. In primal societies, it is true, art is usually representational, according to Anderson, even though human, animal, and plant forms are often highly stylized; for obvious reasons, the use of art to record and transmit information about the environment through art is essential in nonliterate societies. Islamic art, however, not only uses stylized natural forms (such as the vine motif, or arabesque) but the truly abstract forms of geometry. Still, the latter have been used consistently according to traditional patterns and in conformity with a theological perspective that is publicly proclaimed. It is the *idiosyncratic* nature of abstract art in modern Western societies that is truly distinctive. This is why, says Anderson, only a small segment of the population actually participates in the world of art. "One repercussion of the social stratification present in our society," he writes, "is that, for better or worse, accurately or not, most people believe that they do not 'understand' contemporary fine arts, even if they have taken a course in 'art appreciation.'"[22]

Even though the post-impressionists were inspired by the art of primal societies and saw themselves as modern "primitives," there was a profound disparity between their works and those of their unknowing mentors. This has been noted concisely and eloquently in "Art and Icon" by Robert Redfield, another anthropologist. According to him, there are two major differences between primal and modern art. The first is a matter of content. Reflecting on Ortega y Gasset's notion of art as a window frame through which a garden can be seen, Redfield explains that

> non-objective painting and sculpture of the extreme modernist is all window. There is no garden. If the work is a symbol, an icon of sorts, it is one private to the artist. We have nothing to attend to but the window. In contrast, the work of primitive art...does have behind it a garden, a wonderfully and complexly designed garden....This is the first respect in which primitive and abstract modern art are unlike: one lies within and may stand for a complex world of traditional meaning; the other does not. Such modern art is a departure from, even a revolt against, the incorporation of these traditional meanings into a work conceived as a work of aesthetic appeal in and of itself, for its newly discovered arrangements of form and color.[23]

Modern art is different from primitive art in a second way as well. In this case, Redfield refers not to the content of art (the presence or absence of meaning whether it be personal or collective, mundane or transcendent) but to its style (which is to say, the patterned use of formal properties).

> The very modern artist creates his own style, one peculiar to himself, or characteristic of his small group, his "movement." He is self-conscious of this; he knows he is departing from the familiar systems of forms to find fresh ones; he and his fellows are creating styles. But the primitive artist is, of course, making works of art within a highly formalized, intensely local and very long established style. If the primitive artist works in true primitive isolation, he is probably largely unaware of the qualities of the style he follows; he uses it as he does his language,

rightly, and without self-consciousness. He is disciplined, but does not have to struggle for the discipline.[24]

The point here is not that modern (avant-garde) art is either superior or inferior to primal art but only that it is based on very different assumptions; these, therefore, provide an inappropriate frame of reference for a discussion of *The Wizard*. Strangely enough, the assumptions on which primal art is based could provide a more appropriate frame of reference. Clear analogies can be drawn between the function of popular movies in American society and art in other societies. *The Wizard's* massive popularity, at any rate, suggests that it corresponds to a traditional (or generally accepted) worldview and that this makes it accessible to most members of society. Its enduring popularity, moreover, suggests that the worldview is successfully transmitted from one generation to another. In other words, this movie promotes cultural stability (as distinct from social change), just as art does in most other societies. Nevertheless, the word "art" is still so heavily associated with the avant-garde that it would be counter-productive to insist on redefining it (or defining it in an anthropological sense alien to scholars working in the fields of art criticism or art history). The (avant-garde) model of art can tell us only what *The Wizard* is *not* or how it does *not* function in our society. If elite culture is identified with the avant-garde, and if the avant-garde is identified (more or less) with art, then *The Wizard* is clearly not good art. According to this aesthetic model, of course, it could be understood only as "bad art" (something of little or no value). This model cannot tell us how *The Wizard does* function or account for its place in American culture.

In primal societies, art is often used for religious purposes. As Anderson points out, to be sure, this is not always the case. According to anthropologists, art may be used for a variety of purposes ranging from the dissemination of practical information to the display of status. Nevertheless, art and religion are almost always closely linked. To the extent that a society has religion, however that may be defined, it is usually given some form of visual expression. Moreover, art and religion function in very similar ways. One of the most common functions of religion, like art, "is the contribution it makes to the maintenance of social stability and cultural homeostasis through its embodiment of both an ethos and a set of ethical principles that are more or less shared by all members of the society."[25] Art and religion also satisfy very similar psychological needs experienced by individuals. Anderson cites the following passage from a study by

Marvin Harris. He writes that art and religion, "are media for expressing sentiments and emotions not easily expressed in ordinary life.
They impart a sense of mastery over or communion with unpredict-
able events and mysterious unseen powers. They impose human meanings and values upon an indifferent world—a world that has no
humanly intelligible meanings and values of its own. They seek to
penetrate behind the facade or ordinary appearance into the true,
cosmic significance of things."[26]

Furthermore, art and religion achieve these goals in very similar
ways. In both cases, arbitrary distinctions are made—between the
beautiful and the ugly, for instance, or between the sacred and the
profane—that become culturally encoded in mythical, ritualistic, or
aesthetic terms handed down from one generation to the next as
tradition (patterns through which the world can be understood by a
community). I suggest, therefore, that *The Wizard* (and other movies
like it) are most appropriately discussed in terms of religion.

*

Because I draw supporting evidence from other movies, television
shows, landscape paintings, hymn books, and a variety of other
sources, my approach must be considered eclectic. This does not
mean, however, that I have selected evidence at random. On the
contrary, each has been selected with a particular purpose in mind.
My reason for doing so is based on practical necessity. If the richness
and depth of a complex cultural phenomenon is to be discerned, it
must be examined through a variety of lenses; it would be foolish,
even arrogant to imagine that any one method could bring to light
everything worth knowing about it. Therefore, I have made use of a
whole range of methods originating in academic fields as diverse as
film studies, art history, symbolic geography, and psychoanalysis.
None of these alone would provide more than a very fragmentary
picture; together, they provide the basis for a comprehensive analysis
of *The Wizard* and its roots in American culture.

In resorting to eclecticism, though, I am in good company. Wendy
O'Flaherty, noted for her work on Hindu mythology, has done the
same thing. In *Siva: The Erotic Ascetic*, she points out the multiplicity
of meanings attached to all Hindu myths. For different people or at
different times they may be entertaining stories, metaphorical stories
about the gods and goddesses, metaphysical stories about cosmic
laws and processes, or folkloric stories about the human search for
meaning in everyday life within a community. O'Flaherty agrees with

Mary Douglas who writes that "no one meaning can be labelled the deepest or the truest....The best words are ambiguous, and the more richly ambiguous the more suitable for the poet's or the myth-maker's job. Hence there is no end to the number of meanings which can be read into a good myth."[27] If the possible meanings of a myth cannot be reduced to one, or even to one level, neither can the possible methods used to study it. O'Flaherty openly advocates metho-dological eclecticism. "Almost every one of the traditional methods is applicable to some portion of some myth," she writes, "though none can explain them all."[28] In this, she is following many other scholars such as Alan Watts who writes that "There is some truth in almost all theories—as that myth is primitive philosophy or science, that its inner meaning is sexual, agricultural or astrological, that it is a projection of unconscious psychic events, and that it is a consciously constructed system of allegories and parables. No one of these theories accounts for all myths, and yet I do not doubt that each accounts for some."[29]

O'Flaherty makes an interesting analogy between the maker of myth and the student of myth. Following Claude Lévi-Strauss, she argues that both are *bricoleurs:* both take scraps from diverse sources and use them to build meaning. Some Hindu myths, for example, really do lend themselves to Freudian analysis. Others are more amenable to Jungian analysis. Still others are best explained in terms of ritual. Speaking not only of myth but of religion in general, Ninian Smart observes that diversity is sometimes preferable to purity. The field of religious studies itself is no longer a closed compartment; other disciplines and approaches overlap.

> Already...I have hinted that it overlaps with depth psychology (Freud and Jung), economic history (Marx and Weber), New Testament studies (Bultmann), the history of religions (Eliade), and philosophy (Wittgen-stein). But equally we could look to literature—you can learn much about worldviews through Shakespeare and Dostoyevsky and Steinbeck; or to art history—you can learn much through Giotto and Indian sculpture; or to music. The symbolic life of human beings ranges across the humanities and the social sciences. The modern study of religion presents a perspective on the whole of human life.[30]

In short, I have tried to avoid reductionism by placing *The Wizard* in a variety of cultural contexts. Each, if taken alone, would be inade-quate; together, they show that the pervasive and abiding popularity of this movie is the result of its ability to evoke a multiplicity of associations deeply embedded in the national ethos.

APPENDIX 2
OZ IN AMERICAN
POPULAR CULTURE

Some references to *The Wizard* are specifically to the book or to characters, events, and places that appear in the various Oz books but not in the movie.

When Frank Drake, an astronomer at the Radio Astronomical Observatory in West Virginia, begins searching for extraterrestrial life, he calls his project "Ozma" after the princess in several Oz books.[1]

Christian fundamentalists remove their children from public schools in Tennessee rather than have them read *The Wizard of Oz* because "it portrays witches as good. I do not want my children seduced into godless supernaturalism."[2]

A textbook on the sociology of religion notes that the difference between ordinary reality and religious reality is marked in tangible ways: "It is as though one had crossed an invisible boundary to a very different country as Dorothy crossed the Great Sandy Desert from Kansas to Oz.[3]

Often, references are more ambiguous. They may allude to either the book or the movie, but they may also allude to both the book and the movie.

Time reports that Andres Duaney, an architect planning a new town in Florida, is dissatisfied with the "populist pettifogging" that has modified the original designs. "We're building Kansas," he says, "but we're getting Oz."[4]

A popular singer writes and records a song called "Goodbye Yellow Brick Road." It includes a reference to the Kansas farmhouse in which

Dorothy was carried aloft by a tornado and wafted to Oz: "Where are you gonna come down? When are you gonna land? I should have stayed on the farm."[5]

State officials in Kansas increase the budget for advertising in order to encourage tourism. "The money helps combat the image of Kansas as the dusty, black-and-white landscape portrayed in *The Wizard of Oz*."[6]

Recalling her life before she took up acting, Cloris Leachman says of the time she was chosen Miss Chicago of 1946: "I felt like Dorothy, whirled away in a big tornado."[7]

Dorothy, one of the Golden Girls on television, is introduced to someone with a vaguely foreign name and asks him: "What kind of work do you do, Mr. Toto?" Before answering, he corrects her: "Oh, just Toto. You're Dorothy and I'm Toto."[8]

Bartlett's *Familiar Quotations* include references not only to the book—the entry for Lyman Frank Baum cites "The Wonderful Wizard of Oz," "The Wicked Witch of the West," and "The Yellow Brick Road" as memorable phrases—but also the filmed version: the entry for Edgar Y. Harburg includes the first verse of his most famous song, "Over the Rainbow."[9]

The International Wizard of Oz Club has been established to meet the needs of serious Ozophiles. Since 1959, it has issued *The Baum Bugle* (popular and scholarly articles on both Baum himself and Oziana in general) three times a year, published *Bibliographia Oziana* (bibliographical material on the "canonical works" of Baum), *Oziana* (an annual of new Ozian stories), and *The Oz Trading Post* (a quarterly sale and exchange list for collectors). The Club has inspired theme parks all over the United States. By 1987, there were about 2,200 members (including two in India). Every year, the "Munchkins" hold their convention in the East, the "Gilikins" in the North and the "Winkies" in the West. The Club also holds auctions of first editions and other Oz memorabilia. It is listed in *The Encyclopedia of Associations*. And contributions are tax-deductible in the United States.[10]

By now, MGM's filmed version has become a spectacular phenomenon in its own right. It is not merely a derivative of the book. Although all adaptations are derived from the book, this one has been so successful that its original features place it in a separate category. It is not just another movie about Oz; it is The Movie about Oz. Consider the following references:

In 1990, the United States Postal Service issues four stamps commemorating four movies made in Hollywood's "golden year," 1939: *Stagecoach, Beau Geste, Gone with the Wind*—and, of course, *The Wizard of Oz*. Although Julian Pugh created first day covers for all of them, the most beautiful may well be the one he designed for *The Wizard*. (Figure 2).

Dan Rather announces on "The CBS Evening News" that a pair of the ruby slippers worn by Judy Garland was sold for $165,000. This is a record: the highest price ever paid for an article of movie memorabilia.[11]

The Wizard is to be one of forty American movies intended to advance Soviet-American relations. The purpose of this film festival is to provide Russian viewers with "different perspectives on the life and people of America."[12]

Commenting in an interview on the research for his latest book. *The Bonfire of the Vanities*, Tom Wolfe tells Bryant Gumbel of NBC's "Today": "So finally, I started heading across the country, and I found that I was like Dorothy in *The Wizard of Oz* in that marvelous scene in which she falls asleep in a field of poppies. She wakes up and she looks over and there is Oz, and there are these sparkling, brilliant, spires rising up from out of nowhere."[13] This scene does not occur in the book.

When the New York apartment of Ferdinand Marcos, ex-President of the Philippines, is examined, a pillow embroidered with a line from the script—"Toto, I have a feeling we're not in Kansas any more"—is found among the possessions.[14]

As Democratic members of Congress assemble at a resort in West Virginia to discuss the party's future, the featured speaker advises them to adopt a new song: it parodies a famous one from *The Wizard:* "Sing it," he tells them, "I'm off to be the Wizard, the wonderful Wizard of Oz. I know I am a whiz of a wiz because of the wonderful things I does."[15]

An advertisement in the *New York Times* announces a revival of *The Wizard* to be presented at Radio City between March 22 and April 9, 1989.[16] That this production is dependent on the movie rather than the book is made quite explicit: "The Hollywood classic comes to life on the great stage." The entire musical score, in fact, has been retained.

In the debut of "Heartland," a situation comedy, the family farm is overtaken by a tornado. Emerging from the storm cellar, Tom explores the debris and then calls down to the others: "There's a dead witch under the house and everything's in color."[17]

Many cartoonists have also used imagery from the movie. In one cartoon from "The Far Side," Gary Larson shows Dorothy and her friends skipping down the Yellow Brick Road when they meet a bunch of Ozian joggers approaching them from the opposite direction.[18] In another, three insects are strolling down the Yellow Brick Road and paraphrasing dialogue in the movie; instead of "Lions and tigers and bears, oh my!" they chant "Spiders and scorpions and insecticides, oh my!"[19] (Figure 3). In still another, a lobster about to be dumped into a pot of boiling water calls out, "Auntie Em, Auntie Em! There's no place like home! There's no place like home!"[20] (Figure 4). That very line appears in one installment of "Doonesbury," by Garry Trudeau. Boopsie returns to a previous incarnation in ancient Rome. When her session of "regression therapy" is over, she must return to present-day California. Departing, she recites the familiar mantra, "There's no place like home! There's no place"[21] (Figure 5). In a slightly earlier series of the same comic strip, Zonker is asked to sit in the House of Lords. Hoping for the demise of Margaret Thatcher, he begins his maiden speech to the House with the Munchkins' song: "Ding Dong, the Witch Is Dead."[22] (Figure 6). Berke Breathed has also referred to the movie in his comic strip, *Bloom County*. In one instalment, for example, Opus daydreams about Steve's adventure "somewhere above the clouds, above the sky." In the next frame, we see Steve being given shock treatment by some aliens. "I don't want my personality flopped," he says, "Turn on the Gephardtization machine," says one of the aliens. In the final frame, Opus sighs, "Somewhere over the rainboooooow"[23] (Figure 7).

Most telling of all are the advertisements referring directly to the movie. Evidently, market researchers can assume that these references will immediately be recognized by nearly everyone. In these advertisements, quotations from the movie may be verbal (songs and dialogue), visual (props, sets, costumes), or both.

During a television commercial for Esso, Dorothy and her friends once again march down the Yellow Brick Road singing "We're off to see the Wizards, most wizardly wizards there was! We're goin' to Expo '86." Suddenly, the Tin Man's arm rusts solid. But Dorothy knows the solution: "Esso!" After a brief visit to the service station for oil, they set off again for Expo—only the black-and-white film suddenly turns into color (a visual transformation made famous by the movie).[27]

In a satirical mail-order catalogue, the "advertisement" for Toto

Tinsulate Underwear shows Jack Haley in his 1939 role as the Tin Man along with a caption that recalls Dorothy's theme song, "Over the Rainbow": "Useful for wear where troubles melt like lemon drops, away above the chimney tops."[28]

An advertisement for Minolta cameras shows Dorothy, the Scarecrow, and the Lion snapping pictures in the Emerald City. "Imagine if you were afraid of photography, like the Cowardly Lion," reads the caption, "yet your first roll of film turned out perfectly! Imagine if you knew nothing about photography, like the Scarecrow, yet your pictures were beautiful! That's what Minolta's 35 mm Autofocus technology can do for you. So join the wizard of autofocus technology and, like Dorothy, you can have wonderful memories"[29] (Figure 8).

A beautiful advertisement for Bloomingdale's, the New York City department store, shows Dorothy and Toto standing on the Yellow Brick Road. Looking into the distance, Dorothy sees the Emerald city shimmering on the horizon at the foot of a rainbow (which does not appear in the book). "Whether you live in New York or Kansas, or somewhere over the rainbow," reads the caption, "what could be easier than shopping our joyous Christmas 1985 catalogue? Bloomingdale's by mail for the holidays. Because there's no place like home" (a line that quotes the movie directly but only paraphrases the book)[30] (Figure 9).

Because references to the 1939 musical have become integral parts of American popular culture, it is not surprising to find references, both explicit and implicit, in other movies.

One of the major characters in *After Hours* (Martin Scorsese, 1985) is a film buff whose favorite movie is *The Wizard*. He is so obsessed by it that he is in the habit of screaming "surrender Dorothy!" at the moment of sexual climax. As most viewers know, these are the words formed by the Witch's phallic broomstick in the sky above the Emerald City.[31]

A direct quotation is found in *Shoot the Moon* (Alan Parker, 1982). In one sequence, we see some children watching *The Wizard* on television. One of them recites the dialogue along with the Witch: "Fool that I am," they say together, "I should have remembered—those slippers will never come off as long as you're alive. But that's not what's worrying me. It's how to do it. These things must be done delicately!" (107).

Another example is found in *Desert Bloom* (Eugene Corr, 1986). After a battle with her husband, Lilly sits down at the piano and sings "Over the Rainbow." At the same time, her daughter, Rose, sneaks out of the house through the bedroom window. Since this movie is set in 1950, the use of "Over the Rainbow" could be explained as a mere attempt at historical accuracy; it would be appropriate for Lilly to sing any song popular at that time. Just the same, the use of this particular song indicates that it is not merely part of the background like the vintage cars and dated costumes; audiences are expected to make specific associations between its use in *Desert Bloom* and its use in *The Wizard.* Lilly and Rose represent two aspects of Dorothy: the former shares her proclivity for passive daydreaming of a happier world and the latter shares here courage to pursue happiness by running off to seek her fortune. Not coincidentally, Rose is accompanied by a male friend, Robin, just as Dorothy is accompanied by Toto.

Sometimes, quotations are neither direct (actual frames or sequences inserted by montage; specific lines or phrases inserted into the script) nor indirect (oblique visual, musical, or other allusions) but something in between (what could be called paraphrases).

Studded with references of this kind is *Good Morning Vietnam* (Barry Levinson, 1987). The hero, Adrian Cronauer, has just arrived in Vietnam as a new disk jockey for the army's radio station. In his opening monologue, he says that the Demilitarized Zone "sounds like something from *The Wizard of Oz.*" According to this parody, America's Vietnamese allies represent the Munchkins; recalling "We represent the Lullaby League" and "Follow the Yellow Brick Road" from *The Wizard's* score, they sing "We represent the ARVN army" and "Follow the Ho-Chi-Minh Trail." Similarly, the Vietcong represent the Witch's guards; they chant "O-i-o, Ho-Chi-Minh." Not surprisingly, Ho-Chi-Minh himself represents the Wicked Witch: "I'll get you my pretty...now little GI, you and your little Tutu too. A-ha-ha-ha-ha-ha! I'm melting! Aha-ha-ha-ha-ha-ha!" But it is Hanoi Hannah, not a good counterpart, who represents Glinda, Good Witch of the North. "Oh my God," says Cronauer, "it's the Wicked Witch of the North, Hanoi Hannah!" Later on, an early morning broadcast begins with a parody of Glinda's song: Instead of "Come out, come out, wherever you are" we hear "Get up, get up, wherever you are." Toward the end of the movie, Cronauer is walking through a forest in hostile territory and observes: "We're not in Kansas any more, Toto." In his final broadcast, just before being sent back home to America, Cronauer bids farewell by paraphrasing Glinda's instructions to Dorothy at the Emerald City: "The ruby slippers, Adrian. Put them on and say, 'There's no place like home, there's no place like home.'"

In the case of *Under the Rainbow* (Steve Rash, 1981), an entire movie refers to *The Wizard.* This is clear from the title alone. The villain of *Rainbow* is a diminutive Nazi agent who evokes clear associations with both the Wicked Witch of the West and the Munchkins. He relentlessly pursues the good, but exiled, Duchess of Luchow and her dog, Strudel. *Rainbow* also includes thinly disguised references to *The Wizard's* structure. At the end of the movie, most of the events are revealed as fantasies that actually took place in a dream (as they were in the earlier movie). Many viewers are probably familiar not only with characters and events from *The Wizard* itself but also with anecdotes about its production. *Rainbow* is actually about the midgets who were invited to Hollywood in 1939 to play the Munchkins. According to gossip columnists, they were a bunch of promiscuous drunkards who indulged in frequent orgies;[29] much of the humor in this movie would be lost without some knowledge of these rumors.

She's Gotta Have It (Spike Lee, 1986) is a black-and-white film that has no obvious connection with *The Wizard*. Nevertheless, the shift from monochromatic to polychromatic film in one sequence is a parody of the heel-tapping episode in which Dorothy returns from a polychromatic Oz to a monochromatic Kansas.[30]

Peggy Sue Got Married (Francis Ford Coppola, 1986) was reviewed in *Time* as *"Back to the Future* meets *The Wizard of Oz.* Kathleen Turner plays an older Dorothy who is transported to the Emerald City of youth, then ruefully returns to the Kansas of middle age."[31] Apart from a general affinity between the two movies—that is, movement back and forth in time—*Peggy Sue* contains some more specific paraphrases of *The Wizard.* Toward the end, for instance, Peggy Sue tries to return to the "present" with the help of her grandfather's lodge brothers; the latter dress up and stage an elaborate ritual only to be revealed as well-intentioned charlatans (and thus reminiscent of the Great Oz himself). But like Dorothy, Peggy Sue returns home simply by waking up.

Labyrinth (Jim Henson, 1986) is also "associated" with *The Wizard.* According to one reviewer, this recent movie "is little more than an innocuous—albeit visually striking—*Wizard of Oz* for the "Sesame Street" set. After successfully wishing that her baby brother be carted off by a gaggle of goblins, a young lass...subsequently rather guilt-ridden, sets out to retrieve the tyke in some mystical kingdom with its own Wizard of Odd."[32] In a promotional trailer, moreover, it is recommended as "the wizardry of George Lucas!" In fact, *Labyrinth* is filled with direct and indirect references to *The Wizard.* A copy of *The Wonderful Wizard of Oz* appears in two scenes: Sarah's bedroom at the beginning and the scrap-woman's shop near the end. A crystal ball, like that of Professor Marvel and the Wicked Witch, is also seen several times; more important is the fact that, on one occasion, a doll inside the ball looks very much like Glinda (whose customary mode of transportation in Oz is a bright, spherical, bubble). The spatial confusion experienced by Dorothy in Oz is paralleled by Sarah's inability to decide which way to proceed in the labyrinth. The labyrinth itself is hemmed in on both sides by walls of brick (recalling the Yellow Brick Road). On several occasions, Sarah paraphrases Dorothy by repeating: "Things aren't what they seem to be, here." Some of the song-and-dance routines (especially that of Sir Dydimus) are taken straight from vaudeville just as they were in *The Wizard*. If characters from Kansas reappear, thinly disguised in Oz, Sarah's dog and some other characters from the real world reappear in the labyrinth. If Dorothy makes good friends in Oz, so does Sarah in the labyrinth. And like the Cowardly Lion, Hoggrel the goblin must learn about courage in the context of friendship. Just as *The Wizard* concludes when Dorothy tells Auntie Em: "There's no place like home" (132), *Labyrinth* concludes when Sarah announces to her father: "Yes, I'm home!"

Still another movie, *Made in Heaven* (Rudolph Blocker, 1987), is about a return passage from home to some very different realm and back home. Just as Dorothy moves from Kansas to Oz and back to Kansas in *The Wizard*, Mike moves from Earth to Heaven and back to Earth in this movie. *Heaven* contains a number of indirect quotations from *The Wizard*. Like the earlier movie, it begins with a black-and-white prologue, switches to color as soon as the hero, Mike, wakes up, as it were, "on the other side." Just as Dorothy leaves home in the prologue to seek her fortune, so does Mike. And if Dorothy is accompanied by her dog Toto, Mike is accompanied by his dog Skunk. Both Dorothy and Mike are transported to another world by encountering some force of nature; Dorothy is wafted into the sky by a cyclone and carried off to Oz; Mike sinks to the bottom of a river and passes away to Heaven. Just as Oz is ruled by a "humbug" (122), Heaven is ruled by someone named Emmet Humburg. Like the Wizard, however, he has a kind heart; he allows Mike to return to Earth but, like the Wizard, he imposes one condition before granting the boon: the hero must pass a test. Both Dorothy and Mike must learn to have confidence in themselves. As Dorothy prepares to leave the Emerald City, Glinda tells her: "You don't need to be helped any longer. You've always had the power to go back to Kansas;" when the Tin Man asks why Glinda did not tell her this long before, Glinda answers: "Because she wouldn't have believed me. She had to learn it for herself" (128). Similarly, Emmet Humburg tells Mike: "It's up to you," and advises him: "believe in yourself." As in *The Wizard*, the characters of *Heaven* are transmogrified from one world to another. Not only does Mike go back and forth between Earth and Heaven, but several other characters do as well. While in Heaven, for example, he is reunited with

Aunt Lisa as well as a friend who had died. Back on Earth, he meets a computer expert from Heaven (now working for Halo Records), Emmett Humburg himself and the parents of his previous incarnation. He even sees a picture that had been painted in Heaven by Aunt Lisa. Both movies feature paranormal modes of transportation. In Oz, characters fly around on broomsticks or in bubbles. In Heaven, they do so through teleportation, levitation, or imaginary flight. Spatial irregularity is a feature of both movies. In the former, this theme is expressed as a road with many branches and no clear direction. In the latter, it is expressed as the window in Aunt Lisa's celestial home; through it can be seen Paris, Florence, or any other place she wishes to paint. Similarly, temporal irregularity is a feature of both movies. In the former, this is expressed primarily in the transition from Oz to Kansas. Though separated by Dorothy's lengthy journey down the Yellow Brick Road, Glinda informs her that "Now those magic slippers will take you home in two seconds" (128). When Dorothy returns to Kansas, she has actually gone back in time to the moment she was hit on the head (as if nothing had happened in Oz); her future as seen from Oz, is thus a return to the past. In *Heaven*, this theme is expressed more directly by the computer expert who tells Mike that in Heaven "there's no time, no time" and by Mike himself who reads that "Heaven is where the future is born." The road, a traditional symbol of the quest, is a specific motif running through both movies. The Yellow Brick Road, of course, is associated with Dorothy's quest in Oz. Quest is also the main narrative theme in *Heaven*. While in Heaven, Mike falls in love with Annie, but she soon leaves Heaven to be born on Earth. Returning to Earth, Mike embarks on a quest for Annie. This is not a visually central motif in *Heaven*. Nevertheless, it is emphasized in at least one scene: Mike has just returned to Earth and is walking across the country. We see him lying down on the highway. In fact, he is lying right on top of a very prominent yellow line which can be seen stretching far back into the countryside. Finally, both movies include epilogues that refer back in obvious ways to prologues. In *The Wizard*, this is accomplished by a return to monochromatic film and the mise-en-scène of Kansas. Although *Heaven* does indeed have a monochromatic prologue, the epilogue does not return to monochrome. But it does bring back Mike's parents (that is, the parents of his previous incarnation) and the prologue's song, "Goodnight Irene."

APPENDIX 3
RELIGION AND SECULARITY
IN AMERICA

At one time, the churches—officially religious institutions—were distinctive for nourishing the imagination and stirring the sense of wonder. Now, secular institutions such as the entertainment industry have largely taken over by default. Ironically, secularity itself is a partial, albeit unintended outgrowth of the religious revolution set in motion by early Protestantism. If knowledge of God was attained through scripture alone, then the world was radically desacralized. This new emphasis on the cognitive dimension of religion undermined the idea that knowledge of God can also be attained through the experience of sacred time and space mediated imaginatively in myth and sensually in ritual. The altar was soon all but replaced by the pulpit. By now, many churches—and not only Protestant ones—have gone much further. The liturgy may be redesigned as a vehicle to promote "community-building." Prayer may be reinterpreted as a source of personal "growth." Salvation may be redefined as "empowerment" and virtually anything else considered psychologically healthy or politically virtuous. If the sacred is a sine qua non of religion, and if it is sui generis—irreducible to any other phenomenon—then these churches have evidently become profoundly secular (which is only to say that what they do may be desirable or useful but not specifically religious). In any case, they have almost abandoned myth and ritual in their search for "relevance," their attempt to legitimate religion in a modern and secular world. But if the need for myth and ritual is a defining feature of the human race (collectively if not individually)—and I agree with Eliade that it is—then people will seek them wherever they can be found. If myth cannot be found in the churches, for instance, it can surely be found in the movie

311

houses or on television—translated, of course, into secular terms. Needs may thus be served that are no longer served, or ineffectively served, by the officially religious institutions. Like the American civil religion, therefore, movies may have strongly religious undertones— even as liturgies have strongly secular ones. *The Wizard of Oz* may be called a "secular myth" because, though not overtly religious, it functions in a modern and ostensibly secular society, to some extent, the way myths function in traditional and religious societies. In this respect, it resembles some other phenomena that reveal the complex and ambiguous relation between American religiosity and secularity. Consider two quintessentially American festivals: Christmas and Memorial Day.

For some Americans, Christmas is a traditional religious festival. They either go to church on Christmas Eve or watch one of the many Christmas liturgies broadcast every year on television. But Christmas in America is not only for believing and practising Christians. The many musical events associated with Christmas (Handel's *Messiah*, for example, and Christmas carols sung by local and visiting choirs) are enjoyed not only by Christians but also by those who reject their Christian backgrounds, and even by those who belong to non-Christian religious communities. For many Americans, Christmas has been removed from even this minimal association with institutional Christianity. Even so, there is some evidence to suggest that Christmas is still an occasion when most Americans either put aside their scientific notions of reality or wish they could do so.

Several very popular movies are interesting in this respect: *Miracle on 34th Street* (George Seaton, 1947) is about a sophisticated little girl who comes to believe in Santa Claus when a department store employee turns out to be the real thing. *It's a Wonderful Life* (Frank Capra, 1946) is about a saintly man who contemplates suicide, believing that his life has been futile and worthless, until a guardian angel shows him what his town would have been like without him. *A Christmas Carol* (Edwin L. Marin, 1938; Brian Desmond Hurst, 1951; Ronald Neame, 1970; Clive Donner, 1984) is about a cynical miser who learns about the joys of family and friendship after being visited by a trio of ghosts. Of these, not one contains so much as a single reference to the Church, the Incarnation or anything else to do with Christian theology. On the other hand, they are about Christmas since the explicit temporal setting of each is either Christmas or the Christmas season. And each involves a fantasy of the supernatural. It is worth noting that these movies are not aimed only at children. In

Montreal, during the Christmas season of 1988, all three were scheduled at times accessible either to children (during the day or in prime time) or to adults (late at night).[1] Whatever the social meanings of such movies (such as celebrating the American family), the fact remains that even for the many Americans who are not affiliated with churches, Christmas is a time when it is legitimate to indulge in thoughts of the supernatural or of some dimension of experience beyond the normal space and time of daily life. These movies are clearly fictional. And since no religious authorities expect people to believe in Santa Claus, the Ghost of Christmas Past, or guardian angels, they need not be taken seriously on a metaphysical level. For this very reason, it is significant that many Americans still express interest in such fantasies associated with Christmas even if only to think "I wish it were so."

For those who do not care to indulge in such direct fantasies of the supernatural, the annual broadcast of *The Nutcracker* (in one version or another) provides a legitimate way to mark the occasion of Christmas. The fantastic events explicitly take place in a dream, not in a theatrical portrayal of real life. More important, this ballet is Art. Nonreligious American adults need not feel embarrassed about indulging in fantasy when it is associated with Tchaikowsky, Baryshnikov, and the American Ballet Theatre. The link between Christianity and *The Nutcracker* is very tenuous indeed. The two are no longer symbolically connected by Christian themes such as renewal (Ebenezer Scrooge in *A Christmas Carol* and George Bailey in *It's a Wonderful Life* are given second chances through "conversion" or "rebirth" just as the cosmos is metaphysically rejuvenated with the advent of Christ) and faith (Susan's belief in Santa Claus defeats commercial cynicism in *Miracle on 34th Street* just as belief in the mystery of the Incarnation defeats spiritual cynicism). They are connected instead by the mere custom of gift giving. Nevertheless, exchanging gifts does express important cultural values associated with family and friendship (no matter how corrupted by commercialism) and these are, in turn, associated with the Christian festival (the Holy Family; the gifts of the Magi). For Americans who never think about the Incarnation or even about Santa Claus, *The Nutcracker* provides a way of joining in the celebration of a festival that cuts across boundaries of age, sex, race, geography, beliefs, and ethnic origin. Consequently, Christmas is a national holiday for Americans (in addition to whatever meaning it has for Christians). Because it is so appealing to so many people for so many different reasons, it is difficult to be an American and not find some way to celebrate Christmas. Its attractiveness to children, for example, causes practising Jews to meet in synagogues every year to discuss "the problem of Christmas." While liberal Jews often decorate trees and exchange gifts at this time, more traditional Jews try to compensate for Christmas by emphasizing the Jewish festival that also occurs in mid-December (even though Hannukkah is not a real counterpart of Christmas since it has very little theological significance within Judaism).

The same ambiguous relation between religion and secularity can be observed in connection with Memorial Day. To anticipate my conclusion; if Christmas has a religious origin related in various ways to secularity, Memorial Day has a secular origin related in various ways to religion. In *American Life: Dream and Reality*, W. Lloyd Warner places Memorial Day in a theoretical context strikingly similar to what Robert Bellah calls "civil religion."

> The ceremonial calendar of American society, this yearly round of holidays and holy days, partly sacred and partly secular, but more sacred than secular, is a symbol system used by all Americans. Christmas, Thanksgiving, Memorial Day and the Fourth of July, are days in our ceremonial calendar which allow Americans to express common sentiments about themselves and share their feelings with others on set days pre-established by society for this very purpose. This calendar functions to draw all people together to emphasize their similarities and common heritage; to minimize their differences; and to contribute to their thinking, feeling, and acting alike.[2]

With this in mind, he describes Memorial Day observances in a small New England town identified as "Yankee City." Symbolic behavior takes place in four stages. The first phase lasts for several months; it consists of separate activities in each of the many civic and fraternal associations as they anticipate the major events of Memorial Day itself. The second begins three or four weeks before the big day; detailed plans are drawn up for participation in public events and some associations stage special public rituals in honor of their own war dead. The third phase begins a day or two before Memorial Day; scores of public rituals are held in cemeteries, churches, and association halls. This phase culminates in the fourth and last one: on Memorial Day itself, all these separate groups come together in the heart of the business district; with their members in uniform, they march through the town, visit shrines and monuments to the heroic dead, and finally enter the cemetery for the formal climax of the day.

E pluribus unum is the motto of America: out of many, one. This is symbolically expressed by the long process that leads up to Memorial Day. Out of many associations, churches, and ethnic groups emerges one collectivity; out of fragmentation, unity is born. This is the theme not only of Memorial Day but of America itself.

War is the unifying symbol. Theoretically, war could be seen as the opposite of unity because it is the ultimate example of human conflict. Even so, war also evokes feelings of intense solidarity. During modern wars, often called "total wars," feelings of social solidarity have run extremely high. Under these circumstances, Warner suggests, conditions are ideal for new sacred forms to be built on the foundations of earlier ones. Most American towns, for instance, experienced the Second World War as a period of heightened identification with the larger goals of the nation. People organized themselves into groups designed to promote the war effort. The various associations carried on activities that were known to be vital. After the war, activities had to be invented to keep people busy; people looked back with nostalgia to the conflict that had given them a sense of meaning and purpose. The same, of course, was true for the soldiers themselves. In all cases, the common enemy outside the community focused attention on solidarity and camaraderie within it. In other words, the war provided many Americans with what Victor Turner calls "communitas." For both Warner and Turner, creating this feeling, or recreating it on a regular basis, is a major task of religious ritual. During rites at the cemetery, for example, wartime unity is reexperienced in the present. Protestants, Catholics, Eastern Orthodox, and Jews take part in a communal ritual at a graveyard with their common dead. Earlier, they had participated in their own separate ceremonies, but the parade and the unity gained by doing everything at the same time, emphasize the collectivity that includes them all. Each ritual also reminds them that the war was an experience in which everyone sacrificed and some died not as members of separate communities but as citizens of a single nation. In other words, chaos is overcome by order as people move from the periphery, in both space and time, toward the center.

Actually, Warner describes Memorial Day as a "cult of the dead." Its rites "are a cult because the members have not been formally organized into an institutionalized church with a defined theology but depend on informal organization to bring into order their sacred activities."[3] This cult gives expression to thoughts and feelings about death common to everyone and not specific to any particular group.

People are afraid of death in spite of the reassurances they have been given since early childhood. Every church provides a response to death, of course, but no single response is held in common by everyone. Memorial Day provides that; it dramatically expresses the unity of all Americans, living and dead, in the face of their common ultimate enemy, death. The unifying and integrating symbols of this cult are the dead themselves. Their graves symbolically unify all the activities of the separate groups; they become the objects of rituals that allow autonomous organizations, often in conflict during the rest of the year, to subordinate themselves and cooperate in jointly expressing national unity through the use of common rites for the collective dead. These rites show respect for all the dead, but especially for those killed in battle for the benefit of everyone. In the cemetery, the dead are classified as individuals (having separate graves); as members of separate social institutions (belonging to specific families, classes, churches, and associations); and as a collectivity (being called "our dead" by all participants in Memorial Day ceremonies). But the boundaries between the living and the dead are safely drawn; the fences surrounding the cemetery place all the dead together and separate all the living from them.

Memorial Day is explicitly recognized as a religious event by the churches, even though the events being recalled have no biblical or theological significance in themselves. On the Sunday before Memorial Day, the sermons in all the churches of "Yankee City" focused on its meaning to the people both as Americans and as Christians. A link was made between the self-sacrifice of Christ and the self-sacrifice of every American soldier. Even though the vast majority of men must be coerced by law into joining the army, Warner notes that "The death of a soldier in battle is believed to be a 'voluntary sacrifice' by him on the altar of his country."[4] Memorial Day is based on the kind of thinking summed up in the words of Christ: "For whosoever would save his life shall lose it, and whosoever loses his life for my sake will find it."[5] Warner makes it clear that "belief in 'the sacrifice of American citizens killed in battle' is a social logic which states in ultimate terms the subordinate relation of the citizen to his country and its collective moral principles."[6] Memorial Day, then elevates both the community and the heroic dead; these are two sides of the same coin "since by symbolically elaborating sacrifice of human life for the country through, or identifying it with, the Christian church's sacred sacrifice of their god, the deaths of such men also become powerful sacred symbols which organize, direct, and constantly revive the collective ideals of the community and nation."[7]

But there are mythic, as well as ritualistic, aspects to Memorial Day. Along with the Unknown Soldier, there is another major symbolic figure associated with Memorial Day: Abraham Lincoln. This is not the historical Lincoln, but the mythical man who has become both Everyman (the "rail splitter") and Founding Hero (the martyr who sacrificed his life so that the nation might be reborn). Like Christ, Lincoln died so that all might live and be equal before the law as they are in the sight of God. "Christ died that this might be true forever beyond the earth," notes Warner, "Lincoln died that this might be true forever on earth."[8] Like all mythic gods and heroes, Lincoln is surrounded by paradox.

> Lincoln, the superior man, above all men, yet equal to each, is a mystery beyond the logic of individual calculations. He belongs to the culture and to the social logics of the people from whom contradiction is unimportant and for whom the ultimate tests of truth are in the social structure in which, and for which, they live. Through the passing generations of our Christian culture, the Man of the Prairies, formed in the mold or the God-Man of Galilee and apotheosized into the man-god of the American people, each year less profane and more sacred, moves serenely toward identification with deity and ultimate godhead. In him, Americans realize themselves.[9]

Warner may exaggerate the divinization of Lincoln, but his point is well-taken: there is a force in American culture, perhaps in any culture, that lifts people and events out of the ordinary world and places them in symbolic contact with the people and events considered "sacred" according to tradition.

From Warner's analysis of Memorial Day, it can be seen that a culture's religious symbol system is not always sharply distinguished from its social, political, or other symbol systems. Memorial Day is about the nation's wars (which are only indirectly, if at all, linked with religion) and yet it has clearly been assimilated to religion (Christianity). But Warner's thesis depends on a purely functional understanding of religion. This is a major problem. Although he demonstrates how Memorial Day functions as a religious event, he does not make it clear how Memorial Day is different from a more purely Christian one such as Easter Sunday. Part of the problem is that his use of the words "religion" and "sacred" is intuitive; consequently, it is also imprecise and occasionally inconsistent. He uses them with reference not only to traditional Christian symbols and rituals but also in the reductionistic sense of Emile Durkheim. On several occasions, for example, he refers to Memorial Day as a "collective representation." In other words, Memorial Day is a symbolic event that expresses collective consciousness (which Durkehim identified with the sacred). It is a collection of visible symbols and invisible beliefs about the American Way of Life. Ceremonies regularly held make people aware of something that transcends them as individuals and that they therefore hold as sacred; for Durkheim, what transcended the individual was not the spirit world but the social order. Warner elaborates on this matter.

> That which is beyond, yet part of, a person is no more than the awareness on the part of individuals and the collectivity of individuals of their participation in a social group. The religious symbols, as well as the secular ones, must express the nature of the social structure of the group of which they are a part and which they represent. The beliefs in the gods and the symbolic rites which celebrate their divinity are no more than men collectively worshipping their own images—their own, since they were made by themselves and fashioned from their own experiences among themselves.[10]

Given this understanding of religion and the sacred, there can be no significant distinction between religion and secularity. In that case, both Memorial Day and Easter Sunday are simply "collective representations." If Memorial Day can be "religious" and Christmas can be "secular," what can either of these words mean? What is distinctive about the former but not of the later? What, in short, is the defining element of religion? Religion, I propose, is characterized by ontological heterogeneity (both sacred and profane), the accessibility of supernatural beings (through ritual or hierophany), the possibility of surviving death (in a different realm or a new incarnation), and emphasis on the symbolic or intuitive.[11] Secularity, by contrast, is characterized by ontological homogeneity (neither sacred nor profane), the absence of supernatural beings, the impossibility of surviving death, and emphasis on the empirical, rational, or pragmatic.[12] A given cultural production may be studied in terms of some or all of these diagnostic features. Instead of assuming that it must be either religious or secular, I suggest that religion and secularity be seen as ideal types at either end of a continuum. If productions may be religious in some ways and secular in other ways, a multiplicity of models becomes available.[13] Using the model of pluralism, for example, religion and secularity are related in ways that promote feelings of exclusion or inclusion. All American "civil religion" (discussed more fully in Chapter 6) is inclusive. It is based loosely on the Judaeo-Christian tradition but is publicly expressed in such a way that almost every citizen can participate without compromising either personal beliefs or denominational loyalty. Another model of the relation between religion and secularity is based on cultural and sociological transformation. Everyone realizes that Christmas originated as a celebration of the Incarnation and has become, for many Americans, a secular festival. According to still another model, religion and secularity are related in terms of what is official or unofficial. Officially, as Warner has observed, Memorial Day is secular; public rituals are held to honor the nation's war dead. Unofficially, Memorial Day is religious; whether these rituals take place in churches or in public squares, they are symbolically linked, at a profound level, to Christian atonement theology. According to the model of change, secularization may be seen either as inevitable progress or lamentable decline. A conflict model, on the other hand, suggests that secularity is a worldview competing with religion and represents either truth or ignorance. According to a model used here, though, religion and secularity may be expressed either explicitly or implicitly. I argue that *The Wizard* is explicitly secular but implicitly religious.

APPENDIX 4
GOING HOME AND GROWING UP ON TELEVISION

It is commonly said that "you can't go home again." According to this modern proverb, coined by Thomas Wolfe, maturity means learning that the past cannot be recovered. In other words, nostalgia is a sign of immaturity. But there is evidence that many Americans think otherwise. Some popular movies and television shows, at any rate, suggest that many people either believe the opposite or wish they could. Consider a case study, *The Wizard of Oz*. Explicitly, it is about Dorothy's passage from Kansas (or home), through Oz, and back to Kansas. Implicitly, though, it is also about Dorothy's passage from childhood, through the perils of adolescence, to adulthood. Dorothy goes home to Kansas, but not before she grows up in Oz. It is in Oz, of course, that she learns not only about wisdom, compassion, and courage, but also about the meaning of friendship, solidarity, and community. The movie ends where it began, in Kansas. Dorothy has gone home again. But she has changed: having grown up, she now understands what it means to be at home in the world. Because she must grow up in order to go home, in other words, the movie suggests that "growing up" *means* "going home." But if that was true in 1939, is it still true? What do "going home" and "growing up" mean in our time? To answer these questions, we must examine the ways both motifs are presented on television, notably during the Christmas season.

It should surprise no one that Christmas is heavily associated with both family and home because both the story and the symbols of Christmas focus attention directly on a family—the Holy Family—and its hardships away from home. Quite apart from any theological content it may have for some Americans, however, Christmas has become the festival of family and home par excellence for most Americans. By now, it is commonplace to note that American airlines are deluged every year in late December by children and grandchildren returning home to visit their families for Christmas or that the American telephone system is severely taxed during the same period by those who cannot make it back home in person. Many Americans spend Christmas at holiday resorts or theme parks, moreover, and often do so as family units. (Remember that being "at home" does not necessarily mean being in a specific location.)

Every year, Christmas comes to television. Not only is the regular schedule studded with Christmas specials, but individual episodes in regular series are often devoted specifically to the festival. Very few, if any, deal either directly or indirectly with the Incarnation (which is actually the central theological message of Christmas). Network television is aimed at the nation in general; theologically oriented shows would be inaccessible to large segments of the population. Consequently, Christmas is a secular festival for television viewers (apart from those who subscribe to specialized religious cable services). Almost all shows dealing with Christmas have either an ethical message (the theme of giving, generosity, or "sharing" usually presented in connection with the motifs of gift giving and Santa Claus), a psychological message (the theme of home usually presented in connection with motifs of nostalgia and childhood), or both. What follows is a brief study of thirteen shows broadcast on American networks between 19 and 26 December 1987.

*

There seem to be at least three basic ways of thinking about "home" in relation to Christmas. One could be called "being (or staying) home." It is represented by shows that provide a rather static interpretation of "home." Things are as they should be. Characters are already "at home." They need only recognize this fact. As it happens, all three shows in this category are about families not based on biological ties.[2]

In "Designing Women",[3] for example, the friends decide to spend Christmas together rather than travel out of town to family homes of their own. Nevertheless, the importance of blood ties is not entirely neglected. One of the presents given by Charlene makes this clear; she sends a ticket to Mary Jo's son so that he can spend Christmas at home with his mother. On Christmas Eve, they all sit around reminiscing about past Christmases. As the episode concludes, they sing "I'll Be Home For Christmas" while viewers are shown pages from a family album with sepia-toned snapshots. The credits are shown against a view of the house lit warmly in the snowy night.

In an episode of "Perfect Strangers,"[4] Larry wants to go back home to Madison for Christmas. Balki has looked forward to being his guest there, but he also misses Christmas back in the old country. When a snowstorm hits Chicago, they find it impossible to leave the city. "It's not going to be Christmas," says Larry, "it's just not there... the Christmas feeling." Reminiscing about past Christmases at home, he feels more and more depressed. Meanwhile, Balki decorates the apartment. When they exchange Christmas presents, he gives Larry a blanket he had been working on for months. Deeply moved, Larry says "Wait a minute...something's happening. Yes, there it is. It's the Christmas feeling. It's back." Then he draws the obvious conclusion: "I thought I was missing Christmas with my family and friends. But I'm not. You're here." What the boys thought was missing was not missing after all. The episode concludes with a rendition of "The First Nowell."[5]

The same pattern emerges in an episode of "The Golden Girls".[5] Dorothy, Rose, Blanche, and Sophia are stranded at an airport on Christmas Eve. Still hoping to get home for Christmas, they sit down in a restaurant. After a bit of persuasion, however, they agree to fill in behind the counter so that the owner can go home for Christmas. Although they cannot be in their own home for the holiday, they all agree that being together as a "family" is what counts. This is the equivalent of being home. What they thought was missing at the beginning is found to be present all along.

*

A second way of thinking about "home" in relation to Christmas could be called "restoring home." It is represented by shows that provide a slightly more dynamic interpretation of "home." They are about distress caused by an abnormal situation. At the beginning, things are not quite as they should be. Something is temporarily lacking. Someone is temporarily missing. By the conclusion, though, normality is restored. In short, the reality of everyday life is reaffirmed and celebrated. In one case, "home" is associated with a biological family; in the other case, it is not. Apparently, the origin of constituent members is not important in this context.

This is the case in a situation comedy, "Rags to Riches."[6] Nick is a single father. As the show opens, he is on the road and having difficulties with his car. "I gotta get home," he says, "it's Christmas Eve." Throughout the episode, he is shown overcoming one obstacle after another in order to get home. Meanwhile, his adopted daughters are visited by a social worker who wants to resettle them in what she considers more normal families. Waiting for Nick, the girls entertain her with stories of how he saved the day for them, both as a father and as a friend. Eventually, Nick arrives. The social worker and the girls settle down to enjoy Christmas Eve with Nick and the man who helped him get home. As the episode concludes, they all sing "The First Nowell." The problem has been solved; normality is restored.

A very similar pattern can be seen in "The Homecoming."[7] This movie became the basis for a massively popular series, "The Waltons." Its basic plot is the struggle of John, the father, to get home for Christmas. Although he works in the city, John manages to get home for holidays. As a result, everyone is eagerly anticipating his arrival on Christmas Eve. But he is very late. Because of an accident reported over the radio, Olivia becomes anxious. She sends John Boy out to find him. But John Boy runs out of gas and has to get help from the Baldwin sisters. Hours later, he comes home with no news of his father. Finally, John returns, safe and sound, and informs the family that he has come home for good this time. Now that everyone is reunited, Christmas can be celebrated. Once again, the problem has been solved and normality has been restored.

Even commercials are often translated into the Christmas idiom. Countless Santas advertise everything from cars to cleansers. But "home" is also used to sell products. One example should suffice. Carrying his suitcase, a young man enters a house decorated for Christmas. He kneels down to be hugged by his kid sister. She watches him enjoy a cup of Folger's coffee.[8] Finally, his parents come downstairs and embrace him. With the family reunited, the problem has been solved and normality restored.

*

A third way of thinking about Christmas in relation to "home" could be called "going" or "returning home." It is represented by shows—as it happens, the vast majority of shows—that depict the normal situation as inherently, and not accidentally or temporarily, inadequate in some basic way; a change is necessary. So a distinction is symbolically made between "home" and "true home." The latter is not where characters are at the beginning of the story, but where they want to be, think they should be, or need to be. In these stories, therefore, some sort of quest is involved. In every case that I observed, "home" is associated with a biological family. Moreover, it is associated with childhood and nostalgia.

A good example is provided by "Dolly."[9] In this musical special, Dolly Parton celebrates a "down home country Christmas." Included among the many acts is a recreation of her childhood celebrations at home. Songs include: "I Remember," "Once upon a Christmas," and, of course, "Down Home Country Christmas." In this nonnarrative context, the particular modality of "home" must be expressed in an abstract form. It could be argued that Parton "is" home because she sings about being home. On the other hand, the fact that many of her songs are nostalgic—almost all of them are about Christmas at some other time and in some other place—indicate that something important is lacking for Parton (which is to say, for most of her viewers through symbolic identification with her).

The same pattern emerges in another musical special. In "Barbara Mandrell: A Family Reunion,"[10] the star's van breaks down on the way home for Christmas. In her imagination, she sees herself and her sisters as children back home. First, she recalls old home movies. Then she recalls the musical productions they put on for family and friends. After each of these reminiscences, the focus shifts back to Mandrell on the road. Told that the fuel line has been broken, she says, "No matter how much you love to travel, you want to be home for Christmas."

Made-for-television movies picked up the same theme. As *The Little Match Girl*[11] opens, the Dutton family is fragmented. Haywood is the patriarch. Having married a Catholic and, even worse, left the family business to work for a crusading newspaper, Joe is banished from his father's house. Just before Christmas, Joe's brother Neville—who, being a playboy, is also unloved by his father—brings home a waif. This is the "match girl." Hoping to reunite the family, she brings Joe's infant son to the Dutton mansion on Christmas Eve; to retrieve their son, Joe and his wife must go to the mansion themselves. At the same time, a protest march takes place in front of the mansion; the marchers are tenants threatened by the Duttons with eviction from their homes on Christmas Day. While Joe calms them down, his wife suddenly goes into labor on the front porch. Having already softened at the sight of one grandson, Haywood relents at the thought of another being born under his own roof. The movie concludes with the private Dutton Christmas party turned into revelry for family, guests, and protest marchers. All members of the family are reconciled. The house is once more a home for everyone. And the tenants know that they will also be in their own homes for Christmas.

Another made-for-television movie, *Christmas Eve*,[12] follows the same pattern. Amanda Kingsley is a kindly matriarch who learns that she is terminally ill. Her only wish is to be reunited with her three grandchildren for Christmas. Because all have been alienated by her son Andrew, she has not seen them for many years. But Andrew is also alienated. In view of her impending demise, Amanda has changed her will, and Andrew is convinced that the family business will suffer because of her proposed donations to charity. In fact, he goes to court challenging the will on the grounds of her insanity. Meanwhile, her private investigator locates all three grandchildren and convinces them to come home to see their grandmother, if not their father, for Christmas. As the movie ends, mother, son, grandchildren, servants, and private investigator all end up having Christmas dinner at the family home. Reconciliation has taken place. The house is once more a home for everyone.

On *A Garfield Christmas*,[13] the cartoon cat is annoyed at having to spend Christmas away from his warm bed at home. He and Odie, the dog, are taken by Jon to spend an old-fashioned Christmas at the family farm. There, they are reunited with Jon's brother, parents, and grandmother. Even Garfield has a good time.

Christmas at home, of course, is also de rigueur on daytime soap operas. The matriarch on "Days of Our Lives,"[14] for example, sighs joyfully as she anticipates the annual holiday gathering: "I've got all my kids home for Christmas." Unlike the other shows in this category, a soap opera—which is, by definition, a continuing drama—can hardly conclude with the resolution of all problems. In any case, the family gathering represents an explicit hope that conflicts can be resolved in a context of love and kinship. Members of the family pay formal (if not always actual) heed to this notion by their presence at the family home on Christmas Eve.

And let us not forget the situation comedies.[15] On "Family Ties,"[16] of course, the connection between Christmas and family life is made very obvious. Working as Santa Claus in a local department store, Alex finds that one little girl cannot believe in him because she knows that her wish will not be granted: her father will not be able to come home for Christmas. Alex takes her home to enjoy Christmas with the Keatons. Meanwhile, the "real Santa" discovers this and enables the father to come for the girl and take her home for Christmas.

In a holiday episode of "Growing Pains,"[17] Ben finds Denise, a homeless girl, in his dumpster. She is asked to spend Christmas at home with the family. At first, she is cynical and sullen. After a while, though, she begins to enjoy herself. Nevertheless, she is very ambivalent about the experience. After everyone has gone to bed, she comes downstairs intending to run off with the presents. When Maggie and Jason come downstairs, Denise hides. Soon she overhears them talking about how glad they are that all the children—including Denise—are enjoying themselves. Next morning, members of the family are shocked to find all their presents gone. After almost everyone denounces Denise, however, the presents are found on the front porch. Apparently, Denise has changed her mind. She is next seen in a telephone booth telling her parents to expect her home for Christmas. The episode concludes with a chorus of "The First Nowell."

*

If many Christmas shows and commercials are about "home," and if many of these, in turn, are about "going home," what is the connection with "growing up"? Given the popularity of the dictum that originated with Thomas Wolfe, "You can't go home again," there would seem to be none at all; the people who quote Wolfe are saying that they see a contradiction between the two; doing one means negating the other. Nevertheless, at least some Americans do see a connection. On television, at any rate, a link is provided by the notion of "family." Both "going home" and "growing up" are, almost by definition, associated with "family."

In every one of the Christmas shows under discussion, "home" is defined in terms of family relationships. In some cases, the family is based on friendship, adoption, or other nonbiological ties ("The Golden Girls"; "Rages to Riches"; "Perfect Strangers"). In other cases, it is based on biological ties ("Barbara Mandrell"; "Christmas Eve"; *The Little Match Girl;* "Family Ties"; "The Homecoming"). In all cases, however, a particular group of people is defined as "special." Being with them for Christmas is of great importance to the characters.

But "growing up" is also defined in terms of family relationships. The life cycle of every individual begins with birth into a family (no matter how a particular culture defines it) and continues through a series of stages such as weaning, going to school, coming of age, marriage, and death. In one sense, Wolfe is correct: healthy individuals in American society must leave the homes of their families and make their way in the world. In another sense, however, the pattern is circular rather than linear; children leave home precisely in order to establish new homes of their own. If "home" is defined existentially or symbolically, it could be said that "growing up" is indeed a matter of "going home." The generational circle is complete. A new one has begun.

From what has been observed of Christmas television, though, many Americans also want to go home in a more practical sense. For them, "going home" is more than a metaphor of the life cycle; it is an emotional need. It is about coming to terms with the past in a way that transforms the present. As a result, it is not unusual for television characters to "grow up" as a direct result of "going home." That is, they learn something about the meaning of home and family that they did not know, realize, or understand before. In "The Golden Girls," for instance, the women learn that being together is what counts, not being in any particular place; as the familiar cliché has it, home is where the heart is. Larry and Balki learn the same thing in "Perfect Strangers." In "Rags to Riches," the social worker learns that even a single adoptive father can provide a good home for a multiracial brood of daughters. Reconciliation is a very popular Christmas lesson. That is what Haywood Dutton learns in *The Little Match Girl*, what Andrew learns in *Christmas Eve*, and what Denise learns in "Growing Pains." Another very popular lesson is the primacy of personal or family relationships over business. This is what the girl's father learns in "Family Ties" and something else that Haywood Dutton learns in *The Little Match Girl*. Even Garfield the cat learns something by going home for Christmas in *A Garfield Christmas:* the value of an extended family. And when nothing new is learned, something old is reaffirmed. In "Rags to Riches," repressed Nick sighs with delight when he comes within the sight of home: "I've never been so glad to see it."

Even when it is possible, going home for Christmas is not always easy. Old wounds are reopened. Unresolved conflicts are brought to the surface. No wonder Oprah Winfrey devoted one of her shows to this subject. Her guests discussed various ways of maintaining harmonious family relationships during the festival season. It would seem that "growing up" does not merely mean learning to leave home; it also means learning to return home (which is to say, learning to integrate the past with the present and future). As it is often presented on television, at any rate, going home for Christmas is a therapeutic experience. Even if this is not the way most Americans actually experience the event, this is the way many *want* to experience it and the way they think they *should* experience it.

Not every Christmas show under discussion explores this theme in any depth. In some, it is reduced to a symbolic cinematic formula: the mere motif of someone on the road and travelling homeward. Nevertheless, the sheer number of shows in which characters do grow up (that is, learn something, no matter how sentimental or trivial) by going home for Christmas cannot be dismissed without explanation. The formula itself, after all, must be taken seriously. Why is it used so often? Any idea so pervasive in a medium known for pandering to popular taste, any idea that can be recognized immediately even when reduced to a symbolic formula, clearly represents some perceived need on the part of viewers.

Why should Americans make this connection between "growing up" and "going home"? Since "family" is the common feature, it seems likely that it has something to do with the state of the American family. There is no need to bring in elaborate studies by social scientists to support the idea that American family life is fairly troubled (or changing very rapidly) at the present time. Blended, or aggregate, families are quickly becoming the statistical norm. Moreover, there is the longstanding mobility of Americans to consider. Even in the eighteenth and nineteenth centuries, Americans were on the move. Although there is no more frontier, Americans commonly study and work in places far removed from other members of their families. In fact, they often move from one part of the country to another several times in the course of their careers. Under these circumstances, it is almost inevitable to find that kinship and friendship are the subjects of many television shows. What do these things mean in an increasingly uprooted and unstable society? What does it mean to say "I'm from Oklahoma City," or "I was brought up in the Baptist Church," or even "my background is blue collar"? In short, how is identity in the present related to identity in the past? What provides continuity between "I am" and "I was"? Judging from popular movies such as *The Deer Hunter* (Kurt Neumann, 1978) and television shows such as "The Waltons" and "Roots"), it would seem that trying to answer such questions is an important feature of contemporary American life. It is not, of course, a unique feature of American life; the search for roots, a sense of belonging, is a major feature of all modern societies. Nevertheless, it is especially characteristic of American life and has been since the first great waves of immigrants began arriving in the United States, since the first great waves of pioneers began moving West—and, indeed, since the first refugees from religious persecution in the Old World began flocking to the New.

Clearly, Christmas is associated with "going" or "returning home." Because it originated as a sacred festival, this is hardly surprising. As Mircea Eliade points out so well and so often, reversibility is a defining element of sacred, or mythic, time.[19] There is evidence, however, that even the secular culture of America generates symbols that focus attention on the idea of "going home." The most obvious example, of course, is baseball. The whole point of this game, after all, is to return home. The highest achievement is to hit a "home run." That is, the expert player hits the ball, leaves "home plate," runs past a series of bases (each of which represents a kind of trial, or test), and returns to "home plate." No matter how secular and trivial, this pattern corresponds to others that are deeply rooted in American culture. The biblical paradigm of exile and return comes to mind here. The symbolic parallel is so obvious, in fact, that it is usually unnoticed. But is it entirely coincidental, one must ask, that Americans should adopt as the "national pastime" a game based on the same motif of exile and return that played such an important part in defining the identity of their ancestors?[20]

The link between "going home" and "growing up" corresponds to a way of thinking with deep roots in both national and religious traditions. The American experience is often understood as a passage from utopian origin (that is, colonial or antebellum harmony and order), through the vicissitudes of history (or present chaos), to utopian destiny (which is to say, either millennial or technological order and harmony). Why has this way of thinking been so prevalent? Why have movies based on it, such as *The Wizard of Oz*, become so popular? An answer is to be found in the religious traditions on which America was founded. In traditional forms of Christianity, reality itself is understood as a cosmic passage from primeval paradise (that is, Eden), through the vicissitudes of time or history (characterized by exile, sin, confusion, conflict, fragmentation, or chaos), to eschatological paradise (the Messianic Age or the Kingdom of God). It is also understood, moreover, as a microcosmic passage of the immortal soul from eternity (or Eden), through the vicissitudes of time (that is, the life cycle), to eternity (which is either Eden or the heavenly Jerusalem). In conclusion, the link between "going home" and "growing up" so prevalent on television at Christmas is nothing new; it corresponds to longstanding traditions both religious and secular. In spite of conventional wisdom which would have it that "you can't go home again," many Americans either believe or would like to believe that you can—if not in the immediate future then in the ultimate future.

*

Ironically, links between the earthly home and some otherworldly one are seldom made in connection with Christmas or Easter (that is, religious festivals). Just the same, there is evidence that many contemporary Americans believe (or would like to believe) in the possibility of returning home to paradise after death. In any case, they are clearly familiar with the idea. The link between home and life after death, in fact, has become a familiar feature not only of popular religion in particular, but also of popular culture in general. References to it are very common on television.

Since television is very often the interface between popular religion and popular culture, it is interesting to note that the word "home" was used recently with precisely this connotation by a well-known television evangelist. Needing more money for his ministry, he told his audience: "We're at the point where God could call Oral Roberts home. Extend my life. Let me live beyond March."[21] Similarly, Rose inherits a pig on one episode of "The Golden Girls." When "Baby" is stricken with homesickness, it is decided to send him back to the farm in Minnesota. Dorothy explains to Sophia that "Baby is going home," and Sophia immediately responds with "May he rest in peace."[22]

One long-running television series, "Highway to Heaven," consistently links "home," "pilgrimage," and "paradise." It is based on the premise that (good) people become angels when they die; they return to earth on missions. As the opening credits roll, viewers see fluffy white clouds—just as they do during the opening credits of *The Wizard*—and hear serene music that suggests "heaven." Then the camera focuses on a rural landscape. A car is moving slowly down the highway. When it stops, Jonathan (the angel) is picked up by Mark (his helper). Continuing along the way together, they discuss their next assignment. In one episode,[23] Mark and Jonathan help Tim Charles accept the death of his son during the Vietnam War. After eighteen years on the missing-in-action list, the boy's body is returned by the Vietnamese; a local newspaper notes that "Timothy Charles

Junior is finally coming home from the war." But when no one attends the funeral, his father succumbs to bitterness. After the son's friends have been located and a memorial scholarship established to honor him, Tim goes to the hangar to see the remains of a plane he had flown in the Second World War. He gets in with Jonathan. As the engines start, Jonathan explains what is happening.

Tim: The old plane doesn't work...there's no propellers... there's...what's this?

Jonathan: Your last mission.

Tim: What are you talking about?

Jonathan: I'm talking about touching the face of God.

Tim: You...you mean that...?

Jonathan: Yeah, I do.

Tim: Then there is something...there is...?

Jonathan: You bet. Time to go.

Traffic controllers at the field, meanwhile, hear the plane taking off and see it on their instrument panels but are amazed to find it moving straight up at an enormous speed. Sitting in the cockpit, Tim finds that the plane operates more easily than it had so many years ago. He turns to Jonathan but finds that a young man is sitting beside him instead. It is Timmy, his son.

Tim: I guess I got to go the rest of the way all alone.

Timmy: What are you talking about, alone?

Tim: Timmy...

Timmy: We're goin' home, Pop, we're goin' home...

A made-for-television movie makes the same point. In *Go toward the Light*,[24] there are several references to death in terms of going home. A little boy, Ben, is dying of AIDS. He asks his father about what it will be like to die.

Ben: Dad, what's it like in Heaven?

Dad: Well, Ben, you know how you feel when you've been somewhere on a trip or a vacation? And even though you had a really great time you can't wait to finally get home?

Ben: Uhuh.

Dad: That's what it's like Ben, it's like going home.

Later on, Ben is seen in the hospital. He is in great pain and wants the suffering to be over as soon as possible. What he learned earlier about death underlies his present state of mind. The following conversation takes place when his mother arrives at his bedside with an orderly.

Ben: I want to go home...

Orderly: I'm afraid that's not possible, Ma'am. He's much too sick to go home now.

Mom: That's not what he means.

Viewers, however, know exactly what he means. They may not believe in life after death themselves, or that this constitutes a return to some kind of life before birth, but they are familiar with such ideas passed down from one generation to another by the founding religious traditions of America.

Figure 9

[Permission to reproduce this advertisement is granted by Bloomingdale's.]

NOTES

Foreword

1. Mircea Eliade, "Methodological Remarks on the Study of Religious Symbolism," *The History of Religions: Essays in Methodology* (Chicago: University of Chicago Press, 1959), p. 86.

2. Gerald Clarke, "1939: Twelve Months of Magic," *Time* (27 March 1989), p. 70.

3. Quoted by Lewis Beale, "The Class of '39," [Montreal] *Gazette* (27 March 1989), p. F1.

4. Clarke, "1939," p. 72.

5. Robert S. McElvain, *The Great Depression: America, 1929-1941* (New York: Times Books, 1984), p. 177.

6. Ibid., pp. 220-221.

7. C. Hugh Holman, *A Handbook of Literature* (New York: Macmillan, 1986), p. 134.

1. Introduction

1. J. Hoberman, "Many Are Cult, Fewer Chosen," review of *The Wizard of Oz* and other films, *Village Voice* (13-19 January 1982), p. 52.

2. Harry Golden, *Only in America* (Cleveland: World, 1958).

3. It should be noted, however, that lovers of Oz probably exist everywhere. There are, for example, two Indian members of The International Wizard of Oz Club. And *India Today* recently commented on the hero of a

337

local movie as follows: "The Chowkidar, with his flaming, henna-tinted, leonine, hair style (not too unlike a character out of *The Wizard of Oz*) protects her to the end" (Madhu Jain, "A Lyrical Ballad," review of *Mirch Masala, India Today* (15 August 1986), p. 158.

4. Aljean Harmetz, "After Forty-Six Years, Hollywood Revisits Oz," *New York Times* (16 June 1985), pp. 2.1, 10.

5. "Oz, Grammy's Lead CBS to Ratings Win," [Montreal] *Gazette* (8 March 1985), p. D9.

6. Ibid.

7. Quoted in Aljean Harmetz, *The Making of* The Wizard of Oz: *Movie Magic and Studio Power in the Prime of MGM, and the Miracle of Production #1060* (New York: Limelight Editions, 1977), p. 292.

8. Ibid.

9. With a 33.9 rating in 1956, it had a 52.7 percent share of the audience. Not only was *The Wizard* unusually popular before the regular broadcasts began, but its popularity has remained unusual ever since. As of July 1975, it was eleventh on a list of the highest-rated shows ever shown on network television; it had also ranked twelfth, fourteenth, sixteenth, twenty-first, twenty-third, and twenty-fifth. No other movie had ever made this list the second time it was broadcast, much less the third, fourth, fifth, seventh, and eighth times. In 1983, it made broadcasting history when it was played for the twenty-fifth time. No other show had ever been repeated on prime-time television even ten times. Moreover, it was rated ninth that week; even *Gone with the Wind* fell far behind at sixteenth place (Harmetz, *The Making*, pp. 291–292).

10. There have been many attempts to "translate" the book into other media. In fact, such attempts began with Baum himself. The first was a very successful stage production; *The Wizard of Oz* opened in Chicago in 1902 and then, beginning in 1903, played on Broadway for eighteen months. Unlike the book, the play was addressed to adults with more "sophisticated" taste in entertainment. After that, it toured the country. Three years later, Baum put together a theatrical production in which he himself provided the narration to accompany photographs representing key events in the story. Beginning in 1910, several one-reel films were produced by Selig Pictures. In 1913, Baum founded the Oz Film Company and produced three five-reel Oz movies: *The Patchwork Girl of Oz; The Magic Cloak of Oz;* and *His Majesty the Scarecrow of Oz.* In the full-length silent movie produced by Chadwick Pictures in 1925, Dorothy was played by Baum's wife and the Tin Woodman by Oliver Hardy ("Following the Yellow Brick Road from *The Wonderful*

Wizard of Oz to *The Wiz,*" *American Cinematographer* (Nov. 1978): pp. 1090-1091. The MGM musical of 1939, however, gave definitive form to the fantasy of Oz.

Nevertheless, the process of adapting the books to other media did not end in 1939. To this very day, Oz books are being written and adapted for stage, screen, radio, and television. As early as 1950, Judy Garland recreated her role as Dorothy for a production of "The Lux Radio Theatre". Twelve years later, Filmation Associates produced an animated version with the voices of Liza Minnelli (Judy Garland's daughter) as Dorothy, Milton Berle as the Cowardly Lion, Margaret Hamilton (formerly the Witch) as Auntie Em, and Ethel Merman as the Witch! A black version, *The Wiz,* opened on Broadway in 1975 and won Tony Awards for best musical, best score, best director, best choreography, best costumes, best supporting actor, and best supporting actress; it also won the 1976 Grammy Award for best original cast show album. Ten years later, *Return to Oz* was produced by the Walt Disney Studio. *Return* was not a remake of the MGM production. In this movie, unlike *The Wizard,* the Scarecrow, Tin Man, and Cowardly Lion play only peripheral roles and other characters from the earlier movie, such as the Munchkins and the Wizard himself, do not reappear at all. *The Wizard* is based on Baum's first Oz book, *The Wonderful Wizard of Oz;* this one is based on two of his later books; *Ozma of Oz* and *The Land of Oz.* Because comparisons with the well-known and well-loved earlier production were inevitable, Disney faced a problem in making *Return.* "The most difficult marketing problem will be to get audiences to come in with an open mind," noted Richard Berger at Disney. "If people come in expecting to see 'Over the Rainbow'" [they will be disappointed] (quoted in Harmetz, "After Forty-Six Years," p. 1). Still, certain concessions were made with the explicit intention of creating some continuity with the earlier movie. Although Baum wrote about Dorothy's silver slippers, they became ruby slippers at MGM and remained ruby slippers at Disney. And although Baum said nothing about characters from Kansas "reappearing" in Oz, they did so at MGM and also at Disney. One of the villains in *Return* even sounds like Margaret Hamilton (the Witch in MGM's production). Most important of all, Dorothy was cast with Judy Garland in mind. "I wanted to find someone who might be Judy Garland's cousin once removed," said director Walter Murch, "so both films can coexist in your mind like two chords" (quoted in Harmetz, "After Forty-Six Years," p. 10). Most recently, the Oz stories were once again animated for television. In 1986, Cinar Films began producing a series that will eventually include two half-hour episodes and four feature films.

11. Quoted in "Following the Yellow Brick Road from *The Wonderful Wizard of Oz* to *The Wiz,*" *American Cinematographer* 59, no. 11 (November 1978): 1090-1091.

12. Quoted in ibid., p. 1090.

13. Lyman Frank Baum, *The [Wonderful] Wizard of Oz* (1900; New York: Ballantine, 1979), n.p.

14. "Fundamentalists Win School Textbook Case," [Montreal] *Gazette* (25 October 1986), p. F12. Stuart Taylor, "Supreme Court Roundup: Justices Refuse to Hear Tennessee Case," *New York Times* (23 February 1988), p. 4.22.

15. Quoted in Aljean Harmetz, *The Making*, pp. 315–316.

16. Ibid., p. 315.

17. Carol Billman, "'I've Seen the Movie'": Oz Revisited," *Literature and Film Quarterly* 9 (1981): p. 241.

18. Ibid., p. 248.

19. Harmetz, *The Making*, p. 18.

20. Ibid., p. 19.

21. For her performance as Dorothy, Judy Garland was promoted by MGM from "featured player" to "star." But that was only the beginning. By the time she died, in 1969, her own identity had virtually fused with that of Dorothy—even though she was also well known for performances in many other memorable movies. To her devoted fans, not to mention millions of other people, Judy Garland *was* Dorothy Gale (Mel Tormé, *The Other Side of the Rainbow: With Judy Garland on the Dawn Patrol* [New York: William Morrow, 1970], pp. viii–ix). In fact, Garland herself recognized the inevitability of this identification (ibid., p. 45). To some extent, she felt it herself. Like Dorothy, she constantly sought the inner peace and security that seemed to elude her. It is no wonder, then, that her "theme song" at concerts was "Over the Rainbow" (Gerold Frank, *Judy* [New York: Harper and Row, 1975], pp. 305; 337; 583). Harold Arlen, who wrote the score, quoted a letter from Garland in which she wrote: "As for my feelings toward 'Over the Rainbow,' it's become part of my life. It is so symbolic of all my dreams and wishes that I'm sure that's why people sometimes get tears in their eyes when they hear it" ("Judy Garland, 47, Found Dead," *New York Times* [23 June 1969], p. 1:31). The song was a bridge between her and the audience; everyone understands, from personal experience, the need for hope in the midst of despair. In the third paragraph of her obituary, we read that "Miss Garland's personal life often seemed a fruitless search for the happiness promised in 'Over the Rainbow,' the song she made famous" (ibid., p. 1:1). The obituary includes a picture of her as Dorothy.

Likewise, the obituary of Bert Lahr includes a picture of him "in his only enduring Hollywood role, that of the Cowardly Lion in *The Wizard of Oz*. Although Mr. Lahr had parts in more than a score of motion pictures, starting in 1931, he never attained the peak of characterization that he managed as a lion" (Alden Whitman, "Bert Lahr, Comic Actor, Dies: Played

Burlesque and Beckett," *New York Times* [5 December 1967], p. 1.1). In another case, even the obituary's headline referred to *The Wizard:* "Jack Haley, Actor, 79, Dead: Was Tin Woodman in 'Oz' (Eric Pace, *New York Times* [7 June 1979], p. 4.23)." In fact, approximately half the obituary is about *The Wizard.* The author notes that this movie "was by far the greatest success of the fifty movies in which Mr. Haley appeared." It includes a picture of him as the Tin Woodman. Once again, the headline of Ray Bolger's obituary immediately establishes a connection with *The Wizard.* "Ray Bolger, Scarecrow in 'Oz,' Dies" (Glenn Fowler, *New York Times* [16 January 1987], p. 4.19)." He is identified in the very first paragraph as the "loose-limbed song-and-dance man who became known to millions as the Scarecrow in *The Wizard of Oz.*" The author continues: "Among his many roles on stage, screen and television in a career that spanned six decades, none captured the public imagination more than his appearance in the 1939 movie." Apparently, Bolger was among the last surviving members of the cast of a film that "is a perennial favorite on television, being shown worldwide at least once a year." Like so many others in the cast, he discovered that "many who watched him in later years were unable to shake the image of the straw-stuffed Scarecrow flopping about on boneless legs as he lurched down the Yellow Brick Road." One of the two pictures shows him in that role.

Even though she was an accomplished actress for many years, Margaret Hamilton is also remembered primarily for her work in *The Wizard:* "Margaret Hamilton, 82, Dies; Played Wicked Witch in 'Oz' (Joseph Berger, *New York Times* [17 May 1985], p. 4.20)." In the very first paragraph, she is described as "the actress whose role as the cackling Wicked Witch of the West unnerved generations of children." In the next paragraph, we read that "Miss Hamilton was a gentle, lively woman who taught kindergarten for years before she began a career of fifty years in the theatre, movies, radio, and television. But she seared a fearsome image on the public consciousness in 1939 when, at the age of 36, she played the Wicked Witch, the terror of Judy Garland's long dream in the classic film. Her screeching laugh sent shivers up the spines of children." According to her son, Hamilton was always concerned over the impact of this performance on children. Like Judy Garland, Bert Lahr, Jack Haley, Ray Bolger and so many others who worked on this movie, she never really escaped from Oz.

22. *The Baum Bugle,* organ of The International Wizard of Oz Club, is devoted exclusively to Oziana; one issue—vol. 33, no. 2 (1989)—included several articles about the movie on its fiftieth anniversary. Books on Oziana include: Allen Eyles, *The World of Oz: A Fantastic Expedition over the Rainbow* (Tucson: HP Books, 1985); David L. Greene and Dick Martin, *The Oz Scrapbook* (New York: Random House, 1977); Michael P. Hearn, *The Annotated Wizard of Oz* (New York: Clarkson N. Potter, 1973); Michael P. Hearn, ed. *The Wizard of Oz,* Critical Heritage Series (New York: Schocken Books, 1983); Raylyn Moore, *Wonderful Wizard Marvelous Land* (Bowling Green, OH: Bowling Green State University Press, 1974).

23. Doug McCelland, *Down the Yellow Brick Road: The Making of* The Wizard of Oz (New York: Pyramid Books, 1976); Stephen Cox, *The Munchkins Remember* (New York: Dutton, 1989); John Fricke, Jay Scarfone, and William Stillman, The Wizard of Oz: *The Official 50th Anniversary Pictorial History* (New York: Warner Books, 1989).

24. Not all of these, however, are of interest in this context. In "A Filmed Fairy Tale as Screen Memory" (*Psychoanalytic Study of the Child* 29 [1974]: 389-410), for example, Sanford Schreiber discusses the effect of this movie on one of his psychiatric patients. A woman suffering from chronic separation anxiety recalled specific sequences from *The Wizard*. Apparently, she had seen the movie as a child at the very time when her mother left home. According to Schreiber, she projected unresolved feelings onto these sequences rather than deal with the pain. Schreiber does not, however, offer an interpretation of *The Wizard*. He merely uses it, as a clinician, to illustrate the effect of unusually vivid screen imagery on a patient.

25. Magder is Canadian. Although this study is concerned primarily with the place of Oz in American culture, I have not restricted myself to American sources. If Canadians (being slightly removed from the centers of American culture) are so familiar with Oz that casual references to it are easily understood, then this is even more true in the United States. I have also referred, therefore, to Canadian newspapers either reporting on the American scene or carrying material originally produced in the United States.

26. David Magder, *"The Wizard of Oz:* A Parable of Brief Psychotherapy," *Canadian Journal of Psychiatry* 25 (1980): 565.

27. Ibid., p. 567.

28. Ibid., p. 566.

29. Ibid., p. 565.

30. Daniel Dervin, "Over the Rainbow and under the Twister: A Drama of the Girl's Passage through the Phallic Phase," *Bulletin of the Menninger Clinic* 42 (1978): 51-57.

31. Harvey Greenberg, *"The Wizard of Oz:* Little Girl Lost—and Found," *The Movies on Your Mind* (New York: Saturday Review Press, 1975), pp. 13-32.

32. Gregory Renault, "Over the Rainbow: Dialectic and Ideology in *The Wizard of Oz,"Praxis* 4 (1978): 169-180.

33. Ibid., p. 177.

34. Linda Hansen, "Experiencing the World as Home: Reflections on Dorothy's Quest in *The Wizard of Oz,"Soundings* 67 (1984): 91-102.

35. Ibid., p. 98.

36. Ibid., p. 98.

37. Ibid., p. 99.

38. David Downing, "Waiting for Godoz: A Post-Nasal Deconstruction of *The Wizard of Oz,*" *Christianity and Literature* 33, no. 2 (1984): 28–30.

39. Ibid., p. 28.

40. Ibid., p. 29.

41. Ibid., p. 30.

42. Ibid., p. 30.

43. Bryan Wilson, "Secularization: The Inherited Model," *The Sacred in a Secular Age: Toward Revision in the Study of Religion,* ed. Phillp Hammond (Berkeley: University of California Press, 1985), pp. 11–12.

44. Peter E. Glasner, *The Sociology of Secularisation: A Critique of a Concept,* International Library of Sociology (London: Routledge and Kegan Paul, 1977), p. 64.

45. Roland Robertson, quoted in ibid., p. 117.

46. In classical Latin, the term *saeculum* referred to the world order in the present age. When parish priests are now called "secular clergy," it is not because they are irreligious but because their vocation is in the world of everyday life rather than in the cloister. This usage, however, has now been largely overtaken by the notion of opposition to religion. The term "secularity" is used in a derived sense. It is always defined in terms of religion; either through indifference or hostility, it is always the negation of religion.

47. Mircea Eliade, *The Sacred and the Profane: The Nature of Religion,* trans. Willard R. Trask (1957; San Diego: Harcourt, Brace Jovanovich, 1959).

2. Sight and Sound

1. The notion of codes is not a recent innovation. It is based on the idea that the interpretation of reality, not reality itself, is transmitted through language (or any other symbol system). As Sapir made clear, language itself is never unmediated. Or, as Lévi-Strauss argued, what can be learned from the analysis of oral or written messages is not what exists in the outside world but what exists in the minds of those who produce and receive them. Thus, we cannot experience reality except in symbolic terms that are encoded

as cultural assumptions. Through language and other symbol systems, culture invents the world by interpreting the givens of nature. "It follows," according to Terence Hawkes, "that, implicated as we all are in this gigantic, covert, collaborative enterprise, none of us can claim access to uncoded, "pure," or objective experiences of a "real," permanently existing world. None of us, in short, is innocent" (*Structuralism and Semiotics* [London: Methuen, 1977], p. 170).

It is the normal presumption of "innocence" that Roland Barthes attacks. He tries to show precisely how language is used in literature to hide social, economic, or political forces and propagate a specific worldview (ideology). For him, literature is a system of "codes," or symbolic patterns functioning as conscious or unconscious mechanisms that determine meaning just as language itself imposes its own mediating, shaping pattern on what we normally consider an objective world "out there." Consequently, analyzed texts reveal not a simple reflection of objective reality but a complex, ambiguous, and multivalent interpretation of reality. He distinguishes literature that is "readerly" *(lisible)*—conventional works or even classics that are assumed to be univocal and are, therefore, easy to read—from that which is "writerly" *(scriptible)*—works that emphasize multivocality and are, therefore, much more difficult to read. For Barthes, however, the readerly text is only apparently univocal or unambiguous. By decoding it, other (hidden) levels of meaning are revealed. This is precisely what he does to the texts of popular culture in *Mythologies* (London: J. Cape, 1972) and to a text of elite culture in *S/Z* (New York: Hill and Wang, 1974).

More recently, the word "code" has been used by Roger Silverstone in *The Message of Television: Myth and Narrative in Contemporary Culture* (London: Heinemann Educational Books, 1981) and "A Structure for a Modern Myth: Television and the Transsexual" (*Semiotica* 49, nos. 1-2 [1984]: 95-138). His work is based on the formalism of Vladimir Propp and the structuralism of Claude Lévi-Strauss and A. J. Greimas. "I define code," he writes, "as a consistent level of the text's articulation, as a consistent level of the process of signification. There are any number of codes and subcodes in a text; in principle everything is meaningful and every meaningful item is dependent on its referability to a code. We can, for example, recognize acoustic, alimentary, physical, cosmological codes, just as we can talk of the codes of a natural language" ("Structure for a Modern Myth," p. 119). Accordingly, he examines geographical, social, technoeconomic, and physical codes. I have used the word "code" in a more restricted sense: it refers to purely formal (cinematic) properties.

Cultural productions clearly owe their existence to the patterned use of symbols, or codes. These codes are generated by culture to "organize" the world in which a community can live. Cultural productions (such as books, advertisements, myths, songs, or movies), in other words, are distillations of these codes. To understand the organizing principles of the larger cultural order, therefore, requires a process of systematically decoding them, calling attention to patterns that would otherwise not be observed. For Barthes and some other semioticians, however, the hidden levels of meaning encoded in these productions are not only to be described but also to be evaluated. Although his anthropological predecessors claimed that language determines the particular way reality is perceived in all cultures and by necessity, Barthes saw the use of codes in modern, Western societies not merely as one example of a universal human phenomenon but as an insidious device used to propagate the values of a particular class (the bourgeoisie). His emphasis on the lack of "innocence" implies not merely naivete on the part of those who receive them but guilt on the part of those who produce them. Such a normative stance must not be construed as an underlying feature of my work on *The Wizard*.

2. Seymour Chatman, *Story and Discourse: Narrative Structure in Fiction and Film* (Ithaca, NY: Cornell University Press, 1978), pp. 146–195.

3. Ethan Mordden, *The Hollywood Musical* (New York: St. Martin's Press, 1981), p. 23.

4. Evidence for this is admittedly ambiguous. As Dorothy moves toward the front door, monochromatic film ends abruptly. But what, precisely, takes its place? This is very difficult to answer. It could be the beginning of polychromatic film. In that case, the colorful scene outside, which becomes visible as the door slowly opens, would not be technically anomalous. But if this really is color film, the effect cannot be seen inside the house. The interior is bathed in a very heavy golden-brown tonality. (The effect might then be very much like that of the heavy varnish that had, for centuries, obscured the brilliant colors of Michelangelo's frescoes in the Sistine Chapel.) In fact, it is only when Dorothy is actually outside the house that viewers can pick out the bright blue of her apron. Whether the frames are *technically* anomalous, however, is beside the point because they are *effectively* anomalous. Even if only because of the remarkable clumsiness of this transition, these frames could well be considered chromatically anomalous in a movie that is so visually sophisticated in every other way.

5. Many of the ideas put forward in this section were suggested to me by Robert MacAlear, a graduate student in the Faculty of Music at McGill University.

6. Martin Gottfried, *Broadway Musicals* (New York: Abrams, 1980), p. 167.

7. I have used the term "naturalism" instead of "realism" for two reasons. In the first place, the term "realism" has been given to particular schools of painting and film making; no connection between these schools and this discussion of music is intended. Moreover, the medieval dispute between "realists" and "nominalists" gives the former term a weightiness that is

inappropriate in this context. Under discussion here is only the extent to which conditions on screen seem to resemble those off screen. In Chapter 3, however, the subject of "reality" will be discussed in more detail.

8. To nonmusicians in the Western world, atonality has been synonymous with dissonance and disorder. This particular motif, moreover, may include an oblique reference to the Devil. The violin is used not to convey a warm, romantic atmosphere (as it is in "Over the Rainbow") but to convey a sinister mood like that of the "Mephisto Waltz" by Franz Liszt ("Der Tanz in der Dorfschenke (First Mephisto Waltz) in *Two Episodes from Lenau's Faust,* 1859-1861); in that piece, the Devil himself takes up the violin and plays with a scraping, machinelike effect, as if the violin were a percussion instrument.

9. For instance, "Over the Rainbow" has the characteristic melodic structure of American popular songs: AABA plus codetta (which is to say, an "antecedent" of eight bars, a repetition, a "consequent" of eight bars, a repetition of the antecedent, and a summarizing passage of eight bars).

10. *San Francisco* (W. S. Van Dyke, 1936) treats the matter in a fairly explicit way. Shout explains that in this extremely successful "vehicle" for Jeanette MacDonald and Clark Gable, opera is identified as an alien musical tradition and contrasted with more familiar American musical traditions. This conflict is symbolically represented by several characters in the story. Mary Blake is the daughter of a country parson who comes to the big city longing for a career in opera. As her name implies, she is innocent, morally sensitive, and virginal. Just the same, she begins by accepting a job in a cabaret on the Barbary Coast. Blackie Norton, on the other hand, is the rugged, hedonistic owner of this cabaret. Being an unstable mixture of populist idealism and cynical realism—his name suggests a "black eye"—he is the most complex of the major characters. Although he falls in love with Mary, this does not prevent him from exploiting her talent and obstructing her plans to join the opera company. Several secondary characters are also worth noting here. Father Tim Mullin runs a mission on the Barbary Coast. As his biblical name suggests, Father Tim is highly moralistic. Having known Blackie since boyhood, he keeps a paternal eye on Mary. Partly with that in mind, he invites her to sing at the mission. Although he is openly contemptuous of the Church, Blackie is fond of his boyhood friend. In fact, he donates money so that Father Tim can buy a new organ for the mission. Jack Burley, on the other hand, is one of the Nob Hill swells Blackie detests. As a patron of the opera, however, Burley can give Mary her chance to become a diva. For a while, he competes with Blackie as Mary's suitor. But it is Maisie, his mother, who legitimates opera for the viewers. Unlike her status-seeking son, she is proud of her humble origins as a washerwoman, and revels in stories of her youth in the "wickedest city on earth." Like most

immigrants, she came to America with nothing but high hopes and the willingness to work hard. If this exemplary pioneer woman can become an opera lover, the movie suggests, then the gulf between elite and popular culture is not so very wide after all. In other words, opera can be appreciated by Americans when divested of its association with European aristocrats and American social climbers.

None of the men in Mary's life can offer her everything she needs. Blackie can give her romance but not social status (respectability). Burley can give her social status but not romance. And Father Tim can give her spiritual guidance but neither romance nor social status. As Shout wisely observes, though, the contest for Mary's loyalty is waged not only by three men but by three musical traditions and, ultimately, by three strands in the cultural fabric of America itself. To find happiness, Mary must find a way of integrating all three of them. And her personal evolution is revealed in her musical evolution as epitomized by successive renderings of the title song. The first is an audition for Blackie. Mary sings it as if it were a hymn. In a cabaret—albeit one named the Paradise—this is inappropriate. By the time she sings it again, she has adapted her style but not her condescending attitude (shaped partly by the influence of Father Tim and partly by her single-minded devotion to opera). This rendition lacks vitality and conviction. Before she can do it "correctly," she must learn to bring together disparate musical traditions (and resolve conflicting feelings). At this point, Mary leaves the Paradise and joins the opera. After successful performances as Marguerite in *Faust* and Violetta in *La Traviata*, Mary finds that she cannot dismiss the world of Blackie. Representing the Paradise in a contest, she finally sings "San Francisco" properly. This time, significantly, "she brings together not only her own European musical heritage and Blackie's creed of ragtime, but a show business heritage that did not yet exist in 1906. Her interpretation suggests not only the MacDonald persona, but Al Jolson, Sophie Tucker, and Libby Holman" (John D. Shout, "The Film Musical and the Legacy of Show Business," *Journal of Popular Film and Television* 10 [1982]: 26). But just when she seems to have resolved her inner conflict (which is also a characteristically American *Kulturkampf*), disaster strikes. As Shout suggests, "The audience may well sense that Mary's dilemma can only be resolved by an earthquake" (ibid., p. 26).

As the movie ends, Mary has been "converted" to Blackie's world (by choosing to leave Burley), and Blackie has been "converted" to hers (by interpreting the earthquake as a call for repentance and prayer). As the ruins of the old San Francisco are replaced by montage with a skyline of the new, Mary leads the crowd of homeless victims in "Nearer My God to Thee." The idea seems to be that she and Blackie, together, have finally integrated the diverse elements out of which a truly vital American tradition can grow. "In fact," writes Shout, "we are to see *San Francisco* as a depiction of the rebuilding of America on both sacred and profane bases" (ibid., p. 26).

11. John Kobal, *Gotta Sing, Gotta Dance: A History of Movie Musicals* (New York: Exeter Books, 1983), p. 103.

12. Harmetz, *The Making*, p. 97.

13. Paul Dybowski, jacket notes for *Pontifikalamt aus dem Dreifaltigkeits —Sergius-Kloster (Pontifical Mass for the Trinity—St. Sergius Monastery), Sagorsk* (Archiv 2533 451), p. 3.

14. Bruce Bohle, ed., *International Cyclopedia of Music and Musicans*, 10th ed. (London: Dent, 1975), p. 156.

15. Peter W. Dykema, ed., *Community Songs for Male Voices: The Blue Book*, Twice 55 Series, no. 4 (Boston: Birchard, 1926), n.p.

16. W. A. H. Birnie, ed., *Reader's Digest Family Song Book* (Montreal: Reader's Digest Association, 1970), p. 192.

17. "Bishop, Henry R.," *New Grove's Dictionary of Music and Musicians*, ed. Stanley Sadie. (London: Macmillan, 1980), vol. 2, pp. 741-745.

18. Donald Albrecht, *Designing Dreams: Modern Architecture in the Movies* (New York: Harper and Row; Museum of Modern Art, 1986).

19. Howard Mandelbaum and Eric Myers, *Screen Deco: A Celebration of High Style in Hollywood* (New York: St. Martin's Press, 1985).

20. Daniel J. Boorstin, *The National Experience*, vol. 2 of *The Americans*, 3 vols. (New York: Random House, 1965), pp. 97-107.

21. Wayne Andrews, *American Gothic: Its Origins, Its Trials, Its Triumphs* (New York: Random House, 1975).

22. "Air Force Academy Chapel," *Architectural Record* (December 1962): 86.

23. See, for example, *The Justice of Otto* by Dirk Bouts (1470-1475) or the *Portinari Altarpiece* by Hugo Van der Goes (1476-1478).

24. Chatman, *Story and Discourse*, p. 121.

25. For this idea, I am indebted to John Galaty of the Department of Anthropology at McGill University.

26. Controversy over this subject is as old as the medium itself; from the beginning, there have been two schools of thought. One is represented by the Lumière brothers, Louis and Auguste, who filmed scenes of everyday life in the streets of Paris around the turn of the century. Although most of their films were "documentaries," some were brief vignettes of daily life. The Lumière brothers were fascinated by an inherent feature of the new medium: the possibility of recording the passing scene quickly and accurately. A very

different approach was taken by Georges Méliès at about the same time. As a magician, he was interested in another inherent feature of the new medium: the possibility of creating fantasies through special effects. Accordingly, he designed elaborate sets and fantastic costumes for use in his productions. In short, he emphasized theatricality. Because both possibilities—film as documentation (projecting reality) and film as artifice (projecting illusion)—are inherent in the medium itself, the debate over the "proper" use and interpretation of film has continued to the present day.

27. Chatman, *Story and Discourse*, pp. 95–145.

28. Ibid., pp. 44–45.

3. Her Own Backyard

1. R. Blane and H. Martin, "Have Yourself a Merry Little Christmas." Copyright © 1943 (renewed 1971) Metro-Goldwyn-Mayer, Inc. © 1944 (renewed 1972) Leo Feist, Inc. All rights of Leo Feist, Inc. assigned to EMI Catalogue Partnership. All rights controlled and administered by EMI Feist Catalog. International copyright secured. Made in USA. All rights reserved. Permission for printing outside the US and Canada granted by International Music Publications.

2. The term has not always been used with precision. When Hortense Powdermaker used it originally, she did so in a deliberately provocative way: "Hollywood is engaged in the mass production of prefabricated daydreams. It tries to adapt the American dream, that all men are created equal, to the view that all men's dreams should be made equal" (*Hollywood, the Dream Factory: An Anthropologist Looks at the Movie-Makers* (Boston: Little, and Brown Co., 1950), p. 39. Elsewhere, she noted that "in this age of technology and the assembly line, many people wish to escape from their anxieties into movies, collective daydreams themselves manufactured on the assembly line" (ibid., p. 12). In doing so, she anticipated the work of Christian Metz and other scholars who have used elaborate psychoanalytical theories to say what observers have intuited since the earliest movies began flickering on screens in darkened theatres.

3. Christian Metz, *The Imaginary Signifier: Psychoanalysis and the Cinema*, trans. Celia Britton, Annwyl Williams, Ben Brewster, and Alfred Guzetti (Bloomington: Indiana University Press, 1975–82), p. 117.

4. Ibid., p. 117.

5. Ibid., pp. 112–113.

6. Ibid., p. 121.

7. Ibid., p. 124.

8. Ibid., p. 127.

9. Ibid., p. 128.

10. Ibid., p. 135.

11. Ibid., pp. 136–137.

12. Dervin, "Over the Rainbow and under the Twister,", p. 55.

13. Ibid.

14. Ibid., p. 52.

15. Ibid.

16. Ibid., p. 54.

17. Ibid., p. 56.

18. Ibid., p. 54.

19. Throughout his article, Dervin points out that the movie comments (intentionally or unintentionally) on the link between dreams and movies. When Dorothy looks behind the curtain and finds that the Wizard is an ordinary man, for instance, she learns that his projected image is not very frightening after all. It is, at any rate, no more frightening than ordinary adult sexuality. In fact, "the movie subliminally suggests that viewing the one is no more terrible than viewing the other! The Wizard, we now see, is only a showman or director manqué, and what has been frightening was not out the window (in nature) or on the dream screen (in the unconscious) but, rather, on a movie screen and in the response conditioned by the child's relatively inadequate mental equipment. What has been frightening occurred in the space, as it were, between the big bed and the little bed, between adult sexuality and the dream screen—a space in which we too can participate if we have the wit to stay and not hide in the cyclone cellar" (ibid., p. 54). Not only is primal scene material presented as content, but the very act of watching a movie involves witnessing a primal scene. The technological devices themselves, according to Freudian tradition, can be likened to a "primal scene as the male image is cast upon the female screen. Of course, it is only the illusion of a primal scene, but then that is the whole point" (ibid., p. 54).

20. Ibid., p. 56.

21. Ibid.

22. Ibid., p. 55.

23. Ibid.

24. Greenberg, *"The Wizard of Oz,"* p. 14.

25. Ibid.

26. Ibid., p. 16.

27. Ibid., p. 15.

28. Ibid., p. 17.

29. Ibid., p. 10.

30. Ibid., p. 23.

31. Ibid., p. 25.

32. Ibid., p. 26.

33. Dervin, "Over the Rainow and under the Twister," p. 51.

34. Ibid.

35. Harmetz, *The Making*, pp. 303-309. A much fuller account of the ruby slippers and their fate over the years can be found in Rhys Thomas, *The Ruby Slippers of Oz* (Los Angeles: Tale Weaver Publishing, 1989).

36. Ibid., p. 308.

37. Bruno Bettelheim, *The Uses of Enchantment: The Meaning and Importance of Fairy Tales* (New York: Random House, 1975), pp. 199-214.

38. Ibid., pp. 225-235.

39. Ibid., pp. 226-276.

40. Harmetz, *The Making*, p. 328.

41. Ibid., p. 184.

42. Greenberg, *"The Wizard of Oz,"* p. 25.

43. Dervin, "Over the Rainbow and under the Twister," p. 56.

44. Some psychoanalysts have retold the story according to "revisionist" principles. Richard A. Gardner's *Dorothy and the Lizard of Oz* (Cresskill, NY: Creative Therapeutics, 1985) is a new version of the familiar fairy tale; it is designed to "correct" what the author considers inappropriate psychological messages.

45. Jung, Carl Gustav, "The Phenomenology of the Spirit in Fairy-Tales," *The Archetypes of the Collective Unconscious*, 2d ed., trans. R. F. C. Hull, Collected Works of C. G. Jung 9.1; Bollingen Series 20 (Princeton, NJ: Princeton University Press, 1969), p. 217.

46. Jung, "The Meaning of Psychology for Modern Man," *Civilization in Transition*, 2d ed., trans. R. F. C. Hull, Collected Works of C. G. Jung 10; Bollingen Series 20 (Princeton, NJ: Princeton University Press, 1969), p. 152.

47. Jung, *Psychological Types*, trans. H. G. Baynes, Collected Works of C. G. Jung 6; Bollingen Series 20 (Princeton, NJ: Princeton University Press, 1971), p. 477.

48. Jung, "Archetypes of the Collective Unconscious," *The Archetypes of the Collective Unconscious*, pp. 5-6.

49. Jung, "Psychological Aspects of the Mother Archetype," p. 101.

50. Jung, "Psychology and Literature," *The Spirit in Man, Art and Literature*, trans. R. F. C. Hull, Collected Works of C. G. Jung 15; Bollingen Series 20 (New York: Pantheon Books, 1966), pp. 122-123.

51. Jung, "The Practical Use of Dream Analysis," *The Practice of Psychotherapy*, 2d ed., trans. R. F. C. Hull, Collected Works of C. G. Jung 16; Bollingen Series 20 (Princeton, NJ: Princeton University Prss, 1966), p. 150.

52. Baum, *The [Wonderful] Wizard of Oz*, p. 2.

53. Marie-Louise von Franz, "The Process of Individuation," *Man and His Symbols* (New York: Doubleday, 1964), p. 169.

54. This is not generally true, however, of the anima. Jolande Jacobi explains this by pointing to the compensatory nature of the unconscious; because women "naturally" tend toward monogamy in their conscious behavior, their unconscious projections would tend toward polyandry (Jolande Jacobi, *The Psychology of Carl Gustav Jung: An Introduction with Illustrations* (1942; New Haven, CT: Yale Univesity Press, 1973), p. 121.

55. Jung, "The Tavistock Lectures: 4, "*The Symbolic Life: Miscellaneous Writings*, trans. R. F. C. Hull, Collected Works of C. G. Jung 18; Bollingen Series 20 (Princeton, NJ: Princeton University Press, 1976), p. 122.

56. Jung, *Mysterium Coniunctionis: An Inquiry into the Separation and Synthesis of Psychological Opposites in Alchemy*, trans. R. F. C. Hull, Collected Works of C. G. Jung 14; Bollingen Seris 20 (1955-1956; Princeton, NJ; Princeton University Press, 1963), p. 432.

57. Ibid., pp. 113, 289.

58. Jung, "The Psychology of the Child Archetype," *The Archetypes of the Collective Unconscious*, pp. 87-88.

59. *New Hymn and Tune Book for the Use of the African Methodist Episcopal Zion Church* (Charlotte, NC: AME Book Concern, 1937) #1060, p. 396.

60. Jung, *Psychological Types*, p. 259.

61. Jung, "Child Archetype," p. 162.

62. Ibid., p. 164.

63. Jung, "Archetypes of the Collective Unconscious," p. 164.

64. Jung, "Child Archetype," p. 165.

65. Carol Pearson, *The Hero Within: Six Archetypes We Live By* (San Francisco: Harper and Row, 1986), p. 14.

66. Ibid., p. 5.

67. Ibid., p. 21.

68. Ibid., p. 26.

69. Ibid., p. 153.

70. Ibid., pp. 49–50.

71. Arnold Van Gennep, *The Rites of Passage* (London: Routledge and Kegan Paul, 1960).

72. Victor Turner, *The Ritual Process: Structure and Anti-Structure*, Symbol, Myth and Ritual Series (Ithaca, NY: Cornell University Press, 1969), p. 105.

73. This pattern is not universal. In both *Summertime* and *Rebel without a Cause*, for example, the pattern is reversed. Both are coming of age stories in which growing up is linked to going home. But the relative importance of growing up differentiates them from *The Wizard*. This can be explained in terms of the historical preoccupations of particular generations. In 1939, going home was a more urgent problem than growing up. By the 1950s, when both *Rebel* and *Summertime* were released, the situation had reversed itself. Going or staying home was no longer a major problem. Growing up, however, had become one. Members of this generation were often far more alienated from their parents (or society). Some no longer saw the need or even the desirability of reintegration into adult society after a temporary withdrawal during adolescence. The gangs went to war against society; the beatniks dropped out of it. In both cases, alternative societies were established. American society was now fragmented, even polarized, by age as well as race. In view of this, it is not surprising to find that movies about coming of age made at this time feature growing up by treating it explicitly, while going home may be treated implicitly. In both *Rebel* and *Summertime*, the protagonist returns home at the end of the last reel. This much is made explicit. But the significance of this is left to the imagination: it is implied, not stated. In any case, it seems clear that an issue as problematic as coming of age, an issue that has been explored in a number of movies, might well form an important subtext in a movie as popular as *The Wizard*.

74. Moreover, this phenomenon is by no means of merely historical interest.

For a detailed study of these themes as currently explored on television, see Appendix 4. Coming of age (ritual initiation into the adult community) seldom, if ever, takes place in the gay community. There, in any case, growing up has a somewhat different meaning—but one that is represented no less effectively by *The Wizard*. This is explained in Jungian terms by Robert H. Hopcke's "Dorothy and Her Friends: Symbols of Gay Male Individuation," *Quadrant* 22, no. 2 (1989): 65-76. This movie is extremely popular among gay men, he notes, as a symbolic equivalent of the particular conflicts they face growing up in a straight world. Because Dorothy eventually finds not only her self but also her persona—a way of mediating between the inner and outer worlds—they are encouraged in their own search for a similar reconciliation between reality and appearance, masculinity and femininity.

4. The Land of *E Pluribus Unum*

1. D. W. Meinig, Introduction, *The Interpretation of Ordinary Landscapes: Geographical Essays*, ed. D. W. Meinig (New York: Oxford University Press, 1979), p. 6.

2. Meinig, "The Beholding Eye: Ten Versions of the Same Scene," in ibid., p. 34.

3. Ibid., p. 35.

4. Garrett Eckbo, *The Landscape We See* (New York: McGraw-Hill, 1969, p. 42. Quoted by Meinig in ibid., p. 35.

5. Ibid.

6. Ibid., p. 36.

7. Among the Vaupés of Brazil's Amazon basin, for example, home is only vaguely defined. Though not true nomads, the Vaupés do a lot of travelling and are made to feel very much at home when staying with associates in other villages. The region is multilingual but well-integrated socially and culturally because of linguistic exogamy: each marries someone who speaks a different language. Most individuals become very familiar with a variety of communities and their ways. Consequently, there is no sense that beyond the immediate territory of kin lies a land of aliens or enemies. They are domifugal. Among the Aranda of Australia, however, extreme importance is placed on the notion of home. Clan territory is made holy by the ancestors tied to it. These ancestors continue to live both in specific places and in their descendents. Stories of the ancestors are always linked to particular places and associated with secret rituals and symbolic markings. They cling to their native soil with every fiber of their being. Love for home and longing to return home are major motifs that recur over and over again in their myths. Even though members of the clan are said to own land, it might be more

accurate to say that the land owns them because they are unable to stay away from it without dying. They are domicentric.

Even within a single society, Sopher observes, the experience of home may be different from one class, gender, or generation to another. Among the Aranda, for example, only men know of the sacred places, rituals, and myths. When a girl reaches puberty, she leaves her own clan and its territory ignorant of its traditions and settles down with a new clan in a new territory without being initiated into local traditions. In such a society, home is best described as the "fatherland." In other societies, however, it could best be described as the "motherland." In upper-class Britain, for example, boys are deliberately uprooted from their homes and sent to boarding schools. Attachment to what Sopher calls their "mythic home" is encouraged as a replacement for the earlier attachment to their "biological homes." The same differentiation can be observed in terms of class. It is generally assumed, notes Sopher, that peasants are profoundly attached to their native landscapes. And yet peasants have always engaged in mass migrations. Peasants, in fact, have been very realistic in their understanding of home. According to a Roman proverb, for example, *ubi bene ibi patria* (where things are good, that is the fatherland).

8. David Sopher, "The Landscape of Home: Myth, Experience, Social Meaning," in Meinig, *Ordinary Landscapes*, 134.

9. Ibid., pp. 134–135.

10. "The So-Called Letter to Diognetus," *The Library of Christian Classics*, vol. I: Early Christian Fathers, ed. Eugene R. Fairweather (London: SCM Press, 1953). Quoted in Sopher, "Landscape of Home," p. 135.

11. The domifugal tendency is incorporated too, however, because the last stage of the life cycle is ideally devoted to pilgrimage; the *sannyasin* leaves home, family, and even caste behind to seek final release from the cycle of birth, death, and rebirth. The classical view thus integrates the two societal forces.

In Judaism, too, the situation is complex. Although the domicentric tendency has had profound significance in Jewish tradition and the liturgies are filled with nostalgic references to the Land of Israel, most of Jewish history has been lived outside the ancestral homeland—very often by choice. In our own time, most Jews have not, in fact, chosen to return. The discrepancy can be explained by restoring the texture of traditional references to the Land of Israel. It is true that Jews have always dreamed of spending "next year in Jerusalem." But that phrase, used in the Passover liturgy, is heavily weighted with messianic connotations. Indeed, support for Zionism among the Hassidim—which was not enthusiastic until very recently—is now based on the belief that we are presently living in messianic times. What Jews have traditionally sought can be best described not as a mere return to the Middle East but as a return to the paradise that exists beyond time and space. Within history, Jews have accepted, often gladly, an attitude similar to that of traditional Christianity. It is worth noting here that *galut* may be translated not only as "exile" (forced absence) but also as "diaspora" (voluntary absence). In *Galut: Modern Jewish Reflections on Homelessness and Homecoming* (Bloomington: Indiana University Press, 1986), Arnold Eisen gives an excellent account of Jewish ambivalence over the meaning of home.

12. T. S. Eliot, *Four Quartets* (New York: Harcourt, Brace, 1943). Quoted in Sopher, "Landscape of Home," p. 134. Excerpt from "Little Gidding" in FOUR QUARTETS, copyright 1943 by T. S. Eliot and renewed 1971 by Esme Valerie Eliot, reprinted by permission of Harcourt Brace Jovanovich, Inc.

13. Ibid., p. 135. The Apapokuva wander endlessly in search of a Land without Evil; they are, therefore, attached to no particular place en route.

14. Ibid., p. 136.

15. Meinig, "Symbolic Landscapes," p. 164.

16. A good example of "boosterism" at work can be seen in the case of Lake Havasu City. This community bought London Bridge, transported it to the Arizona desert, and reassembled it over an artificial waterway. In 1970, its population was 4,411; by 1980, its population has soared to 15,737 (*World Almanac and Book of Facts* [New York: Pharos Books, 1988], p. 544.

17. *The National Atlas of the United States of America* (Washington, DC: Department of the Interior, 1971), pp. 336–417.

18. Meinig, "Symbolic Landscapes," p. 167.

19. "A Stop at Willoughby," "The Twilight Zone," CBS, WCAX-TV, Burlington, VT, 6 May, 1960.

20. Marc Scott Zicree, *The Twilight Zone Companion* (New York: Bantam Books, 1982), p. 117.

21. In a very similar episode, "Walking Distance," another executive from the big city returns to a small town. This time, though, it is the small town (appropriately named "Homewood") of his own childhood. These episodes take an overtly positive attitude toward the small town. Other episodes, however, are more ambiguous. In "The Monsters Are Due on Maple Street," a community is invaded by aliens from outer space; when neighbor turns against neighbor out of fear and suspicion, the result is mass hysteria. This may be a small town. It may also be a suburb. In any case, the episode is about a feature of all human communities, the tendency toward mob violence, and not about the advantages or disadvantages of any particular form of community.

22. Zicree, *Twilight Zone Companion*, pp. 118–119.

23. Richard Zoglin and John D. Hull, "Back to the Time Warp: The

Mayberry Clan Joins the Trend toward TV Reunions," *Time* (3 March 1986), p. 61.

24. Richard V. Francaviglia, "Main Street U.S.A.: A Comparison/Contrast of Streetscapes in Disneyland and Walt Disney World," *Journal of Popular Culture* 15, no. 1 (1981): 141-145. Margaret J. King, "Disneyland and Walt Disney World: Traditional Values in Futuristic Form," *Journal of Popular Culture* 15, no. 1 (1981): 116-140. Elizabeth Walker Mechling and Jay Mechling, "The Sale of Two Cities: A Semiotic Comparison of Disneyland with Mariott's Great America," *Journal of Popular Culture* 15, no. 1 (1981): 166-179.

25. Meinig, "Symbolic Landscapes," p. 167.

26. Ibid., p. 182.

27. Ibid., pp. 182-183.

28. Styskal, cartoon, *Newsweek* (10 August 1987), p. 11. Frank Trippett, "Highway to Homicide: California's Road Wars Go on and, in One Case, Go Airborne," *Time* (17 August 1987), p. 18. Mickey Kaus and Janet Huck, "Gunplay on the Freeway: In Los Angeles, It's 'Out of My Way, or Make My Day,'" *US News and World Report* (10 August 1987), p. 6.

29. Meinig, "Symbolic Landscapes," p. 183.

30. Dickran Tashjian, "Engineering a New Art," *The Machine Age in America, 1918-1945* (New York: Brooklyn Museum; Harry N. Abrams, 1986), p. 257.

31. H. Arlen and E. Y. Harburg, "Follow the Yellow Brick Road." Copyright © 1938, 1939 (renewed 1966, 1967) Metro-Goldwyn-Mayer, Inc. assigned to Leo Feist, Inc. All rights of Leo Feist, Inc. assigned to EMI Catalogue Partnership. All rights controlled and administered by EMI Feist Catalog, Inc. International copyright secured. Made in USA. Used by permission. All rights reserved. Permission for printing outside the US and Canada granted by International Music Publications.

32. In common parlance, "the West" is associated with both "wilderness" and "frontier." Very often, it is assumed that these two words are synonymous. They are not. Each has its own symbolic associations based on a way of life that has left a profound impression in the collective memory of Americans. Before proceeding, therefore, the differences must be made clear. To do this, I have made use of *Virgin Land: The American West as Symbol and Myth* by Henry Nash Smith (1950; Cambridge, MA: Harvard University Press, 1978); and *The Machine in the Garden: Technology and the Pastoral Ideal in America* by Leo Marx (New York: Oxford University Press, 1964).

Smith suggests that American history can be fully understood only in terms of the West as it has existed in the collective imagination. "One of the most persistent generalizations concerning American life and character," he observes, "is the notion that our society has been shaped by the pull of a vacant continent" (Smith, *Machine*, p. 3). His final chapter, in fact, is devoted to Frederick Jackson Turner, whose "frontier hypothesis" gave classic expression to this school of thought at the end of the nineteenth century. Turner claimed that the characteristic features of American society could be explained by the availability of free land in the West; the continuing interaction between wilderness and civilization on the frontier generated the distinctive quality of American life. Turner distinguished between two Wests. One lay beyond civilization: this was the wilderness, and it was empty. The other lay just within civilization: this was the frontier, and it was a garden. The frontier, then, is defined as the meeting place between "savagery" (nature) and "civilization" (culture). Smith points out that Turner was ambivalent about the frontier. On the one hand, he assumed the primacy of nature in determining the course of American history. That is, the forces shaping it were thought to be inherent in the landscape itself (vast areas of free land cultivated as family farms) and not in the cultural traditions inherited from the Old World. This emphasized the unique features of American life. From this point of view, the frontier was "good." On the other hand, Turner also believed in the evolution of civilization through various stages. The effect was to stigmatize the frontier as socially, culturally, and even morally primitive compared to the more sophisticated and evolved world of the urban East. From this point of view, the frontier was "bad." I have discussed Turner's hypothesis, albeit briefly, because it continues to provoke controversy and is still one of the best-known interpretations of American history. Why should this be so? What does the sheer popularity of such a theory say about the people who respond to it, in one way or the other, with such passion? What role does it play even now in American culture? "Since the enormous currency of the theory proves that it voices a massive and deeply held conviction, the recent debate over what Turner actually meant, and over the truth or falsity of his hypothesis, is much more than a merely academic quibble. It concerns the image of themselves which many—perhaps most—Americans of the present day cherish, an image that defines what Americans think of their past, and therefore what they propose to make of themselves in the future" (Smith, *Machine*, p. 4).

In this way, Smith's aim in discussing Turner is like my own in discussing *The Wizard*. In both cases, the topic is a phenomenon of lasting and extensive popularity: an explicit theory of American history and identity in the first case and an implicit one in the second. In both cases, moreover, symbolic significance rather than historical veracity is of paramount importance: what it reveals about emotional, cultural, or even spiritual concerns. Whether expressed directly in a historical theory that continues to intrigue scholars or indirectly in a popular movie that continues to charm viewers, images of the wilderness and the frontier continue to haunt the American imagination and are frequently invoked to define collective identity—especially in relation to the urban and industrial imagery that currently defines the reality of everyday life for most Americans.

33. Peter J. Schmitt comments on several related subjects in *Back to Nature: The Arcadian Myth in Urban America* (New York: Oxford University Press, 1969). These include novels about life in the wild, the development of suburbs and garden cities, the rise of summer camps and the scouting movement, the promotion of urban parks as a way of improving the health of urban children, the establishment of national parks to preserve the wilderness and primitivism, or instinctivism, as a worldview. Schmitt points out that although Americans in the late nineteenth and early twentieth centuries liked the idea of going "back to nature," they did not like the idea of going "back to the land" nearly as much. Theirs was an urban response to nature. The latter was fine—on weekends or in fantasies.

34. Linda H. Graber discusses the positive aspects in *Wilderness as Sacred Space*, Monograph Series 8 (Washington: Association of American Geographers, 1976). The wilderness, she observes, has been associated with "geopiety." Through verbal images (nature writing) and visual images (purist landscape photography) Americans have glorified the wilderness as the functional equivalent of sacred space in traditional forms of religion. This has been articulated not only by isolated artists but also by political pressure groups. Graber concludes that the environmentalist movement has become a kind of religion in secular dress. Although she has little to say about Eden as the prototypical wilderness (the "wild" or "natural" garden), she does comment at length on the universal need for sacred space.

Roderick Nash comments on the ambiguous connotations of wilderness in American history. In *Wilderness and the American Mind* (New Haven, CT: Yale University Press, 1967), he describes the gradual transition from wilderness as a moral and physical wasteland suitable only for conquest to wilderness as a moral and physical treasure existing as an end in itself.

35. Phillipe de Montebello, Foreword, *American Paradise: The World of the Hudson River School* (New York: Metropolitan Museum of Art, 1987), p. xi.

36. John C. Howat, "Frederick Edwin Church," *American Paradise*, p. 251.

37. The definitive work on the wilderness in American art is Novak's *Nature and Culture: American Landscape Painting 1825–1875* (New York: Oxford University Press, 1980). Novak discusses the effects of religion and romanticism on attitudes toward nature (the primeval wilderness as revelation and as the sublime) and how these are related to landscape painting. Both painters and scientists in the nineteenth century, for example, tended to see themselves as quasi-mythic heroes on a quest for divine truth; conse-

quently, they often went off together on expeditions to study the mysteries of nature.

38. Cathleen McGuigan, "The Search for Paradise Lost: The Hudson River School Saw America as Eden," *Newsweek* (12 October 1987), pp. 82–83.

39. Oswaldo Rodriguez Roque, "The Exaltation of American Landscape Painting," *American Paradise*, p. 30.

40. Howat, "Frederick Edwin Church," p. 252.

41. John P. Guttenberg, "Edward Hicks: A Journey to the Peaceable Kingdom," *American Art and Antiques* 2, no. 3 (1979): 76.

42. Isa. 11:6.

43. Marx, *Machine*, p. 41.

44. Ibid., p. 43. By "desert", he refers to the hostile and threatening aspect of the wilderness in general rather than to the hot and dry form of wilderness in particular.

45. Perry Miller, *Errand into the Wilderness* (Cambridge, MA: Harvard University Press, 1956).

46. St. John de Crèvecoeur, *Letters from an American Farmer*, ed. Warren Barton Blake (London: Everyman's Library, 1912). Quoted in Marx, ibid., p. 111.

47. Andrew Gordon, "*Star Wars:* A Myth for Our Time," *Literature and Film Quarterly* 6 (1978): 318.

48. In 1939, however, she was also the functional equivalent of any dictator threatening world peace. Her winged monkeys flying off in formation to capture Dorothy look very much like dive bombers flying off to attack a city. Although Hitler's *Blitzkrieg* on Warsaw was still a few weeks in the future when *The Wizard* opened on August 17, most viewers had long since become familiar with such scenes from newsreels of air attacks during the Spanish Civil War and the Japanese invasion of China.

49. Although the West has produced important cities, the East has produced America's prototypical cities. San Francisco, for example, has always been considered something of an anomaly (which is to say, an Eastern city that happens to be located in the West) and Los Angeles has entered the collective imagination as a collection of suburbs surrounding the Hollywood studios.

50. Raymond A. Mohl, "The Preindustrial American City," *The Urban Experience: Themes in American History*, ed. Raymond A. Mohl and James F. Richardson (Belmont, CA: Wadsworth, 1973), pp. 1–13.

51. Richard Guy Wilson, Dianne H. Pilgrim, and Dickran Tashjian, *The Machine Age in America, 1918–1945* (New York: Brooklyn Museum; Harry N. Abrams, 1986).

52. Robert Hughes, "Back to the Lost Future: A Remarkable Show Revives the Machine Age, Fins and All," *Time* (22 December 1986), p. 46.

53. David Albrecht, *Designing Dreams: Modern Architecture in the Movies* (New York: Harper and Row; Museum of Modern Art, 1986).

54. For Meinig, the American city's symbolic ties with family life, home, and community are inadequate to replace the three earlier symbolic land-scapes. He writes that "for most Americans, the old cliché 'a nice place to visit, but I wouldn't want to live there' has expressed their feelings well, and in recent years they are much less interested in, or even fearful of, an occasional visit ("Symbolic Landscapes" 181)." Nevertheless, Meinig does suggest the possibility that a new kind of city (identified with the Western metropolis) may do what the earlier kind (specifically, the Eastern metropo-lis) cannot do. San Francisco, he argues, may be the prototype of an urban environment that unambiguously affirms family life, home, and community. He notes that it has provided fertile soil for experiments in the arts, religion, psychology, and education. Moreover, it has been at the center of various ecological movements. Most important, it has challenged national attitudes toward unlimited growth, consumption, and technological progress. San Francisco, therefore, has become famous for the assertion of new patterns of individual and group consciousness. More specifically, it has been "gradually recognized through a self-sorting of people not by class or income, nor even very firmly by ethnicity or race, but by life-style, resulting in "voluntary districts"... formed out of the search for a way of life which may be quite at variance with what have been the cultural norms. It is conceivable that from such developments San Francisco might shed its old anomalous status and serve as the chief basis for a new generalized concept of urban life featuring attractive townhouse living, the vibrancy of social heterogeneity, a greater appreciation of townscape, a deeper sense of history and of place, and a greater emphasis upon the humane rather than the material aspects of life so that the core becomes increasingly more a central social district than a central business district" (Meinig, "Symbolic Landscapes," p. 187).
Reading this in the early 1990s, it is difficult not to think that the author, using language so characteristic of the 1960s and early 1970s, is somewhat naive. In the first place, the way of life he describes was even then restricted to a very affluent and well-educated segment of the population. Moreover, there is no evidence to suggest that San Francisco, popular though it may be, has replaced the Eastern metropolis as an image of urban life in the United States. As the quintessential American city, New York is still a powerful symbolic landscape attracting both the ambitious (those seeking success defined in terms of money, power, and prestige) and the domestic or foreign

poor (those seeking security from the vast social service bureaucracy). One has only to think of the Manhattan skyline to realize its profound impact not only in the United States itself but all over the world; it is a universal symbol of hope, opportunity, even adventure.

55. James E. Vance, "California and the Search for the Ideal," *Annals Association of American Geographers* 62, no. 2 (1977): pp. 182-210. Quoted in Meinig, "Symbolic Landscapes," p. 181.

56. H. S. Reuss and W. E. Simon, "Is New York Worth Saving?" *US News and World Report* (10 November 1975), pp. 32-34.

57. Martin E. Marty, *Righteous Empire: The Protestant Experience in America* (New York: Dial Press, 1970). In the past few decades, liberal Protestant theology has taken a very different approach to the metropolis. By far the most famous (and still controversial) celebration of the city and modernity is Harvey Cox's *The Secular City: Secularization and Urbanization in Theological Perspective*, rev. ed. (New York: Macmillan, 1966).

58. Sam Bass Warner, *The Urban Wilderness: A History of the American City* (New York: Harper and Row, 1972), pp. 3, 4. Quoted in Meinig, "Symbolic Landscapes," p. 181.

59. One stands out as an illustration. Made in 1944, only five years after *The Wizard* and at the height of the Second World War, *Meet Me in St. Louis* reveals both the anxiety and social disorder caused by historical events beyond the control of anyone. Millions of Americans were leaving home. The young men were sent off to fight overseas. Many others, however, were migrating from farms and small towns to the cities where they found work in war industries. This movie, however, does not affirm the massive social changes that were taking place; it is a frankly nostalgic look at life in small-town America at the turn of the century. The visual structure of *Meet Me in St. Louis* emphasizes this. Corresponding to the eternal rhythm of nature itself, each of its four segments opens with a sepia-tinted photograph of the Smith family house in a different season; the implication is that this is not only the way things once were but the ways things should be and will be once again (after the war).

In one rather disturbing sequence, Tootie and her friends build a bonfire in the street as part of their Halloween revelry. Then the other children assign her the task of scaring one of the neighbors (who happens, not coincidentally, to have a foreign name). When he opens the door, she throws flour in his face and screams "I hate you!" The Halloween episode is one of the very few that takes place outside the house. It must be seen, therefore, in relation to those that take place inside; it is a commentary, so to speak, on the house and everything it represents. In a way, the house is the real "star" of *Meet Me in St. Louis*. It is always bathed in warm, glowing light. The house represents not only the family that lives there but a whole way of life characterized by peace, order, security, harmony, intimacy—all things lacking in wartime. War, after all, is chaos. Significantly, the Halloween sequence is followed by one in which nocturnal fears are banished and reassurance is provided. It could be argued that the ghostly, demonic atmosphere of the earlier sequence is carnivalesque; like the ancient and universal rites of carnival, the movie implies that normality (order) will return after a brief interlude of abnormality (disorder). In the context of 1944, the confluence of these sequences could be seen as an indirect (and nonthreatening) acknowledgment that the war really was reversing both the natural order (parents mourning their sons) and the cultural order (women in charge of families and working outside the home) but also as an assertion that both forms of disorder would soon be replaced by order.

Chaos, or disorder, is symbolically represented not only by the easily contained threat of a children's festival but also by the much more serious threat of the big city. Father is planning to move the family from St. Louis to New York. He is the only one, though, who wants to move there. Everyone else is horrified at the very idea. They want to remain where they belong. And they belong in what appears to be a small midwestern town of the kind described by Meinig. There are no shots of St. Louis itself. Viewers see only gracious Victorian homes with front porches and spacious lawns on tree-lined streets. Eventually, Father is touched by the attachment of his family to their house, their friends, and their way of life. He decides not to move after all. In the concluding sequence, he takes the family out to see the World's Fair and everyone agrees, in effect, that there is no place like home. "We don't have to leave home on a train or stay in a hotel," exclaims Rose, "it's all right here in our own home town." Almost immediately, Esther reinforces this sentiment: "I can't believe it," she sighs, "right here where we live. Right here in St. Louis." On that note, the movie ends. Both girls suggest, just as Dorothy does in *The Wizard*, that the safe and happy world of one's own backyard is preferable to the exciting and glamorous, but also threatening and dangerous, world beyond. In 1944, they had good reason to long for life as they had known it before the war; it was to preserve that way of life, after all, that they were fighting in the first place. Implicitly, then, *Meet Me in St. Louis* told Americans that the anxiety, confusion and dislocation of the war years was only temporary; this interlude would be followed by a return to peace, security, order, stability and everything associated with the word "home." Explicitly, however, *Meet Me in St. Louis* told Americans that home was not to be found in a big city such as New York.

60. Alain Silver and Elizabeth Ward, eds., *Film Noir: An Encyclopedic Reference to the American Style* (Woodstock, NY: Overlook Press, 1979) 3.

61. Foster Hirsch, *The Dark Side of the Screen: Film Noir* (New York: Da Capo Press, 1983), p. 13.

62. Silver and Ward, *Film Noir*, p. 34.

63. Hirsch, *Dark Side*, pp. 13-15.

64. Ibid., p. 15.

65. Ibid., p. 17.

66. Ibid., p. 17.

67. Kurt Anderson, "Spiffing up the Urban Heritage: After Years of Neglect, Americans Lavish Love and Sweat on Old Downtowns," *Time* (23 November 1987), pp. 64-79.

68. Dianne H. Pilgrim, "Design for the Machine," in Wilson, Pilgrim, and Tashjian, *Machine Age in America*, p. 271.

69. Franklin Delano Roosevelt, "First Inaugural Address," *The President Speaks: From William McKinley to Lyndon Johnson*, ed. Louis Filler (New York: Capricorn Books, 1964), p. 200.

70. Following Leo Marx, I use this term in referring to a pictorial symbol (whether visual or verbal) of our relation to the environment. In other words, it represents the relation between nature and culture. This relation is not the projection of any particular age or society; it is inherent and universal. Examples would be the wilderness (nature over culture), the city (culture over nature), and the garden or farm (mediation between nature and culture).

71. Marx, *Machine*, pp. 42-43.

72. Smith, *Virgin Land*, pp. 123-124.

73. Ibid., pp. 151-152.

74. Sidney Howard, *Gone with the Wind: The Screenplay* (1939; New York: Macmillan, 1964), p. 81.

75. Ibid., p. 243.

76. Ibid., pp. 413-414.

77. I refer here to a version of the garden that flourished in the North, Midwest, and West; eventually, it replaced the Southern version and could thus be called the "American" version.

78. Smith, *Virgin Land*, p. 191.

79. Ibid., pp. 192-193.

80. Ibid., p. 124.

81. Ibid., p. 187.

82. Charles Reagan Wilson, *Baptized in Blood: The Religion of the Lost Cause, 1865–1920* (Athens: University of Georgia Press, 1980), pp. 5, 27, 61.

83. Smith, *Virgin Land*, p. 187.

84. Following Leo Marx, I use this term in referring to a "poetic idea displaying the essence of a value system *(Machine*, p. 42)." Like the symbolic landscape, the root metaphor is culture-specific; unlike the ecological image, in other words, it is not inherent in the relation between nature and culture that pertains universally. But the root metaphor, as I use this term, is the original, prototypical, symbolic landscape on which later versions are based; it is the "type" that corresponds to one or more "antitypes." Perhaps this distinction between root metaphor and ecological image did not occur to Marx (who seems to use the two interchangeably) because he (like Smith) virtually ignored the Christian traditions on which American culture is based. It is true, of course, that the United States was founded on notions of civic virtue and republican idealism derived from ancient Greece and Rome. American culture has been enriched, therefore, by additional root metaphors originating in the classical tradition. Since this book is about the function of popular culture, however, and since classical allusions have been accessible only to an elite stratum of society, I have considered the biblical root metaphors primary and the classical ones secondary. An example would be the biblical Garden of Eden (or the classical Arcadia) corresponding to the frontier farm (a specifically American symbolic landscape).

85. J. B. Jackson, "The Order of a Landscape: Religion and Reason in Newtonian America," in Meinig, *Ordinary Landscapes*, pp. 153-163.

86. Ibid., p. 155.

87. Ibid., p. 156.

88. Ibid., p. 158.

89. Ibid., p. 160.

90. The definitive work on American revivalism is G. McLoughlin's *Revivals, Awakenings and Reform: An Essay on Religion and Social Change in America, 1607–1977*, Chicago History of American Religion (Chicago: University of Chicago Press, 1978). The author includes material on America as the new Eden, American mythology, and the problem of cognitive dissonance. The theological background of American revivalism is examined very thoroughly in Ernest L. Tuveson's *Redeemer Nation: The Idea of America's Millennial Role* (Chicago: University of Chicago Press, 1968).

91. Larry James Gianakos, *TV Drama Series Programming: A Compre-*

hensive Guide, 1959–1975 (Metuchen, NJ: Scarecrow Press, 1978), p. 559.

92. Set in Virginia during the Depression, it is technically incorrect to discuss this show in terms of the frontier; it is linked to the frontier, nevertheless, by the dominant image of an isolated family homestead nestled comfortably somewhere between wilderness and metropolis.

93. Even though Theocritus is sometimes considered the first pastoral poet, Marx sees Virgil as the "fountainhead" of this genre.

94. Marx, *Machine*, p. 21.

95. Ibid., p. 22.

96. Ibid., p. 23.

97. Ibid., p. 3.

98. Marx has nothing but contempt for this sort of thing. "Whenever people turn away from the hard social and technological realities," he writes, "this obscure sentiment is likely to be at work" (ibid., p. 5). He looks with particular disapproval on some of the effects of nostalgic sentimentality (such as what he considers the inflated power of the farming lobby in Congress and state electoral systems that give the rural population a share of political power grossly out of proportion to its size or contribution). Of more immediate concern to Marx, however, is the pernicious influence of this form of pastoralism on the arts: "There can be little doubt that it affects the nation's taste in serious literature, reinforcing the legitimate respect enjoyed by such writers as Mark Twain, Ernest Hemingway, and Robert Frost. But on the lower plane of our collective fantasy life, the power of this sentiment is even more obvious. The mass media cater to a mawkish taste for retreat into the primitive or rural felicity exemplified by TV westerns and Norman Rockwell magazine covers" (ibid., p. 6).
Such cultural detritus is generated by "the yearning for a simpler, more harmonious style of life, an existence 'closer to nature,' that is, the psychic root of all pastoralism—genuine and spurious" (ibid., p. 6). This yearning, he explains is universal. Still, he believes the American experience of nationhood has clearly invested it with a peculiar intensity. "The soft veil of nostalgia that hangs over our urbanized landscape," he writes, "is largely a vestige of the once-dominant image of an undefiled green republic, a quiet land of forests, villages, and farms dedicated to the pursuit of happiness" (ibid., p. 6). It is not only anachronistic, according to Marx, it is also reactionary. He argues that this "spurious" pastoralism has consistently been used in the service of ideologies that hide the realities of life in an industrial civilization. In this, he is in agreement with several other "discerning, politically liberal historians of American thought" (ibid., p. 6) such as Smith and Richard Hofstadter. To support his position, he brings in Ortega y Gasset and even

Sigmund Freud. The former scorned those who appreciate the benefits of technology but not the principles on which it is founded; such people believe that their material comforts are givens of the natural order rather than the results of specific cultural forces (urbanization and industrialization). The latter argued that the benefits of civilization are enjoyed at the cost of repressing the primordial need for sexual gratification; they are, as a result, both appreciated and resented at the same time. For Marx, then, the "popular and sentimental" mode of pastoralism is not only anachronistic and reactionary (Hofstadter; Smith) but also foolish (Ortega) and even neurotic (Freud).

99. Examples of this can be found in the history of both European and American painting. Like their European counterparts, American painters of the nineteenth century were still imitating the idyllic landscapes of Claude Lorraine. In the seventeenth century, he created an idealized vision of the Italian countryside that has haunted artists ever since. It is a dreamlike world of shepherds and shepherdesses (glorified peasants), contemplating the ruins of ancient Rome. Claude introduced several formal devices that have been widely imitated. These include the use of figures in the foreground, a glassy lake or inlet shimmering in the middle distance, and hazy mountains rising in the background. On one side of the foreground are trees; on the other side are more trees or, perhaps, a ruin of some kind. The setting sun bathes this bucolic world in the golden glow of a perpetual afternoon. That creates an evocative, reflective, and slightly melancholy or wistful atmosphere. Nevertheless, the landscape is characterized by order, serenity, and harmony. It is, of course, the landscape of Virgil's Arcadia.

American pastoralism is associated with the Hudson River school. Sometimes, the American version was a literal rendering of the Claudean idiom. Carrie Rebora writes, for example, that in *Harvest Scene* (1875), Jasper Cropsey turned rural New Jersey into the Italian *campagna*. "The harvesting activity, the clothing, and the architecture set the scene for an American provincial myth in which a farmer Apollo meets his countrified Venus in a field of sweet, freshly cut grain.... The picture records the Cooley estate as its proprietor's bountiful, personal Arcadia" ("Jasper Cropsey," *American Paradise*, p. 202). Sometimes, however, painters "translated" Claude into American terms. In these cases, no attempt was made to disguise the American context; it was seen, nevertheless, from the perspective of European pastoral traditions. In *The Old Hunting Ground* (1864), Worthington Whittredge contemplates a peaceful spot in the eastern woodlands. The scene is framed by dark trees on the right and left of the foreground. In the center, a canoe is floating on the shore of a lake or pool. The middle ground is dominated by water that reflects a sunlit forest of birch trees in the background. "For artists of the second generation of the Hudson River School who depicted the national landscape," writes Esther T. Thyssen, "the use of Claudean conventions invoked pastoral associations and helped reinforce the developing myth of America as a new Eden" ("Worthington Whittredge," in ibid., p. 180). Of particular interest here is the way Whittredge assimilated the Indians—those distinctively North American inhabitants—with the European pastoral tradition. Thyssen comments that "the decaying Indian canoe establishes on the landscape concrete evidence of previous human presence and so endowed the land with an ancient history. Thus the Indians were seen to have fulfilled a function in America's forests that was similar to the pastoral duties of European peasants" (ibid., p. 182). Like the ruin of an ancient Roman temple, the ruin of an Indian canoe serves as a vehicle for contemplation of the transience of history or nostalgic meditation on a lost golden age of innocence and harmony. A slightly more ambiguous version of American pastoralism is noted by Gwendolyn Owens in the work of David Johnson. Commenting on *Natural Bridge* (1860), she observes that viewers who did not know that the painting depicts a natural land formation in Virginia could very easily assume that it is an ancient Roman aqueduct overgrown with vegetation. This painting is an Arcadian vision. "Whether seen as a ruin or a natural wonder, this distant view of the bridge shows a world of old and new elements—an ancient form depicted in the agrarian context of the nineteenth century" ("David Johnson," in ibid., p. 274).

Even when machine technology appears in American landscape paintings of the nineteenth century, it often confirms rather than challenges his pastoral vision. Although Marx refers mainly to literature, he does mention a painting by George Inness as a classic visual statement of the pervasive belief that the machine (technology) can be integrated into the "middle landscape." At first Inness did not want to accept a commission by the Lackawanna Railroad Company to paint the setting of its operations. He did not know how to assimilate a roundhouse, a repair shop, or a smoking locomotive to the Arcadian tradition of Virgil and Claude. The result, however, is often considered to be his finest work. Far from causing disharmony, the train is part of the landscape. Buildings are softened by trees and integrated into the hills in the middle distance. Sharp lines, which would divide cultural artifacts from natural terrain, are avoided. The cottony puffs rising from the locomotive and the roundhouse echo the puffy clouds rising behind the church. Animals in the pasture continue to graze or rest peacefully even as the train approaches. Tree stumps indicate that a forest has been felled, to be sure, but the solitary human figure reclining beneath a tree in the foreground indicates that changes of this kind, made in the name of progress, are not disruptive. He may not hold a crook, but he contemplates the landscape of Pennsylvania with the serenity of a good shepherd contemplating the beauty of Arcadia. Although Inness has acknowledged the presence of the machine in the garden, he has not acknowledged the inherent conflict between them. For Marx, therefore, paintings of this kind trivialize modernity; they foster naive and optimistic illusions. They are examples of "popular and sentimental" pastoralism.

100. Marx, *Machine*, pp. 9–10.

101. Ibid., p. 25.

102. Ibid., p. 365.

103. Karin Blair points out in "The Garden in the Machine: The Why of *Star Trek*" (*Journal of Popular Culture* 13 [1979]: 310–320) that a surprising number of episodes feature the search for a garden paradise. Such episodes include: "The Menagerie," "Shore Leave," "This Side of Paradise," "The Apple," "The Way to Eden," "Who Mourns for Adonais?" "The World Is Hollow and I Have Touched the Sky," "The Return of the Archons," "The Mark of Gideon," "The Paradise Syndrome," and "Metamorphosis." Blair notes approvingly that "Star Trek" generally takes a negative attitude toward the garden as an externalized image of paradise. Those who try to find paradise on some remote planet are always disappointed. For Blair, the garden "out there" is no longer an adequate symbol; it represents a regressive desire for the abandonment of culture and reunion with nature (lack of differentiation or individuation, unconsciousness, and even death). According to her, "Star Trek" reinterprets the garden in accordance with more progressive ways of thinking (which is why, she argues, it has become an American myth). "Once the garden has been transferred to the psyche it incorporates the polarities which are the inevitable result of individuality and difference. The machine is no longer the instrument of opposition, war and destruction; it has become a vehicle which both sustains and expresses the human psyche which created it. Within it traditionally opposing forces can recombine and generate energy and motion; our heritage from the past can evolve into fuller awareness of the present and hope for the future.

"In this way the human community or "garden" on board the *Enterprise* can move by means of the machine through conscious construction into new unknown territories including the future. Outside the gravitational pull of 'Mother Earth'—Mother Nature and her paradisal garden—there is no falling but only flying" (ibid., p. 318). I think Blair is too hasty in suggesting the demise of the garden. Whatever "Star Trek" says about the garden as an image of the frontier, however, it unmistakably affirms the frontier as such. Floating through the wilderness of outer space, the starship *Enterprise* is a dynamic new version of the American frontier.

104. Nancy R. Gibbs, "Paradise Found: America Returns to the Garden," *Time* (20 June 1988), p. 62.

105. Ibid., p. 64.

106. Ibid., p. 69.

107. James Howard Kunstler, "Would You Like to See My Motherworts: More Than Hollyhocks Can Bloom in Your Garden," *GQ* (April 1989), pp. 54ff.

108. This notion of literature is consistent with the avant-garde notion that artists stand apart from their culture and challenge it. As I have tried to show in terms of the visual arts, this definition of art is by no means universal. Nevertheless, it represents prevailing attitudes in this society at this time; it is, therefore, appropriate in Marx's discussion of literary works that do expose, provoke, challenge, or question cultural assumptions. For him, the relation between popular and elite culture is dichotomous and even dualistic. The distinction he makes between "popular and sentimental pastoralism" (popular culture), on the one hand, and "imaginative and complex pastoralism" (elite or "high literary" culture), on the other, is both aesthetic and moral. The former is bad and even dangerous; the latter is good and even salvific. "The work of serious writers," he observes, "is different, clearly, in most of the ways that works of art differ from the glow of casual, undisciplined expression that makes up the general culture" (Marx, *Machine*, p. 10). Although he admits that "an initial receptivity to the pastoral impulse is one way in which our best writers have grounded their work in the common life" (ibid., p. 11), he also indicates that in doing so they risk contamination by the vulgarity and sentimentality of that common life. It would almost seem that Marx feels a need to apologize for the pastoral preoccupation of these writers by ascribing a salvific role to them: the artist descends into hell to rescue humanity and bring it to heaven. Indeed, his thesis is that these "serious" writers transform pastoralism from effete escapism into a valiant struggle with the complexity of modern life. For ordinary people, pastoralism "is the starting point for infantile wish-fulfillment dreams, a diffuse nostalgia, and a naive, anarchic, primitivism" but for heroes it is "the source of writing that is invaluable for its power to enrich and clarify our experience" (ibid., p. 11). Marx abhors any expression of fantasy or longing unless linked to (and thus mitigated by) some expression of practical or "realistic" concern. It may be that he does so in the context of art but would not do so in the context of myth. In any case, he makes it clear that the only artistically legitimate attitude toward Arcadia is rejection; pastoral literature, in fact, is not literature at all (as distinct from some more degraded form of human expression) unless it uses antipastoral imagery (the "counterforce") to threaten the pastoral dream. Similarly, the pastoral ideal is morally legitimate only when it "enhances some token of a larger, more complicated order of experience" (ibid., p. 25). The success of American pastoralism in "serious" literature, then, is caused by its repeated juxtaposition of pastoral (rural or agrarian) and nonpastoral (urban, industrial, or technological) imagery. The power of this technique to move people "derives from the magnitude of the protean conflict figured by the machine's increasing domination of the visible world. This recurrent metaphor of contradiction makes vivid, as no other figure does, the bearing of public events upon private lives. It discloses that our inherited symbols of order and beauty have been divested of meaning. It compels us to recognize that the

aspirations once represented by the symbol of an ideal landscape have not, and probably cannot, be embodied in our traditional institutions" (ibid., p. 364). My intention here is not to reverse Marx's literary hierarchy. I do not claim here that popular culture ("popular and sentimental pastoralism") is superior to "imaginative and complex pastoralism" (elite culture); there is a real need for the latter. I do argue, however, that Marx's dualistic approach to works of the imagination prevents him from understanding the former. It, too, may serve real human needs (albeit different ones). As I have already indicated, for example, "bad art" may be "good myth."

109. Ibid., p. 356.

110. Indeed, that painting has been called the "American Mona Lisa." Its fame extends far beyond the world of art historians. Wood's sister, who posed for it, complained recently that she is still troubled, after almost sixty years, by unflattering remarks about the painting. When a parody of it appeared in *Hustler*, she sued the magazine (and lost). When Johnny Carson made ribald remarks about it during his monologue on "Tonight", she was given the opportunity to appear on the air and receive a public apology ("Fifty-Eight Years Later, Model Still Smarts from Knocks on *American Gothic,*" [Montreal] *Gazette* [6 June 1988], p. C16). Plainly, a great many Americans are familiar with this painting even if they cannot name the painter.

111. Wanda M. Corn, *Grant Wood: The Regionalist Vision* (New Haven, CT: Yale University Press, 1983), p. 62.

112. James M. Dennis, *Grant Wood: A Study in American Art and Culture* (New York: Viking Press, 1975), p. 13.

113. Ibid., p. 212.

114. Richard Hofstadter, *The Age of Reform: From Bryan to F. D. R.* (New York: Alfred Knopf, 1972).

115. Dennis, *Grant Wood*, p. 212.

116. Included in this category are decorative, monumental, and highly formalized paintings designed to glorify American farmers and their way of life. Single figures face the viewer as if waiting to be photographed for a family album. They represent the inherent and eternal plenitude of nature. "Like the farmscape itself, Wood's farmers, animals, fruits and vegetables are fecund forms, ripe and robust. . . . They exist as pure symbols, ready to bestow the produce yielded by the bountiful garden upon the world. Ideal-ized, washed and sorted, they present themselves as the agrarian fruits of Iowa" (ibid., p. 217–218).

117. Ibid., p. 219.

118. Corn, *Grant Wood*, p. 90.

119. Wood is also ambivalent toward nature, but much less so. Generally speaking, he presents the idyllic aspect of nature; the tranquil beauty of spring and summer prevail in *Stone City* (1930), *Young Corn* (1931), *Arbor Day* (1932), *Spring Turning* (1936), and most of his other landscapes. But Wood is neither naive nor sentimental. Occasionally, he allows winter—cold, dark, and barren—to enter the scene. The harshness of nature strips the trees, blankets the ground and darkens the sky. Early winter in the Midwest could provide some entertaining diversions as in *December Afternoon* (1941), but soon became tedious and bitter as in *March* (1940) and *February* (1941). For him, rural America is at least one step removed from Eden. But for Wood, unlike some of the other agrarian painters, such intrusions of nature's fury are brief. They are transient phases in a natural cycle that continually generates new life. Wood's Iowa is a snug and happy world, not a threatening or sinister one.

120. When a machine does dominate the Woodian garden, it does so in a very negative way. A good example of this is *Death on the Ridge Road* (1934). In fact, it corresponds to what Marx calls the "counterforce" (whatever negates the idyll in "imaginative and complex" pastoralism). Taking a very direct and even melodramatic form, it is represented by one car about to collide with another. A sinister black limousine tries to regain the right side of the road after illegally passing a slower car; bent on destruction and death, the oncoming red truck drives toward it over the hilltop. Space is contorted. Shadows are deep. Time stands still. Sweeping in from the upper right corner, a massive storm seems to suggest a natural counterpart to cultural malevolence. It is no coincidence that one of the very few paintings by Wood to include such ordinary manifestations of culture as utility poles and wires is heavy with the foreboding atmosphere of an impending collision. The symbolic message is clear: allow the machine into the garden and the result will be death and destruction.

121. Dennis, *Grant Wood*, p. 216.

122. Corn, *Grant Wood*, p. 74.

123. Dennis, *Grant Wood*, p. 222.

124. Ibid., p. 105.

125. "Art: U.S. Scene," *Time* (24 December 1935), p. 25.

126. Considering the collected works of Wood rather than isolated individual paintings, however, the analogy becomes more appropriate. Most of Wood's farmscapes are warm and sunny, it is true, but some of them are icy

and gloomy. Similarly, most of his paintings show the implicit presence of benevolent technology, but some of them (as I have noted) show the explicit presence of malevolent technology. The same is true of *The Wizard*. Although the Yellow Brick Road meanders through the ripening fields and verdant meadows of rural Oz, it also passes through a "temperamental" orchard and a haunted forest. And the dazzling urban splendor of the Emerald City is dimmed upon discovery that the Wizard uses technology to foster the illusions of gullible citizens. In short, it could be argued that both Woodian and Ozian landscapes symbolically represent the confusing, ambiguous, and sometimes dangerous world of everyday life in modern America—even though both appear superficially to be childlike lands of make-believe that need not be taken seriously as "real."

5. The Sweet Vales of Eden

1. Mircea Eliade, *The Sacred and the Profane: The Nature of Religion*, trans. Willard R. Trask (1957; San Diego: Harcourt Brace Jovanovich, 1959), p. 30.

2. Ibid., p. 64.

3. Mircea Eliade, *The Myth of the Eternal Return or, Cosmos and History*, trans. Willard R. Trask, Bollingen Series 46 (1949; Princeton, NJ: Princeton University Press, 1959), p. 22.

4. Ibid., pp. 21–33.

5. Ibid., p. 165.

6. Another frontier is located in the depths of inner space. If I focus more attention on outer space, it is because American attitudes toward the frontier of inner space are more ambivalent. Despite the potential blessings of new birth technologies and genetic engineering, many people find the potential curses profoundly disturbing.

7. Rudolf Bultman, Gerhard von Rad, and Georg D. Bertram, "Zao," *Theological Dictionary of the New Testament*, ed. Gerhard Kittel, trans. and ed. Geoffrey W. Bromiley (Grand Rapids, MI: Eerdmans, 1964-1976), vol. 2, pp. 832-875.

8. Louis Ginzberg, ed., *Legends of the Jews*, tr. Henrietta Szold (1937; Philadelphia: Jewish Publication Society of America, 1968), p. 30. Based on Gen. Rab. 25:3.

9. For a detailed study of this subject, see Ulrich Simon's *Heaven in the Christian Tradition* (New York: Harper, 1958).

10. Frank E. Manuel and Fritzie P. Manuel, "Sketch for a Natural History of Paradise, *Daedalus* 101, no. 1 (Winter 1972), p. 83. Two much more detailed studies have been published recently. For the history of specifically Christian doctrines of heaven, see Colleen McDannell and Bernhard Lang, *Heaven: A History* (New Haven: Yale University Press, 1988). For a broader approach, including both cross-cultural and psychoanalytical perspectives, see Richard Heinberg, *Memories and Visions of Paradise: Exploring the Universal Myth of a Lost Golden Age* (Los Angeles: J. P. Tarcher, 1989). Heinberg's conclusions about the notion of returning to a primeval paradise are consistent with my own.

11. Harry Levin, *The Myth of the Golden Age in the Renaissance* (Bloomington: Indiana University Press, 1969), p. 29. An excellent study of the paradisian garden in Central and South Asian cultures is Elizabeth Moynihan's *Paradise as a Garden: In Persia and Mughal India* (New York: Braziller, 1979).

12. Levin, *Myth*, p. 30.

13. Ibid., p. 40.

14. Ibid., p. 33.

15. I am not suggesting that mysticism and myth are synonymous. What I am suggesting is that both involve an experiential dimension not involved in the doctrinal theology and legal analysis characteristic of orthodoxy. Doctrinal theology and legal analysis depend solely on cognitive processes; mysticism and myth depend on intuitive and imaginative ones. Mysticism, however, also involves cognition. Although mystics use verbal or visual imagery strongly resembling that of myth to describe their visions, this is used self-consciously as a way of alluding metaphorically either to ineffable experiences or to complex philosophical and theosophical ideas. Myth itself, on the other hand, does not involve that kind of self-conscious reflection. Moreover, myth is not esoteric; on the contrary, it is the "cultural property" of an entire community.

16. A precursor of Eden was Dilmun. In Sumerian mythology, Dilmun was a paradise "clean and bright." It was a land of harmony and plenty. The following passage is quoted by S. N. Kramer in *Sumerian Mythology: A Study of Spiritual and Literary Achievement* (Philadelphia: American Philosophical Society, 1944):

> In Dilmun the raven uttered no cries,
> The kite uttered not the cry of the kite,
> The lion killed not,
> The wolf snatched not the lamb...
>
> The sick-eyed says not "I am sick-eyed,"
> The sick-headed says not "I am sick-headed,"
> Its [Dilmun's] old woman says not "I am an old woman,"
> Its old man says not "I am an old man" (ibid., p. 55)

Although Eden was at first considered the primeval paradise, it eventually came to be considered the eschatological paradise as well in postbiblical Judaism and Christianity. The preceding passage seems to prefigure Isaiah's eschatological paradise (Is. 11), but Dilmun never actually acquired such connotations.

17. Manuel and Manuel, "Sketch," p. 87.

18. Ibid., pp. 97-99.

19. Levin, *Myth*, p. 33.

20. In Chapter 4, I discussed traditions associating America itself with Eden. I did so, however, primarily in terms of symbolic landscapes and the visual arts. For other aspects, see the following: R. W. B. Lewis, *The American Adam: Innocence, Tragedy and Tradition in the Nineteenth Century* (Chicago: University of Chicago Press, 1955); Charles Sanford, *The Quest for Paradise* (Urbana: Univesity of Illinois Press, 1961).

21. Norman Cohn, *The Pursuit of the Millennium: Revolutionary Messianism in Medieval and Reformation Europe and Its Bearing on Modern Totalitarian Movements*, 2d ed. (New York: Harper and Row, 1961).

22. Manuel and Manuel, "Sketch," p. 122.

23. Ibid., pp. 122-123.

24. Ibid., p. 123.

25. *The Daily Prayer Book; Ha-sidur ha-shalem*, trans. Philip Birnbaum (New York: Hebrew Publishing Company, 1949), p. 604.

26. Levin, *Myth*, p. 34.

27. William Alexander McClung, *The Architecture of Paradise* (Berkeley: University of California Press, 1983), p. 14.

28. Rev. 21: 18-21.

29. McClung, *Architecture of Paradise*, p. 41.

30. Ibid., p. 19.

31. Ibid., p. 39.

32. Ibid., p. 38.

33. Ibid., p. 19.

34. Ibid., p. 24.

35. Katharine Smith Diehl, *Hymns and Tunes: An Index* (New York: Scarecrow Press, 1966).

36. For convenience, "heaven" and "paradise" will be considered synonymous.

37. H. Richard Niebuhr, *Christ and Culture* (New York: Harper and Row, 1951).

38. I Cor. 13:12.

39. Mrs. Frank A. Breck (1855-1934), "Face to Face with Christ My Saviour," *The Hymnal, Army and Navy*, ed. Ivan L. Bennett (Washington: U.S. Government Printing Office, 1941) #527, p. 489 [The Life Beyond] [6].

40. John Newton (1725-1807), "While, With Ceaseless Course, the Sun," *New Hymn and Tune Book for Use of the African Methodist Episcopal Zion Church* (Charlotte, NC: A. M. E. Zion Book Concern, 1937), #956, p. 355 [Time and Eternity: Brevity and Uncertainty of Life] [11].

41. Isaac Watts (1674-1748), "Our God, Our Help in Ages Past," *The Hymnal: Containing Complete Orders of Worship* (1941; St. Louis: Eden; General Synod of the Evangelical and Reformed Church, 1955) #63 [God the Father: His Eternity and Majesty] [67] Reproduced with permission as published in *The Hymnal*, copyright 1985, United Church, Press, New York, NY.

42. Wilhelm Andreas Wexels (1797-1866), "Some Day, I Know, the Mist," trans. S. D. Rodholm, *American Lutheran Hymnal* (Columbus, OH: Wartburg Press, 1930), #640, p. 548 [Meditation].

43. James Lewis Milligan (1876-), "There's a Voice in the Wilderness Crying," *Hymnal Containing Complete Orders of Worship*, #94 [Our Lord Jesus Christ: His Advent] [5].

44. Charles A. Tindley (1856-1937), "Nothing Between," *The Broadman Hymnal*, ed. B. B. McKinney (Nashville: Broadman Press, 1940), #66 [The Christian: Consecration] [1].

45. Clifford Bax (1886-1962), "Turn Back, O Man," *Christian Worship and Praise*, ed. Henry Hallam Tweedy (New York: A. S. Barnes, 1939), #574 [The Nations] [2].

46. Maltbie Davenport Babcock (1858-1901), "Be Strong," *The Methodist Hymnal: Official Hymnal of the Methodist Episcopal Church, The Methodist Episcopal Church, South, The Methodist Protestant Church* (New York: Methodist Book concern, 1935), #300 [Integrity] [13].

47. William Augustus Muhlenburg (1796-1877), "O Cease, My Wand'ring Soul," *The New Christian Hymnal*, ed. H. J. Kuiper (Grand Rapids, MI: Eerdmans, 1929), #246 [The Christian Life; Refuge] [3].

48. E. Taylor Cassel (1849-1930), "I Am a Stranger Here," ibid., #197 [The Church" Means of Grace] [3].

49. Jessie H. Pounds (1861-1921) and Mrs. C. M. Alexander, "Anywhere with Jesus," ibid., #399 [Songs For Children] [5].

50. Elizabeth Cecilia Clephane (1830-1869), "Beneath the Cross of Jesus," *The New Church Hymnal*, ed. H. Augustine Smith (New York: Appleton-Century, 1937), #154 [Suffering and Death] [41].

51. Gen. 2:23-24.

52. Johan Olof Wallin (1779-1834), "To Realms of Glory I Behold," trans. C. W. Foss, *American Lutheran Hymnal*, #458, p. 391 [The Church Year: Ascension] [1].

53. John Ross Macduff (1818-1895), "Christ is Coming! Let Creation," *New Hymn and Tune Book*, #1016, p. 377 [Time and Eternity: Judgment and Retribution] [8].

54. Harrit E. Buell (1834-1910), "My Father Is Rich in Houses and Lands," *New Baptist Hymnal Containing Standard and Gospel Hymns and Responsive Readings* (Philadelphia: American Baptist Publication Society, 1926), #342, p. 271 [Gospel Hymns: Invitation] [5].

55. Charles Wesley (1707-1788), "And Let This Feeble Body Frail," *New Hymn and Tune Book*, #1032 [Death: Judgment, Heaven] [3].

56. Augustus Montague Toplady (1740-1778), "Your Harps, Ye Trembling Saints," ibid., #633, p. 232 [The Christian Life: Trial, Suffering, Submission] [2].

57. Bernard of Cluny (twelfth century), "The World Is Very Evil," trans. John M. Neale, *The Lutheran Hymnal* (St. Louis: Concordia; Evangelical Lutheran Synodical Conference of North America, 1941), #605 [The Last Things: Judgment] [12].

58. William Williams (1717-1791), "Guide Me, O Thou Great Jehovah," trans. Peter Williams, *The Hymnal of the Protestant Episcopal Church in the United States of America* (1940; New York: Church Pension Fund, 1961), #434 [General Hymns] [1].

59. Thomas Rawson Taylor (1807-1835), "I'm But a Stranger Here," *Lutheran Hymnal*, #660 [Carols and Spiritual Songs] [1].

60. Elizabeth Mills (1805-1829), "O Land of Rest, for Thee I Sigh," *New Baptist Hymnal*, #398, p. 327 [Gospel Hymns: Heaven] [5].

61. John Fawcett (1739-1817), "Lord Dismiss Us with Thy Blessing," ibid., #23, p. 18 [Adoration: Close of Service] [1].

62. Frederick William Faber (1814-1863), "Hark, Hark, My Soul!" *The Student Hymnary*, ed. Edward Dwight Eaton (New York: Barnes, 1937), #404, p. 360 [The Life Eternal] [46].

63. William Henry Burleigh (1812-1871), "Lead Us, O Father, in the Paths of Peace," *The Hymnal* (Philadelphia: Presbyterian Board of Christian Education for the Presbyterian Church in the United States of America, 1933), #262 [The Life in Christ: Aspiration] [25].

64. Isaac Watts (1674-1748), "O That the Lord Would Guide My Ways," *The Concordia Hymnal: A Hymnal for Church, School and Home* (1932; Minneapolis: Augsburg, 1946), #320, p. 288 [Christian Life: Following Christ] [11].

65. Horatius Bonar (1808-1889), "I Heard the Voice of Jesus Say," *Methodist Hymnal*, #210 [Forgiveness] [54].

66. Anon., "I Am a Poor Wayfaring Stranger," *Broadman Hymnal*, #74 [1].

67. George Rundle Prynne (1818-1903), "Jesus, Meek and Gentle," *Hymnal of The Protestant Episcopal Church*, #4 [General Hymns] [15].

68. Philip Doddridge (1702-1751) and John Logan (1748-1788), "O God of Bethel, by Whose Hand," *Christian Worship: A Manual* (Philadelphia: Judson Press, 1941), #174 [God: Love and Mercy] [34].

69. Anon., "I Am a Poor Wayfaring Stranger."

70. Henry Francis Lyte (1793-1847), "Know My Soul, Thy Full Salvation," *New Baptist Hymnal*, #215, p. 157 [The Christian Life] [1].

71. Hans Adolf Brorson (1694-1764), "I Walk in Danger All the Way," *Lutheran Hymnal*, #413 [Sanctification: New Obedience] [3].

72. David Nelson (1793-1847), "My Days Are Gliding Swiftly By," *New Baptist Hymnal*, #288, p. 220 [Heaven] [9].

73. P. A. Peter, "Who Shall Ope for Us the Portals," *American Lutheran Hymnal*, #364, p. 301 [The Church Year: Sylvester Eve] [1].

74. Arelius Clemens Prudentius (348-413), "Despair Not, O Heart, in Thy Sorrow," *Concordia Hymnal*, #418, p. 379 [Last Things: Death and Burial] [3].

75. George Gallup, "Fifty Years of Gallup Surveys on Religion," *Gallup Report* 236 (May 1985): 53-54.

76. *Religion, Spirituality and American Families: A Report from the Editors of Better Homes and Gardens Magazine* (Des Moines: Better Homes and Gardens Magazine, 1988), pp. 17-18.

77. Ray Palmer (1808-1887), "My Faith Looks up to Thee," *Christian Worship: A Hymnal*, #355 [Faith and Hope] [53].

78. Edward Arthur Dayman (1807-1890), "Sleep Thy Last Sleep," *The Hymnal and Order of Service* (1925; Rock Island, IL: Augustana Book Concern; Evangelical Lutheran Augusta Synod, 1949), #595, p. 487 [Last Things: Death and Burial; The Life Eternal] [6].

79. Berhardt Severin Ingemann (1789-1862), "Through the Night of Doubt and Sorrow," trans. Sabine Baring-Gould, *The Hymnal*, #345 [The Church and the Sacraments: Christian Fellowship] [37].

80. Sigmund Speth, *A History of Popular Music in America* (New York: Random House, 1948), p. 56.

81. Maymie R. Krythe, *Sampler of American Songs* (New York: Harper and Row, 1969), pp. 40-61.

82. John Howard Payne (1792-1852), "'Mid Pleasures and Palaces," *Concordia Hymnal*, #349, p. 315 [Home, Childhood, and Youth: Home] [4].

83. T. J. L., "'Tis a Sweet and Glorious Tho't That Comes to Me," *The Richard Allen A. M. E. Hymnal* (Philadelphia: African Methodist Episcopal Book Concern, 1946), #386, p. 332.

84. David Denham (1791-1848), "'Mid Scenes of Confusion and Creature Complaints," *New Hymn and Tune Book*, #1054, p. 392 [Time and Eternity: Heaven] [6].

85. H. Arlen and E. Y. Harburg, "Over the Rainbow." Copyright © 1938, 1939 (renewed 1966, 1967) Metro-Goldwyn-Mayer, Inc. assigned to Leo Feist, Inc. All rights of Leo Feist, Inc. assigned to EMI Catalogue Partnership. All rights controlled and administered by EMI Feist Catalog, Inc. International copyright secured. Made in USA. Used by permission. All rights reserved. Permission for printing outside the US and Canada granted by International Music Publications.

86. Albert Midlane (1825-1909), "There's a Friend for Little Children," *Hymnal, Army and Navy*, #542, p. 503 [Children's Services] [16].

87. Charles Wesley (1707-1788), "Still out of the Deepest Abyss," *New Hymn and Tune Book*, #681, p. 252 [The Christian Life: Trial, Suffering, Submission] [1].

88. Fanny J. Crosby (1820-1915), "Jesus Is Tenderly Calling Thee Home, *Hallowed Hymns New and Old for Use in Prayer and Praise Meetings, Evangelistic Services, Sunday Schools, Young People's Societies and All Other*

Departments of Church Work, ed. Allan I. Sankey, special Gipsy Smith ed. and supp. (Chicago: Biglow and Main, 1919), #147 [13].

89. John Lovell, *Black Song: The Flame and the Forge: The Story of How the Afro-American Spiritual Was Hammered Out* (New York: Macmillan, 1972), p. 367.

90. Ibid., p. 368.

91. Ibid., pp. 258; 369.

92. Ibid., pp. 367–369.

93. Philip Friedrich Hiller (1699-1760), "O Son of God, We Wait for Thee," *Concordia Hymnal*, #430, p. 390 [Last Things: Christ's Return] [4].

94. Selina Huntingdon (1707-1791), "When Thou My Righteous Judge," *New Christian Hymnal*, #96 [Jesus Christ: Second Coming] [5].

95. DeWitt C. Huntington (1830-1912), "O Think of the Home over There," *New Baptist Hymnal*, #393, pp. 322-323 [Gospel Hymns: Heaven] [4].

96. Benjamin Schmolck (1672-1737), "Heavenward Still Our Pathway Tends," trans. Frances E. Cox, *Hymnal: Containing Complete Orders of Worship*, #421 [Eternal Life] [5] Reproduced with permission as published in *The Hymnal*, copyright 1985, United Church Press, New York, NY.

97. Magnus Brostrup Landstad (1802-1880), "I Know of a Sleep in Jesus' Name," *American Lutheran Hymnal*, #299, p. 250 [The Christian Life: Death and Burial] [5].

98. Lovell, *Black Song*, p. 370.

99. Henri Abraham Cesar Malan (1787-1864), "It Is Not Death to Die," trans. George W. Bethune, *Lutheran Hymnal*, #602 [The Last Things: Death and Burial] [12].

100. James Montgomery (1771-1854), "Forever with the Lord," *New Baptist Hymnal*, #294, p. 255 [Heaven] [31].

101. DeWitt C. Huntington (1830-1912), "O Think of the Home Over There."

102. M. Falk Gjersten (1947-1913), "I Know a Way Besieged and Thronging," trans. Oscar R. Overby, *Concordia Hymnal*, #306, p. 275 [Christian Life: Following Christ] [1] Reprinted from *The Concordia Hymnal*, copyright © 1932 Augsburg Publishing House. Used by permission of Augsburg Fortress.

103. Bernard of Cluny (twelfth century), "For Thee, O Dear, Dear Country," trans. John M. Neale, *Lutheran Hymnal*, #614 [Life Everlasting] [18].

104. Peter Abelard (1079-1142), "O What Their Joy and Their Glory Must Be," trans. John M. Neale, *Hymnal of the Protestant Episcopal Church*, #589 [General Hymns] [14].

105. Henry Alford (1810-1871), "Forward! Be Our Watchword," *New Baptist Hymnal*, #220, pp. 162-163 [The Christian Life] [25].

106. Mary Ann Kidder (1820-1905), "We Shall Sleep, but Not Forever," *Hymnal and Order of Service*, #604, p. 495 [Last Things: Death and Burial] [2].

107. F. B. P. (ca sixteenth century), "O Mother Dear, Jerusalem," *New Baptist Hymnal*, #277, p. 210 [Heaven] [18].

108. Gustav Friedrich Ludwig Knak (1806-1878), "Let Me Go, Let Me Go," trans. H. R. Krauth, *American Lutheran Hymnal*, #642, p. 550 [Meditation] [1].

109. Lionel B. C. L. Muirhead (1845-1925), "The Church of God a Kingdom Is," *Hymnal of the Protestant Episcopal church*, #387 [General Hymns] [5].

110. William Orcott Cushing (1823-1902), "Beautiful Valley of Eden," *New Baptist Hymnal*, #312, p. 241 [Occasional: Death] [4].

111. John R. Clements, "Though Burdens Heavy We Here Must Bear," *Hallowed Hymns*, #10.

112. Sarah Josselyn Wilson (1893-), "The Land We Love Is Calling," *New Hymnal for American Youth*, ed. H. Augustine Smith (New York: Appleton-Century, 1935), #276, p. 231 [Fatherland] [5].

113. Fanny J. Crosby (1820-1915), "My Saviour First of All," *Hallowed Hymns*, #121 [4].

114. John 1:1-2.

115. John 1:14.

116. John 20:17.

117. Charles Wesley (1707-1788), "Hark! A Voice Divides the Sky," *New Hymn and Tune Book*, #1001, p. 370 [Time and Eternity: Death and Resurrection] [2].

118. John Samuel Bewley Monsell (1811-1875), "O'er the Distant Mountains Breaking," *Lutheran Hymnal*, #606 [The Last Things: Judgement, Advent] [9].

119. Johnann Steuerlein (1546-1613), "The Old Year Now Hath Passed

Away," trans. Catherine Winkworth, *Lutheran Hymnal*, #125 [New Year] [5].

120. John Byrom (1690-1763), "Christians Awake, Salute the Happy Morn," *Hymnal of the Protestant Episcopal Church*, #16 [Christmas] [22].

121. Robert Seagrave (1693-1757), "Rise, My Soul, and Stretch Thy Wings," *Christian Worship: A Hymnal*, #573 [The Life Eternal] [27].

122. Hugh R. Haweis (1838-1901), "The Homeland! O the Homeland," *Hallowed Hymns*, #165 [11].

123. Benjamin Schmolck (1672-1737), "Heavenward Still Our Pathway Tends," trans. Frances E. Cox, *Hymnal: Containing Complete Orders of Worship*, #421 [Eternal Life] [5]. Used by permission (United Church Press).

124. Benjamin Schmolck (1672-1737) and Hans Adolf Brorson (1694-1764), "Why Art Thou Cast Down, My Soul?" trans. Carl Doving, *Concordia Hymnal*, #294, p. 263 [Christian Life: Trust and Confidence] [2].

125. Charles Wesley (1707-1788), "O Glorious Hope of Perfect Love!" *New Hymn and Tune Book*, #542, p. 199 [The Christian: Sanctification and Growth] [1].

126. Abraham Joshua Heschel, *The Earth Is the Lord's and The Sabbath* (New York: Harper and Row, 1966).

127. Frederick William Faber (1814-1863), "O Paradise! O Paradise! Who Would Not Win Thy Rest?" *Christian Worship and Praise*, #659 [Eternal Life] [1].

128. Benjamin Schmolck (1672-1737), "Light of Light, Enlighten Me," trans. Catherine Winkworth, *Hymnal*, #21 [Times of Worship: The Lord's Day] [20].

129. William Hiley Bathurst (1796-1877), "Oh, for a Faith That Will Not Shrink," *Lutheran Hymnal*, #396 [Consecration: Sanctification] [33].

130. Gen. 1:9.

131. Northrop Frye refers to these as "apocalyptic" and "demonic" respectively. I find the former unhelpful because it is heavily associated with a particular literary genre and a particular theological tradition. By "divine," I refer to anything or anyone associated with God; by "satanic," I refer to anything or anyone associated with Satan.

132. Green, as I have indicated, is generally associated with holiness. But there are exceptions. A green person, for instance, would carry very different connotations. The Witch's green complexion seems unnatural and distorted. This emphasizes her role as a satanic counterpart to the divine Glinda. In modern folklore, too, alien visitors up to no good are often "little green men."

133. Eschatological events are normally said to include the final battle between Christ and the Antichrist, the last judgment, resurrection of the dead, and Christ's rule over a world beyond the ravages of time (not necessarily in that order). Also included, according to some traditions, is the conversion of the Jews. Because Paul said that "a hardening has come upon part of Israel, until the full number of Gentiles come in, and so all of Israel will be saved" (Rom. 11:25), such a belief is hardly surprising. There may be an interesting parallel to this in *The Wizard* (albeit one that would be disturbing to Jews). After the Witch is killed, her murderous hordes are "converted." They hail Dorothy for having liberated them from tyranny.

134. Northrop Frye, *The Great Code: The Bible and Literature* (Toronto: Academic Press, 1982), pp. 80-81.

135. Ibid., p. 139.

136. Gen. Rab. 25:3. Quoted in Ginzberg, *Legends of the Jews*, p. 30.

137. Frye, *Great Code*, p. 129.

138. In the *felix culpa* tradition, both the serpent in Eden and Judas in Gethsemane are ambiguous in status. Both represent betrayal. Nevertheless, the former was "necesssary" because the human race would not otherwise have needed redemption, while the latter was "necessary" because Christ would not otherwise have been crucified and resurrected to bring about the joy of redemption.

139. By "church history," I mean not so much the sequence of events in the development of an institution but the lived experience of a community of saints and sinners in covenant with God through Christ.

140. Frye, *Great Code*, p. 72.

141. Ibid., p. 171; see also pp. 76; 129; 137; 145; 159.

142. Marty, *Righteous Empire*, p. 48.

143. Ibid., p. 46.

144. Quoted in ibid., p. 46.

145. Ibid., p. 23.

146. Laurel Arthur Burton believes that some are outstanding in their power to evoke religious feelings, observing that *"Star Wars* took the country by storm and renewed a religious fervor not seen since *The Wizard of Oz"* (Laurel Arthur Burton, "Close Encounters of a Religious Kind," *Journal of Popular Culture* 17, no. 3 (1983) p. 143).
Following Robert Jewett and John Lawrence, moreover, Burton argues that the return to Eden has been incorporated into the structure of the

American "monomyth." The "monomyth" is represented by the western and other genres using the same formula: heroes enter a supernatural realm, triumph over evil, return to the world of everyday life, and grant boons to grateful mortals. Heroes who bring salvation are not quite divine figures but (having special power, wisdom, control, and courage) they are more than mere mortals; if not divine beings, they are nevertheless messianic figures (deliverers). "Frequently," writes Burton, "it is by violence, always justified, that the Messiah dispatches the evil one and restores the community to its Eden" (ibid., p. 142). But the parallel between this American "monomyth" and traditional religious myths presents two problems if the former is represented by *The Wizard*.

In the first place, *The Wizard* has a heroine who comes from within the community and not from beyond it. In this sense, *The Wizard* is less traditional than the "horse operas" and "space operas." The biblical tradition, after all, makes it quite clear that deliverance is ultimately a gift of divine grace (even though that may involve the active participation of recipients). And Burton may oversimplify the relation between popular movies and traditional religion with reference to the origin of evil. "The point," he writes, "is that evil is external to the community just as many understand the evil of Eden as external" (ibid., p. 142). But on what grounds can it be said that the evil of Eden is external? The origin of evil in the biblical story is either in Adam and Eve or in the serpent: all existed together within Eden. In *The Wizard*, the source of evil is more ambiguous. The evidence from this movie can be interpreted in two ways. If we argue that Miss Gulch comes from Kansas (as distinct from Oz), then the source of evil is within the community; this would place *The Wizard* close to religious tradition. But if we argue that Miss Gulch comes from another farm (as distinct from Dorothy's) or from town, then the source of evil is beyond the community; this would place *The Wizard* further from religious tradition. In either case, I argue, the movie ends in a return to paradise.

6. Conclusion

1. Richard Anderson, *Art in Primitive Societies* (Englewood Cliffs, NJ: Prentice-Hall, 1979).

2. Gregor Goethals, *The TV Ritual: Worship at the Video Altar* (Boston: Beacon Press, 1981).

3. The term "icon" refers generally to visual images. Nevertheless, as Charles Peirce has shown *(Collected Papers of Charles Sanders Peirce*, ed. Charles Hartshorne and Paul Weiss [Cambridge, MA: Harvard University Press, 1933], vol. 3, p. 211), it can be used with much more precision as one symbolic device among many. Redfield uses the term in cross-cultural per-

spective. For him, the artifacts of primal societies are iconic not only because they are visual images but, more specifically, because they refer beyond themselves to a world of meaning shared by the entire community. Very often, they are sacred images conveying the presence of sacred beings or the experience of cosmic order. They reveal the "garden" behind the "window." They are really doing what the images in churches have always done. It is in this sense that Goethals refers to the images of television as icons; they may not refer to a sacred order but they do refer to a cultural order.

4. For John Wiley Nelson, popular culture is not only like religion, it *is* religion. In *Your God Is Alive and Well and Appearing in Popular Culture*, (Philadelphia: Westminster, 1976), he explains that popular culture gives symbolic, even mythic expression to the core beliefs of American society. The American popular religion, in short, is popular culture. Like Geertz, Nelson assumes that any symbol system providing a sense of order and meaning qualifies as religion. Although popular culture entertains, it does a great deal more. "Simultaneously," he writes, "the shared values we hold as Americans are being reaffirmed, dramatically—in the same way that the rituals of worship services undergird and reaffirm religious beliefs" (ibid., p. 16). He returns to this theme over and over again. For Nelson, popular culture supports commonly held beliefs and patterns of behavior. In this, it is unlike contemporary art, which supports an elite community and is generally out of touch with the ideas and feelings of ordinary people. It could be argued here that religion does the opposite. In some forms of contemporary Protestantism, for example, it is maintained that the chief function of religion is to challenge the culture rather than support it. Nevertheless, there is some truth in what Nelson says. "Institutional religions...do not hold worship services to give the believer a chance to challenge the beliefs and values of the religion. On the contrary, such services are mortar to the bricks of faith. In the worship ritual, all that is affirmed in the religion is integrated in a dramatic style, explicitly designed to more fully establish the foundation of life-meaning advocated by the religion. The same case can be made for popular culture in America. The success of any unit of popular culture is directly proportionate to its ability to perform satisfactorily the religious function of affirming and supporting beliefs already held in the dominant American cultural belief system. Popular culture is to what most Americans believe as worship services are to what the members of institutional religions believe. That, in a nutshell, is our thesis" (ibid., p. 16).

In fact, he argues that it competes directly with Christianity for the soul of America. The only difference is that the churches are explicitly religious, and popular culture is implicitly religious. The difficulty for Christians (such as Nelson himself) who are seeking to propagate the Gospel is not that Americans are secular (that is, either indifferent or hostile to religion), but that they already have a religion that provides satisfying answers to their problems and a symbol system that gives it expression in public life.

Considering the subject under discussion here, though, Nelson's link between religion and popular culture should be helpful (even though he himself is hostile to this rival of Christianity). After all, he would surely have no difficulty with the idea of *The Wizard* as a modern American myth. But his theory is very problematic. He argues that the role of popular culture is always to affirm and propagate the established social and cultural order. But if popular culture is a religion, then the same must be true of more traditional religions. In fact, he does justice to neither religion nor popular culture. Although it is true that both can and do function in this way, it is also true that both can and do function in other ways too. Some popular singers affirm the status quo, for example, but this could hardly be said of Woodie Guthrie, Joan Baez, or Bruce Springsteen. Similarly, some members of the clergy affirm the values of the dominant society, but this could hardly be said of William Sloan Coffin, Martin Luther King, or Daniel Berrigan. Moreover, Nelson's definition of religion is just as vague as that of Geertz. Almost anything produced by popular culture can be considered religious. Consequently, words like "religious" and "secular" can have no meaning.

5. In discussing the avant-garde, I have already noted that artists have marginalized themselves; Goethals says much the same thing. Whatever the merits or demerits of television images, one thing is clear: they are far more accessible than those of contemporary art. By and large, artists have not chosen (in recent times) to transmit public images. Although they continue to produce visual images, as such, they no longer provide public ones. That is, the images they produce are addressed to and understood or appreciated by a small segment of the population. This development did not take place overnight. Goethals refers specifically to the rise of abstract (aniconic) art since the 1940s, the very period when television was becoming America's mass medium par excellence. Consequently, the gulf between what could be called popular art and elite art was deepened. On the one hand, there was nonobjective (nonrepresentational) art that consisted of forms, shapes, and colors (as in abstract expressionism, for example, or minimalism); on the other hand, there were the ubiquitous, incessant, and lifelike images of television.

Recognizable images have provided television viewers with concrete references to everyday experience; abstract works provided no such common references. In view of this, people began asking a question that often seemed irrelevant to the artists themselves: what does it mean? In reviews of art shows, the critics have tried to answer this question in several ways. Some explain that art is its own metaphor, that traditional metaphors (such as the family, nature, or even technology) are too limiting. Others repeat the classic dictum: art for art's sake. The fact remains, however, that the critics are necessary as intermediaries between the artists and the public because the former no longer use a lingua franca known by the latter. Ordinary people generally accept an eroded confidence in their ability to understand or appreciate art but still consider it important. According to Goethals, for example, trips to the museum on Sundays take on overtones of pilgrimages to sacred shrines (often built in the form of temples).

Television appropriated the old metaphors that nonobjective art had discarded. Whatever the value of art to the artists themselves, or to the group with intellectual and financial access, its cultural value—its ability to disseminate commonly shared ideas about the way things are—is now severely limited. No matter how trivial the television images may appear on the surface (judged from an aesthetic point of view), they "become for many Americans a means of locating themselves in an ordered world. Where traditional institutions of high art do not provide meaningful public symbols, television images rush in to fill the void" (Goethals, *TV Ritual*, p. 4).

But Goethals overstates his case. He might have acknowledged that not all societies have tried to produce naturalistic or lifelike images. The artifacts of many or even most societies are highly stylized and conventionalized (abstracted) versions of plants, animals, people, or other elements of the natural order. Their value depends on the fact that everyone knows what these symbols represent; everyone can immediately recognize them, relate them to myths and appropriate them through public rituals. It is this, not merely representational art as such, that is lacking in contemporary art.

6. Anglican Church of Canada, *The Book of Common Prayer* (Toronto: Macmillan, 1959), p. 550.

7. Goethals may have oversimplified the link between Protestantism and the rise of television. It is true that Protestantism has generally discouraged ritual and visual representation; this does not, however, make Protestantism unique. Indeed, at least one other major aniconic tradition should be noted in this context. In Islam, too, a tradition of secular art developed to meet the need for visual images banned by theology. Illuminated manuscripts, for example, provided illustrations for books of Arabic and Persian folklore (not to mention treatises on medicine, science, and geography). In a way, medieval Islam represents a reverse of the situation Goethals describes: the elite strata had access to secular art that was representational (the manuscripts), while the great masses had access only to religious art that was abstract (public architecture). The fact is, however, that even the abstract forms that cover Islamic buildings have a meaning accessible to all the faithful. These forms do not express the private thoughts and feelings of individual artists; on the contrary, they are used consistently as terms in a symbolic language consciously or unconsciously understood by everyone (although they may also refer to esoteric symbol systems). Even to a non-Muslim, the repetition of geometric forms suggests cosmic order and infinity. Islamic art is in no way idiosyncratic; it perfectly expresses the publicly acknowledged and commonly shared worldview of society.

8. Goethals, *TV Ritual*, p. 143.

9. Ibid., p. 142.

10. Ibid., pp. 143-144.

11. Johan Huizinga, *Homo Ludens: A Study of the Play Element in Culture* (1950; Boston: Beacon Press, 1955).

12. The distinction between myth and other traditional narrative genres (such as the folktale, fable, legend, or fairy tale) remains problematic. Not only do scholars disagree on how to classify traditional stories by content, they also disagree on how these genres originated. Nevertheless, the word "myth" is not meaningless. Most scholars agree that whatever else myths may be, they are stories about supernatural beings (deities). Stories about super-human beings (such as heroes with special powers) are sometimes included in the category of myth, for instance, but stories about the deities are never excluded. Because *The Wizard* is not about the latter, a case must be made for calling it a myth. But its resemblance to myth is strong enough to call for an explanation.

13. I have chosen not to use the structuralist theory of myth associated with Claude Lévi-Strauss. Lévi-Strauss himself analyzed only the cultural productions of nonliterate societies. Nevertheless, followers such as Edmund Leach have turned their attention to the cultural productions of literate societies. It would not be difficult to show through structural analysis that *The Wizard* is indeed a myth. But doing so would bypass the domain of religion and its relation to secularity (which is, after all, the underlying concern of this book). For Lévi-Strauss, myth had little or nothing to do with religion. He was interested in myth primarily as a way of understanding universal structures of the human mind. In fact, it was more akin to science than anything else. "This science of the concrete," he wrote with reference to myth, "was necessarily restricted by its essence to results other than those destined to be achieved by the exact natural sciences but it was no less scientific and its results no less genuine" *(The Savage Mind* [Chicago: University of Chicago Press, 1966], p. 16). Elsewhere, he wrote that "the kind of logic which is used by mythical thought is as rigorous as that of modern science and...the difference lies not in the quality of the intellectual process but in the nature of the things to which it is applied" ("The Structural Study of Myth," *Journal of American Folklore* [1968]: 444). From this point of view, the story itself is irrelevant. To uncover the paradigmatic structures, syntagmatic ones may be ignored. Whether the narrative includes gods and goddesses or human heroes and animal ancestors—or gangsters and cops—is of no importance. Actually, I have done a structural analysis of *The Wizard* and intend to see it published. This method reveals a great deal about American society. More specifically, it identifies some forms of ambivalence that were characteristic of American society long before 1939 and that remain so to this day: country versus city (nature versus culture) and America versus Europe (the familiar versus the alien). These are

expressed symbolically through the use of formal (cinematic) properties as bipolar oppositions (such as red versus green, European versus American music and mise-en-scène, subhuman versus superhuman characters, polychromatic versus monochromatic film and so forth). But structural analysis reveals little or nothing about American religiosity. Since that is the specific subject under discussion here, other ways of studying myth are more useful.

14. Eliade, *Myth and Reality*, trans, Willard R. Trask (New York: Harper and Row, 1963), p. 201.

15. Ibid., pp. 200–201.

16. Ibid., p. 201.

17. Ibid., pp. 201–202.

18. Eliade, *The Quest: History and Meaning in Religion* (Chicago: University of Chicago Press, 1969), p. 126. See also Eliade's "Survivals and Camouflages of Myths" in his *Symbolism, the Sacred, and the Arts*, ed. Diane Apostolos-Cappadona (New York: Crossroad, 1985), pp. 32-52.

19. There are a few exceptions. In "Film as Hierophany" (*Religion in Film*, ed. John R. May and Michael Bird [Knoxville: University of Tennessee Press, 1982], pp. 3–22), Michael Bird discusses film and the sacred. Because art (including film) makes visible what would otherwise be invisible, he avers, it is like a hierophany as described by Mircea Eliade; just as the sacred is always manifest through the profane, the transcendent is always known through the mundane. Consequently, art reveals the truly Real hidden by the superficially real. As he puts it, film cannot show the face of God but it can show people seeking the face of God. His argument is heavily based on Paul Tillich's notion of "theology from below" and his existentialist outlook (since the motivation for seeking the transcendent in the first place is the threat of nonbeing caused by some encounter with finitude or meaninglessness). From this, it follows that the religious film is one that focuses attention on the profane (ordinary) level of reality in order to reveal the sacred (profound) level hidden within it. In other words, a film's style (realism) and not its content or structure makes it religious. Given the purpose of this book, the problem with Bird's theory is its provincialism: religion is defined in a way that is peculiar to some modern forms of Protestantism; for him, religion is a form of existentialism. For him, as for Tillich himself, religion is synonymous with "ultimate concerns." This reduces religion to the psychological experiences of individuals or even of communities. It says nothing of religion as a cultural system, as a tradition of public symbols (myths and rituals). Similarly, his theory is provincial in defining it as the attempt to transcend (point beyond or challenge) culture; one function of art in other societies is, on the contrary, to propagate culture.

The same problem is found in "Visual Story and the Religious Interpretation of Film" by John R. May (*Religion in Film*, pp. 23–43), although his work offers richer possibilities for the analysis of popular movies such as *The Wizard*. He begins by discussing three approaches to the study of religion and film; these are derived from the work of Paul Tillich. A "heteronomous" approach evaluates film according to the standards of religious faith (that is, standards extrinsic to the film itself). Consequently, a film may be called religious merely because its director had a certain religious background or wanted to communicate a certain religious idea; this may or may not be evident in the film itself. Both Tillich and May reject this approach. Tillich, of course, favors a "theonomous" approach. Neither film nor religion is supreme since God is the source of both. But, since God is defined as "ultimate concern," almost any human quest for meaning can be called religious. May himself prefers an "autonomous" approach to film and religion. For him, film must be evaluated on its own terms. If a film is religious, it is because of something intrinsically cinematic. Some movies, for example, are open to a religious worldview. This openness is to be discerned from direct examination of their formal structures. These pose the visual and aural analogues of religious questions. And these questions, according to May, are the ones listed by Huston Smith as universal religious questions: (1) The question about God: are we alone in an indifferent cosmos, alienated by a hostile one, or nurtured in a friendly one? (2) The question about society or evil: are we isolated from each other or are we interdependent? (3) The question about salvation: is liberation attained through knowledge or through compassion?

In short, a religious movie is one that raises these questions through cinematic narrative. As visual stories, movies may be the cinematic equivalents of myth or parable. Following John Dominic Crossan, May regards these as the two basic paradigms for all religious stories. For Crossan, myths are stories that establish and propagate a worldview; parables are those that challenge and subvert one. Applying this, along with Herbert Richardson's work on myths of transcendence, to Smith's three religious questions, May comes up with a definition of the religious film. It may be either a myth or a parable. If the former, it will be about reconciliation in terms of (1) the cosmos (separation and return), (2) society or evil (division and unity), or (3) salvation (conflict and vindication). If the last, it will be about unresolved tension in terms of (1) the cosmos (risk as opposed to security), (2) society or evil (weakness as opposed to strength), or (3) salvation (death as opposed to life).

Although May's theory might be useful here in one way—*The Wizard* would be classified as a myth (that is, a religious movie)—it is not so useful in other ways. Religion, for example, is defined in strictly cognitive terms. If Bird's theory reduces religion to experience, this one reduces it to philosophy or ethics. If Bird overemphasizes the style of a movie, May overemphasizes its content. The problem is not that May and Bird are incorrect about art and religion but that they are only partially correct. Moreover, this is so primarily in the context of contemporary Christianity in the West. Neither even attempts to examine either art or religion on a cross-cultural basis. What they write is interesting from the perspective of theology (a normative discipline) but not from the perspective of comparative religion or the history of religions (descriptive disciplines).

20. Roland Barthes, *Mythologies*, trans. Annette Lavers (London: J. Cape, 1972).

21. M. Darrol Bryant, "Cinema, Religion, and Popular Culture," *Religion in Film*, p. 103.

22. Ibid., p. 102.

23. Ibid., p. 104.

24. Ibid., p. 105.

25. Ibid., p. 106.

26. Ibid., pp. 109-110.

27. Ibid., p. 113.

28. Ibid., p. 106.

29. Lee Drummond, "Movies and Myth: Theoretical Skirmishes," *American Journal of Semiotics* 3, no. 2 (1984): 4-5.

30. Ibid., pp. 4-5.

31. Ibid., pp. 15-16.

32. Ibid., p. 6.

33. Drummond, "The Story of Bond," *Symbolizing America*, ed. Hervé Varenne (Lincoln: University of Nebraska Press, 1986).

34. Conrad Phillip Kottack, "Social-Science Fiction," *Psychology Today* (February 1978), pp. 12 ff.

35. Margaret Bourke-White and Archibald MacLeish, "Franklin Roosevelt's Wild West," *Life* (23 November 1936), pp. 9-12.

36. Peter G. Filene, *Americans and the Soviet Experiment, 1917-1933* (Cambridge, MA: Harvard University Press, 1967).

37. A massive protest was generated in 1911 when Russian-American Jews were denied visas to visit their relations in Russia; this led to abrogation of an 1832 commercial treaty with Russia. On the other hand, as Filene points out, many Americans admired Russian ballet, music, and literature.

They had a sentimental image of the downtrodden, quasi-mystical, freedom-loving Russian peasant.

38. Edwin Reischauer, Foreword, *Russia: The Roots of Confrontation*, by Robert V. Daniels (Cambridge, MA: Harvard University Press, 1985), p. vi.

39. Robert V. Daniels, in ibid., p. 2.

40. The Bolsheviks, observes Daniels, were depicted as monsters. Bolshevism was identified with chaos (anarchy) as well as despotism. The new regime was linked to wholesale murder and the destruction of civilization itself. This was true especially after similar (but unsuccessful) revolutions in Germany and Hungary after the First World War. Then came the Red Scare at home. Organized labor initiated strikes out of frustration at being excluded from postwar prosperity. This was interpreted as a conspiracy against the United States by traitors at home who were being directed by foreign agents. The hysteria finally subsided when the public learned how few labor leaders were actually involved in socialist politics. But the damage had been done. American attitudes hardened into suspicion and hatred.

41. In 1918, according to Daniels, rumors spread about the "nationalization of women." According to hearsay, women were required to register with a "bureau of free love" at the age of eighteen; they would then be assigned husbands without giving their consent, or they would take husbands without requiring consent. In short, atheism was associated with destruction of the family and, thus, of civilization itself.

42. Filene, *Soviet Experiment*, p. 214.

43. Robert Fyne, "From Hollywood to Moscow," *Literature/Film Quarterly* 13, no. 3 (1985): 196.

44. Thomas R. Maddux, "Red Fascism, Brown Bolshevism: The American Image of Totalitarianism in the 1930s," *The Historian* 49 (1977): 85-103.

45. Alexis de Tocqueville, *Democracy in America*, trans. Henry Reeve and Francis Bowen, ed. Phillips Bradley, 2 vols. (1835-1840; New York: Vintage Books, 1945), vol. 1, pp. 314-318; vol. 2, pp. 152-153.

46. George Gallup, "Fifty Years of Gallup Surveys on Religion," *Gallup Report* 236 (1985): 5.

47. By the late 1930s, when Gallup surveys were being used to measure religiosity, seven Americans in ten were church members, and four in ten went to church in a typical week. In 1938, Gallup reported that the Bible was the most popular item on American bookshelves (slightly ahead of *Gone with the Wind*) although this does not, of course, indicate how often, if ever, it was actually read. A year later, Americans were asked if their parents

went to church more often, or less often, than they themselves did; although 50 percent said more often, 18 percent said less often, and 32 percent reported no difference. In short, religion was a common feature of American life in all sectors of the population; most people had some connection with religious life. By and large, Americans could not have been described as a secular people.

A few years later, in 1947, Americans were asked about their personal religious convictions; nine in ten reported that they believed in God. This was the highest reported for any nation polled; in France, for instance, only two in three said they believed in God. Similarly, seven Americans in ten reported that they believed in an afterlife; only five in ten did so in Britain and Sweden. But another survey done that same year indicated that the quality of religiosity left much to be desired from the perspective of religious leaders; even though almost all Americans reported belief in God, it was by no means clear that this represented belief in the personal God of the Bible.

After the war, a period of growth sent affluent Americans to the suburbs where they built churches as well as homes and schools. In fact, they attended worship more often than ever before. Moreover, the sale of religious books increased as did the popularity of religious persons such as Billy Graham, Norman Vincent Peale, and Bishop Fulton J. Sheen. This period is not considered a religious revival, or "awakening," however, due to the lack of depth involved. According to a survey of 1950, only half of those polled could name even one of the gospels; four years later, only a third knew that Jesus had given the Sermon on the Mount.

Massive social changes were reflected in American attitudes toward religion during the 1960s. The boom was over. In spite of attempts by the clergy to make religion "relevant" (by participating in movements to promote social justice, modernizing theology, and rewriting liturgies), church attendance and membership declined dramatically. In 1957, only 14 percent of Americans believed that religion was losing its influence on society; this figure rose to 31 percent in 1962 and 72 percent in 1969. It is important to note, according to Gallup, that the drift away from the churches and traditional religion was not a universal phenomenon; it was prevalent mainly among the young, especially those in the academic environment. To be sure, some theologians declared that God was dead. But for most Americans, God was still very much alive. They continued to report strong belief in God that gave them comfort and support. In fact, most continued to believe in a personal God who could be reached through prayer rather than a vague, impersonal force.

Due to the disillusionment and cynicism characteristic of the 1970s (which is to say, after the Vietnam War and the Watergate scandals), the optimism and activism characteristic of the previous decade declined. Although surveys showed that Americans had not lost faith in the nation's future, they also showed that Americans had lost faith in institutions of all kinds—including the (liberal) churches. Among Protestant and Catholic clergy under forty, according to a survey of 1971, four in ten reported that they had seriously considered leaving religious life; among rabbis, the figure was six in ten. They complained of many things, including the inability to communicate with their parishioners, confusion over their roles, too many rules and regulations, and even the irrelevance of religion. "Much survey evidence from the early 1970s could be cited to show that religion had fallen on difficult days, but it is important to note that discontent among the clergy and laity at the time stemmed not from a weakening of religious convictions, but from a reluctance to accept certain aspects of institutionalized religion" (ibid., p. 9). This was particularly true in the Roman Catholic Church: a survey of 1971 revealed that six Catholics in ten who were over forty, and seven in ten who were under forty, expressed opposition to the Church's teaching on birth control. The drop in church attendance between the late 1950s and early 1970s was traced almost entirely to falling attendance among Roman Catholics.

Nevertheless, the population as a whole continued to affirm traditional aspects of religiosity. In the United States, unlike Europe, no significant change in the level of American religiosity has occurred since scientific studies began in the 1930s. "And while the mood of Americans during the 1970s was one of disillusionment revealing a lack of confidence in key American institutions, confidence in the church or organized religion was higher than in seven other key institutions tested" (ibid., p. 9). In fact, the 1970s witnessed what really could be called a religious revival. Long quiescent, the Evangelicals became a prominent feature of public life. According to one Gallup poll in 1976, 34 percent of Americans said that they had been "born again" (that is, reached a turning point in their lives and committed themselves to Jesus Christ). This meant that approximately 50 million Americans over the age of eighteen were Evangelicals. Even when the definition of "born again" was narrowed to include only those who also believed in biblical inerrancy and had encouraged others to accept Jesus as their personal savior, this meant that one-fifth of the adult population claimed to be intensely religious. At the same time, many Americans turned to less familiar manifestations of the inner, or spiritual, life. Approximately 6 million were involved in transcendental meditation, 5 million in yoga, 3 million in the charismatic movement, 3 million in mysticism, and 2 million in Eastern religions.

By 1976, the religious "slump" was over. Church attendance rose slightly after fifteen years of decline. All the same, church affiliation (membership and attendance) is inadequate as a measure of religiosity. This was the finding of a major study conducted for the Religious Coalition to Study the Backgrounds, Values and Interests of Unchurched Americans by the Gallup Organization and Princeton University. It was found that many Americans separated believing from belonging. Most of the unchurched reported that they continued to be devoutly religious in one way or another; at least half of them said that they could imagine circumstances under which they would return to active participation in a worshiping community. During this period, 56 percent of Americans reported that their religious beliefs were very important to them. This contrasts sharply with the 27 percent of Europeans who said so. "The only major nation in which the importance of religion exceeded the United States," notes Gallup, "was India. In India, 81 percent said their religious beliefs were very important to them" (ibid., pp. 9-10).

Given the questioning of religious authority in the 1970s, it was possible to predict a postreligious era in the near future. So far, no evidence suggests that such a prediction has come true. According to a study of 1985, 95 percent of Americans believe in God or a Universal Spirit; 75 percent believe in Jesus as God; 90 percent pray; and 56 percent say that religion is an important part of their lives. Moreover, 90 percent state a denominational preference; 68 percent belong to a church or synagogue; 65 percent have confidence in organized religion; and 40 percent participate in public worship during a typical week. Religion also has a high profile in public life. During the 1980 presidential race, all three of the major candidates (Ronald Reagan, Jimmy Carter, and John Anderson) claimed to have been "born again." The Moral Majority (a political movement founded by the Rev. Jerry Falwell to serve the needs of Protestant fundamentalists) tried to defeat candidates who disagreed on specific issues; its 4 million members actively campaigned against candidates who took what they considered unacceptable stands on issues such as prayer in the public schools or abortion.

In 1984, after "mainline" churches expressed concern that the television evangelists were drawing money and members away from local congregations, the Gallup Organization conducted a survey with the Annenberg School of Communication and found that the real competition to organized religion came not from religious television (that is, from the "televangelists") but from secular television (ibid., p. 12). This suggests that secular television meets at least some of the needs not being met by organized religion. Whatever else the churches do, observes Andrew Greeley ("When Religion Cast off Wonder, Hollywood Seized It," *New York Times* [27 November 1977], section 2, p. 1), they do not generally provide the imaginative environment in which fantasy or myth can flourish; that, he says, is provided by Hollywood. Those churches that are growing, the resurgent conservative and fundamentalist churches, prefer cognitive forms of expression such as doctrine to imaginative ones such as myth. This is extremely important in connection with what has been said about *The Wizard* as a "secular myth." Apparently, religion and myth have parted company.

Equilibrium seems to be returning to the Roman Catholic Church after years of upheaval. The proportion of Americans who describe themselves as Roman Catholics is higher now (at 20 percent in 1984) than at any time since the 1940s. Although some of these may be nominal Catholics, many others are traditional Catholics recently arrived from Latin America. By now, many Catholics consider it possible to disagree with the Church's unpopular teachings and even to disobey some of its rules (especially on birth control or abortion) and still be good Catholics. Attendance at mass is still much lower than it was before Vatican II but has remained steady for several years. "In examining the trends of the last half century, it should be borne in mind that most of the changes have been relatively small and have been most pronounced among young adults... [consequently] the most appropriate word to describe the religious character of the nation as a whole is...'stability.' Basic religious beliefs today differ little from the levels recorded fifty years ago" (Gallup, "Fifty Years," p. 5).

But not all indicators are so stable. Even though church attendance has remained stable for the churches in general, it has changed for certain traditions in particular. As already noted, the Roman Caholic Church has experienced a dramatic decline in attendance at mass. Some Protestant churches have experienced similar losses, while others have gained. Between 1973 and 1983, Evangelical (or conservative) churches showed a net gain in members: 71 percent for the (Pentecostal) Assemblies of God; 40 percent for the (Mormon) Church of Jesus Christ of Latter Day Saints; 34 percent for the Seventh Day Adventists; 22 percent for the Church of the Nazarene; and 15 percent for the Southern Baptist Convention. By contrast, mainline (or liberal) churches showed a net loss during the same period: 15 percent for the Presbyterian Church (USA); 13 percent for the Christian Church (Disciples of Christ); 8 percent for the United Methodist Church; 4 percent for the (Anglican) Protestant Episcopal Church; and 3 percent for the Lutheran Church in America. Moreover, one surprising trend has been noted: more students have been attending religious services on college campuses, reporting that religion is an important part of their lives and taking courses on religion.

48. Kenneth A. Briggs, "America's Return to Prayer," *New York Times Magazine* (18 November 1984), p. 107.

49. Ibid., p. 117.

50. David G. Leitch, "The Myth of Religious Neutrality by Separation in Education," *Virginia Law Review* 71 (1985): 127-172.

51. Leitch turns his attention specifically to church-state relations and the public schools. In recent years, debate over this particular issue has intensified because of the growing realization that education is inherently "religious." In the first place, it always involves the propagation of a worldview that, in turn, shapes beliefs. Then, too, nontraditional, even nontheistic, worldviews such as "secular humanism" are now competing directly with traditional forms of Judaism and Christianity in the pedagogical marketplace of ideas. Leitch traces the move away from interpreting the First Amendment in terms of absolute separation. This has been caused by recognition of the

fact that neither government nor religion can be defined in ways that make an absolute separation practical or even desirable. The reach of government, for example, has been extended into areas (such as public funding of private schools) once assumed to be matters of private control. Moreover, the definition of religion has been expanded from the theistic (or deistic) notions prevalent in the eighteenth century. It is becoming increasingly obvious that secular ideologies and worldviews are often functional equivalents of traditional forms of religion; allowing them—but not traditional forms of religion— to be represented in the classroom discriminates in favor of the former and against the latter (thus violating the "establishment clause"). A further complication, adds Leitch, is that the word "religion" appears only once in the First Amendment and refers to both the "establishment clause" and the "free exercise clause." The wording does not indicate that the framers had two different definitions of religion in mind, and yet it is very difficult to find a single definition that would do justice to both clauses. A broad definition of religion (one that would include both traditional and nontraditional, theistic and nontheistic worldviews) is desirable in connection with the latter because there is a general consensus favoring religious liberty for individuals. A broad definition would be less desirable in connection with the former, on the other hand, because it would render unconstitutional the humanitarian—but not necessarily theistic—basis for a great deal of legislation aimed at improving society.

Leitch notes that the controversy surrounding church-state relations often touches the symbolic core of national life. In 1943, for example, the Court struck down a statute requiring pupils to salute the American flag and recite the Pledge of Allegiance (West Virginia Board of Education v. Barnette). It was noted that compulsory deference even to national symbols was unconstitutional, as it forced pupils to declare beliefs when they might wish to remain silent or even to express dissent. In 1963, religious exercises in public schools were ruled unconstitutional; since then, the courts have consistently struck down efforts to include prayers and scripture reading in class. But surveys ("Prayer in Public Schools," *Gallup Reports* 229 [1984]:7) consistently show that most Americans want prayer and scripture reading in the public schools; according to a Gallup poll of 1984, 69 percent were in favor and only 28 percent opposed to class prayers.

52. Henry Warner Bowden, "A Historian's Response to the Concept of American Civil Religion," *Church and State* 17 (1973): 495-505. James Garret, "'Civil Religion': Clarifying the Semantic Problem," *Journal of Church and State* 16 (1974): 187-195. Robert T. Handy, "A Decisive Turn in the Civil Religion Debate," *Theology Today* 37 (1980): 342-350. Robert D. Linder, "Civil Religion in Historical Perspective: The Reality That Underlies the Concept," *Journal of Church and State* 17 (1975): 399-421. Joan Lockwood, "Bellah and His Critics: An Ambiguity in Bellah's Concept of Civil Religion," *Anglican Theological Review* 57 (1975): 395-416. Martin E. Marty, *A Nation of Behavers*

(Chicago: University of Chicago Press, 1976). Sidney E. Mead, "The 'Nation with the Soul of a Church,'" *Church History* 36 (1967): 262-283. Herbert W. Richardson, "Robert Bellah's 'The Broken Covenant.'" *Anglican Theological Review* 57 (1975): 480-490. John F. Wilson, "The Status of Civil Religion in America," *The Religion of the Republic*, ed. Elwyn A. Smith (Philadelphia: Fortress Press, 1971), pp. 1-21.

53. Robert N. Bellah, "Civil Religion in America," *Daedalus* 96, no. 1 (1967): 1.

54. Ibid., pp. 3-4.

55. Ibid., p. 8.

56. Bellah has been attacked for eulogizing the American civil religion. Even in his first essay, though, he acknowledged that it has not been an unmixed blessing. It has been invoked to legitimate unworthy causes as well as worthy ones, for instance, and to promote intolerance as well as tolerance. But, he argues, it has been difficult to use the words of Jefferson or Lincoln to support inequality or to undermine liberty. Those who defended slavery before the Civil War eventually came to reject the mentality that had produced the Declaration of Independence itself; some of them turned against both Jeffersonian democracy and Reformation religion; their vision was of a South dominated by medieval chivalry and divine-right monarchy. Although members of the radical right today often display overt religiosity, their relation to the civil religious consensus is very tenuous. The misuse of civil religion, however, is not confined to the domestic scene. According to Bellah, the nation has now entered a "third time of trial" in which Americans must find a responsible way of integrating themselves into the larger world community. In his earlier works, at any rate, Bellah believed that this process need not disrupt the continuity of American civil religion because it was based not on worship of the nation itself but on an understanding of American history in the light of an ultimate and universal reality; in that case, he has argued, a world civil religion would be the fulfillment, not the denial, of American civil religion.

57. Ibid., p. 10.

58. Ibid., p. 10.

59. Ibid., p. 11.

60. Fred Davis, *Yearning for Yesterday: A Sociology of Nostalgia* (New York: Free Press, 1979), p. 104.

61. His failure to mention *The Wizard* is probably due to the fact that it has never been revived; on the contrary, it has been a part of American life

ever since it was first released in 1939. At any rate, it clearly evokes nostalgia for an earlier, simpler and safer America that, nevertheless, has undergone massive social changes.

62. The fact that Dorothy is ostensibly a little girl, of course, may evoke this kind of therapeutic nostalgia for childhood among adolescent viewers. But *The Wizard* addresses their psychological needs in much more powerful ways. Besides, nostalgia is not notably characteristic of teenagers because they are strongly oriented toward the future.

63. Davis, *Yearning*, p. 59.

64. Mircea Eliade, *Patterns in Comparative Religion* (New York: New American Library, 1958), p. 408.

Appendix 1. Methodological Notes

1. Like most (but not all) movies, *The Wizard* is considered popular culture. It is thus distinguished from elite culture—what is sometimes known as "high culture" or simply as "Culture". By definition, popular culture is intellectually, socially, and economically accessible to the entire population and not restricted to an elite stratum of society. The kind of social stratification that this implies, however, is not universal. In small-scale traditional societies, there may be no elite group with its own separate traditions; everyone may participate in a common "folk" tradition. In more complex traditional societies such as India, according to A. K. Ramanujan (Foreword, *Folk Tales of India*, ed. Brenda E. F. Beck et al. [Chicago: University of Chicago Press, 1987], pp. xvi-xix), a distinction is made between Little Tradition and Great Tradition. The former corresponds to folk culture. It is produced in local languages by and for the inhabitants of specific regions within the larger civilization. The latter corresponds to elite culture. It is produced in a classical or sacred language by a learned class and disseminated across regional lines. Because the classical scholars are also participants in regional traditions, however, there is a great deal of overlapping; similar material can be found in both Little and Great Traditions and may be differentiated mainly according to context and function (rather than content). In modern or early modern societies, folk culture often persists as a rural phenomenon; popular culture, on the other hand, distinguishes the masses from the elite in urban settings. Popular culture has the same relation to elite culture as folk culture but includes productions (such as prints and novels) that presuppose some level of literary and more sophisticated technology. With the coming of industry and advanced technology in the field of communication, it becomes proper to speak more specifically of "mass

culture" (that is, popular culture disseminated through mass media such as radio, television, and film). This term, therefore, is more precise for a discussion of Hollywood movies. In a study comparing the popular culture of a modern society with that of a traditional society, it would be necessary to call the former "mass culture." In this book, though, the reference to mass media is assumed; the terms "mass culture" and "popular culture" are used interchangeably.

2. M. Gottdiener, "Hegemony and Mass Culture: A Semiotic Approach," *American Journal of Sociology* 90 (1985): 982.

3. Ibid., pp. 982–983.

4. Ibid., p. 984.

5. Ibid., p. 989.

6. There is no truly adequate term for people who "receive" mass entertainment. The word "user" is too mechanistic for use in describing a complex and subtle process such as the creation of meaning. Gottdiener sometimes uses the word "consumer," which is too heavily weighted with connotations of a purely economic transaction. Other words present merely technical problems. The word "audience" actually refers to people who listen to cultural productions such as radio shows or concerts; words such as "viewers" or "spectators" refer to people who watch cultural productions such as television or silent movies. Although there is no word in English for people who do both at the same time (as they do in the case of television or sound movies), these words have become virtually synonymous; I have used them interchangeably.

7. This is necessary because terms such as "object" and "artifact" generally refer only to material culture. He may have avoided terms such as "text" and "document" because of their strong associations with the literary world. In common use among anthropologists, however, is the word "production." It is the most general; movies, television shows, novels, amusement parks, and songs can all be called cultural "productions."

8. Diana Crane, *The Transformation of the Avant-Garde: The New York Art World, 1940–1985* (Chicago: University of Chicago Press, 1987), p. 13.

9. Ibid., p. 1

10. Ibid., p. 11.

11. Ibid., p. 12–13.

12. Ibid., p. 16.

13. The case of Andrew Wyeth is an interesting illustration of the polariza-

tion between high and low, elite and popular culture. Richard Corliss notes that Wyeth's most famous painting, *Christina's World*, has "become an indelible part of postwar America's visual vocabulary." He also writes that "the spare, meticulous, compassionate vision...has made Wyeth a beloved icon to American museum goers and a nettlesome anachronism to the art establishment." In the same article, he quotes the former curator of twentieth century art at the Metropolitan Museum of Art; according to Henry Gold-zahler, "Wyeth's philosophy is *Poor Richard's Almanack.* His skies have no vapor trails. His people wear no wristwatches. He is the Williamsburg of American painting—charming, especially when seen from a helicopter" (*Time* [18 August 1986], p. 55).

Although Robert Hughes reports that "the time is past when one could dismiss Wyeth as nothing more than a sentimental illustrator, as critics irked by his popular appeal did a decade or more ago," he does precisely this himself. Comparing one of Wyeth's portraits to Manet's *Olympia*, he writes that there is a world of difference "between the harsh confrontational skills of a great talent and the tepid virtuosity of a popular one (*Time* [June 1987], p. 77).

Wyeth may or may not be a great artist. Undoubtedly, however, he is a massively popular one. This fact cannot be ignored in any discussion of his place in American culture. In fact, it is precisely his popularity that seems to prevent him from achieving status within the art world. The avant-garde art establishment values "harsh confrontational skills." One cannot be harsh or confrontational and still be popular. Ergo, one cannot be a good artist and still be popular. As M. Stephen Doherty suggests in an article on the recent nationwide tour of Wyeth's paintings and drawings, the controversy over him is symptomatic of a larger problem in the art world. "These exhibitions...are certain to rekindle the debate about paintings by the Wyeths and, by implication, all realist artists. Magazines, newspapers, and radio and television programs will repeat the negative criticism of those who have invested themselves in the Modernist point of view, and the media will also report on the phenomenal attraction these forthcoming exhibitions will have for millions of people. As the public becomes better informed and more appreciative of the Wyeths, the critics seem to become more vituperative. In a recent article in *The New York Times*, Edmund P. Pillsbury, the director of the Kimbell Art Museum in Fort Worth, said that Andrew Wyeth is 'not a good draftsman, and he's a sentimental artist. His paintings tell stories. They're anecdotal, not profound, backward-looking and not forward-looking'" (*American Artist* 1 [May 1987]: 10).

Clearly, the work of Andrew Wyeth "speaks" to the American people in a way that the work of Jasper Johns or even Andy Warhol does not. If Wyeth is not producing good art, he is obviously producing something—whatever one chooses to call it—that fills a deep need. I do not argue that the critics are wrong for preferring their own definition of art. I only point out the polarization between "taste cultures."

14. "Sunday Today," NBC, WPTZ, Plattsburgh, NY, 10 July 1988.

15. Anderson himself refers, reluctantly, to "primitive societies." By this, he means societies that depend on a relatively simple technology, occupy a relatively small space, consist of a relatively small population, and have a relatively limited degree of specialization. As he explains, this word has unfortunate (and false) connotations of inferiority. Since my purpose in discussing these societies is to contrast them with modern societies (not only in Europe and America but also in Japan or other parts of the world), I could refer instead to "traditional societies" characterized by an emphasis on maintaining the cultural traditions handed down from one generation to another rather than by an emphasis on creating new cultural forms. But some traditional societies—as in China, India, Islam, and medieval Europe —are clearly different from both modern societies and those discussed by Anderson. For want of a better word, I have used another term now favored by some anthropologists: "primal."

16. Anderson, *Art in Primitive Societies*, p. 11.

17. Ibid., p. 98.

18. Ibid., p. 48.

19. Ibid., pp. 36–37.

20. Ibid., p. 202.

21. John Dominic Crossan, *The Dark Interval: Towards a Theology of Story* (Niles, Ill.: Argus Communications, 1975).

22. Anderson, *Art in Primitive Societies*, pp. 200–201.

23. Robert Redfield, "Art and Icon," *Anthropology and Art: Readings in Cross-Cultural Aesthetics*, ed. Charlotte M. Otten (1959; Austin: University of Texas Press, 1971), p. 47.

24. Ibid., p. 48.

25. Anderson, *Art in Primitive Societies*, p. 49.

26. Marvin Harris, quoted in ibid., p. 49.

27. Mary Douglas, quoted in Wendy O'Flaherty, *Siva: The Erotic Ascetic* (Oxford: Oxford University Press, 1973), p. 2.

28. Ibid., p. 14.

29. Alan Watts, quoted in ibid., p. 14.

30. Ninian Smart, *Worldviews: Cross-Cultural Exploration of Human Beliefs* (New York: Scribner's, 1983), p. 11.

Appendix 2. Oz in American Popular Culture

1. Richard Flaste, "Listening for Life Among the Stars," *New York Times Magazine* (15 September 1985), p. 38.

2. "Fundamentalists Win School Textbook Case," p. 12.

3. Robert S. Ellwood, *Introducing Religion from Inside and Outside* (Englewood Cliffs, NJ: Prentice-Hall, 1978), p. 11.

4. Kurt Andersen, "Building a Dream-Home Utopia: Florida's Seaside Is a New Kind of New Town, Circa 1930," *Time* (4 November 1985), p. 55.

5. Elton John and Bernie Taupin, *Goodbye Yellow Brick Road* (London: Dick James Music, 1973).

6. Phillip O'Connor and Kate Miller, "Kansas Looks for Spot on Tourism Map," [Montreal] *Gazette* (14 February 1987), p. I13.

7. Mary Vespa, Crowning Moments," *People* (15 Septembr 1986), p. 84.

8. Robert Bruce and Martin Weiss, "Three on a Couch," "Golden Girls," NBC, WPTZ, Plattsburgh, NY, 12 May 1987.

9. John Bartlett, *Familiar Quotations: A Collection of Passages, Phrases, and Proverbs Traced to Their Sources in Ancient and Modern Literature*, ed. Emily Morison Beck, 15th ed. (Boston: Little Brown, 1980), pp. 677; 842.

10. Notice issued by The International Wizard of Oz Club, March 1987.

11. Dan Rather, "CBS Evening News," CBS, WCAX-TV, Burlington, VT, 21 June 1988.

12. Fred M. Meyer, "Oz in the News," *Baum Bugle* 32, no. 2 (1988): 26.

13. Tom Wolfe, interview, "Today" NBC, WPTZ, Plattsburgh, NY, 12 March 1987.

14. "From Wine Cellar to Disco: Manhattan Townhouse Shows Marcos Decadence," [Montreal] *Gazette* (1 March 1986), p. A11.

15. "Democrats in Oz," *New Republic* (1 April 1985), p. 6.

16. Radio City Music Hall, "The Hollywood Classic Comes to Life on the Great Stage," advertisement, *New York Times* (19 February 1989), p. H11.

17. Don Reo, "The Tornado," "Heartland," CBS, WCAX-TV, Burlington, VT, 20 March 1989.

18. Gary Larson, *The Far Side Gallery* (Kansas City: McMeel and Parker, 1984) [p. 9].

19. Larson, *The Bride of The Far Side* (Kansas City: Andrews, McMeel and Parker, 1984) [p. 43].

20. Larson, *In Search of The Far Side* (Fairway, KS: Andrews, McMeel and Parker, 1984) [p. 2].

21. Garry Trudeau, "Doonesbury," cartoon, [Montreal] *Gazette* (15 January 1988), p. C10.

22. Ibid., (24 December 1987), pp. E14, E15.

23. Berke Breathed, "Bloom County," cartoon, [Montreal] *Gazette* (17 March 1988), p. D15.

24. Lisa Malo, "Wizzards," storyboard of commercial for Esso, 16 April 1986.

25. Alfred Gingold, *More Items from Our Catalogue* (New York: Avon, 1983), p. 2.

26. Minolta Corp., "Now You Don't Have to Be a Wizard to Get Perfect Pictures," advertisement, *Newsweek* (1 July 1985), p. 5.

27. Bloomingdale's By Mail Ltd., "Open a Bloomingdale's Near You," advertisement, *Mademoiselle* (September 1985), p. 81.

28. Bruce Bailey, "Weird *After Hours* a Comic Winner," review of *After Hours*, [Montreal] *Gazette* (17 October 1985), p. B10.

29. Harmetz, *The Making*, pp. 188-194.

30. Bailey "Weird *After Hours* a Comic Winner," p. B10.

31. "Best of '86," *Time* (5 January 1987), p. 83.

32. Bill Brownstein, *"Labyrinth:* The Key Word Is 'Boring' as David Bowie Plays Wizard of Odd," review of *Labyrinth*, [Montreal] *Gazette* (31 January 1987), TV times, p. 63.

Appendix 3. Religion and Secularity in America

1. During the last two weeks of 1988, according to *TV Guide* (17-23, 24-30 December 1988), *Miracle on 34th Street* could be seen in prime time on December 24 (8:00 P.M.) and late at night on December 25 (12:30 A.M.). *It's a Wonderful Life* could be seen in prime time on December 19 (9:00 P.M.) and late at night on December 22 (11:30 P.M.). And one version or another of *A Christmas Carol* could be seen during the day on December 22 (1:00 P.M.), December 24 (1:00 P.M.), and December 25 (10:45 A.M.); in prime

time on December 21 (9:00 P.M.), December 22 (9:00 PM.), December 24 (8:00 and 9:00 P.M.); and late at night on December 21 (11:30 P.M.) and December 24 (11:30 P.M.). These listings are for the Montreal region. There is no reason to think, however, that listings for regions in the United States differ in any significant way.

2. W. Lloyd Warner, *American Life: Dream and Reality* (Chicago: University of Chicago Press, 1953), p. 2.

3. Ibid., p. 23.

4. Ibid., p. 25.

5. Matt. 17:25.

6. Warner, *American Life*, p. 25.

7. Ibid., p. 26.

8. Ibid., p. 15.

9. Ibid., p. 16.

10. Ibid., p. 23.

11. I have tried to avoid defining religion too broadly. The definition of Clifford Geertz appears in "Religion as a Cultural System," *Reader in Comparative Religion: An Anthropological Approach*, ed. William A. Lessa and Evon Z. Vogt, 4th ed. (New York: Harper and Row, 1979), pp. 78–79. "Religion," he observes, "is (1) a system of symbols which acts to (2) establish powerful, pervasive and long-lasting moods in men by (3) formulating conceptions of a general order of existence and (4) clothing these conceptions with such an aura of factuality that (5) the moods and motivations seem uniquely realistic." If religion is a society's core symbol system, then communism is surely a religion. But is there no significant difference between communism and Christianity or any other traditional religion? Likewise, I have tried to avoid defining religion too narrowly. Melford Spiro defines the term in "Religion: Problems of Definition and Explanation," *Anthropological Approaches to the Study of Religion*, ed. Michael Banton, ASA Monographs 3 (London: Tavistock, 1966), pp. 85–126. According to him, religion is "an institution consisting of culturally patterned interactions with culturally postulated superhuman beings" (ibid., pp. 89–90). Idiosyncratically, Spiro separates religion from the sacred. The latter is defined in relation to "ultimate concerns." Something may thus be religious but not sacred or sacred but not religious. Neither Geertz nor Spiro can offer an adequate understanding of religion or its relation to secularity. If the broad approach is followed (underemphasizing the difference between religion and secularity), religion becomes synonymous with culture or with any organizing principle of culture; almost anything could be

classified as religious. If the narrow approach is followed (overemphasizing the difference), religion is trivialized; it is confined to personal beliefs in, or experience of, superhuman beings; this would eliminate much of what is normally considered religious. I have chosen diagnostic features that are broad enough to include phenomena not normally included in the category of religion but that, nevertheless, are linked to certain distinctive character-istics of religion—especially the dialectic of sacred and profane as described by Eliade.

12. Although some scholars have defined secularity in normative terms, I have used it in a purely descriptive sense. Secularization is a tendency to be found in modern societies. It must be taken seriously. Consequently, it is appropriate to consider secularity an ideal type, for heuristic purposes, along with religion.

13. I have rejected two normative models. According to one, secularization is either inevitable progress or lamentable decline. According to the other, secularity is a worldview competing with religion and represents either truth or ignorance.

Appendix 4. Going Home and Growing up on Television

1. Actually, Thanksgiving has the same connotations and may be even more widely observed as Jews and other non-Christians can participate more easily; nevertheless, the intensity of emotion generated by Christmas is unparalleled.

2. It is quite possible, of course, that other shows in this category might involve biological families.

3. CBS, WCAX-TV, Burlington, VT, 21 December 1987.

4. ABC, WMTW, Poland Spring, MD, 23 December 1987. Originally broad-cast in 1986.

5. NBC, WPTZ, Plattsburgh, NY, 26 December 1987. Originally broadcast in 1986.

6. NBC, WPTZ, Plattsburgh, NY, 20 December 1987.

7. CBS, WCAX-TV, Burlington, VT, 24 December 1987. Originally broadcast in 1971.

8. CBS, WCAX-TV, Burlington, VT, 20 December 1987. Like all commercials, this one was broadcast many times; moreover, it was rebroadcast in 1988, 1989, and 1990.

9. ABC, WMTW, Poland Spring, ME, 20 December 1987.

10. CBS, WXAX-TV, Burlington, VT, 25 December 1987.

11. NBC, WPTZ, Plattsburgh, NY, 21 December 1987.

12. NBC, WPTZ, Plattsburgh, NY, 23 December 1987. Originally broadcast in 1986.

13. CBS, WCAX-TV, Burlington, VT, 21 December 1987.

14. NBC, WPTZ, Plattsburgh, NY, 24 December 1987.

15. This study was conducted in Montreal. Like most Canadian cities, Montreal is within the viewing area of American networks. The criterion for selecting shows, however, is origination in the United States. During the period under discussion, Canadian networks broadcast reruns of American shows. These have been included in the study. They were originally made by and for Americans, and individual channels all across the United States were broadcasting these episodes, or others like them, during the same period.

16. CTV, CFCF, Montreal, Que., 20 December 1987.

17. ABC, WMTW, Poland Spring, ME, 22 December 1987. Originally broadcast in 1986.

18. "Coping with the Family Holidays," "The Oprah Winfrey Show," NBC, WPTZ, Plattsburgh, NY, 22 Decemer 1987.

19. Mircea Eliade, *The Myth of the Eternal Return, or, Cosmos and History*, Bollingen Series 46 (Princeton, NJ: Princeton University Press, 1954).

20. It could be argued here that football is becoming even more popular than baseball, but that would make no difference in the context of this discussion. My goal has not been to prove that exile and return is the only paradigm informing American culture or that the distinction between sacred and profane is the only paradigm informing American notions of time but only that these paradigms are very common.

21. Quoted in "Loosetalk," ed. Deborah Mitchell, *Us* (23 February 1987), p. 19.

22. Robert Bruce and Martin Weiss, "Bringing up Baby," "The Golden Girls," NBC, WPTZ, Plattsburgh, NY, 3 October 1987.

23. Dan Gordon, "To Bind the Wounds," "Highway to Heaven," NBC, WPTZ, Plattsburgh, NY, (17 December 1985).

24. CBS, WCAX-TV, Burlington, VT, 1 November 1988.

INDEX

This book is interdisciplinary. It discusses *The Wizard* on three levels that are seldom brought together (that of the psyche's passage through childhood and adulthood, the nation's passage through wilderness and frontier, and the soul's passage through time and eternity). It thus brings together a number of divergent fields (including religious studies, film studies, American studies, symbolic geography, art history, psychoanalysis, popular culture, and cultural anthropology). Not surprisingly, the subjects discussed are related in extremely subtle and complex ways. As a result: (1) entries from various fields are thrown together; (2) many of these refer to discussions from at least three points of view; and (3) some represent a vocabulary that includes terms either found nowhere else at all or nowhere else with the same connotations. Because most people are unlikely to make connections that would give them access to more than a few familiar terms, and thus to more than a partial exploration of what this book says about any given subject, some help is provided in the form of "see also" references. These do not necessarily refer readers to other entries with more information on specific aspects of the *same* subject; they may refer readers to other entries on *closely related* subjects. Important links are thus made among entries ranging from the obviously related to the seemingly remote and from the linguistically familiar to the newly coined. Each "see also" represents a cluster of similar (and possibly contrasting) ideas. Under "Paradise," for example, readers are encouraged to consult entries including "Arcadia," "Dilmun," "Eden," "Emerald City," "Eschatology," "Garden," "Going home," "Growing up," "Hudson River school," "Jerusalem," "Kansas," "Metropolis," "Nostalgia," "Pastoralism," "Sin," "South," "Utopia," "West," and "Wilderness." Even though there appears to be little or nothing in common between Paradise and Kansas, say, or Metropolis, there is an underlying unity linking them. One function of this index, then, is to make the connections more accessible.

(Italic numerals indicate illustrations.)